Effective Methods of Teaching Business Education in the 21st Century

National Business Education Association Yearbook, No. 41

2003

Editor
Martha H. Rader
Arizona State University
Tempe, Arizona

Assistant Editor
Linda A. Kurth
Phoenix College
Phoenix, Arizona

Published by

National Business Education Association
1914 Association Drive
Reston, VA 20191-1596
(703) 860-8300 • Fax: (703) 620-4483
www.nbea.org

TABLE OF CONTENTS

Part III: The Business Education Curriculum—Methods and Resources

Part IV: Organizational and Professional Responsibilities

PREFACE

The *2003 NBEA Yearbook* presents the latest research, teaching strategies, and suggested resources for all areas of business education. The *Yearbook* contains a wealth of information for experienced teachers who wish to improve their teaching skills or teach a new business subject or course. The *Yearbook* also can be used as a methods book for undergraduate and graduate business education students.

This *Yearbook* includes 20 chapters written by leading business educators who are experts on the topics of their chapters. Part I, Business Education Perspectives, includes the following three chapters: Chapter 1, The Foundations of Business Education; Chapter 2, Delivery Systems for Business Education; and Chapter 3, Current Trends in Business Education. These chapters discuss the history, philosophy, and goals of business education; the role of business education programs in traditional and nontraditional settings; and current trends affecting business education programs.

Part II, Instructional Concepts for Business Education, contains four chapters: Chapter 4, Planning for Instruction; Chapter 5, Providing for Students' Learning Styles and Differences; Chapter 6, Managing the Classroom and Technology Lab; and Chapter 7, Evaluating and Assessing Student Performance. These chapters discuss aligning curriculum with national and state curriculum standards and developing lesson plans; addressing learning styles, multiple intelligences, diversity, and students with special needs; managing student behavior in the classroom and technology lab; and evaluating and assessing student performance.

Part III, The Business Education Curriculum—Methods and Resources, contains the following chapters: Chapter 8, Input Technologies; Chapter 9, Information Technology; Chapter 10, Communication; Chapter 11, Accounting and Business Computation; Chapter 12, Business Foundations and Management; Chapter 13, Economics and Personal Finance; Chapter 14, Business Law; Chapter 15, Entrereneurship and E-Commerce; Chapter 16, International Business; Chapter 17, Marketing; and Chapter 18, Cooperative Education and Work-Experience Programs. These chapters present the latest research, current teaching practices, and suggested resources for each subject in the business education curriculum.

Part IV, Organizational and Professional Responsibilities, includes Chapter 19, Sponsoring Student Organizations, and Chapter 20, Lifelong Professional Development. Chapter 19 discusses student organizations, activities, and responsibilities of the sponsoring teacher. Chapter 20 outlines the importance and benefits of participation in business education professional organizations and the necessity for lifelong professional development and learning.

The *2003 Yearbook* was written by 29 business educators who invested an enormous amount of time, energy, and work in conducting research and writing the chapters. I would like to express my appreciation to the authors for their wonderful contributions, their willingness to share their expertise, and their dedication to the profession.

I also express my appreciation to the 54 individuals who served as chapter reviewers. Their advice and helpful suggestions served as a major contribution to the quality of the *Yearbook*. I especially thank Linda Kurth, Assistant Editor of the *Yearbook*, for her many hundreds of hours of assistance; the NBEA Publications Committee, the NBEA staff, and editorial assistants Dana Fladhammer and Michelle Crary for their help in innumerable ways.

Finally, I extend a special thanks to Robert Gryder, James Calvert Scott, and Kenneth L. Gorman for their inspiration, encouragement, and mentorship.

Martha H. Rader, Editor
Arizona State University
Tempe, Arizona

ACKNOWLEDGEMENTS

The following business educators devoted their time, effort, and expertise to reviewing the *2003 NBEA Yearbook, Effective Methods of Teaching Business Education in the 21st Century*:

Mary Ellen Adams	John P. Manzer
Marcia A. Anderson	Arthur McEntee
Sherri Lee Arosteguy	Peter F. Meggison
Martha E. Balachandran	Mary Etta Naftel
Beverly A. Block	Patricia G. Odgers
Dianna Briggs	Sharon Lund O'Neil
Jean M. Buckley	Larry G. Pagel
Richard Clodfelter	Heidi R. Perreault
John E. Clow	Donna H. Redmann
Donna J. Cochrane	Cynthia B. Redmond
Lonnie Echternacht	Abigail R. Reynolds
Marie E. Flatley	Ginny Richerson
Judy Fleming	Harriet D. Rogers
Connie M. Forde	Robert J. Scherrer
Steve Golen	James Calvert Scott
Kenneth L. Gorman	Jean Anna Sellers
Mary Ellen Guffey	Wanda Stitt-Gohdes
Dana Harader	Allen D. Truell
Janice C. Harder	Darlene Voeltz
Dianna S. Hart	Kelly L. Wilkinson
Thomas Haynes	Christopher Williams
Linda Hefferin	Karen Schneiter Williams
William Hoyt	Patricia Wilson
Marcia L. James	Martha C. Yopp
Carol A. Johnson	Marilyn Zarzecki
Carol Larson Jones	Nancy D. Zeliff
Dennis LaBonty	
Judith J. Lambrecht	

The Foundations of Business Education

Mary Margaret Hosler

University of Wisconsin–Whitewater

Whitewater, Wisconsin

Business education has been a part of the American school system since the early colonists initiated their version of education. This early education offered penmanship and bookkeeping as business subjects, the objective of the business education programs being strictly "vocational." But from 1600 to the present, business education has expanded its mission to include (a) educating students *about* business by encouraging them to become effective citizens, and (b) educating students *for* business by preparing them to enter the workplace. This chapter discusses the evolution of business education from its inception to the present, with emphasis on the history of its federal funding and laws, curriculum, philosophy, and organizations.

ELEMENTS OF BUSINESS EDUCATION

Business education is often referred to in the context of vocational education, or career and technical education. A definition of each of these terms will provide an explanation of each concept and how the three are related.

Business Education

Business education or *commercial education* (an earlier term for business education) is a term dating back hundreds of years. In several statements in the past, the Policies Commission for Business and Economic Education (PCBEE) has defined business education. Its Statement No. 71, 2002 (PCBEE), reiterates that business education is "education *for* and *about* business." Education *about* business means preparing all learners for the various roles they will play as economically literate citizens. Education *for* business means building on these general understandings about business in a way that prepares learners to be employed in a variety of careers.

The *National Standards for Business Education* (2001), published by the National Business Education Association (NBEA), describes the present mission of business educators as one that seeks to develop competencies in students and equip them with a mastery of business foundamentals and skills essential for a successful life.

Vocational Education

The term *vocational education* historically has meant instruction designed to prepare individuals for the world of work. Early vocational education served to provide workers with agricultural, industrial, and homemaking skills. As business education and marketing education were added to the curriculum, they were included in the term "vocational" education, since the courses prepared students for the world of work. The 1968 Vocational Education Amendments specifically excluded preparation for professional-level jobs (generally requiring a baccalaureate degree) from the definition of federally aided vocational education, except for the training of students and teachers preparing to become teachers in a vocational education program (Roberts, 1971).

Career and Technical Education

After many years of discussion about the word "vocational," the American Vocational Association (AVA) at its December 1998 convention voted to change its name to the *Association for Career and Technical Education* (ACTE) (Roberts, 1999). The Association for Career and Technical Education defines *career and technical education*:

> Career and technical education prepares both youth and adults for a wide range of careers, from registered nurse to computer technician, that require varying levels of education—from high school to postsecondary certificates to two- and four-year college degrees (ACTE, 2002).

Following the adoption of the new name, state associations and student organizations began changing to the new terminology (Roberts, 1999).

THE EVOLUTION OF BUSINESS EDUCATION

Business education dates back to ancient civilizations (see Chapter 2). The history of business education presented in this section focuses on the last four centuries, with an emphasis on federal legislation that has provided money to support career and technical education programs in the twentieth century. Federal legislation has played a major role in the evolution of business education because funding has motivated changes in methods of delivery and content offerings. The following section discusses business education in the United States from the seventeenth century to the opening of the twenty-first century.

Seventeenth and Eighteenth Centuries

A dual and differentiated system of education existed in the 1600s. The provisions of the English Poor Law of 1601 that were adopted by the colonists encouraged an apprenticeship system by requiring parishes to place the children of poor families with masters to teach them a trade. To serve the children of the elite, Boston Latin Grammar School, a college preparatory school for boys, opened in 1645; Harvard, the first college, opened in 1636 (Thompson, 1973). Vocational education became the preparation for learning a trade, while students entering the Latin Grammar School went on to a profession. Private schools operating on a tuition basis offered a curriculum of handwriting, arithmetic, bookkeeping, and English. Governing boards, usually the churches, dominated public schools. In these schools commercial courses such as handwriting, arithmetic, and bookkeeping were offered. Only a few admitted girls (Bartholome, 1997).

Discussions continued in the 1700s about control over public versus privately run schools. In 1779 Thomas Jefferson stated that for the public schools to serve the entire public, they must be free from religious or private control; this concept eventually became accepted. In the public schools, which would be established and maintained by the states, vocational education could develop as the states saw fit (Thompson, 1973).

Nineteenth Century

Three events in the early 1800s—the Embargo Act, the Non Intercourse Act, and the War of 1812—closed American markets to foreign manufactured goods. These events led to the promotion of vocational education or training as a national economic policy because a large labor force was needed to produce goods (Thompson, 1973).

First business college. The first business college was established in 1824 with instruction in reading, penmanship, arithmetic, algebra, astronomy, history, geography, commercial law, and political economy (Bartholome, 1997). The first chain of private business colleges was opened in 1853 by Bryant and Stratton. Their mission was to prepare workers for a growing economic system in the industrial age. Many of the business college chains failed because of the Civil War and subsequent economic depression during the 1860s. With the invention of the first workable typewriter in 1868, the business colleges again experienced growth.

First federal aid—The Morrill Act. In the first half of the 1800s, the agricultural sector of the economy demanded vocational and practical education, leading Congress to pass the Morrill Act in 1862 (Gordon, 1999). This act, the first legislation passed by the federal government to support collegiate-level vocational education, established land-grant colleges that offered programs in agriculture, mechanical arts (engineering), and military science.

Twentieth Century

At the turn of the twentieth century, private business schools taught typewriting and shorthand, along with the traditional business subjects of the past. As comprehensive high schools began to form at the beginning of the century, "commercial" courses moved into the secondary curriculum. From 1900-1910, as business education slowly moved into the developing public high schools, business education enrollments grew from 42,000 students to 111,000 students (Thompson, 1973). By the 1920s, business education began to experience significant enrollments at the high school level (Hosler, 1971).

Marketing education. At one time, the concept of training workers for jobs in retail sales was nonexistent. Lucinda Wyman Prince, a member of the Women's Educational and Industrial Union in Boston, conducted the first comprehensive investigation of retail occupations in 1905. At that time sales clerks' wages were low; the job was looked down upon and lacked social approval. As a result of her findings, she concluded that sales clerks could be trained to sell. She proposed to the management of W. A. Filene's ready-to-wear store that a few clerks be sent to her at the Union for training in how to sell merchandise. A condition imposed was that the company would increase the wages of each trainee. Nichols (1979) comments that the lowest increase was 50 cents a week and the largest was $14. Thus, retail store training had begun. As an aside, it is interesting to note that the first cooperative education program was established in 1914 by a business teacher—the head of the commercial education department at Fitchburg High School in Massachusetts arranged with local employers to take his seniors for a few hours a week because he believed that his students would benefit from real office experience (Nichols, 1979).

For some educational leaders, the next move was to get high schools to include retail store training in their business education programs. Boston's superintendent of schools became convinced of the need for retail training and attempted to lead the effort, but the heads of business departments and business teachers were opposed. In their view, stenographic jobs were more attractive than store jobs, for the latter had traditionally been considered unskilled labor. Besides, they reasoned, the retail courses would "drain from the enrollment in the shorthand courses" (Nichols, 1979, p. 115).

Smith-Hughes Act. An advocacy group called The National Society for Vocational Education formed in 1906 to obtain support for vocational education for several years as Congress considered different bills. On February 23, 1917, President Wilson signed into law the Smith-Hughes Act (PL 64-347), providing federal funding for vocational education in secondary schools. The Act specified that before a state could receive funds, it must establish a responsible state vocational board to develop a state plan for how the federal funds would be used (Thompson, 1973). The boards fostered the notion of vocational education as separate from academic education (Gordon, 1999).

Although the Smith-Hughes Act did not appropriate funds for business education programs, it did provide assistance to states to conduct studies, investigations, and reports. The Act created a seven-member Federal Board for Vocational Education that provided for one position for business education. Because of the work he had done on behalf of business education, F. G. Nichols, an administrator for the New York City Schools, who later became a professor at Harvard University, was appointed to the Board to represent business education. In October 1933, the administrative functions of vocational education were transferred to the U.S. Office of Education, and the Federal Board continued in an advisory capacity until President Truman abolished it in 1946 (Nichols, 1979).

Nichols believed that retail selling education should be placed in the business department, and that it should be regarded as a type of business education. *Bulletin No. 22* issued by the Federal Board for Vocational Education and written by Nichols, carried this statement: "This Board has decided, after careful investigation, to consider training for retail selling as belonging in the commercial department of vocational training" (Nichols, 1979, p. 141).

Economic education. Economic education in the business education field started with the Junior Training course developed by Nichols in the early 1920s. The emphasis in economic education shifted during the Depression years of the 1930s from the junior business model, that enabled those who did not complete the high school program to get a job, to an emphasis on consumer behavior such as budgeting and thrift, and then to the study of economic principles in later years (Bahr & Wegforth, 1976).

After writing a series of books on junior business training, Nichols authored in 1936 *Junior Business Training for Economic Living*, designed for the ninth and tenth grades. He commented in 1979 that the text was an attempt to move away from the vocational emphasis of the curriculum towards economics—an introduction to the fundamentals of thrifty living, or making the most of one's resources.

Vocational education legislation, 1929-1946. Following the trend of federal support for business education, the next half-century would see the passage of a series of laws that expanded the field even further. The federal government continued to support those vocational areas funded by the Smith-Hughes Act by passing the George-Reed Act of 1929 (PL 70-702) that provided funding for vocational home economics education and vocational agricultural education. The George-Ellzey Act of 1934 (PL 72-245) provided additional funding for vocational education in agriculture, trades and industry, and home economics. The George-Deen Act of 1936 (PL 74-673) authorized close to $14 million a year for vocational education to agriculture, home economics, and trade and industrial education (Gordon, 1999). This Act was particularly significant because *distributive* (marketing) occupations were recognized for the first time with an authorization of $1.3 million (Thompson, 1973). The law was passed in the middle of the Depression, when much had been written about the inefficiency of the distribution system. In this economic atmosphere the George-Deen Act was designed as an inservice program for employed individuals, as the Act stipulated that students in a supported program must be employed 15 hours a week. Subsequently, some states and schools began requiring their vocational education students to work 15 hours a week to meet the stipulation of the law. The 1963 Vocational Education Act removed this requirement.

The George-Barden Act (PL79-586) of 1946 doubled the money authorized for annual appropriations for marketing education. Funding was limited to supporting only cooperative education (part-time) programs and evening courses for employed workers (Gordon, 1999).

Student organizations. With the expansion of business education programs came the rise of student organizations. College and secondary students formed academic clubs that enriched business education with extracurricular activities. The student organizations Future Business Leaders of American (FBLA) and Distributive Education Clubs of America (DECA) were formed during this period of time. The first charter of FBLA was granted in 1942 to Science Hill High School, in Johnson City, Tennessee (Hosler & Hosler, 1992). FBLA was originally sponsored by NBEA; in 1969, however, the executive board of NBEA voted that FBLA and its collegiate counterpart Phi Beta Lambda (PBL) would become independent organizations (Hosler & Hosler, 1992).

DECA began in 1947 as the Distributors Clubs of America, with the first conference held that year in Memphis, Tennessee. In 1950 the name was changed to Distributive Education Clubs of America, or DECA. In 1961, a postsecondary division, Delta Epsilon Chi, was established (Gordon, 1999).

A third student organization was established in the 1960s, known first as the Vocational Office Education Clubs of America (VOECA), later changed to the Office Education Association (OEA), and in 1988 becoming Business Professionals of America (BPA) (Gordon, 1999). In July 1966 an organizational meeting was held with representatives from Iowa, Kansas, and Wisconsin to form BPA; the collegiate division was initiated in 1974 (Sims, 1976).

Vocational Education Act and Amendments. The 1960s and 1970s saw a round of federal legislation that infused new life into business education. In the early 1960s unemployment was high, and vocational education was criticized for failing to respond to manpower trends. At the same time, a concern for persons with special needs began to emerge. In 1961 President Kennedy appointed a panel of consultants to study vocational education. The report resulting from this panel set the stage for the passage of the Vocational Education Act of 1963 and the 1968 Amendments.

After the report of the panel of consultants in 1962, President Kennedy sent an education bill to Congress that included one section dealing with vocational education. This bill eventually became the Vocational Education Act of 1963 (PL 88 210).

The bill, signed into law by President Johnson in December 1963, originally read that the Act was to maintain, extend, and improve existing programs of vocational education. The original wording specified continued funding for agriculture, home economics, marketing education, and trade and industrial education, but *not* business education.

A committee consisting of Hamden L. Forkner, Russell J. Hosler, and Paul Lomax was appointed to attempt to have business education included in the 1963 Act. The committee had the support of the U. S. Office of Education, the executive director of American Vocational Association (AVA), now ACTE, and the National Education Association.

Business education had not been supported with previous acts mainly because of lobbying by the private business schools that did not want their competition supported with public funds. However, by 1963 the private business schools had diminished in numbers and their argument was never presented. The committee members met with legislators in Washington, D.C., including Representative Carl D. Perkins of Kentucky. According to Hosler (1971), they were able to convince Representative Perkins to include the term "business education" within the bill. The Act now read: "...those programs which were previously supported and business education for the office."

For a period of time after the passage of the Act, a separation developed among those who would define the objectives of business education. Hosler (1969, p. 243) wrote:

> There appears to be a tendency on the part of some to identify the objectives of business education with the source of financial support. Some would suggest that 'vocational business education' is that which is reimbursed, and if it is not reimbursed, it is 'general business education.'

The Vocational Education Amendments of 1968 (PL 90-576) helped to address that split by setting forth a list of rigid specifications necessary to qualify for the monies allocated. Consequently, both state and federal governments exerted more direct control over local programs of vocational education than ever before. The first priority of the Act was to support vocational education programs designed to assist the "hard to reach and the hard to teach" (Thompson, 1973, p. 79). The 1968 Amendments discontinued categorical aids that had started with the Smith-Hughes Act; all areas of vocational education had to compete for the appropriated funds. However, the Amendments did insert new categories for funding that included special needs, cooperative education, and innovative programs (Thompson, 1973).

A National Advisory Council on Vocational Education was created, and each state was required to establish a State Advisory Council. President Johnson appointed the National Council in 1969.

The Vocational Education Amendments of 1976 (PL 94-482) extended and increased funding of the Vocational Education Act of 1963 and the 1968 Amendments. In addition, states were given assistance in overcoming sex discrimination and sex stereotyping in their vocational programs (Gordon, 1999).

In 1983 the National Commission on Excellence in Education published *A Nation at Risk* that observed the U.S. was losing ground in international economic competition and attributed the decline to low standards and poor performance of the American educational system. Perhaps in reaction to the Commission's report, the Carl D. Perkins Vocational Education Act of 1984 (PL 98-524) was passed. The Act amended the 1963 Act and replaced the amendments of 1968 and 1976. It changed the emphasis of federal funding in vocational education from primarily expansion to program improvement, including support for at-risk populations. The Perkins Act emphasized equity in vocational education by providing relevant training for the disadvantaged, reducing sex stereotypes by enrolling students in nontraditional programs, and serving special populations more effectively (National Commission on Secondary Vocational Education, n.d.).

Changes in the business curriculum. The changes fostered by this era of federal educational support were significant. In 1961 Tonne noted that typewriting, short-hand, and bookkeeping were the most popular business courses at the secondary level at that time. Other business courses included business arithmetic, business law, consumer education, introduction to business, and office, clerical, and secretarial practice. By 1970 the principal subjects taught in the business program continued to be typewriting, bookkeeping, shorthand, but now general business and business arithmetic would occupy the most popular category alongside them. The enrollment in typewriting and distributive (marketing) training had tremendously increased (Tonne & Nanassy, 1970). The Vocational Education Act and its Amendments had successfully fostered increased interest and greater enrollments in business education.

In the late 70s and early 80s, new terms were coming into the vocabulary of business educators and questions were raised about curriculum design. The *1980 NBEA Yearbook* contained a chapter on data processing where Drum (p. 53) recommended, "…all business students should take at least an introduction to data processing course." Topics to include in that introductory course included data processing and the punch card. In the same yearbook, Anderson (p. 60) wrote "considering the demand for secretaries who can take dictation, it is evident that business is still a long way from the total concept of word processing…." In 1985 Wood wrote, "The microcomputer, with its wide availability and use in the home, business, industry, government, and educa-tion, has launched us into the new century. Every discipline and level within education must deal with the advent of the small computer and the power, problems, and promise that it brings to education" (p. 72).

The business education curriculum changed rapidly, and debates were taking place about typewriters versus computers in the classroom. Questions were being raised about the value of shorthand in the curriculum; bookkeeping had taken on the label of accounting; and typewriting was soon to become keyboarding.

Carl D. Perkins Vocational and Applied Technology Act. This act of Congress, signed by President George Bush in 1990 (PL 101-392), amended and extended the Perkins Act of 1984. The new name given to the Act indicated Congressional interest in both academic and career and technical skills to prepare for work in a global society. The Act carried appropriations of $1.6 billion a year through 1995 for state and local programs that taught the skill competencies necessary to work in a technologically advanced society (Reese & Thompson, 2002). In addition, the legislation initiated support for the concept known as *Tech Prep,* the cooperative arrangement that combines academic and technical courses at the secondary and postsecondary levels.

The Act had a three-pronged approach for better workforce preparation: (a) integration of academic and career and technical education, (b) articulation between segments of education engaged in workforce preparation (Tech Prep), and (c) closer linkages between school and work (Gordon, 1999). The Act, which was a departure from previous acts that had tended to separate career and technical education from the rest of the school, now emphasized integration with academic instruction. States were required to develop systems of performance measures and standards for secondary and postsecondary career and technical education.

The SCANS reports. Two reports in the early 1990s emphasized the need for new skills in the high-tech workplace. The Secretary's Commission on Achieving Necessary Skills (SCANS) report in 1991, *What Work Requires of Schools,* outlined a plan for making Americans more competitive for high wages by increasing high-tech skills. The Commission issued a second report in 1992, *Learning a Living: A Blueprint for High Performance,* which concluded that educators need to teach in context, so that learning to "know" would not be separated from learning to "do." The report also indicated that an improved match needed to be made between what work requires and what students are taught, by changing how instruction is delivered and how students learn. These two reports undoubtedly set the stage for Congress to enact legislation incorporating the recommendations of the Commission.

Standards-based legislation. In 1994 Congress passed three acts that were intertwined in purpose and action: (1) The School-to-Work Opportunities Act, (2) Goals 2000: Educate America Act, and (3) the National Skills Standards Act. The connection among all three acts was the development of standards (Kaufmann & Wills, 1999).

The School-to-Work Opportunities Act (STWOA) (PL 103-239) was intended to address the national skills shortage (Gordon, 1999). The Act, signed by President Clinton, gave grants totaling more than $1.6 billion to support programs that included internships, career academies, apprenticeships, and job shadowing. After October 2001 states would no longer have federal support for these programs. Administered by the Departments of Education and Labor, the Act encouraged the integration of academic and career and technical courses and work-based learning.

Goals 2000: Educate America Act established voluntary national education goals to promote coherent, systematic education reform. The objective was to establish standards for student achievement upon completion of grades 4, 8, and 12. Goals 2000 defined three types of standards: content standards, performance standards, and opportunity-to-learn standards. This last standard was later removed by other legislation (Kaufmann & Wills, 1999).

The National Skill Standards Act was Title V of Goals 2000. This legislation created the National Skill Standards Board that was to construct a voluntary system of skill standards to cover nearly all institutions concerned with worker skills. Standards were to be used for developing curricula and instructional materials at the various educational levels (Kaufmann & Wills, 1999).

Workforce Investment Act. The Workforce Investment Act (PL 105-220) passed in 1998 made one-stop career centers the key vehicles for employment and training programs funded by the Labor Department (Hosler, 2000). The one-stop career center system, funded by grants to states by the U.S. Department of Labor beginning in 1994, become key in the workforce delivery system (Kaufmann & Wills, 1999).

Carl Perkins Amendments. President Clinton signed the 1998 Carl D. Perkins Vocational-Technical Education Act Amendments (PL 105-332) that required states to report student achievement more extensively than in the past and called for career and technical students to meet challenging academic standards. The Amendments did not define the term "challenging," (Hosler, 2000) however. This legislation supported improvement of programs to increase both the career and academic preparation of students (Lynch, 2000). The Act allowed more state and local flexibility in providing services that included Tech-Prep education.

The technology curriculum. By the1990s the curriculum for business education had changed, reflecting the use of computers at all levels of education, the advancements in technology, and the legislation enacted by Congress. Keyboarding was now offered at the elementary level, thus taking the keyboard out of the exclusive control of the business educator. Terms such as database, desktop publishing, globalization, spreadsheet, telecommunications, and the Internet became part of the curriculum. Business educators had the opportunity to integrate technology with subject matter to provide students with greater breadth and depth of information. Standards for business education were developed by states in reaction to the accountability measures required by various federal laws.

Twenty-First Century

No federal act that directly affects career and technical education has yet been passed since the turn of the 21st century. According to ACTE, Congress continues to fund programs for career and technical education, such as the Tech Prep demonstration project.

Impact of federal legislation. Although federal legislation has provided funding for career and technical education and specifically business education for many years, the legislation has drawn both criticism and support. Federal funds were intended to stimulate the development of new programs, and gradually state and local funds were to be allocated to support these programs (Thompson, 1973). For example, the School to Work Act that ended in 2001 forced states to find ways to continue programs that were started with federal seed money after the federal funding was discontinued.

Benefits of federal funding include the following:

- development of curriculum and curriculum standards at all educational levels,

- professional leadership at the local and state levels,

- education and business linkages,

- promotion of career and technical programs,

- upgrading and maintenance of classroom equipment,

- professional development for teachers,

- access to many classroom resources,

- expansion of accountability measures,

- support for student organizations,

- initiatives for new programs, and

- opportunities for K-12 career education.

Without federal support and monies, business education would not have been able to develop the excellent programs that are now available to students at all levels of education.

THE PHILOSOPHY OF BUSINESS EDUCATION

Business education relies upon its policy makers to speak as one voice for the profession in defining the mission, objectives, and philosophy of the discipline. Four major groups carry out these roles, namely, the Association for Career and Technical Education (ACTE); Delta Pi Epsilon (DPE); the National Business Education Association (NBEA); and the Policies Commission for Business and Economic Education (PCBEE). A brief history of each group is outlined here; additional information about these organizations is presented in Chapter 20.

Association for Career and Technical Education

The Association for Career and Technical Education (ACTE) is the largest national education association dedicated to the advancement of education that prepares youth and adults for careers. Its mission is to provide educational leadership in developing a competitive workforce (Association for Career and Technical Education, 2002).

ACTE, known as the American Vocational Association (AVA) from 1926-1998 (Hosler, 2000), originally provided for six divisions with commercial (business) education as one of the six. In 1948 this division was split into two disciplines: Business Education and Marketing (Distributive) Education (Barlow, 1986). Official recognition of business education as a division did not take place until 1957, and then it lasted only one year due to lack of membership. In 1964-65 the ACTE Board of Directors granted official recognition for the business education division (Lee, n.d.).

The Association has 12 divisions and 5 geographic regions. Business education is one of the 12 divisions. Within the Business Education Division, three affiliated groups are organized—(1) National Association of Classroom Educators of Business Education (NACEBE), representing secondary and postsecondary classroom educators; (2) National Association of Supervisors of Business Education (NASBE), with membership from business education supervisors at the state, region, or local education agency; and (3) National Association of Teacher Educators for Business Education (NATEBE), with membership from teacher educators and graduate students in business education (ACTE, 2002).

Delta Pi Epsilon

Delta Pi Epsilon (DPE) is a national graduate honorary society for professionals who support and promote scholarship, leadership, and cooperation toward the advancement of education for business. The Commercial Teachers Club, established at New York University in 1936, was the forerunner of Delta Pi Epsilon. Paul Lomax was its first sponsor, and according to Dr. Herbert A. Tonne, "…we had dances, lectures, stimulating discussions and much, much socializing" (Sapre, 1981).

Membership comes from affiliated university chapters, state-based chapters, and the national chapter. The national executive board oversees the work of the society and makes appointments to national standing committees, national ad hoc committees, and other interorganizational groups such as the Policies Commission for Business and Economic Education and the Joint Committee on Economic Education. DPE hosts an annual national conference, conducts research projects, publishes journals and other literature, sponsors research awards annually, and provides research grants through its National Research Foundation, Inc. (Delta Pi Epsilon, 2002).

National Business Education Association

The National Business Education Association (NBEA) is the nation's largest professional organization devoted exclusively to serving individuals and groups engaged in instruction, administration, research, and dissemination of information for and about business (National Business Education Association, 2002a). The National Business Education Association evolved from many prior organizations beginning with Business Educators' Association in 1892 (Hosler & Hosler, 1992). Two organizations, however, are recognized as having the earliest national impact on business education: the National Commercial Teachers Federation (now North Central Business Education Association) and the Eastern Commercial Teachers Association (which became the Eastern Business Teachers Association). Mergers of other organizations in business education occurred and led to the formation of the United Business Education Association (UBEA) in 1946. UBEA was to grow into the National Business Education Association in 1962, as independent regional associations joined NBEA. The unification of all business education regions in the country did not occur until the Eastern Business Teachers Association became the Eastern regional affiliate of NBEA in 1972 (Hosler & Hosler, 1992).

NBEA now comprises five regional associations and two divisional associations. The regional associations are Eastern Business Education Association (EBEA), Southern Business Education Association (SBEA), North Central Business Education Association (NCBEA), Mountain-Plains Business Education Association (M-PBEA), and Western Business and Information Technology Educators (WBITE). The two divisional associations, with their separate membership and dues structures, are the U.S. Chapter of the International Society for Business Education (ISBE) and the National Association for Business Teacher Education (NABTE) (NBEA, 2002b).

Policies Commission for Business and Economic Education

In 1958, the executive board of UBEA (NBEA) authorized President Dorothy Travis to issue an invitation to the Delta Pi Epsilon president to meet in Washington, D.C., to discuss the possible formation of a committee that would issue statements of suggested policies for business education. As a result of their meeting, a Commission for the Advancement of Business and Economic Education was established under the joint sponsorship of NBEA and DPE, with financial responsibility divided equally (Hosler & Hosler, 1992).

When the Commission was established in 1959, it became the Policies Commission for Business and Economic Education. It later expanded its membership to include representation from the Business Education Division of the Association for Career and Technical Education. The aim of the Commission is to identify and define both existing and emerging issues in business and economic education.

Since its inception through 2003, the Commission has issued seventy-three statements. These statements "serve as yardsticks against which legislative leaders, business people, parents, as well as professional educators are able to assess the effectiveness of the components of business education and the total discipline" (PCBEE, 1997a, p. vi).

The PCBEE has published several statements that present the mission of business education. When the Commission started, it appeared to place business education at the secondary and postsecondary levels, as reflected in statements issued in the early years. Not until 1977 in Statement 23 (1997b), did the Commission include elementary schools in describing the mission of business education. Then in 1995 with Statement No. 57, an expanded mission was assigned to business education:

> We believe that business education programs should develop a broader client base that will become larger and more diverse, beginning with students at the elementary level and continuing throughout life. Elementary and middle schools will more frequently be sites for instruction in economic education, keyboarding, computer applications, and business career exploration (Policies Commission for Business and Economic Education, 1997c, p. 122).

SUMMARY

Business education has changed from a field that emphasized typewriting, shorthand, and bookkeeping at the secondary level to a multi-level discipline that embraces technology beginning at the elementary school level. With the support of federal dollars provided through numerous laws and, in particular, the landmark 1963 Vocational Education Act, business educators were able to expand curriculum offerings to students at various levels of instruction. Federal dollars also fostered the growth of student organizations, DECA, FBLA/PBL, and BPA, which enrich the education of students with activities beyond the classroom.

Professional groups—the Association for Career and Technical Education, Delta Pi Epsilon, the National Business Education Association, and the Policies Commission for Business and Economic Education—have defined the philosophy of business education and made many other contributions to the discipline of business education as it continues into the twenty-first century.

REFERENCES

Anderson, R. I. (1980). Word processing. In M. H. Johnson (Ed.), *The changing office environment* (Yearbook No. 18, pp. 55-65). Reston, VA: National Business Education Association.

Association for Career and Technical Education. *About ACTE/divisions.* (2002). Retrieved July 16, 2002, from http://www.acteonline.org

Association for Career and Technical Education. (2002). *About ACTE/who we are.* Retrieved July 16, 2002, from http://www.acteonline.org

Bahr, G., & Wegforth, R. P. (1976). A historical development of an economic emphasis in business education. In R. B. Woolschlager & E. E. Harris (Eds.), *Business education yesterday, today, and tomorrow* (Yearbook No. 13, pp. 20-40). Reston, VA: National Business Education Association.

Barlow, M. L. (1986). The growth of the AVA family. *Vocational Education Journal, 61*(8), 27-31.

Bartholome, L. W. (1997). Historical perspectives: Basis for change in business education. In C. P. Brantley & B. J. Davis (Eds.), *The changing dimensions of business education* (Yearbook No. 35, pp. 1-16). Reston, VA: National Business Education Association.

Bliven, B., Jr. (1954). *The wonderful writing machine.* New York: Random House.

Delta Pi Epsilon. (2002). Retrieved July 16, 2002, from http://www.dpe.org

Drum, W.O. (1980). Data processing. In M. H. Johnson (Ed.), *The changing office environment* (Yearbook No. 18, pp. 45-54). Reston, VA: National Business Education Association.

Gordon, H. R. D. (1999). *The history and growth of vocational education in America.* Boston: Allyn and Bacon.

Hosler, M. M. (2000). *A chronology of business education in the United States 1635-2000.* Reston, VA: National Business Education Association.

Hosler, R. J. (1969). Objectives of business education. *Balance Sheet, L,* 243.

Hosler, R. J. (1971). *Discussion on the history and development of business education.* Seminar presentation at the University of Wisconsin-Madison, Madison, WI.

Hosler, R. J., & Hosler, M. M. (1992). *The history of the National Business Education Association.* Reston, VA: National Business Education Association.

Kaufmann, B. A., & Wills, J. L. (1999). *User's guide to The Workfore Investment Act of 1998* (E. Ries, Ed.). Alexandria, VA: Association for Career and Technical Education.

Lee, J. D. (n.d.). *History Business Division of American Vocational Association 1927-1981.* Unpublished manuscript, State Department of Public Instruction, Indianapolis, IN.

Lynch, R. L. (2000). *New directions for high school career and technical education in the 21st century* (Information Series No. 384). Columbus, OH: ERIC Clearinghouse on Adult, Career, and Vocational Education, The Ohio State University.

National Business Education Association. (2002a). *Mission and purpose.* Retrieved July 16, 2002, from http://www.nbea.org/about/aboutmission.html

National Business Education Association. (2002b). *Regional and divisional associations.* Retrieved July 16, 2002, from http://www.nbea.org/about/aboutrda.html

National Business Education Association. (2001). *National standards for business education: What America's students should know and be able to do in business* (2nd ed.). Reston, VA: Author.

National Commission on Secondary Vocational Education. (n.d.). *The unfinished agenda: The role of vocational education in the high school.* Columbus, OH: The National Center for Research in Vocational Education.

Nichols, F. G. (1979). *Frederick G. Nichols' memoirs, 1878-1954: The early view of business education.* St. Peter, MN: Delta Pi Epsilon.

Policies Commission for Business and Economic Education. (1997a). *Policy Statements 1959-1996.* Cincinnati, OH: South-Western Educational Publishing.

Policies Commission for Business and Economic Education. (1997b). This we believe about the mission of business education, Statement 23, 1977. *Policy Statements 1959-1996.* Cincinnati, OH: South-Western Educational Publishing.

Policies Commission for Business and Economic Education. (1997c). The evolving vision of education for and about business, Statement 57, 1995. *Policy Statements 1959-1996*. Cincinnati, OH: South-Western Educational Publishing.

Policies Commission for Business and Economic Education. (2002). *This we believe about the need for business education*, Statement 71, 2002. Reston, VA: National Business Education Association. Retrieved May 6, 2002, from http://www.nbea.org/curfpolicy.html

Reese, S., & Thompson, J. (2002). A new age of technology. *Techniques. 77*(2), 38-43.

Roberts, M. (1999). The making of a leader. *Techniques, 74*(8), 20-22.

Roberts, R. W. (1971). *Vocational and practical arts education* (3rd ed.). New York: Harper and Row.

Sapre, P. M. (Ed.). (1981). *Early leaders in business education at New York University*. Reston, VA: National Business Education Association.

Secretary's Commission on Achieving Necessary Skills. (1991). *What work requires of schools: A SCANS report for America 2000*. Washington, DC: U.S. Department of Labor.

Secretary's Commission on Achieving Necessary Skills. (1992). *Learning a living: A blueprint for high performance: A SCANS report for America 2000*. Washington, DC: U.S. Department of Labor.

Sims, R.R. (1976). *A comparison and contrast of the 1976 national programs of the Office Education Association and the Future Business Leaders of America-Phi Beta Lambda, Inc.* Unpublished manuscript, North Texas State University, Denton, TX.

Thompson, J. F. (1973). *Foundations of vocational education*. Englewood Cliffs, NJ: Prentice-Hall, Inc.

Tonne, H. A. (1961). *Principles of business education*. New York: McGraw-Hill Book Company.

Tonne, H. A., & Nanassy, L. C. (1970). *Principles of business education*. New York: McGraw-Hill Book Company.

Wood, M. (1985). Implementing an information processing program. In J. A. Hibler & B. C. Fry (Eds.), *Information processing in the business education curriculum* (Business Education Forum 39 (8), April-May, pp. 72-78). Reston, VA: National Business Education Association.

Delivery Systems for Business Education

Lloyd W. Bartholome
Utah State University
Logan, Utah

The purpose of this chapter is to provide a framework or structure to the delivery of business education instruction from elementary school through college. The chapter presents an overview of the business curriculum at the various levels of instruction, as well as a review of how technology has affected and continues to affect the content and delivery of business education. A crucial part of delivering business education is the teacher, and a review of qualities necessary for a good teacher is part of this chapter. Finally, this chapter includes a brief description of accrediting agencies, which assist in ensuring that educational institutions provide quality programs and that business teachers are qualified to deliver instruction effectively. Additional discussion of the delivery of business education, including analyses of instructional technology, teaching methods, and curriculum are presented in subsequent chapters.

DELIVERY SYSTEMS DEFINED

Systems are interdependent parts that are separated by a boundary from their surrounding environment. The parts are units from within a system such as individuals, work groups, or subdivisions of an organization, and a boundary refers to the perimeter or outer limits of the system. The exact boundary around a system is arbitrarily defined by the person conducting the analysis, who may be an academic researcher or a manager bent on solving a particular problem. Thus, there is no right or wrong way to define a boundary around a system; only as the purpose of the analysis is determined can a boundary definition be drawn and evaluated (Farace, Monge, & Russell, 1977).

A system is usually part of another system, either a suprasystem or a subsystem. A *suprasystem* is a larger system that incorporates the system under scrutiny while *subsystems* are parts of larger systems, which themselves show boundaries (Farace et. al., 1977). Thus, instruction in business education is part of a larger suprasystem of the whole context of teaching and learning, while delivery systems in business education are subsystems of instruction in business education.

Delivery systems are defined in this chapter as macro descriptions of instruction in business education. These business education delivery systems are the various business subjects to be taught at different levels of instruction and the communication processes, both human and technical, to ensure that the subjects are learned.

THE IMPACT OF TECHNOLOGY

Technology has affected business since the invention of the abacus in the Middle East around 500 B.C. (Courter & Marquis, 1997). Two inventions in the 1800s, the telephone and the typewriter, probably influenced business more than any other technology up to that time. The computer, especially the personal computer, probably has affected the business world even more than the telephone and the typewriter. In fact, the personal computer was the single invention that led to the demise of the typewriter (Bartholome, 1997). A brief history of technology and its impact on business and education are discussed in this section.

During the early to middle 1900s, typewriting courses were the single most important business courses taught in the public schools (Bartholome, 1997). Now, typewriting instruction has been replaced with computer classes. This technological change actually began in the early 1800s, when Charles Babbage completed his first diagram of a steam-powered difference engine and, subsequently, an analytical engine. Babbage's "difference engine" was the first machine to calculate numbers using a punch card system, the forerunner of the mainframe computer. Herman Hollerith at the U.S. Census Bureau was the first to mechanize the census process. He worked on a machine to tabulate census information. Hollerith used punch cards like Babbage did, but in a different way. He used the cards to record specific pieces of census data. Hence, the Hollerith code was developed.

World War II prompted the next breakthrough in the history of technology. The U.S. government needed a way to tabulate massive amounts of data. In 1943 John Mauchly, an instructor at the Moore School of Engineering at the University of Pennsylvania, and John Eckert, a graduate student at the school, submitted a proposal to the U.S. Army to create a general-purpose computer for analyzing its data. Finally, in 1946, just after World War II, and three years after the computer was conceived, Mauchly and Eckert unveiled the electronic numeral integrator and computer, the ENIAC, the first general purpose computer. This early computer included 18,000 vacuum tubes and weighed 30 tons. In the late 1940s and 1950s, mainframe computers came into their own.

A milestone equally as important as the general purpose computer was the development of the semiconductor in 1948 by Bell Laboratory physicists. The first semiconductors consisted of germanium, a metalloid element resembling silicon. Other semiconductors were discovered, and finally silicon, which is made easily from the raw materials of rocks or sand, was used to develop semiconductors. These semiconductors are called transistors, still in use today in various forms. In 1971 a small company named Intel, currently the world's foremost chip manufacturer, put all the critical components of the computer into one chip, the microprocessor. Today Intel is still the main producer of microprocessor chips.

The first commercial microprocessor was available in 1971, and in 1976 the Apple II was released. Personal computers became a reality after a few visionary people ignored those who said that it couldn't be done. Bill Gates was one of those people, the past president and chairman of the board of Microsoft Corporation, one of world's largest companies. At the age of 15, Gates began getting paid for writing computer programs, and at 21, started Microsoft with his friend Paul Allen. By the late 1990s Bill Gates was ranked by *Forbes* magazine as the world's richest private citizen with an estimated worth of almost $20 billion (Courter, 1997).

Nearly 50 million personal computers are sold annually in the U.S., and now the majority of U.S. households have personal computers. Furthermore, almost 90 percent of teenagers use computers at least several times a week. Teens from lower income homes use computers as often as teens from wealthier families, but they get their access at school (Computer Almanac, 2002). The personal computer is a necessary business tool that is used in almost every area of business.

Technology to Enhance Instruction

When the technology revolution began to occur earlier in the twentieth century, technology similar to the personal computer was being used to enhance instruction. In the late 1920s Sidney Pressey advocated the use of "teaching machines" to handle drill and informational material. He developed a machine that resembled a typewriter carriage with a window that revealed a question with four answers. The user pressed a key that corresponded to the correct answer. In 1958 B.F. Skinner developed a machine based on Pressey's model; he noted that the machine kept the student active and busy and would not allow the student to proceed until the material was understood. Skinner's ideas launched the programmed instruction movement in the United States (Hypertext History of Instructional Design, 2002).

It was not until the advent of the personal computer, however, that computer programs were developed as true teaching machines to enhance instruction. Then, with the advent of the Internet, those teaching machines could be used by anyone who might be connected electronically to the World-Wide Web. A similar pathway from basic machine to complex digital system is traceable in the delivery of the classroom lecture.

During the late 1940s and 1950s, teachers began to use overhead projectors as lecture aids. They could face their students and write on a projection system that would show on a white board or screen. Now these teaching aids have become sophisticated, computer-controlled systems for instruction that allow teachers to show videotapes and films. Accompanying projection systems allow teachers to write on a flat-panel screen for immediate viewing, and to incorporate videotape, film, or slides into their lectures. The introduction of presentation software such as PowerPoint has made it much easier for teachers to outline and present their lectures and make the lectures readily available for students to review.

The World Wide Web

The development of the computer allowed for the gradual evolution of the World-Wide Web, a tool that has revolutionized research and access to information. The Internet actually had its roots in 1957 when Russia launched Sputnik. The U.S. Department of Defense developed a research project known as Advanced Research Projects Agency (ARPA). ARPA, working with the Rand Corporation, developed the model for the communication network called "packet switching," which allowed data to be transferred in nonsequential chunks and then reassembled at the destination. Thus, if a certain key computer were down, the information could be rerouted to other computers on the network.

In 1969 ARPA developed the ARPA-Net in conjunction with four institutions of higher education acting as hosts. These institutions included the University of California at Los Angeles, University of California-Santa Barbara, the University of Utah, and the Stanford Research Institute. The ARPA-Net was the beginning of the Internet, and at that time Telnet and File Transfer Protocol (FTP) were developed. In 1982 Transmission Control Protocol/Internet Protocol (TCP/IP) was created, which permitted easier packet switching of data with appropriate checking for transmission errors. Thus, the system for communicating data was built. In 1991 Tim Burners-Lee developed the first code for the World-Wide Web.

The first Web browser was Mosaic, invented in 1993 by Mark Andreessen, who later co-founded Netscape Communications Corporation and marketed Netscape Navigator. At about the same time Bill Gates and Microsoft developed Internet Explorer, another Web browser. Now almost everyone in the world has some access to electronic mail and the World-Wide Web through the use of the Internet (How Did the Internet, 1997).

Users had difficulty finding data on the Internet before search engines were developed. Now they can go to Infoseek (www.infoseek.com), Alta Vista (www.altavista.com), or Google (www.google.com) and find information about any topic in the world. Thus, many business teachers use the Internet in their business classes to teach students how to find business-related information. The Internet can stretch the imagination of business teachers by enabling them to incorporate technology into their daily lesson plans.

Technology Certification

Technology certification is sponsored by industry, and is not usually required of business teachers by their school systems. Still, a number of business teachers have been quick to take advantage of certification in order to become expert in the computer technology that they have the opportunity to teach.

The first company to offer certification using various hardware and software programs was Novell, with its Certified Network Administrator (CNA), Certified Network Engineer (CNE), and Certified Network Instructor (CNI). In most cases a private consultant provided the instruction, after which the sponsoring software company would administer a test. Instruction and tests were generally very expensive; however, in most instances the certification was offered as an educational benefit to workers and paid for by companies. More companies soon began to offer certification, and eventually public schools began to be offer it in high schools and vocational or applied technology postsecondary schools. Some of the common certifications today include Novell certification; CISCO Certified Network Associate (CCNA); Microsoft Certified Professional (MCP); Database Development Certification sponsored by Oracle/Sun; Microsoft Certified Systems Administrator (MCSA); Microsoft Certified Systems Engineer (MCSE); and CompTIA certification, which is a certification measuring the competency of service technicians and Internet networking professionals (Information Technology Programs, 2001-2002; LearnKey, 2002). In many instances states and school districts will sponsor teachers for certification in order to qualify them to teach certification courses in turn. After students complete the appropriate coursework and pass the industry sponsored test, they receive a certificate indicating the software and hardware skills in which they have become certified.

Instructional Technology

Business teachers are closely associated with instructional technology teachers. *Instructional technology* as a discipline is an outgrowth of auxiliary services for teachers called *audio-visual services* in the 1940s and 1950s. During that period individuals preparing to be teachers learned how to thread a 16-mm projector and how to develop programs to place on films. These audio-visual departments changed to departments of instructional systems and library science in the 1960s. By the 1970s these departments were titled some variation of the term, "instructional media department." During the late 1970s the discipline and the professional associations related to the discipline changed their names to *instructional technology*. Instructional technologists have assisted teachers greatly in the use of the current technology to enhance instruction with techniques such as videotaping, developing tutorials for students, and using technology to design instruction (C. Stoddard, personal communication, May 28, 2002).

Distance Learning

Today, both instructional technologists and teachers develop and offer courses on the Internet. Two of the most common programs used to offer online courses are Blackboard and WebCT. Business teachers who learn how to design instruction for use with these programs can conceivably teach classes on the Internet to anyone, anywhere in the world.

THE BUSINESS CURRICULUM: WHAT IS BEING TAUGHT?

Other chapters in the yearbook identify specific curriculum components that are used when teaching business subjects. This section provides a general overview of business content taught from elementary school through college.

Curriculum is generally interpreted to be "all of the planned experiences of the learners under the school's guidance" (Hass, 1987, p. 5). It is a program of education whose purpose is to achieve broad goals and related specific objectives based upon theory and research in past and present professional practice (Hass, 1987). The curriculum includes all planned school activities, such as library, health care, assemblies, food services, and intellectual studies. In fact, the curriculum is the social system within the school designed to provide experiences for students.

When discussing the business curriculum, one must consider whether the experiences are planned for personal business use or for career use, because the business curriculum encompasses both areas. The first step in planning is the task analysis phase, in which a teacher determines objectives and must decide how to "deliver" the material to the students. The planning of instruction is a major part of the curriculum process. During the planning process, the teacher must also consider the unique nature of each individual, of the local community, and of the subject matter content (Mager, 1997). Teachers must themselves be aware of their objectives, and then clearly communicate desired outcomes to learners. Broad goals and specific objectives should be determined through (a) the consideration of the demands of society and the job, (b) the characteristics of the students, and (c) the potential contributions from related fields that will enrich the learning experience (Mager, 1997). For a detailed discussion of the planning process, see Chapter 4. Programs have often failed when teachers and other curriculum planners have failed to recognize the need for adequate planning. Planning is of prime importance in the curriculum development process.

A Curriculum Vision by NBEA

In 1983 the National Business Education Association (NBEA) appointed a task force on new concepts and strategies to predict how business education should relate at the various levels of instruction. The task force concluded that (a) the personal computer should be part of all business instruction from elementary school through college, (b) that elementary school students must learn to keyboard to use computers effectively, and (c) that business teachers must accept responsibility for teaching computer software and hardware use at all levels of instruction (NBEA Task Force, 1983).

The NBEA task force on new concepts also developed and implemented a list of curriculum standards for teaching business subjects. NBEA printed its first curriculum publication in 1988. A subsequent revision entitled, "The National Standards for Business Education" was printed in 1995 and updated in 2001. The standards, which address every business subject at every level of the curriculum, have been incorporated and used in most states. The next section provides an excerpt from the standards (at each academic level) followed by a summary description of those standards.

The Elementary School Curriculum

The *National Standards for Business Education* states the following regarding the elementary school (grades K-6) curriculum.

> "Business educators at this level begin with the assumption that learning is lifelong. They serve as resource persons, technology coordinators, peer coaches, media specialists, or team teachers. By partnering with elementary teachers, business educators integrate technology and career awareness into the curriculum" (NBEA, 2001, p. xi).

At the elementary school level, keyboarding is probably the business subject that has had the most effect on the curriculum. One reason for this is that students are learning to read, write, and spell, and keyboarding enhances this instruction. As early as the first typewriting study, conducted in 1929, researchers concluded that typewriting (keyboarding) enhances the learning process in language arts. Evidence showed that (1) elementary school children can learn to key correctly and well, (2) keyboarding experiences accelerate language arts skills and competencies, (3) keyboarding helps improve penmanship, (4) creative composition expression can be stimulated by work at the computer keyboard, (5) elementary school children submit neater papers and make more projects and displays when their materials are typed, and (6) added use of the computer and the typewriter improved attitude towards schoolwork (Bartholome & Long, 1986; Nanassy, Malsbary, & Tonne, 1977). Research on the use of the typewriter and computer keyboards and its effect on the improvement in basic skills has just begun, and additional research needs to be done.

Probably the single most important event that happens in a child's educational experience is learning to read, write, and spell. "There are counties in California that use third grade reading scores to plan their prison populations for 20 years down the road," stated Alan Hoffmeiser, director of the Reading for all Learners project at Utah State University ("Apache Educators," 2002, p. A-3).

Keyboarding instruction at the elementary school is often led by business educators. In many instances, however, computer laboratory instructors teach the keyboarding with the help of the business teachers, or business teachers act as advisors to the computer laboratory instructors or the classroom teachers. Goals for keyboarding in the elementary schools are to be able to key 25-30 words a minute in the third grade with gradual improvement through the sixth grade. Early keyboarding skills are just beginning-level skills, since employment-level skills using the computer keyboard require a considerably higher level. It is important that additional keyboarding and word processing be taught in the middle school/junior high school and high school levels to ensure progressive skill development.

Keyboarding effectively requires more skill than 25-30 words a minute. Highly skilled people in industry are able to keyboard at 70-100 words a minute. Chapter 8 provides a thorough discussion of keyboarding instruction at all educational levels.

The Middle/Junior High School Curriculum
Middle schools usually consist of grades 6-8, and junior high schools, usually grades 7-9. However, other combinations may occur in the public middle/junior high schools. The *National Standards for Business Education* states:

"In middle/junior high school business educators teach students to use technology effectively in the learning process, regardless of subject matter. Students are introduced to basic business entrepreneurial and personal finance concepts and how these are integrated into a business venture. In realistic simulations learners apply technology skills and demonstrate the soft skills needed to become effective and successful in the business world" (NBEA, 2001, p. xi).

The middle/junior high school curriculum, while an exploratory and career awareness period, is still building on basic skills of reading, spelling, writing, and computing. Typical business-oriented classes include information literacy, which teaches students how to use the Internet to research information and write reports; career awareness and technology careers classes, which introduce students to the world of work; and basic business and personal finance, which provide students with basic business and personal accounting principles. Various keyboarding applications are continued in the middle/junior high school, such as introduction to word processing. (Central City Public Schools, 2002; Kelly Middle School, 2002; Utah Link, 2002).

In many systems the ninth grade is part of the high school, and students at that level begin to learn foundation skills for business and industry. Some of the skills taught are word processing and technology education, including the use of the Internet, multimedia, and the computer for communication. While business classes in the elementary school may consist of a keyboarding class for one half hour, two or three days a week, business classes in the middle/junior high school are for longer periods of time and usually continue for at least 9 to 18 weeks, with the students meeting every day. Because the middle/junior high school is a period in which students start to think about their future careers, they take more intensive career-related subject matter classes.

The High School Curriculum
The high school curriculum usually consists of grades 9-12 or 10-12. The *National Standards for Business Education* states:

"Business educators at the secondary [high school] level facilitate learning in a student-centered environment, guiding learners as they develop the skills needed to be effective consumers, citizens, workers, and business leaders. Learning is customized. Learners select projects based on personal and career interests working independently or in teams to use a wide range of technologies to solve unstructured problems. All of these opportunities support students' desires for independence and creativity as well as their need for collaboration. Learners continue to explore careers, apply work-based skills, gain business experience, and participate in student organizations" (NBEA, 2001, p. xii).

The high school is a time when students refine their basic skills and become seriously involved with their future career skills.

Business teachers have been at the forefront of the computer revolution; therefore, almost all business subjects at the high school level have some relationship with the use of the personal computer. Many high schools require students to take at least a one-semester computer literacy course, which is usually taught by a business teacher.

Typical business courses at the 10th-grade level include economics, accounting, information processing, word processing, keyboarding, business law, business mathematics, business communication, telecommunications, using the Internet, foundations of technology, and various multimedia and communications technology courses. Tenth grade students also begin to learn to understand how a computer works, and computer maintenance courses are taught beginning at the tenth grade.

Tenth-grade classes may also include beginning marketing, international marketing, and E-commerce (marketing on the Internet), as discussed in Chapters 15 and 17. Fashion merchandising and sports marketing also are popular marketing courses. Similar business and marketing classes are taught in grades 11 and 12, and often 10th, 11th, and 12th-graders are all grouped in the same classes, depending on the number of electives they are allowed to take with their required courses. Business and marketing classes are usually elective subjects, except for a semester or two of required technology. Thus, students in 11th and 12th grade continue to take advanced marketing courses, as well as advanced computer classes, word processing, accounting, entrepreneurship, economics, desktop publishing, telecommunications, and multimedia, and other courses (Utah Link, 2002), as discussed in Chapters 8 through 17. Business and marketing teachers also provide work-based learning through cooperative education programs and business internships, which are discussed in Chapter 18.

As discussed previously, technology certification is a popular entry to the 11th and 12th-grade high school classes. Courses such as the Microsoft Certified Professional program, Oracle certification, CISCO Certified Networking Associate program, the Novell-sponsored Certified Network Administrator, and other industry certifications are popular entries in the 11th- and 12th-grade high school business education curriculum. These certifications begin in high school and continue at the postsecondary levels of instruction. Computer programming is also usually introduced in grades 11 and/or 12, and grade 12 may also include some of the necessary skills for management, including introduction to management, administrative management, and banking and finance (Information Technology Programs, 2001-2002).

Business teachers at the high school level must provide quality programs and "sell" their programs to the students and to the parents, since business classes are high school electives, and the number of electives available is oftentimes restricted because of the various requirements of the local school districts.

Vocational/Technical Schools

The *National Standards for Business Education* lists two-year postsecondary/community colleges or technical colleges as one area. However, because the role of the two schools is somewhat different, the vocational technical school and the community college are discussed separately. The *National Standards for Business Education* states:

"Two-year postsecondary/community colleges or technical colleges are ideal places for providing education and training to people who want to broaden their educational experiences, change careers, expand employability options, and/or upgrade technological skills. Certificate and degree programs, when combined with practical work experience, can smooth the transition from high school to two- and four-year colleges or to the business world. A variety of available learning formats affords students the opportunity to develop advanced technological skills, refine their understanding of economic principles and systems, and enhance their proficiency and communication, critical thinking, management, personal finance, problem solving, team building, and decision making" (NBEA, 2001, p. xii).

Vocational and technical schools emerged as a result of federal funding during the early and middle 1900s. Business programs became eligible for vocational funding as a result of the Vocational Education Act of 1963 and subsequent federal legislation. The primary purpose of these schools is to provide jobs for the unskilled and underskilled populations. The federal government generally distributes the money to the states; states then add their own funds and determine how the vocational/technical schools should be organized. In some states these schools have their own governing board; in some states they are part of the state higher education governing board; and in other states public school boards govern them.

The primary difference between vocational/technical schools and community colleges is that the role of a vocational/technical school is to provide job training, whereas the community college provides general education as well as education for careers. Typical business programs in vocational/technical schools are programs to prepare accountants, office personnel, and computer technology workers. However, some computer technology programs, such as programming and computer repair, may be taught in other technology divisions of vocational/technical schools.

Many vocational/technical schools are open entry, open exit. That is, students can come at any time and leave when they have completed the objectives and requirements of the job for which they are preparing. Most vocational/technical schools provide job placement assistance for their students. Many of these programs are intensive, all-day programs lasting for six months to a year, while others are taught in the evening for employed individuals. Vocational/technical schools also offer highly specialized short-term training at the request of local businesses. In some instances vocational/technical schools over the years have expanded their roles and become community colleges.

Community Colleges

Community colleges do exactly what the name suggests—they serve a local population in a way that other colleges do not. Community colleges were originally developed to provide the first two years of college for the local population, but now they have multiple roles. One role is to provide those first two years of college to those who intend to transfer to a four-year institution; another role is to provide employable skills for those who do not wish to continue any further in college; a third role is to provide ongoing education for people who have already been to college and are retraining, or who are working and want to improve their job skills. Classes are typically taught in the evening, since most students who wish this type of education are not able to attend during the day. Some states have community colleges that are part of the higher education system.

States with highly organized community college systems usually have separate community college governing boards. For example, the state of California community college governing board provides leadership and technical assistance to 108 community colleges and 72 community college districts. This board is responsible for allocating state funding to the colleges and districts. The California community college system is the largest system of higher education in the world, serving over 2.5 million students who have a wide variety of education and career goals (California Community Colleges, 2002).

Teaching at the community college level generally requires a master's degree; however, instructors are sometimes hired with bachelor's degrees, especially in occupational/vocational education programs. Many community college instructors begin teaching at the community college level part-time, either during the day or in the evening.

Community college business programs build upon the skills learned in high school and in some cases may even duplicate some of those skills. Typical classes taught at the community college include technology including word processing, spreadsheet, database, programming, and various industry certification classes such as Novell, CISCO, and Microsoft. Community college students who plan to transfer to other business programs at four-year colleges take some of their prerequisites at the community college. These may include courses in business law, business communication, marketing, economics, management, as well as completing general education courses needed to enter a four-year college. Business teachers may contribute to the general education program by teaching such transfer subjects as economics, business statistics, finance, business law, and computer literacy.

Besides providing industry certification, community colleges usually offer associate degrees. The Associate of Arts and/or Science degree program is a degree program of primarily general education for students who wish to transfer to a four-year school. Although some career preparation may be involved, at least one-third or more of the program is related to general education. The Associate of Applied Science is the other associate degree program usually offered at community colleges. This degree prepares students for employment in a variety of fields, including business. Students generally work toward an Associate of Applied Science degree in business fields such as office systems, accounting, and information technology.

Private Business Schools

Private business schools are generally established by individuals or corporations and do not receive state funding, as discussed in Chapter 1. Some private business schools are approved to provide college classes that are transferable to other colleges and universities. However, many private business schools are not accredited by regional accrediting agencies, and thus, colleges and universities will not accept their transfer credit. Students must be careful when attending private business schools to verify that the credit is transferable to colleges and universities, if transfer is desired.

Colleges and Universities

The *National Standards for Business Education* does not address college and university business curricula, because that area is very broad. To teach at the four-year college or university, an instructor normally has a doctorate degree. Typical business degrees include majors in finance, marketing, accounting, information systems, economics, office systems, and management. All business students must take what is called a "common body of knowledge" in the business field, the content of which is specified by the Association for the Accreditation of Collegiate Schools of Business (AACSB). Those specifications require that an undergraduate curriculum in business have a general education component of at least 50% of the student's four-year program. This requirement means that at least half of the program must be offered outside the College of Business. The standards also specify that the curriculum must include knowledge in behavioral science, behavioral economics, mathematics and statistics, and written and oral communication.

In addition, the curriculum requires business courses consistent with the mission of the college and the program. These courses usually include classes in information systems, economics, law, finance, marketing, production, and business strategies (The International Association for Management Education, 2001).

Concurrent/Dual Enrollment

Because a definite division between high school and collegiate classes does not always exist, and because many bright high school students are ready for college classes during their senior year, many schools have developed concurrent/dual enrollment plans. *Concurrent/dual enrollment* means that students take high school courses and receive both high school credit and college credit for a course. Usually students must be accepted at a college to qualify for this type of credit. High school credit is then granted by the high school based upon the standards set by the State Office of Education. Concurrent/dual enrollment courses are frequently offered in business education. Typical courses include computer applications, beginning accounting, and word processing. Concurrent/dual enrollment allows high school students to enter college with some college credits already accrued. For high school teachers to teach concurrent/dual enrollment classes in a high school, they must be certified or approved by the collegiate institution offering the credit, or a community college instructor may go to the high school and teach the class.

HUMAN DELIVERY SYSTEMS

Human delivery systems consist of the people who develop, teach, and evaluate the curriculum. These individuals include school librarians, instructional technologists, principals, superintendents, and other administrators. Of course, the most important human delivery system is the classroom teacher. This section identifies traits, characteristics, and skills necessary to be a good business teacher.

Traits of Effective Teachers

Effective business teachers must know the subject matter content and how people learn. They must be able to plan, teach, and evaluate objectives to ensure that learning takes place, as discussed in Chapters 4 and 7. The National Board for Professional Teaching Standards (2002), a volunteer organization to recommend standards and certify teachers at the national level, has studied traits of good teachers and has identified five core propositions that good teachers should know and be able to do. These propositions are summarized as follows:

1. *Teachers are committed to students and their learning.* This statement means that teachers make knowledge accessible to all of their students, and they believe that all students can learn. They treat students equitably. At the same time, they recognize individual differences. They adjust their teaching based upon what they observe about their students. Accomplished teachers must understand how students develop and learn. They also must foster students' self-esteem, motivation, character, civic responsibility, and their respect for individual culture, religious, and racial differences.

2. *Teachers know the subjects they teach and how to teach those subjects to students.* Teachers must have a thorough knowledge and understanding of the subjects they teach. They must use this knowledge to develop the critical and analytical

capacities of their students. They understand where difficulties may occur in instruction, and they modify their practice accordingly.

3. *Teachers are responsible for managing and monitoring student learning.* Teachers set and maintain the instructional setting, and they capture and sustain the interest of their students. Good teachers command a range of instructional techniques and know when to apply each. They know when to engage groups of students to ensure a disciplined learning environment and how to organize instruction to allow the school's goals for students to be met. Good teachers assess the progress of all of their students individually and as a group.

4. *Teachers think systematically about their practice and learn from experience.* Good teachers are models of educated persons, and they seek to inspire their students to increase their curiosity, tolerance, honesty, fairness, respect for diversity, and appreciation of cultural differences. They draw on their knowledge of subject matter and instruction to make judgments about sound teaching practices.

5. *Teachers are members of learning communities.* Good teachers contribute to the effectiveness of the school by working collaboratively with other teachers and administrators in the school on instructional policy, curriculum development, and staff development. They are aware of specialized school and community resources that can help their students, and they are skilled at employing these resources. They work collaboratively and creatively with parents, engaging them with their students and the school.

Characteristics of Effective Business Teachers

The characteristics of good business teachers can be summed up in one sentence. Good teachers must have passion, skill, enthusiasm, sensitivity, heart, and humor. In a survey of principals who hire teachers, the word *passion* was repeated over and over by principals ("What Qualities Do Principals," 2002). Principals said that teacher candidates must have a passion for knowledge, a passion for teaching, and a passion for students.

Good teachers who have the necessary skills will be successful. These skills include the ability to provide strong curriculum content to students by defining objectives, providing lesson plans, understanding the audience, and presenting appropriate and stimulating instruction. Proper use of instructional methods, including technology, is also important. General methods are discussed in Chapters 4 through 7, and specific content methods are discussed in Chapters 8 through 18.

Good teachers must be enthusiastic. Because teachers are role models, they impart their enthusiasm to their students. Enthusiastic teachers have a positive attitude, are self-assured, and want their students to have a positive attitude and good self-esteem.

Good teachers are sensitive to the needs of the students and parents, as well as sensitive to colleagues. Being sensitive means being a good listener, noticing when students are having learning problems, and assisting them with those problems.

Good teachers have heart—they are open and receptive to teaching students. They are people want to be where they are, and who believe that teaching is one of the greatest of all professions.

> Good teachers have a sense of humor. Humor gets teachers and their students through the daily challenge of learning. To use humor appropriately, teachers need to understand the characteristics and backgrounds of their students ("What Qualities Do Principals," 2002).

TEACHING AND PROGRAM STANDARDS

Teaching and program standards ensure quality of the delivery systems. Various professional agencies ensure that standards are met and programs and institutions are accredited. This section introduces various agencies involved in the accreditation of business teacher education programs.

State Standards

Every state accredits its own teacher education programs. In many instances reciprocal certification agreements are made among states to enable a teacher who has completed an accredited program in one state to be eligible for certification in another state. State teaching standards are usually performance-based and relate to all phases of the delivery system, including the curriculum and the success of the teacher in the curriculum. In some states the National Business Education Association Teaching Standards are used as guidelines for the subject matter content of the standards. To be certified/licensed as business teachers, most states require teachers to complete a business teacher education program in secondary education that includes a student teaching experience. Many states also require business teachers to pass a teaching proficiency and/or content area proficiency test. Most business teachers have vocational education/career and technical education certification or endorsement in addition to secondary education certification/licensure. Vocational education or career and technical certification requires specific courses, generally one year of work experience in business and industry, and specific endorsement such as cooperative education.

Professional Accreditation Bodies

The primary accreditation body for the accreditation of teacher education is the National Council for Accreditation of Teacher Education (NCATE). The U.S. Department of Education and the Council for Higher Education Accreditation recognize NCATE as a professional accrediting body for teacher preparation. Most higher education institutions with quality teacher education programs belong to NCATE.

NCATE is the teaching profession's mechanism to help establish high quality teacher preparation. NCATE accredits schools, colleges, and departments of education and works closely with state departments of education. NCATE's accreditation is a performance-based system. NCATE also works closely with all areas of teacher education, including business teacher education. The NBEA standards, as well as state-sponsored standards for business education, are incorporated as part of ongoing NCATE reviews of teacher education institutions (National Council for Accreditation of Teacher Education, 2002).

National Board for Professional Teaching Standards (NBPTS)

The National Board for Professional Teaching Standards was created in 1987. Its mission is to establish high and rigorous standards for what accomplished teachers should know and be able to do. National Board certification is offered to teachers on a voluntary basis and is valid for ten years. The certification does not replace state licensure. In each state, school districts and schools decide how best to use the standards process. The standards are portfolio-based. Students develop a portfolio based upon their experiences in the classroom, including their student teaching experiences. National Board certification demonstrates a teacher's practice measured against high and rigorous standards and is above and beyond state certification ("What Teachers Should Know," 2002).

The Association to Advance Collegiate Schools of Business (AACSB)

The Association to Advance Collegiate Schools of Business (AACSB) began its accreditation functions in 1919 and accredits business schools. From the 1950s through the 1990s, AACSB also included business teacher education programs as part of its business school accreditation, when teacher education programs were housed in the business schools. Its most recent accreditation standards eliminated the accreditation of business teacher education programs in collegiate schools of business; however, business teachers should be aware of AACSB accreditation so that they can advise their students to attend accredited business schools. The role of AACSB is to ensure that the accredited institutions produce outstanding graduate programs with qualified faculty and structured learning through relevant curricula. More than 700 business schools in collegiate higher-education institutions exist, and more than 400 of those are accredited by AACSB (The Association to Advance Collegiate Schools of Business [AACSB], 2002).

SUMMARY

Technology has affected business instruction since the invention of the abacus. The typewriter, the telephone, and especially the computer, are technological advances that have dramatically affected business instruction. Computers have a profound affect on business instruction by providing e-mail, the Internet, technology certification, and various methods for business teachers to deliver instruction at a distance, as well as in the classroom. Business instruction enhances basic skills in the lower grades. The business curriculum gradually broadens to include personal and occupational business skills, as students progress through the various levels of instruction. Teachers who have the appropriate background of subject expertise and teaching expertise, as well as characteristics of passion, enthusiasm, sensitivity, and humor, ensure that the business content is delivered in a quality manner. Quality controls for business programs and instruction include general teacher education accreditation bodies, as well as accreditation bodies and standards for business education. All of these components ensure that quality instruction is delivered to business students.

REFERENCES

Apache educators study cache reading. (2002, May 3). *Herald Journal*, Logan, UT, p. A3.

Bartholome, L. (1997). Historical Perspectives: Basis for Change in Business Education. In C. Brantley & B. Davis (Eds.), *The changing dimensions of business education.* (Yearbook No. 35, pp. 1-16). Reston, VA: National Business Education Association.

Bartholome, L., & Long, I. (1986). Teach keyboarding to elementary school students. *National Association of Laboratory Schools, I*(4), 22-28.

California Community Colleges, Sacramento, CA. (2002). Retrieved May 7, 2002, from http://www.cccco.edu/about/about/htm

Central City Public Schools, Central City, NE. (2002). Retrieved February 11, 2002, from http://www.cecps.esu7org

Computer Almanac. (2002). *Computer use in homes and work.* Retrieved May 9, 2002, from http://www-2.cs.cmu.edu/afs/cs.cmu.edu/user/bam/www/numbers/html

Courter, G., & Marquis, A. (1997). *The learning guide to computers.* Alameda, CA: SYBEX, Inc.

Farace, R., Monge, P., & Russell, H. (1977). *Communicating and organizing.* Reading, MA: Addison-Wesley Publishing Company.

Hass, G. (1987). *Curriculum planning* (5th ed.). Newton, MA: Allyn & Bacon, Inc.

Hopkins, Gary (1998). What qualities do principals look for in a new teacher? (2002). *Education World.* Retrieved January 31, 2002, from: http://www.education-world.com/a_admin/admin071.shtml

How did the Internet get to be such a big deal? (1997). Wilsonville, OR: Franklin, Beedle & Associates.

Hypertext History of Instructional Design. (2002). Retrieved August 7, 2002, from http://www.coe.uh.edu/courses/cuin6373/idhistory

Information Technology Programs. (2001-2002). Salt Lake City, UT: Utah State Office of Education, Applied Technology Services.

Kelly Middle School, Eastpointe, MI. (2002). Retrieved February 11, 2002, from http://www.misd.net/macombschools/eastdet.pdf

LearnKey Training. (2002). (Volume 19). St. George, UT: LearnKey, Inc.

Mager, R. F. (1997). *Preparing instructional objectives.* Atlanta, GA: The Center for Effective Performance, Inc.

Nanassy, L., Malsbary, D., & Tonne, H. (1977). *Principles and trends in business education.* Indianapolis, IN: Bobbs-Merrill Company.

National Board for Professional Teaching Standards, National Board Certification. (2002). Retrieved February 11, 2002, from http://www.nbpts.org/nat_board_certification/index.html

National Business Education Association. (2001). *National Standards for Business Education: What America's students should know and be able to do in business* (2nd. ed.). Reston, VA: Author.

National Council for Accreditation of Teacher Education. (2002). Retrieved May 30, 2002, from http://www.ncate.org/ncate/m_ncate.htm

NBEA Task Force on New Concepts and Strategies. (1983). Future direction and recommended actions for business education. *Business Education Forum, 38*(2), 3-11.

The Association to Advance Collegiate Schools of Business. (2002). Accreditation. Retrieved May 14, 2002, from: http://www.aacsb.edu/accreditation/

The International Association for Management Education. (2001, February 14). *Standards for business accreditation.* St. Louis, MO: Author.

Utah Link. (2002). Curriculum courses, grades k-12. Retrieved May 7, 2002, from http://www.uen.org/lessons

What teachers should know and be able to do. (2002). National Board for Professional Teaching Standards. Retrieved February 11, 2002, from http://www.nbpts.org/standards/stds.cfm

Current Trends in Business Education

Martha C. Yopp
University of Idaho–Boise Center
Boise, Idaho

The current trends in business education suggest a bright future for the field. These are exciting times for business educators and future business educators, who have an unprecedented opportunity to approach the future with optimism and vigor to ensure that programs thrive. Today the business curriculum is moving into the middle and elementary grades, while new levels of technological and occupational certification are becoming available in secondary and postsecondary programs.

With its publication of the *National Standards for Business Education* in 2001, the National Business Education Association (NBEA) stands at the center of the developmental growth trends in the 21st century. The Standards provide business educators at all levels with a dynamic model for curriculum excellence, encompassing teaching, learning, and assessment. This chapter begins with an overview of the *National Standards* statement, and moves through a description of the following current trends that have been identified as significant in recent business literature.

- Adding value to business education,

- The emerging role of business educators,

- Enrollment trends,

- The shortage of business teachers,

- Alternative certification,

- The growth of computer technology,

- The emergence of knowledge management principles and practices,

- Globalization of the economy,

- Integration of business courses into the academic curriculum,

- School reform, and

- Assessment and accountability mandates.

NATIONAL STANDARDS FOR BUSINESS EDUCATION

The National Business Education Association publishes the *National Standards for Business Education* every five to six years. The latest *National Standards* describes what all K-14 students should know and be able to do in business (National Business Education Association, 2001). These standards are based on the philosophy that business education competencies are essential for all students. An education for and about business offers students the opportunity to master the fundamental knowledge and skills needed to succeed in business and in life.

Business teachers "play a prominent role in preparing students to become responsible citizens capable of making astute economic decisions that benefit their personal and professional lives"(NBEA, 2001, p. vii). Business teachers introduce students to the basics of personal finance, consumer economics, economics, and international business. Business educators need to continue to promote the philosophy that now, more than ever, all students need to be literate in business and economics. All students need to practice the interpersonal, team, and leadership skills that will help them function successfully in adverse international business environments. All students need to embrace lifelong learning skills that foster flexible career paths and confidence in adapting to a workplace that demands constant retraining and acceptance of change. All students must be able to use technology to interact effectively with other people, solve problems, and complete routine tasks.

The *National Standards* recommend that at the completion of their secondary or postsecondary preparation, students should be able to (1) function as economically literate citizens, (2) understand how businesses operate, and (3) demonstrate interpersonal, team, and leadership skills. Students also should develop an awareness of career opportunities and be able to select and use technology as a tool for making personal and business decisions. They need well-developed communication skills and should understand how accounting is used to make decisions about the allocation of valuable resources. Students should understand the principles of law, appreciate the value of having an entrepreneurial spirit, and understand that the various functions of business are not separate but are interrelated. Critical-thinking skills are imperative for students to move into adult life and the multiple roles they will assume as citizens, consumers, workers, managers, business owners, and directors of their own economic futures.

The *National Standards* incorporate a four-tier developmental approach to business education. In the elementary grades, business educators partner with elementary teachers to integrate technology into the curriculum, mainly in the forms of keyboarding and the introduction of students to career awareness. Not only can elementary students learn to type, but those who do type improve their language arts skills. There is fairly consistent evidence that the keyboard's influence on spelling is more favorable than on any other subject tested in the Stanford Achievement Test. Elementary teachers have found that children with keyboarding skills are more careful about the beginnings and endings of their sentences, and they recognize structure better and pay more attention to details.

In junior high or middle school, business educators introduce students to concepts of basic business, entrepreneurship, and personal finance. Students learn to apply technology skills and work to develop the "soft," or interpersonal skills needed to become successful in the business world.

At the secondary level, business educators "facilitate learning in a student-centered environment…[where] learning is customized: students select projects based on personal and career interests. Working independently or in teams, students use technologies to solve unstructured problems…Learners continue to explore careers, apply work-based skills, gain business experience, and participate in student organizations" (National Business Education Association (NBEA), 2001, p.xii).

At the postsecondary level, business educators offer certificate or degree programs that enable students to develop "advanced technological skills; refine their understanding of economic principles and systems; and enhance their proficiency in communication, critical thinking, management, personal finance, problem solving, team building, and decision making" (NBEA, 2001).

Perhaps the most important new trend that the *National Standards for Business Education* emphasizes is that "learning is customized." Curriculum and classroom activities cannot be a "one-size-fits-all" variety. Students should be encouraged to select unstructured projects, work independently or in teams, and use a wide range of technologies to solve problems. A customized approach poses great challenges and opportunities for business teachers and their students.

ADDING VALUE TO BUSINESS EDUCATION

Economists speak frequently about the importance of adding value to goods and services as a way of increasing profits and maximizing utility. Judith Olson-Sutton (1998), former NBEA president, draws a parallel by suggesting ways to add value to business education. Olson-Sutton believes that the business education curriculum encourages students to develop competencies in information technology, international business, and entrepreneurship. At the same time, students need competency in soft skills such as teamwork, human relations, problem solving, and decision making, as well as professionalism, ethical conduct, appreciation and respect for others, self-confidence, and integrity.

To keep pace with dynamic changes in the workplace, business educators must help to add value to their students and their expectations for success. Ways to help accomplish this goal include the following strategies (Olson-Sutton, 1998):

- Assist students in their personal development.

- Demonstrate a positive attitude toward learning.

- Exhibit a passion for business education.

- Evaluate programs and curriculum continuously.

- Establish a vision to provide future direction for business education.

- Provide a broad-based curriculum that incorporates technology.

- Prepare students for a global community.

- Serve as an advocate for students and programs.

THE EMERGING ROLES OF THE BUSINESS EDUCATOR

In Policy Statement 68, *This We Believe About the Emerging Roles of the Business Educator,* the Policies Commission for Business and Economic Education (2001) acknowledged that the 21st century presents many opportunities and challenges for business education. Creating an environment where students learn to think and embrace the challenges of societal and technological change is a top priority. Individuals who are able to communicate, collaborate, value diversity, and effectively use technology will be in high demand. Substantive changes in students, learning environments, delivery systems, and technologies will continue. These changes transform the business educator's role to that of facilitator, educational designer, collaborator, mentor, political advocate, and lifelong learner.

Business educators will be expected to facilitate experiences that allow students to become independent learners, as well as team members who are accountable for their own knowledge and performance. Toward this end business educators should employ the following strategies (Policies Commission for Business and Economic Education, 2001, pp. 14-15):

- Use collaborative, project-based learning activities in which students share thoughts and ideas to solve problems;

- Encourage students to locate, retrieve, evaluate, and use information from traditional and emerging resources;

- Create a positive environment in which learners take educated risks and experience trial-and-error learning;

- Encourage students to develop and apply criteria for assessing individual and group achievement; and

- Assist students in the development of their educational plans.

ENROLLMENT TRENDS

Enrollments in business education courses and programs should benefit from the fact that the number of students in grades 9-12 is high and is projected to remain high through the year 2010 (Lynch, 2000). In addition, more male students are enrolling in computer-related business courses. Program improvements, business-education partnerships, student interest in computers and technology, and a growing sense that students need some employment skills have increased interest in business courses.

Business leaders want educators to provide students with the knowledge and activities necessary for them to develop essential workplace skills. This effort should positively support enrollments in business courses and programs. Stephen Marriott, senior vice president of culture and lodging sales recruiting, Marriott International, believes that educators need to hold students accountable for their work. To promote teamwork and leadership skills, students also need to work on group projects that teach them how to solve problems and get along with others. Marriott also emphasizes the fact that internships and work experience are increasingly important to employers (NBEA, 2001).

The skills that students bring to the workplace should be those that businesses need. If business teachers have close contact with employers in their communities, they will be able to seek their advice about curriculum (NBEA, 2001). Career cluster or career pathway programs provide business educators with an opportunity to improve the marketing and delivery of the curriculum. These programs include a business curriculum structured around broad business, marketing, finance, and management clusters in which the teaching of academic skills is embedded in business courses. Subject content is presented in a problem or project-based manner, using examples drawn from the local and regional economic base (Grubb, 1996). This approach provides opportunities for business educators to become advocates for high school students to participate in well-articulated postsecondary education opportunities. The mutual benefits of career pathway programs to local employers and to the students in their midst not only strengthen communities, but also create crucial support for business education in the schools.

THE TEACHER SHORTAGE

A shortage of business teachers exists in some areas of the United States, and the shortage is expected to become more widespread. Up to 50% of business teachers who were in classrooms in 2000 are expected to retire or leave the profession within the next 5 to 10 years (Wilson & Plutsky, 2001). At the same time, the number of business teacher education preparation programs has declined. *Business Education Forum* lists 104 institutions offering degrees or licensure in business education in 37 states (NBEA, 2001).

The shortage of business teachers is being addressed in various ways. A number of states have adopted alternative paths for certification of individuals with a four-year college degree in business plus real-world business experience.

ALTERNATIVE PREPARATION AND CERTIFICATION

The National Association for Business Teacher Education (NABTE) has adopted a position statement, as follows: "…both traditional and alternative business teacher licensure/certification programs must be designed and offered by accredited colleges and universities" (Perreault et al., 2001, p.14). The NABTE report adds that the National Center for Educational Information (NCEI) has identified 12 states that have developed exemplary alternative teacher certification routes. The more effective alternative teacher certification programs require a strong academic coursework component, a bachelor's degree, a successful classroom internship, and collaboration with state departments of education. A fairly strong public interest exists in allowing people to teach when they are perceived to have content knowledge and related work experience.

COMPUTER TECHNOLOGY

For an example of a time when alternative certification might answer a program's need for business expertise the classroom, the computer revolution is a good place to look. Computer technology has affected business education in a variety of ways. Computers have replaced typewriters; but more importantly, the computer has changed what business educators teach and how they teach it. Introductory keyboarding is now offered in elementary school, in shorter time frames (Jennings, 2001). This approach provides opportunities for business teachers to collaborate with elementary school teachers to ensure that students are being taught the touch system when they begin using a computer for composition.

Business teachers are often hired to teach keyboarding, computer applications, and/or career awareness at the middle school and junior-high level. Business education at this level provides students with a solid foundation for developing good keyboarding techniques and computer skills that secondary teachers can build and expand upon.

Business educators need to promote keyboarding in ways that add value to the K-12 curriculum. Empirical evidence indicates that teaching keyboarding improves language arts skills and spelling (Bartholome, 1999). Providing keyboarding instruction at a single grade level is not enough. Students should learn the keyboard early and should be provided with opportunities for skill reinforcement as they advance through the grades.

In some states and districts keyboarding and computer applications are required for high school graduation. Business educators should work through their local, state, regional, and national professional organizations to promote business technology requirements in their districts.

Karen Schmohe, Executive Editor for Keyboarding/Office Technology at South-Western/Thomson, suggests that "new key learning" is not the same as keyboarding mastery (2001). Business teachers need to emphasize and provide incentives for students to develop keyboarding mastery by reinforcing touch-typing skills using the correct fingers. Solid keyboarding skills are essential in today's high-tech world. Business professionals who have keyboarding skills are more productive than those who do not (Jennings, 2001).

Technology is very powerful and promises to improve productivity and the quality of life in the United States as well as other parts of the world. Computer applications courses are popular with many students and provide business teachers with an opportunity to integrate basic business concepts, office procedures, and accounting into the computer application courses. Teachers should design realistic projects that support a business theme and require using computer applications. Real-world applications can involve developing actual projects for the school or for local businesses. Business teachers now have an excellent opportunity to use and teach the latest versions of popular office software, become proficient in voice-recognition software and wireless technology, and continue to work closely with students involved in organizations such as Business Professionals of America, Future Business Leaders of America, and DECA in their quest to compete successfully in regional, state, and national competitive events.

KNOWLEDGE MANAGEMENT

Another curriculum initiative that provides mutual benefit to schools and businesses is the teaching of "knowledge management," which grows out of a need identified by businesses for improved performance of office personnel. The term "knowledge management" appears frequently in the literature about business and organizational learning; it is the effective management and use of an organization's knowledge resources. The concept of knowledge management includes both recorded documentation and unrecorded information that exists through the knowledge and experiences of the employees of an organization (Read-Smith, Ginn, & Kallaus, 2002).

Knowledge management requires in-depth thinking about knowledge, the form it takes, the processes used to create it, and its financial value to the organization. This concept advocates the sharing of information to generate efficiency and foster innovation. Business leaders and consultants regard knowledge as the chief asset of organizations and the key to a sustainable competitive advantage (Davenport & Prusak, 1998). Recent studies to determine what skills businesses want office professionals to possess emphasize both recordkeeping and records management.

Knowledge management is broader than records management or records and information management; however, records and information management are important components of a comprehensive knowledge management system. Knowledge management principles and practices should be integrated into the business education curriculum; filing and records management modules and units can be included in various business education courses such as, computer applications, keyboarding, general business, management, marketing, accounting, office procedures, and cooperative office education.

GLOBALIZATION OF THE ECONOMY

The teaching of economics has always been aligned with the mission of business education. Fundamental economic principles, microeconomic principles, macroeconomic principles, and broad social goals are part of a business educator's required curriculum for business teacher certification. Grounding students in the study of economics is essential, as business teachers assume responsibility for international business and economics courses in their classes. The globalization of the world economy necessitates that students be aware of the impact of international trade on Americans' employment opportunities and their standard of living.

One in five jobs in the United States depends on international trade (Pool & Stamos, 1994). Business educators can promote understanding and appreciation of other countries and their people, culture, economic systems, languages, religions, customs, and human rights records by integrating cross-cultural education into the K-12 curriculum early and frequently. Now and in the future, appreciation, tolerance, and the valuing of diversity will be a fact of life for economic efficiency in the United States and around the world. Business educators can find creative ways to integrate international issues and activities into their curriculum at all levels.

SCHOOL REFORM

Career and technical education programs, including business education, are being affected by the national movement toward school reform. Highly effective schools may be characterized by rigorous academic content with real-world applications and authentic assessment. Schools need to set valid standards and high expectations that help graduates perform in the real world, rather than focusing primarily on passing standardized tests (Lynch, 2000).

A successful school reform model is High Schools That Work, which combines the content of the college preparatory curriculum with career and technical education. High Schools That Work is based on the concept of education through occupations, as well as education for occupations. Students study specific skills to prepare for employment but are also expected to meet academic standards that enable them to pursue postsecondary education. Key practices include high expectations for student learning, rigorous career and technical courses, more required academic courses, learning in work environments, collaboration among academic and career and technical teachers, and an individualized advising system. Students are also provided with tutors and extra help after school and during the summer (Lewis, 2002).

The career and technical education curriculum is organized around career clusters and activities that promote effective decision making for life and work. Students identify the career clusters in which they are most interested and have realistic expectations for success and future growth. The *Standards for National Board Certification: Vocational Education* (1997) identified career clusters in business, marketing, information management, and entrepreneurship. Other clusters that align well with business programs include business and administrative services, financial services, information technology services, hospitality and tourism, and retail/wholesale sales and services.

Business teachers today are already facilitators of knowledge. Increasingly, they "are saying 'no' to lecture and 'yes' to self-directed learning opportunities, interactive environments, multiple forms of feedback, choice of assignments, and use of varied resources to create personally meaningful educational experiences"(Glenn, 2000, p.14). Assignments and activities are customized to meet the interests and needs of individual students.

THE INTEGRATED CURRICULUM
The integration of business principles, skills, and practices with the traditional academic curriculum is sound educational practice. For it to be accepted with enthusiasm by teachers, administrators, parents, students, and the business community, business educators must be proactive in linking the business curriculum to academic standards. Business topics, concepts, and modules lend themselves to the development of communication skills, computational skills, economics and personal financial management competencies, career exploration and related work experience, entrepreneurship, the entrepreneurial spirit, active learning, project-based activities, teamwork, and more.

Business educators must identify how content areas meet or exceed the academic standards being required for graduation. In addition, they must market the business education curriculum effectively to help ensure its adoption.

ASSESSMENT, ACCOUNTABILITY, AND ACADEMIC STANDARDS

"Assessment," "accountability," and "academic standards" are terms proliferating in the literature at all levels of education in the United States. Although the business education curriculum is not included in most mandatory testing throughout the country, it is nonetheless affected by academic assessments. Business educators must take a proactive stand to develop assessment procedures and standards that demonstrate that many of the core competencies required for high school graduation can be taught in business education courses.

For example, Nebraska business educators have developed assessment models for each of Nebraska's business education standards called "essential learnings." Nebraska's 50 models link business education essential learnings to the content standards for other disciplines (Sibert, 2001). Business educators in other states are engaged in similar projects to link business competencies to academic standards.

SUMMARY

The future for business education lies in the hands of those who embrace change and use it to their advantage. Business educators have an excellent model to lead them into the future in the *National Standards for Business Education,* which provides a blueprint for success. Current trends call for business teachers to add value to business education, customize the curriculum, utilize more real-world projects, and have students work in teams. The business curriculum is changing because of the growth and interest in computer technology, emphasis on knowledge management principles, globalization of the economy, and the integration of business courses into the academic curriculum. The school reform movement, with its assessment and accountability mandates, also has affected business education.

REFERENCES

Bartholome, L. W. (1999). *Typewriting/keyboarding instruction in elementary schools.* Utah State University, Logan, UT. Retrieved December 27, 2001, from http://bis.usu.edu/people/typewrit.htm

Davenport, T. H., & Prusak, L. (1998). *Working Knowledge.* Boston: Harvard Business School Press.

Glenn, J. M. L. (2000). Teaching the net generation. *Business Education Forum, 54*(3), 6-14.

Grubb, W. N. (1996). The new vocationalism: What it is, what it could be. *Phi Delta Kappan, 77*(8), 535-546.

Jennings, S. E. (2001). National keyboarding trends. *Business Education Forum, 55*(3), 46-48.

Lewis, M. V. (2002). *Needs, feedback, and the future: Need sensing activities in 2001* (Grant No. V051A990004). Ohio State University: National Dissemination Center for Career and Technical Education. (PDF257KB). Retrieved November 12, 2002, from http://www.nccte.org/publications/infosynthesis/r&dreport/NeedsFeedbackFuture_Lewis-3.pdf

Lynch, R. L. (2000). *New directions for high school career and technical education in the 21ˢᵗ century* (Information Series No. 384). Columbus, OH: ERIC Clearinghouse on Adult, Career, and Vocational Education, Ohio State University. (ERIC Document Reproduction Service No. ED 444037)

National Board for Professional Teaching Standards. (1997). *Standards for National Board Certification: Vocational Education.* (1997). Southfield, MI: Author

National Business Education Association. (2001). *National standards for business education: What America's students should know and be able to do in business* (2ⁿᵈ ed.). Reston, VA: Author.

National Business Education Association. (2001). Institutions offering degrees or licensure in business education. *Business Education Forum, 56*(1), 61-64.

National Business Education Association. (2001). Business leaders discuss essential workplace skills. *Keying In, 12*(2), 2.

Olson-Sutton, J. (1998). Recognizing and adding to the value of business education. *Business Education Forum, 53*(2), 4.

Perreault, H. R., Chalupa, M. R., Richerson, G. L., Groneman, N., Bartel, K., Joyner, R. L., & LaBonty, D. (2001). Alternative teacher education licensure/certification for business educators. *NABTE Review, 28,* 14-24.

Policies Commission for Business and Economic Education. (2001). This we believe about the emerging roles of the business educator, Policy Statement 68. *Business Education Forum, 56*(1), 14-15.

Pool, J. C., & Stamos, S. C. (1994). *Exploring the global economy.* Winchester, VA: Durell Institute of Monetary Science.

Reed-Smith J., Ginn, M. L., & Kallaus, N. F. (2002). *Records management* (7ᵗʰ ed). Cincinnati: South-Western Educational Publishing.

Schmohe, K. (2001). The way I see it. . . keyboarding/office technology. *Balance Sheet, 4*(1), 1. Retrieved October 24, 2001, from   http://www.swep.com/swepstuff/balancesheet/archives/0101/0101a.html

Sibert, B., Krejci, D., Schoenrock, R., & Sydow, S. (2001). Learning from Nebraska's assessment system. *Business Education Forum, 55*(2), 46-49.

Wilson, B. A., & Plutsky, S. (2001). The demand for business education teachers in California as perceived by middle school and high school principals. *NABTE Review, 28,* 42-45.

Planning for Instruction

Herbert F. Brown, III
University of South Carolina
Columbia, South Carolina

Cheryl D. Wiedmaier
University of Central Arkansas
Conway, Arkansas

Planning for instruction, one of the most important steps in teaching, is a systematic process wherein the teacher carefully and thoughtfully creates instructional materials that are effective for both teacher and student. An educator who follows this process will be well organized and ready to teach. Planning permits educators to reach all of their students in a personal way, enabling the students to reach their fullest potential. This chapter provides an overview of planning for instruction and addresses how the entire planning process should be highly integrated. Topics include course planning from the syllabus to the unit plan, individual lesson plans, and lesson activities.

STANDARDS

A variety of standards and competencies are available to assist teachers in planning course content and assessment activities. The National Business Education Association's *National Standards for Business Education: What America's Students Should Know And Be Able To Do In Business* is a good starting point to guide in the development of course content. Business educators and business professionals were brought together and formed into groups in order to review and revise the standards for a number of courses included in the business curriculum (NBEA, 2001). Educators also may review industry, state, and local standards/competencies as a guide in course planning.

Industry Standards

Employment standards are available for many industries and may be obtained from industry organizations. Some of these standards have been identified through industry certification testing, such as Microsoft, CompTIA (A+, Network+, etc.), Novell, and Cisco. The standards used in industry may serve as a guide to educators, as they work to develop activities and learning environments that are based on the real world. Educators may also wish to use the following resources:

- The *Dictionary of Occupational Titles* (http://www.oalj.dol.gov/libdot.htm) to determine the worker actions, tools, and equipment used; materials, products, and services provided; and the instructions and problem-solving activities used for specific job titles.

- The *Occupational Outlook Handbook* (http://www.umsl.edu/services/govdocs/ooh20002001/1.htm) for further information about employment, training, and other qualifications; licensure and advancement requirements; and the job outlook, earnings, and related occupations for job titles.

- The National Skill Standards Board (NSSB) for skill standards in 15 industry sectors, compiled by voluntary groups consisting of business, industry, community, and education leaders. The NSSB Web site at http://www.nssb.org contains documents and links related to national and international skill standards.

- The V-TECS organization (a consortium for innovative career and workforce development resources) for documents about developing curriculum based on occupational analysis and skill standards. Products may be purchased from V-TECS, while many helpful documents can also be found at their Web site at http://www.v-tecs.org.

- Licensing/certification organizations for information about the processes and competencies needed to pass the various industry exams. For example, information about the Microsoft MOUS certifications is available at http://www.microsoft-certification.com.

- Local advisory board members for a list of industry standards used by their organizations and for job descriptions and job specifications that apply to their employees.

State Standards

Educators need to check with their state departments of education in order to determine the state standards in place for students enrolled in business classes in their schools. Required state standards must be incorporated into course planning. Many states have developed performance-based competencies based upon the *National Standards for Business Education* (NBEA, 2001). These competencies may be presented by course title and suggested units and lessons. Some states have prepared checklists that educators may use to record the proficiency level or achievement of each student in the class. Examples of the state standards/competencies lists are found in the South Carolina Web site at http://www.myscschools.com/offices/cate/competencies/bus_mkt;

the Missouri Web site at http://www.dese.state.mo.us/divvocedbiz_be_competencies.htm; and the Virginia Web site at http://www.pen.k12.va.us/VDOE/Instruction/CTE/be.

Local Standards

The mission of a school district also must be considered in determining content for courses. Individual school districts may have developed a set of competencies or standards that graduating students must achieve before graduation. Exit exams are common for school districts and individual programs. These standards must also be incorporated into the business curriculum.

COURSE PLANNING

Course planning is an essential task for any teacher. For the new teacher, planning can be a daunting task. Effective planning involves much more than selecting a textbook and calling the chapters in the text "units." Course planning should include everything from examination of national curriculum standards to workplace skills. The National Association for Business Teacher Education (NABTE) (1997) suggests that curriculum should integrate real work experiences and should include the development of cognitive, affective, and psychomotor learning objectives for courses, units, and other experiences. Gagne, Briggs, and Wager (1992) define these three areas as follows: *Cognitive* refers to mental processes of learning. *Affective* refers to attitudes toward people and things, including qualities such as work ethics, morals, and values. *Psychomotor*, or motor skills, refers to physical actions such as keyboarding or collating papers.

Learning processes must also be examined and integrated into the planning process to ensure the effectiveness of the course planning. NABTE (1997) suggests that curriculum development should be structured and sequenced to optimize learning. The course planning process begins at the most general level, the syllabus, and ends at the most specific level, the lesson plan and lesson activities. The entire progression from syllabus, to unit, to lesson planning should show a natural and clear linkage, as each element is a component of the previous element.

Syllabus

The first step in the planning process is to develop a syllabus that outlines the entire course and shows how it will be structured, managed, and taught. The *course syllabus* is a contract between the teacher and the student that outlines the competencies that the student will gain/master, the topics for the course, and the policies and procedures that will be used to manage the learning environment. A syllabus typically includes the following parts:

- A header containing general course information (course title, time, location, instructor, etc.)

- A list of general competencies/abilities to be mastered by the end of the course

- Overall course goals

- The unit objectives and topics to be covered (This section outlines the entire course content by general topic. Determine these topics by finding a textbook that meets the overall course goals and model its structure or conduct a content analysis of the topics that support the overall course goals.)

- Outline of the course content

- Required materials, including textbook(s) and other materials, such as laboratory supplies

- Policies, procedures, and rules for the class

- Grading scale and information on how the grade will be determined

Students should be able to read a syllabus and know what is expected of them, how they will be evaluated, how they are to act, and what the teacher's role is in the learning process. The syllabus sets the tone for the course early in the instructional process.

Course Content

A syllabus should include an outline of the main *course content*, which includes the main topics or competencies that will be covered in the course. The outline of the course content gives the students and the teacher a clear framework from which to begin and progress through the instructional process. This outline is not a detailed account of every minor topic that will be covered, but a categorization of the entire course into main topics or units. These units are best determined by creating a detailed outline of everything to be covered in the course. The outline should then be condensed to no more than a dozen first-level headings. The headings then become the units of instruction. The remaining subheadings of the outline help an educator create the individual lessons that make up each unit of instruction. The general organization of planning elements from most general to most specific is syllabus, unit, and lesson. When planning the course content, the business teacher must determine the framework and sequencing of the lessons, units, and other instructional experiences (NABTE, 1997).

To determine what should be taught in the specific topic area, educators should examine available local, state, and national curriculum standards. As previously mentioned, the *National Standards for Business Education* (NBEA, 2001) are a good starting point for planning a course. These standards can help educators determine what should be a unit (achievement standards) and what should be at the lesson level (performance expectations). The *National Standards* also provide a developmental level framework, allowing an educator to determine which content should be taught at the various educational levels (elementary, middle, secondary, or postsecondary, and referred to as "developmental learning levels") (NBEA, 2001). These developmental levels can also help to establish course prerequisites, since performance expectations identified at earlier levels should be considered prerequisites for higher level performance expectations.

UNIT PLANNING

Once the syllabus and the detailed outline are created to organize the course content much of the unit planning work is completed. Burden and Byrd (1999) define *unit planning* as "developing a sequence of daily plans that addresses the topic of the unit in a cohesive way" (p. 56). They further identify the following six steps for unit planning:

1) Select the overall goals and the more specific objectives for the unit.

2) State the rationale for the unit.

3) Outline or organize the content.

4) Plan a sequence of daily lessons with appropriate instructional activities.

5) Plan and prepare for ways that students will be evaluated.

6) Gather and prepare the materials needed for instruction (pp. 57-58).

Unit plans for each of the units identified on the syllabus can be generated using the materials already created.

Organizing Unit Content

The first step is to take the outline that was created for the complete course and examine the subheadings identified under the unit. These subheadings should become the individual lesson topics within the unit plan. Once the lesson topics have been identified and recorded, lesson objectives can be generated to determine specifically what outcomes are expected from the students. While determining the lesson objectives, the teacher should determine how best to assess or evaluate the completion of the unit. All of these elements are combined to create the unit plan.

Creating Unit Plans

Each unit plan begins with header information identifying the course, unit topic, sequence number (1, 2, 3... the order of the units), and any other identifying information that may be useful. The unit objectives should then be identified and correlated with local, state, and national standards/competencies.

In the next section of the unit plan, the teacher outlines and lists the individual lessons by topics (designed to meet unit objectives), listing the specific lesson objectives that will be used to meet the requirements of each lesson. Adhering to the listing process allows for effective flow and sequence from one document to another and provides advanced planning for individual lesson plans yet to be created.

The lesson portion of a unit plan should constitute the bulk of the plan. Specific materials and supplies that are needed to complete the unit should also be recorded, so that they may be obtained prior to beginning the unit and individual lessons. The teacher should outline the type of assessment that will be used during the unit and during individual lesson delivery within the unit plan. Identifying evaluation processes is particularly important if unit tests are used to measure student understanding. The evaluation/assessment part of the unit plan may specify the number of formal assessments (e.g. tests, quizzes, and projects) that will be given and the lesson topics/content to be included in each.

Consideration should be given in the unit planning process to ensuring that all students are properly accommodated in the learning process. A statement as to how the unit can be adjusted for special needs students might be included to address this consideration.

The unit plan should be a good "snapshot" of what will take place during the implementation of the unit. A unit plan is similar to a lesson plan in format, but more general in the statement of topics and objectives. Table 1 shows a partial unit plan. (This unit plan is not complete and shows only the lesson objectives for the lesson shown in Table 2.)

LESSON PLANNING

After developing the unit plan, the teacher's focus should shift to generating the individual lesson plans that will constitute the major part of the planning process. Because the unit plans already identify the lesson topics and objectives, the teacher will transfer those elements to individual lesson plans for further planning. Some debate exists regarding the format for lesson plans; however, the following section provides details on the most common elements that generally constitute a lesson plan. When planning lessons, a teacher should consider the components or *events of instruction*. Gagne, Briggs, and Wager (1992) suggest the following nine events of instruction that should be considered when planning:

1) Gaining attention

2) Informing learner of the objective

3) Stimulating recall of prerequisite learning

Table 1. Partial Unit Plan

Computer Technology I – Unit 1
Microsoft Word

Unit Objectives:

1. Create documents with word processing software.
2. Edit and format documents.
3. Create large documents.
4. Integrate and modify graphics.
5. Incorporate advanced desktop publishing features.
6. Exhibit expert-level competence in Microsoft Word.

National Standards Correlation:

NBEA—Information Technology, V: Identify, evaluate, select, install, use, upgrade, and customize application software; diagnose and solve problems resulting from an application software's installation and use.

Unit Lessons:

1. Opening a Word document
2. Editing and document formatting
   a. Identifying the options on the formatting toolbar
   b. Formatting text using the formatting toolbar
   c. Modifying the formatting toolbar options
3. Working with graphics
4. Creating large documents
5. Doing desktop publishing with Word

Materials and Supplies:

Instructor computer with LCD projector
Microsoft Word (XP)
Textbook: *New Perspectives Office XP*, Course Technology, 2003
Activity Sheets 1-16

Unit Evaluation:

Unit application of Microsoft Word objectives
Unit lessons application test (1-5)
Activity sheets as basis for homework grade

4) Presenting stimulus material

5) Providing learning guidance

6) Eliciting the performance

7) Providing feedback about performance correctness

8) Assessing the performance

9) Enhancing retention and transfer (p. 203)

Most of these nine events should be incorporated into the "instructional activities" heading of the lesson plan format detailed in the next section.

Lesson Plan Format

Lesson planning is greatly simplified if the syllabus and the unit plans are already generated, since the lesson plan topics and lesson objectives have already been determined. At this stage, each lesson topic that was identified on a unit plan should be expanded into a complete lesson plan. When developing the lesson plans, the teacher must remember that the individual lesson plans should be specific enough so that a substitute teacher (or anyone other than the classroom teacher) can pick up the lesson plan and teach from it. Foremost, a lesson plan has to be usable. Schrag and Poland (1987) recognize most of the following components as part of a typical lesson plan:

- **Header** includes the lesson topic, order number, course information, classroom location, time/schedule for the class, and any other identifying information.

- **Lesson objectives** include measurable and specific objectives beginning with action verbs. Objectives should be short, concise, and written so that they could begin with the phrase "the student will…" (i.e., student-centered not instructor-centered). Local, state, and national standards should also be correlated to these lesson objectives. Lesson objectives will be discussed in more detail later in this section.

- **Prerequisites to learning** specify any information and skills students should already possess before beginning the lesson.

- **Materials and equipment** lists the materials and equipment, including text books, handouts, audio-visual aids, and computer technology that are needed to complete the lesson. This category may be subdivided into those materials and equipment needed by the student and those needed by the instructor.

- **Attention-getter/Anticipatory set/Advance organizer** attracts the students' attention and allows them to relate previous knowledge to the current lesson, or otherwise prepare them for the activity of the day by linking this activity with the activities to come. For example, the teacher might ask students to relate a court case that occurred recently in the news to the day's activity in a business law course. The anticipatory set could also be an activity that students plunge into immediately upon entering the classroom, with little or no initial direction. This "bell work" activity could be written on the board for students to begin as soon as they arrive. It should be tied to the day's lesson and not be mere busywork. For example, if the day's lesson covers job applications, the students could be instructed to retrieve a newspaper upon entering the classroom and begin searching for an ideal job. This example activity gets the students into the right frame of mind for the instructional activity and engages them in the day's topic the minute they enter the classroom.

- **Instructional activities** include instructor-centered steps that are used to deliver the instruction. These steps need to be specific enough so that a substitute teacher could teach the lesson (provided that adequate resources are available). Some suggest indicating approximate time allotments for each activity to help the execution. Time estimations can be very helpful for planning purposes; however, the teacher must make certain that plenty of extra work is available if that "20-minute" activity takes only 10 minutes. Within the instructional activities, the lesson is skills-based and should include a skills practice or reinforcement segment at the beginning of the lesson.

  Instructional activities based on the constructivist view would typically be more student-centered. These activities might include "discovery learning" and "student exploratory" types of activities, or student-guided projects that allow the students to organize their own paths to learning. One size does not fit all learning when it comes to instructional activities and general lesson delivery. Teachers should be prepared to adjust the lesson process and be flexible in accommodating all student learning styles.

- **Closing activity/Summary/Assessment/Evaluation** includes elements that give resolution to the lesson. Evaluations and assessments may be formal or informal, as discussed in Chapter 7, and the lesson may include a summary or closing activity to bring closure and reinforcement to the lesson.

- **Special needs accommodations** include a descriptive paragraph detailing how the lesson should be adjusted to meet the needs of students with learning disabilities, physical disabilities, or limited English proficiency. Provisions should be made to accommodate all students in the classroom. If special needs planning is included early in the planning process, the teacher will be much more prepared to accommodate all student learning appropriately.

Table 2. Completed Lesson Plan

Computer Technology I
Unit 1 – Word
Room 120B – M. Jones

Lesson Topic: Editing and Document Formatting – The Formatting Toolbar

Lesson Objectives:
The students will
1. Identify the options on the formatting toolbar.
2. Format text using the formatting toolbar.
3. Modify the formatting toolbar options.

Curriculum Standards Alignment:
1. Apply font formats (SC-5020-2).
2. Select and change font and font size (SC-5020-11).

Prerequisites:
Students should have completed activity sheets 1-5 in Microsoft Word.

Materials and Equipment:
Computers and LCD projector
Microsoft Word
Textbook: *New Perspectives Office XP*, Course Technology, 2003
Handout – Activity sheet 6 – "Word Formatting Toolbar".

Anticipatory Set/Advance Organizer:
Write the following activity on the board: "Record on a piece of paper the top ten text formatting features you would be likely to use when writing a report."

Instructional Activities:
1. Discuss the formatting features the students recorded for the anticipatory set; write the common ones on the board. "These features make word processing easier to use. Let's see how many of these formatting elements are already on the formatting toolbar."
2. Show the formatting toolbar on the LCD projector (or overhead). Move the cursor over each option working left to right and show the students the "pop-up" balloon help name that appears. Discuss the use of each.
3. Review the options, show the main menu item, FORMAT/FONT, and discuss the dialog box that appears—What are the similarities and differences between the toolbar choices and the full FONT options?

4. Have the students key their lists into a new Word document. (Students follow along as the teacher highlights each keyed formatting feature and uses each formatting option on a different line of text. Discuss each feature while displaying it on the LCD projector.)
5. Review student progress and clarify comprehension with questions.
6. Hand out Activity Sheet 6 and review the instructions with the students.
7. Instruct students to follow the directions and complete the activity sheet before the end of class.
8. Move around the class, observe progress, and provide assistance as needed.

Special Needs Accommodations:
The handout activity sheet 6 should have the font size changed to 48-point font and printed for visually impaired students (marked with an * on the seating chart).

Evaluation:
1. Grade and record the activity sheet.
2. Give unit quiz on Friday.

Comments:

- **Comments** are optional but provide the teacher a space to make notes about what went well or poorly during the lesson, with ideas on changes to be made the next time the lesson is taught.

Table 2 shows a completed lesson plan. Note that the lesson objectives correlate with the lesson objectives and topic listed on the unit plan example (see Table 1). The evaluation or assessments also match the activity sheet #6 listed on both documents.

Lesson Objectives
Lesson objectives are the cornerstone of a good lesson plan. Objectives clearly define what the students should learn in the lesson. Good lesson objectives should be designed so that they could begin with the stem "The student will . . .." Applying the common stem to the front of the objective ensures that they are student-centered and not instructor-centered. Objectives should begin with action verbs that identify what the student is expected to do; for example, "Define computer terms." This example is a very specific objective and clearly directs the student to complete an action. Notice that it could begin with the stem, "The student will . . .." The objective is also measurable, meaning that educators can assess whether the objective has been met. Numerous ways exist to assess whether a student can define computer terms (e.g., multiple choice, completion, matching questions, and more). When writing objectives, avoid verbs

such as "understand," "know," and "learn," because these qualities are not easily measurable. Contrast the verbs in this example: "Know computer terms" vs. "Define computer terms." ("Know" is not an action verb and is not readily measurable, whereas "Define" gives clear instruction and is easily measurable in an assignment and/or a quiz.) The selection of verbs is essential to writing good lesson objectives.

Objectives also should refer to a specific behavior or action. Consider the example, "The student will demonstrate formulas in Microsoft Excel." This objective is too general and fails to specify whether it means simple adding and subtracting, complex functions, or basic formula syntax. The way to measure this objective is unclear, because the activity to be completed is unspecific. Choosing a specific task ("Master basic formula syntax") improves the objective's assessment capability.

The *constructivist* viewpoint amplifies the approach to designing objectives and learning environments by suggesting that objectives be strictly learner-oriented, thus allowing students to select their own paths through the learning process. This method, known as discovery learning, allows students to explore and discover the solution to a problem without directed instruction from the teacher. The constructivist viewpoint focuses on the idea that students learn in different ways and, therefore, should be given more freedom to determine their own learning paths based upon their individual preferences. Objectives based on the constructivist viewpoint should describe standards of excellence in terms of a general procedure or a general product (Gronlund, 2000). The objectives are more specific at the introductory knowledge level, and become more general at the advanced knowledge level, allowing the learners to have more control over their learning experiences (Jonassen, 1991). The teacher may propose a problem, and the students are required to solve it through their own process of exploration and discovery, generating their own paths to learning. Teachers omit step-by-step directions, in favor of independent task organization by the student. For example, in a constructivist mode, the objective that "Students will research three companies and rank them as an investment" could be arrived at in a variety of ways— deduction, induction, or a combination of both, depending on the student's preferred learning pattern.

Learning Domains

Because students do learn in different ways, instructors should design their planning to deliver different types of instruction. Some instruction may involve hands-on, skills-based learning activities, or the *psychomotor domain*. Other instruction may be designed to deliver basic information and promote information processing, or the *cognitive domain*. Finally, an instructor may want to help students develop values and behaviors that are appropriate for the world they live in, part of the *affective domain*. The cognitive domain is used most often in the classroom, as it primarily involves the conveying of knowledge, facts, and information (Good & Brophy, 1995).

Table 3. Sample Verbs for Writing Cognitive Objectives	
Knowledge	**Comprehension**
Cite Recite Count Record Define Relate Draw Repeat Identify Select Indicate State List Tabulate Name Tell Point Trace Quote Write Read	Associate Express Classify Extrapolate Compare Interpret Compute Interpolate Contrast Locate Describe Predict Differentiate Report Distinguish Restate Explain Review Estimate Translate
Application	**Synthesis**
Apply Order Calculate Predict Complete Practice Demonstrate Relate Dramatize Report Employ Restate Examine Review Illustrate Schedule Interpret Sketch Interpolate Solve Locate Translate Operate Use	Arrange Integrate Assemble Manage Collect Organize Compose Plan Construct Prepare Create Prescribe Design Produce Detect Propose Formulate Specify Generalize
Analysis	**Evaluation**
Analyze Distinguish Appraise Experiment Contrast Infer Criticize Inspect Debate Inventory Detect Question Diagram Separate Differentiate Summarize	Appraise Measure Assess Rank Choose Rate Critique Recommend Determine Revise Estimate Score Evaluate Select Grade Test Judge

Note. From *Maricopa Community College District Curriculum Procedures Handbook*, www.dist.maricopa.edu/eddev/curric/cphb/crsvl.html, retrieved April 4, 2002. Reprinted with permission of Maricopa Community Colleges.

Bloom (1956) identified six levels of understanding that can influence higher levels of cognitive learning based on the appropriate use of verbs. The first three groups of verbs identify learning at a lower level (the knowledge, comprehension, and application levels) such as "define," "describe," and "apply." The second three groups of verbs identify learning at a higher level (the analysis, synthesis, and evaluation levels) such as "compose," "prepare," and "recommend." Depending on their use, a number of verbs can be appropriate for more than one level. Table 3 displays a list of cognitive action verbs by level (Maricopa Community Colleges, 2002).

Instructional planning should address some of the higher level cognitive objectives in the lesson. Teachers who include these higher level cognitive objectives provide students the opportunity to strengthen their critical thinking skills.

A lesson objective, for example, may state one of the following directives: define terms; compare and contrast features; critique data. Notice that the verbs are at different levels of understanding. To "define a term" implies rote memorization and recall. To "compare and contrast features" requires the students to have a greater understanding of the features and why one is better than others. To "critique data" requires a higher level of understanding of the material. These levels also apply to the other two domains (psychomotor and affective). For example, if students are learning to key (psychomotor), they begin by learning the keystrokes and then practicing until they master the process and it becomes second nature. If an educator is trying to instill good work behaviors in the classroom, the lowest level is for the students to know the rules (which may be assessed similarly to the low-level cognitive domain, with multiple-choice questions). Eventually the objective would be for students to demonstrate and then incorporate and exhibit these behaviors in their everyday activities. The higher level affective objectives are typically assessed with such tools as affective check sheets (or behavior check sheets) that document that the students are actually displaying these desired behaviors in their daily actions. Table 4 provides examples of objectives at two general levels.

Standards Alignment

In addition to planning for maximum student learning, educators need to ensure that they are teaching what is required by industry, the local district, the state department of education, and national standards. As previously noted, these types of documentation can help an educator plan the structure of a course. However, standards correlations may also be required to show proof that the lesson has met all state requirements. Individual state standards, which are the most commonly used for lesson planning, are generally based on the *National Standards for Business Education*. The best way to document the relationship between lesson objectives and local, state, or national competencies is to correlate state standards or competencies with lesson objectives. Therefore, clear documentation is provided that shows where and when the student met the required standard or competency.

Table 4. Examples of Objectives by Level

Lower Level

Define computer terms.

Key home row keys.

Identify professional behaviors.

Demonstrate proper keyboarding technique.

Higher Level

Solve management problems using spreadsheet applications.

Generate appropriate business documents from spreadsheet data.

Display professionalism.

Real and Relevant Curriculum

Relevant curriculum helps motivate students to learn because it prompts students to understand the importance of the skills, behaviors, and knowledge they are mastering in the standards-based curriculum and courses (NBEA, 2001). To prepare students for success in the workplace, a performance-based curriculum should provide real-world problems and experiences. In order to align classroom activities and assignments with real-world work experiences, educators may consider the following activities:

- Consult with advisory board members to determine the skills, knowledge, and behaviors actually performed in their organizations.

- Conduct observations of workers in area organizations to record the skills, knowledge, and behaviors used by workers in specific job titles.

- Review actual job descriptions and policy/procedure manuals for job titles in organizations that may employ the students.

- Provide job-shadowing experiences for students and have them report their experiences to the class.

Losh (2000) discussed the use of scenarios in developing contextual learning activities. *Scenarios* involve case study situations or simulations that integrate more specific academic and workplace skills. When developed correctly, scenarios incorporate the use of skills standards, technical skills, workplace skills, academic skills, and higher-order thinking skills in a real-world situation found in business/industry, community, or other related settings.

Learning activities incorporating real-world situations may also be utilized in the constructivist problem-solving environment. Jonassen (1994) explained that constructivist environments should support "a meaningful, authentic context for learning and using the knowledge they construct" (p. 37) by utilizing real-world, case-based problems. The constructivist approach also includes collaboration among the students with the teacher acting in a coaching/mentoring role. Real-world learning activities might include operating a school-based enterprise such as a school store or "investing" in the stock market.

ASSESSMENT

Assessment is an important component in the planning of curriculum and courses. The assessment should measure achievement of learning objectives. Students must demonstrate that they have learned the necessary skills, knowledge, and behaviors to the proficiency level set by the standards of the educator, the state, the school district, and the industry. A variety of assessment activities may be necessary for students to demonstrate actual learning. Traditional paper-and-pencil assessments are not always appropriate for students to demonstrate all they have learned. Educators must determine the assessment method that best validates student learning. Domain categorization and the learning levels of the lesson objectives help determine the types of assessments that should be implemented. Chapter 7 provides an overview of assessment and assessment methods in business education. The NABTE *Business Teacher Education Curriculum Guide and Program Standards* reinforces the use of formal and informal assessment measures to be used in assessing student progress (NABTE, 1997).

SUMMARY

Planning for instruction is a process. Educators plan course content and syllabi, units, lessons, and assessments based upon the goals for learning and upon industry, state, local, and the *National Standards for Business Education* (NBEA, 2001) and/or related competencies. Thorough planning helps educators become more effective in the classroom. Well-planned courses, units, and lessons provide students with an organized learning environment that results in better retention of the material and a more meaningful learning experience. While developing lessons and assessments, educators should address multiple learning domains to provide meaningful learning experiences for every student.

The integration of essential skills and course content must be a part of the planning process. When skills, behaviors, and knowledge are learned in real-world situations, students can identify the importance or relevance of their learning. Teaching in context leads to increased student retention of content. Assessment should also be conducted in a real-world context and account for differences in learning styles. Students should be allowed to demonstrate what they know, as well as what they can do.

REFERENCES

Bloom, B. S. (1956). Taxonomy of educational objectives. *Handbook I: Cognitive domain*. New York: David McKay Co.

Burden, P. R., & Byrd, D. M. (1999). *Methods for effective teaching*. Boston: Allyn and Bacon.

Fulkert, R. F. (2000). Authentic Assessment. In J. Rucker & R. J. Schoenrock (Eds.), *Assessment in Business Education* (Yearbook No. 38, pp. 71-91). Reston, VA: National Business Education Association.

Gagne, R. M., Briggs, L. J., & Wager, W. W. (1992). *Principles of instructional design*. Fort Worth, TX: Harcourt Brace Javanovich College Publishers.

Good, T. L., & Brophy, J. (1995). *Contemporary educational psychology* (5th ed.). White Plains, NY: Longman Publishers.

Gronlund, N. E. (2000). *How to write and use instructional objectives*. Columbus, OH: Prentice Hall.

Jonassen, D. H. (1991). Evaluating constructivistic learning. *Educational Technology, 31*(9), 28-33.

Jonassen, D. H. (1994). Thinking technology: toward a constructivist design model. *Educational Technology, 34*(4), 34-37.

Losh, C. L. (2000). *Using skill standards for vocational-technical education curriculum development*. Retrieved February 13, 2002, from http://www.v-tecs.org/Documents/Using%20Skill%20Standards.pdf

Maricopa Community Colleges. (2002). Suggested verb list for writing behavioral objectives. *Maricopa Community Colleges District Curriculum Procedures Handbook*. Retrieved April 4, 2002, from the Maricopa Community College Web site http://www.dist.maricopa.edu/eddev/curric/cphb/crsvl.html

National Association for Business Teacher Education (NABTE). (1997). *Business teacher education curriculum guide and program standards*. Reston, VA: National Business Education Association.

National Business Education Association. (2001). *National standards for business education: What America's students should know and be able to do in business* (2nd ed.). Reston, VA: Author.

Schrag, A. F., & Poland, R. P. (1987). *A system for teaching business education*. New York: McGraw-Hill.

Zeliff, N. D. (2000). Alternative Assessment. In J. Rucker & R. J. Schoenrock (Eds.), *Assessment in Business Education* (Yearbook No. 38, pp. 91-103). Reston, VA: National Business Education Association.

Providing for Students' Learning Styles and Differences

Beryl C. McEwen

North Carolina A&T University

Greensboro, North Carolina

Students learn in a variety of ways. Some prefer to focus on facts or data, while others prefer visual forms of information such as pictures or diagrams. Some students prefer verbal forms such as written or spoken information, and some must be actively involved to learn (Felder, 1996). Understanding how students learn and keeping them actively engaged in the learning process can lead to self-empowerment, self-direction, and higher academic achievement.

This chapter discusses learning styles, multiple intelligences, and diversity. It explores a variety of instructional strategies that business educators can use to ensure that all students have the opportunity to learn in their preferred style. The chapter also discusses how business educators can serve students with special needs, including students with disabilities, second-language learners, and gifted students.

THE BUSINESS EDUCATION CLASSROOM

Business educators teach courses that are designed to prepare students for their multiple roles as citizens, consumers, workers, managers, business owners, and directors of their own economic futures (National Business Education Association, 2001). The courses include accounting, business law, career development, communication, computation, economics and personal finance, entrepreneurship, information technology, international business, management, and marketing.

Business education classrooms in public schools typically attract students who are at middle school or high school levels. These students reflect the diversity of society. The

National Center for Education Statistics (2002) reports that in 2000, 39% of public school students were considered to be part of a minority group, an increase of 17% from 1972. The greatest increase was for Hispanic students—up from 11% in 1972 to 17% in 2000. Like society in general, business education classrooms include a diverse group of students, a variety of learning styles and intelligences, and students with special needs.

Learning Styles

Dunn and Dunn (1993) suggest that effective instruction demands that teachers consider a wide variety of learning styles among students, as well as help students to use their learning styles to maximize their academic performance. *Learning styles* are the ways in which people think, solve problems, and learn (Litzinger & Osif , 1992). Each person has a dominant or preferred learning style, and teachers need to be aware of these styles and develop appropriate instructional strategies and materials (Kolb, 1985). Education literature suggests that students who are taught using their preferred learning style are more empowered to participate in the learning experience and experience greater academic achievement.

A wide variety of learning style models are described in the literature. For example, the Myers-Briggs Type Indicator (Myers, 1978) measures extroversion versus introversion, sensing versus intuition, thinking versus feeling, and judging versus perception. Riechmann and Grasha's (1974) social interaction model addresses how students interact in the classroom and classifies learners as independent, dependent, collaborative, competitive, participant, and avoidant. Dunn and Dunn's (1978) Learning Styles Model is based on the premise that most individuals can learn, but individuals have different strengths. As shown in Table 1, this model has 21 elements grouped across five basic stimuli categories, including environmental preferences, emotional preferences, sociological preferences, physiological preferences, and psychological (cognitive processing) preferences.

Dunn and Dunn (1993) also describe learning styles more simply, in terms of students' physiological stimuli—visual, auditory, and kinesthetic. *Visual learners* benefit from diagrams, charts, pictures, films, and written directions. *Auditory learners* benefit from lectures, speeches, and reading aloud. *Kinesthetic learners* benefit from touching, feeling, and handling.

The literature suggests that one of the most widely accepted models is Kolb's (1984) Experiential Learning Model, which theorizes that experience is the source of learning and development. Table 2 shows the main characteristics of Kolb's model, which is based on four types of learner classifications—pragmatists (feel), reflectors (watch), theorists (think), and activists (do) (Kolb, 1984). Analysis of the model presented in Table 2 is drawn from the work of Kolb, Rubin, & Osland (1995), Hartman (1995), Felder (1996), and Clark (1999).

Table 1. Dunn and Dunn's Learning Style Elements	
Stimuli Categories	**Learning Style Elements**
Environmental Stimuli Preferences	Sound Preference Light Preference Temperature Preference Design Preference
Emotional Stimuli Preferences	Motivation Preference Persistence Preference Responsibility Preference Structure Preference
Sociological Stimuli Preferences	Self Preference Pair Preference Peers Preference Team Preference Adult Preference Varied Preference
Physiological Stimuli Preferences	Perceptual Preference Intake Preference Time Preference Mobility Preference
Psychological Stimuli Preferences	Global/Analytic Style Hemisphericity Preferences Impulsive/Reflective Preference
Note. From "Background of the Dunn and Dunn Learning Styles Model," (n.d.). North Carolina Distance Education Partnership in Special Education Project, Dr. David Lillie, Director. This grant was funded by the U.S. Department of Education. Retrieved November 15, 2002, from http://www.unc.edu/depts./ncpts/publications/learnstyles.htm	

Kolb identified these learning styles as a continuum that learners move through over time; however, he believed that learners usually prefer and rely on one style over others. Business educators are challenged to understand their teaching styles and to identify and respond to the learning styles of their students as a precondition for designing learning activities that can positively affect performance. A Teaching Style Inventory adapted from Dunn and Dunn (1993) is available at http://snow.utoronto.ca/Learn2/mod3/tchstyle.html.   Students' learning styles may be identified by using Kolb's Learning Style Inventory (1985) or the Dunn, Dunn, and Price Learning Styles Inventory (1985).

Table 2. Kolb's Learning Style Model

Types	Learner Characteristics	Instructor Roles
Pragmatists— Concrete Experiencers (CE)—*feeling*	Enjoy skills application, tutorials, labs, experiential learning, and observations.	Be a coach/facilitator/ helper.
Reflectors—Reflective Observers (RO)— *watching*	Enjoy brainstorming, logs, journals, and lectures.	Provide expert interpre- tation; be a taskmaster/ guide.
Theorists—Abstract Conceptualizers (AC)—*thinking*	Enjoy lectures, papers, analo- gies, case studies, readings, and thinking alone.	Allow time for reflection and withhold expert opinions.
Activists—Active Experimenters (AE)— *doing*	Enjoy problem solving, group discussions, simulations, case studies, peer feedback, and homework.	Project a very orga- nized, professional image.

Multiple Intelligences

The theory of multiple intelligences emerged from the research of Howard Gardner (1983), who defines *intelligence* as "the capacity to solve problems or to fashion products that are valued in one or more cultural settings." His view of intelligence differs from the traditional view, which recognizes two primary intelligences: verbal and computational. Gardner proposed that at least seven relatively autonomous intellectual capacities exist that individuals use to solve problems and create products. Brualdi (1996) described Gardner's seven intelligences as follows:

- *Linguistic intelligence*—involves mastery of the language, including the use of language as a means to remember information.

- *Logical-mathematical intelligence*—involves the ability to reason deductively and think logically and is most often associated with scientific and mathematical thinking.

- *Spatial intelligence*—allows one to manipulate and create mental images to solve problems. This intelligence is not limited to visual domains, as Gardner notes that it is also formed in blind children.

- *Musical intelligence*—allows one to recognize and compose musical pitches, tones, and rhythms.

- *Bodily-kinesthetic intelligence*—involves the use of one's mental abilities to coordinate one's own bodily movements.

- *Interpersonal intelligence*—involves the ability to perceive and understand other individuals, including their moods, desires, and motivations.

- *Intrapersonal intelligence*—involves the ability to understand one's own feelings and motivations.

Gardner (1993) believes that individuals possess varying degrees of all intelligences, and that teachers should consider all intelligences as equally important. Business educators should include instructional methods that appeal to multiple intelligences—role playing, cooperative learning, and reflection.

Diversity
Diversity is defined as those human qualities that are different from our own (University of Maryland, 2001). These qualities include age, ethnicity, gender, physical abilities/qualities, race, and sexual orientation as primary dimensions of diversity. Characteristics that can change, such as educational background, geographic location, income level, marital status, military experience, parental status, religious beliefs, and work experience are considered secondary dimensions of diversity. This definition clearly suggests that a typical classroom is a diverse environment.

Although some researchers have found links between cultural diversity and learning style preferences, for example Griggs and Dunn (1996) and Swisher (1991), one should not assume that students from the same culture have the same dominant learning style. Neither should teachers assume that students with similar types of disabilities have the same dominant learning styles. Instead, all teachers should try to understand the differences that exist among their students and value these differences in terms of what they bring to the learning environment. Teachers need to take time to understand how students learn and use a variety of instructional strategies that appeal to all students.

INSTRUCTIONAL STRATEGIES
Although education literature describes a variety of instructional strategies that are appropriate for the business education classroom, too often business educators limit themselves to the few with which they are most comfortable. The following instructional strategies appeal to a variety of learning styles and multiple intelligences.

Lecture/Central Presentation
The teacher is the central figure during a lecture/central presentation, which is best used to communicate facts, ideas, and theories. A *lecture* is a structured presentation and may be enhanced with visuals such as slides, transparencies, or electronic supports such as PowerPoint. Information should be presented in a logical way that allows students to build on what they already know. The students' main role is to listen.

Students should be taught to take notes, as note taking can enhance listening and provide material for review.

The lecture is an effective way to present an overview of learning materials, such as reading assignments, group activities, and classroom discussions. It has the potential to offer more current information than that which is contained in textbooks.

Lecture/Discussion

A *lecture/discussion* actively involves students in the learning process. Students may brainstorm, analyze, problem solve, and share their opinions; teachers listen as much as they speak. The interaction ensures that more students are engaged in the learning process. Simmons (1990) offers several tips for leading a discussion: sharing the learning goals of the discussion with students, maintaining eye contact with students, circulating around the room, asking relevant open-ended questions, asking students to elaborate on their responses, and incorporating students' contributions by building on their ideas.

Socratic Instruction

Socratic instruction involves the use of questions to drive the instruction. This method fosters critical thinking, evaluation, and knowledge application in students. The teacher is responsible for developing the questions that will drive the instruction. To be effective, Socratic instruction should be well planned, with attention to the following details (North Central Regional Educational Laboratory (2002b).

- Avoid using 'yes-no' questions, as they do not promote thinking or discussion.

- Use a variety of open-ended and closed question. *Closed questions,* which have one correct answer, are used to focus attention. *Open-ended questions,* which ask for a response in the student's own words, promote critical thinking.

- Be sure that students have the background and experiences to respond to the questions.

- Allow 'wait time' for thinking before asking a student to respond. Stahl (1994) recommends that teachers wait in silence for three seconds or more before calling on another student to respond to the question.

- Include clarifying questions or statements to help students reach the right responses.

Demonstration

Teacher-led demonstrations have a long history of use in business education. Essentially, *demonstrations* are step-by-step, show-and-tell sessions that are often used in skills training. Demonstrations are useful for arousing interest in a topic or for showing in practice what could only be inadequately explained (Johnson, 1971). Good demonstrations should include an explanation of what is happening and should allow for student questions. To be effective, demonstrations must be well planned, sequenced, and conducted flawlessly. A teacher should take time to rehearse the demonstration before the class begins, to minimize the chances that errors or mishaps may detract from the lesson. Demonstrations should be followed by individual practice aimed at skill development.

Modeling/Guided Practice
The guiding of novices—beginning learners—by expert teachers has been an accepted instructional strategy for a long time (Stoddart, 1990). Novices learn by watching an expert work and then by being coached by the expert as they practice the skill. In guided practice, the skill to be learned is broken into small pieces, presented and demonstrated to the learners, and followed immediately by independent student practice and teacher feedback. The basic steps are as follows: (a) model the behavior, (b) conduct the guided practice, (c) allow for independent practice, and (d) provide feedback to students (Allsopp, 1999).

Modeling/guided practice improves on demonstrations by actively engaging students in the learning process. The teacher typically begins by giving an overview followed by working through the activity, showing and discussing in small units of instruction, and immediately requiring student practice. This process may be repeated several times throughout the lesson.

Case Study
Case studies are stories that have an educational message. Case studies allow students to deal with situation-specific dilemmas (Herreid, 1997). Each case study should have a specific learning outcome and include questions to help students target their discussions and/or focus their analyses and presentations. Careful planning helps to anticipate possible student difficulty. In preparing a case study, the teacher should answer the following basic questions:

- Is the case study appropriate for the students (consider the issue or issues addressed, the content, and the grade-level appropriateness)?

- Why am I using this case, what do I hope to achieve, and what are the learning outcomes?

- What basic questions should students consider as they respond to the case?

In responding to case studies, students should be required to read, gather information, evaluate options, and make decisions. Careful planning helps in anticipating possible student difficulty and in providing for active participation in any classroom discussion that relates to the case.

Simulation

A *simulation* is an instructional strategy that allows for learning through problem solving in a realistic environment (Christopher, 2002). In many ways, simulations are like case studies. However, not only do students have to read, gather information, evaluate options, and make decisions, but they also have to implement the solution. Simulations are usually effective because they can be highly motivating.

Simulations can be assigned as individual or group projects. As with case studies, the teacher should make the goal of the simulation very clear to students, who should be provided with appropriate guidance and feedback about their progress and achievement. A well-designed simulation presents a problem to be solved, allows the learner to make decisions, gives the consequences of the decisions, and rewards the learner when the activity is successfully completed. Simulations are problem-based and do not have cut-and-dried answers (Christopher, 2002). In a simulation, learners experience the consequences of their decisions as they fulfill their roles in a professional manner.

Role Playing

Role playing allows students to improvise behaviors and skills that illustrate specific business situations and get immediate feedback from the instructor. Role playing transforms students from passive observers to active participants who take responsibility for their own learning. It encourages thinking and creativity in a nonthreatening setting. O'Donnell and Shaver (1990) offer several key elements for an effective role play:

- Develop a scenario that clearly shows the skill or behavior to be learned.

- Assign character roles and warm-up time for the roles.

- Simulate the roles or the actual acting.

- Debrief—discuss the simulation.

Debriefing is probably the most important part of role playing because it gives teachers a chance to question the students, to draw conclusions, and to pull everything together. Role playing builds problem-solving skills while promoting interpersonal relations and social interactions among class members. Role playing is a creative, participatory teaching technique that has high student involvement, while facilitating meaningful and fun learning. Role playing allows students to learn valuable skills such as empathy and the ability to see the situation from multiple perspectives. To help to reinforce learning through role play, students may be asked to prepare a written reflection at the conclusion.

Discovery Learning/Constructivism

Constructivism, considered to be as much of a philosophy as a teaching strategy, is an approach to teaching and learning that is based on the premise that learning results from mental construction—students learn by linking new information to what they already know (North Central Regional Educational Laboratory, 2002a). In discovery learning/constructivism, the teacher's role is that of facilitator instead of director, while students explore and discover knowledge. Through trial and error, students balance their old and new experiences to develop new levels of understanding. Student autonomy and initiative are encouraged as they engage in dialogue with the teacher, who reinforces or helps them to reevaluate their ideas (Brooks & Brooks, 1993). Discovery learning often involves individual or group projects such as conducting library or Internet-based research; developing experiential, written or media-based projects; or conducting experiments. Learning is assessed through ongoing activities such as performance-based projects or portfolios, instead of traditional objective tests or written responses.

In constructivist learning environments the teacher is a facilitator who focuses on guiding the student through the learning processes—making connections between facts and fostering new understanding. The constructivist approach encourages thinking, analysis, and synthesis that lead to good problem solving and decision making (Brooks & Brooks, 1993). The teacher is a colearner who is considered to be the virtual "guide on the side," instead of the "sage on the stage."

Cooperative Learning

Cooperative learning is defined as the instructional use of small groups, so that the students work together to maximize learning (Johnson, Johnson, & Smith 1991). Cooperative learning encourages students to work together to accomplish shared learning goals.

Effective work groups are the basis of cooperative learning. North Central Regional Educational Laboratory (2002b) offers some excellent suggestions for establishing effective groups: (a) establish heterogeneous groups; (b) establish group size; (c) designate group work areas; (d) designate any specific group member responsibilities; (e) provide clear directions, time constraints, rules, and procedures; (f) provide necessary materials; (g) establish leader selection process; (h) minimize exchange of information between groups; (i) watch for conflict; and (j) encourage and praise (reward) group support.

To foster group cooperation, students should be encouraged to model good communication habits such as listening, speaking, being courteous, and allowing others to participate in the conversation. The teacher must develop a comfortable, supportive environment in which students might observe, participate, and evaluate one another. Students should be provided with meaningful, interesting activities that push them to develop critical thinking skills.

Effective cooperative learning encompasses more than requiring students to work in groups. Activities are structured to ensure that all students contribute and are accountable for their learning. Teachers should assign activities that have group goals and allow for individual accountability. Several models are used to enhance the effectiveness of cooperative learning groups, as outlined below.

(a) **Jigsaw.** In the *Jigsaw* model students are divided into basic work groups and given the assignment. Each member of each work group is also assigned to a research team to learn about a specific aspect of the project. The goal of each research team is to become an expert on the part of the project that it was assigned. The teacher may provide "expert sheets" that outline readings and questions to help each research group get started and focus on the topic being studied. Upon completion of the research, members of the research teams return to their work groups, where members share the information gathered in their research teams, essentially teaching the other members of their groups. A class discussion, role play, or question-and-answer can follow to share information with the entire class (Aronson & Patone, 1997).

(b) **Group investigation.** The *Group Investigation* model is more student-directed in its approach. The teacher presents an introduction of the topic or unit; students discuss what they have learned and outline topics for further examination. Each work group chooses a topic from the list and determines any needed subtopics. Each group member is responsible for a specific part of the research and prepares a brief report for his or her group. The work group then designs a presentation for the class. Peer evaluation of each presentation can be an effective way of providing additional feedback to the work groups (Sharan & Shachar, 1988).

(c) **Think-pair-share.** In the *Think-Pair-Share* model, students pair with a partner to share responses to a question or mini-case. Students are asked to share their responses with the entire class. One way to facilitate the sharing with the class is to have the entire class stand up, and as each student responds, he or she sits down. The teacher may allow anyone with a similar response to sit down. This process continues until everyone is seated. For questions that require very short answers, the teacher may move quickly around the room, while allowing each student to give an answer (Andrini, 1991).

SERVING STUDENTS WITH SPECIAL NEEDS
The Center for Education Policy (2002) reports that approximately 6.5 million children (11% of all school children) with disabilities have been identified and are receiving special education services. They noted that 30 years ago, only one of every five children with disabilities was educated in a regular school. In contrast, today about 96% of children with disabilities learn in classrooms with nondisabled children, rather than in state institutions or separate facilities. About 75% of these students spend at least 40% of their day in a regular classroom with nondisabled peers rather than in separate rooms. Almost half of the students with disabilities spend at least 80%

of their day in regular classrooms. Regulations based on the Individuals with Disabilities Education Act (IDEA) now specifically require that students with disabilities have access to the general curriculum.

1997 IDEA Amendments

The 1975 landmark federal law guaranteeing educational rights to children with disabilities was called the Education for All Handicapped Children Act, popularly known as Public Law 94-142 (Center on Education Policy, 2002). In 1990 the name of the law (Public Law 101-476) changed to the Individuals with Disabilities Education Act (IDEA), as it is known today. Prior to the 1997 Amendments, the law did not specifically address general curriculum involvement of students with disabilities. The 1997 Amendments (IDEA '97) shifted the focus of the IDEA to one of improving teaching and learning, with the Individualized Education Program (IEP) as the main tool for enhancing the student's progress in the general curriculum (National Association of State Directors of Special Education, 1998).

IDEA '97 identifies the following disabilities: mental retardation; hearing impairments, including deafness; speech or language impairments; visual impairments, including blindness; severe emotional disturbances; orthopedic impairments; autism; traumatic brain injury; other health impairments; specific learning disabilities; deaf-blindness; or multiple disabilities. Attention deficit disorder (ADD) and attention deficit hyperactivity disorder (ADHD) are listed as conditions that could make a child eligible under the "other health impaired" category of IDEA (National Association of State Directors of Special Education, 1998).

Working with the Special Education Department

The 1997 IDEA amendments require that Individualized Education Programs (IEPs) be developed as the primary tool for enhancing the progress of students with disabilities. An IEP is a written document developed by the Local Education Agency (LEA) and the parent(s). It describes the educational program for a student with a disability and is a management tool to help ensure that the student receives the needed special education and related services in the learning environment. The 1997 amendments require that the team for each child's IEP must include at least one of the student's regular teachers, together with special education teachers, parent(s), and LEA representative if the child is, or may be, participating in the regular education environment (National Association of State Directors of Special Education, 1998). To help students who have disabilities to be successful in business classes, business educators should maintain a working relationship with special education colleagues.

Attending IEP Meetings

IDEA requires that IEP meetings be held at least annually. Based on the student's needs, meetings to review and revise the IEP may be held more frequently. The regular education teacher is expected to participate in the development, review, and revision of the IEP, including the determination of appropriate positive behavioral interventions, appropriate teaching strategies, supplementary materials, and services consistent with the IEP (Office of Special Education Programs, 1999). The main role of the teacher is to participate in the discussions about the student's involvement and performance in the general classroom environment. Once the IEP has been developed, it is available to each regular classroom teacher, special education teacher, and other service providers who are responsible for implementing it.

Adapting Lessons and Materials for Students with Special Needs

Awareness of the multiple intelligences and learning styles of students with disabilities or other special needs is important for planning effective delivery of instruction in the regular classroom. Business teachers should be aware of assistive devices, technologies, and other resources that can be used to enhance the delivery of instruction to students with special needs. Assistive tools include Braille and high-resolution monitors for the visually impaired; telecommunication devices for the deaf; speech digitizers and synthesizers; and electronic writing tools, including text- and graphics-based software that support the writing process. Switches, optical pointers, voice-controlled devices, and voice-recognition software can also help students with physical disabilities. Apart from these tools, students with special needs might also benefit from the following teaching strategies:

(a) *Multi-level instruction*—teacher delivers each lesson with variations for individual students;

(b) *Activity-based learning*—hands-on, interactive approaches that appeal to the senses;

(c) *Student-directed learning*—students participate in decision making about curriculum, content, learning strategies, and evaluation;

(d) *Multi-age classrooms*—classroom includes students of similar academic levels rather than similar ages; and

(e) *Heterogeneous groups*—varied and flexible groups that allow opportunities for students to interact with diverse peers (Johnson, 1999).

Adapting Lessons and Materials for Second Language Learners

Diverse classrooms often include students for whom English is a second language. As compared with English-proficient students, the instructional time for Limited English Proficiency (LEP) students might need to increase, affecting the coverage and learning of content. The appropriate response is never to limit the educational experiences of the students, but to understand how they learn and to design learning experiences that appeal to their learning styles. Teachers can draw on these students' culture and involve their parents and others in the community in school activities.

When planning instruction, remember that LEP students may benefit from some additional time and from written instructions instead of, or in addition to, oral instructions. Peer tutoring can be helpful for LEP students. Cooperative learning strategies can be particularly helpful, especially the Jigsaw method that allows members of each group to develop expertise in a particular aspect of the project and then assist the other members of the team. LEP students in Jigsaw, formed homogeneously according to English proficiency, may develop greater language proficiency when being taught at a language level that is appropriate.

LEP students may benefit from maintaining journals in which they reflect on daily events. Journals provide evidence of progress in vocabulary development, mechanics, grammar, and spelling, in addition to content (Cooper, 1997). Business teachers can utilize the Internet, including e-mail discussion groups for support material and access to other students who speak the same language. Using the English language keyboard and English vocabulary can help LEP students improve their writing skills (Canney, Kennedy, Schroeder, & Miles, 1999). Teachers should remember that while their language deficiencies can limit LEP students' ability to construct meaning, they usually possess the intellectual abilities to be successful in their courses. Campbell (1996) suggested the following strategies:

- Provide a key-word outline and use terms such as "first," "second," and "finally" to indicate the introduction of topics and transitions to new ones.

- Use an overhead projector or electronic slides to help students take accurate notes and write words correctly.

- Give students specific tasks that require them to use new vocabulary.

- Provide resources for students to use out of class to build expected prior knowledge.

- Use visuals as much as possible to help students learn the new vocabulary.

- Provide students with good samples of the quality of work that is expected of them—for example, research papers and journal entries.

Adapting Lessons and Materials for Gifted Students

Although all students need a challenging learning environment, gifted and talented students require more than longer assignments. These students need materials and interactions that offer greater intellectual rigor. Resources should be dictated by students' abilities. An understanding of multiple intelligences and learning styles is very important when planning instruction for gifted and talented students. White (2000) suggests the following strategies in adapting lessons and materials for gifted students:

- Allow self-pacing and incorporate problem solving, inquiry, and creativity into the classroom activities.

- Use contract work and encourage individual research. Involve mentors who have specific expertise.

- Use curriculum compacting. Pretests can confirm knowledge and free up time for these students to engage in special individual projects.

- Plan a range of activities that offer choice. Include a variety of activities that relate to various learning styles and multiple intelligences.

- Provide work that is meaningful and appropriate to the ability level of the student. Some gifted students have physical or learning disabilities, but these students will not be motivated by work that is below their cognitive ability.

Business educators can challenge gifted and talented students by involving them in peer tutoring activities. When cooperative learning activities are assigned, gifted and talented students should be part of heterogeneous groups that include both average students and students with special needs.

SUMMARY
The typical business education classroom is a culturally diverse environment that includes students with special needs, as well as a variety of learning styles and multiple intelligences. The challenge for business teachers is to develop instructional experiences that meet the learning needs of all their students.

Effective instruction should include a variety of strategies that appeal to the learning styles and multiple intelligences of the diverse student body. Instructors who are aware of their teaching styles, understand the learning styles of their students, and put forth the effort to become adept with a variety of instructional strategies should be able to appeal to the preferred learning styles of their students. Various instructional strategies include lecture/central presentation, lecture/discussion, Socratic instruction, demonstration, modeling/guided practice, case study, simulation, role playing, discovery learning/constructivism, and cooperative learning. Special efforts must be made to adapt instructional strategies to meet the needs of students with disabilities, students with limited English proficiency, and gifted students.

REFERENCES
Allsopp, D. H. (1999). Using modeling, manipulatives, and mnemonics with eighth-grade math students. *Teaching Exceptional Children, 32*(2), 74-81.

Andrini, B. (1991). *Cooperative learning and mathematics: A multi-structural approach.* San Juan Capistrano, CA: Kagan Cooperative Learning.

Aronson, E., & Patone, S. (1997). The *jigsaw classroom: Building cooperation in the classroom* (2nd ed.). New York: Addison Wesley Longman.

Brooks, J. G., & Brooks, M. G. (1993). *In search of understanding: The case for constructivist classroom.* Alexandria, VA: Association for Supervision and Curriculum Development.

Brualdi, A. C. (1996*). Multiple intelligences: Gardner's theory.* (Clearing House No. TM026059). Washington, DC: ERIC Clearinghouse on Assessment and Evaluation. (ERIC Document Reproduction Service No. ED410226). Retrieved July 23, 2002, from httpp://www.ed.gov/databases/ERIC_Digests/ed410226.html

Campbell, A. (1996). Ideas for working with students who speak English as a second language. *Teacher Talk, 2*(2). Retrieved July 22, 2002, from http:// education.indiana.edu/cas/ tt/v2i2/ideas.html

Canney, G. F., Kennedy, T. J., Schroeder, M., & Miles, S. (1999). Instructional strategies for K-12 limited English proficiency (LEP) students in regular classroom. *Reading Teacher, 52*(5), 540.

Center for Education Policy. (2002). *Educating children with disabilities: The good news and the work ahead.* Retrieved July 17, 2002, from http://www.ctredpol.org/ specialeducation/25yearseducatingchildren.pdf

Christopher, P. (2002). *Simulations: An overview.* Retrieved July 23, 2002, from http:// www.gsu.edu/~mstswh/courses/it7000/papers/newpage.htm

Clark, D. (1999). *Kolb's learning styles.* Retrieved July 18, 2002, from http:// www.nwlink.com/~donclark/hrd/history/kolb.html

Cooper, J. D. (1997). *Literacy: Helping children construct meaning* (3rd ed.). Boston: Houghton Mifflin.

Dunn, R., & Dunn, K. (1978). *Teaching students through their individual learning styles: A practical approach.* Upper Saddle River, NJ: Prentice Hall.

Dunn, R., & Dunn, K. (1993). *Teaching secondary students through their individual learning styles: Practical approaches for grades 7-12.* Boston: Allyn & Bacon.

Dunn, R., Dunn, K., & Price, G. E. (1985). *Learning styles inventory (LSI): An inventory for the identification of how individuals in grades 3 through 12 prefer to learn.* Lawrence, KS: Price Systems.

Felder, R. M. (1996). Matters of style. *ASEE Prism, 64*(4), 18-23. Retrieved July 18, 2002, from http://www.ncsu.edu/felder-public/Papers/LS-Prism.htm

Gardner, H. (1983). *Frames of mind.* New York: Basic Books, Inc.

Gardner, H. (1993). *Multiple intelligences: Theory and practice.* New York: Basic Books.

Griggs, S., & Dunn, R. (1996). *Hispanic-American students and learning style.* Urbana, IL: Clearing House on Elementary and Early Childhood Education. (ERIC Document Reproduction Service No. ED393607). Retrieved July 17, 2002, from http:// www.ed.gov/databases/ERIC_Digests/ed393607.html

Hartman, V. F. (1995). Teaching and learning style preferences: Transitions through technology. *VCCA Journal, 9*(2), 18-20. Retrieved July 22, 2002, from http:// www.br.cc.va.us/ vcca/hart1.htm

Herreid, C. F. (1997). What is a case? *Journal of College Science Teaching, 27,* 92-94.

Johnson, D. W., Johnson, R. T., & Smith, K. A. (1991). Cooperative learning: Increasing college faculty instructional productivity. *ASHE-ERIC Higher Education Report No. 4.* Washington, DC: The George Washington University, School of Education and Human Development. Retrieved July 23, 2002, from http://www.fis.ncsu.edu/ugs/ cooperat.htm

Johnson, E. (1971). *Teaching: A basic guide.* London: George G. Harrap & Co. Ltd.

Johnson, G. M. (1999). Inclusive education: Fundamental instructional strategies and considerations. *Preventing School Failure, 43*(2), 72-79.

Kolb, D. A. (1985). *Learning styles inventory technical manual.* Boston: McBer and Company.

Kolb, D. A. (1984). *Experiential Learning: Experience as the source of learning and development.* Englewood Cliffs, NJ: Prentice Hall, Inc.

Kolb, D., Rubin, I., & Osland, J. (1995*). Organizational behavior, an experiential approach.* Englewood Cliffs, NJ: Prentice Hall, Inc.

Litzinger, M. E., & Osif, B. (1992). Accommodating diverse learning styles: Designing instruction for electronic information sources. In L. Shirato (Ed.) *What is good instruction now? Library instruction for the 90s.* Ann Arbor, MI: Pierian Press.

Myers, I. (1978). *Myers-Briggs type indicator.* Palo Alto, CA: Consulting Psychologists Press.

National Association of State Directors of Special Education. (1998). *Involvement of general education teachers in the IEP Process.* (Clearing House No. EC306978). Alexandria, VA: Project FORUM Staff. (ERIC Document Reproduction Service No. ED426542).

National Business Education Association. (2001). *National standards for business education: What America's students should know and be able to do in business* (2nd ed.). Reston, VA: Author.

National Center for Education Statistics. (2002). *Participation in education: Elementary/secondary schools.* Retrieved July 23, 2002, from http://nces.ed.gov/programs/ coe/2002/section1/indicator03.asp

North Central Regional Educational Laboratory. (2002a). *Constructivist teaching and learning models.* Retrieved July 17, 2002, form http://www.ncrel.org/sdrs/areas/issues/ envrnmnt/drugfree/sa3const.htm

North Central Regional Educational Laboratory. (2002b). *Effective teaching strategies.* Retrieved July 17, 2002, from http://www.ncrel.org/sdrs/areas/issues/envrnmnt/ drugfree/ sa3effec.htm

O'Donnell, N., & Shaver, L. (1990). *The use of role play to teach communication skills.* (Clearing House No. JC910437). (ERIC Document Reproduction Service No. ED336160). Retrieved July 17, 2002, from http://www.askeric.org/plweb-cgi/

Office of Special Education Programs. (1999). *Regular education teachers as IEP team members.* Retrieved July 11, 2002, from http://www.ed.gov/offices/OSERS/Policy/ IDEA/brief3.html

Riechmann, S., & Grasha, A. (1974). A rational approach to developing and assessing the construct validity of a student learning style scales instrument. *Journal of Psychology, 87,* 213-23.

Sharan, S., & Shachar, C. (1988). *Language and learning in the cooperative classroom.* New York: Springer-Verlag.

Simmons, P. (1990). *Teaching tips for leading a discussion.* Retrieved November 1, 2001, from http://www.isd.uga.edu/teaching_assistant/ta-topics/discuss.html

Stahl, R. J. (1994). *Using "think-time" and "wait-time" skillfully in the classroom.* (Clearing House No. SO024197). (ERIC Document Reproduction Service No. ED370885). Retrieved July 17, 2002, from http://www.ed.gov/databases/ERIC_Digests/ed370885.html

Stoddart, T. (1990). *Perspectives on guided practice.* (Clearing House No. SP033003). East Lansing, MI: National Center for Research on Teacher Education. Technical Series 90-1. (ERIC Document Reproduction Service No. ED330682).

Swisher, K. (1991). American Indian/Alaskan native learning styles: Research and practice. (Clearing House No. RC018175). (ERIC Document Reproduction Service No. ED335175). Retrieved July 17, 2002, from http://www.ericfacility.net/ericdigests/ed335175.html

University of Maryland. (2001). The University of Maryland definition of diversity. Retrieved July 19, 2002, from http://www.inform.umd.edu/EdRes/Topic/Diversity/Reference/ diversity.html

White, S. (2002). *Gifted and talented students: Meeting their needs in New Zealand schools.* Wellington: Learning Media Ltd.

Managing the Classroom and Technology Lab

Martha H. Rader
Arizona State University
Tempe, Arizona

Proficiency in classroom management is essential for successful teaching. Good classroom management skills foster a positive learning environment that promotes student achievement and discourages student misconduct. This chapter discusses classroom management research and theory and outlines a number of strategies for effective classroom management. The chapter also discusses the causes of student misbehavior and suggests appropriate responses to various types of student misconduct.

CLASSROOM MANAGEMENT

Effective teachers manage the events in their classrooms, including their students' behavior. *Classroom management* is defined as "the actions and strategies teachers use to establish an effective climate for learning and for maintaining order in the classroom" (Burden & Byrd, 1994, p. 160). Current views of classroom management have shifted from a reactive, or after-the-fact approach focusing on discipline, to a proactive or preventive approach (Cruickshank, Bainer, & Metcalf, 1995). Effective classroom management enhances the efficiency of instructional time, improves students' motivation, reduces disruptive behavior, and increases achievement (Wang, Haertel, & Wallberg, 1993).

Classroom control is an important component of classroom management. *Classroom control* is the process of controlling students' behavior in the classroom (Callahan, Clark, & Kellough, 2002). This term is used today rather than the older term *classroom discipline*, which was associated with use of strict punishment to control students' misbehavior. The discipline approach to classroom control fell out of favor in the

1970's because it was found to be ineffective. Research on discipline revealed that student misbehavior significantly increased after teachers were asked to increase their punishment of students who misbehaved (Becker, Engelmann, & Thomas, 1975). Today teachers use punishment very seldom and only as a last resort to control the behavior of students who have failed to respond to a more positive approach to classroom management.

Classroom management is essential to student learning (Wong & Wong, 1998). Effective teachers manage their classrooms and teach their students with very little wasted time, disruptions, or confusion. Well-managed classrooms are characterized by a task-oriented learning environment, where the students know exactly what is expected of them.

New teachers are often apprehensive about classroom management, and experienced teachers may occasionally experience problems maintaining order in the classroom. Effective classroom management occurs when a teacher consistently prepares well-planned lessons and materials; provides a positive, supportive atmosphere for learning; establishes and reinforces classroom procedures and rules; and deals quickly and firmly with distractions and inappropriate student behaviors. An effective teacher maintains order in the classroom by being prepared, fair, and consistent (Kellough & Kellough, 1999).

CLASSROOM MANAGEMENT RESEARCH

Current concepts of classroom management have evolved since the 1960's from the work of behavioral theorists such as Skinner, Canter and Canter, Dreikurs, Glasser, and Kounin. Today's concept of classroom management has its roots in behaviorist theory that originated with research on behavior modification.

B. F. Skinner's Learning Theories

Strategies for effective classroom management are based on behavior modification research that began with B. F. Skinner's learning theories about the use of *reinforcers* (rewards) to shape behavior (1971). Reinforcers comprise the following techniques:

(a) *Social reinforcers* include verbal attention; praise; and nonverbal behavior, such as body language, smiling, or frowning.

(b) *Graphic reinforcers* consist of handwritten or stamped letters, numerals, and symbols that provide feedback about student performance.

(c) *Privilege reinforcers* include activities such as games, special computer privileges, free time, or the opportunity to help the teacher.

(d) *Tangible reinforcers* consist of rewards such as candy, pizza, certificates, student-of- the-week awards, etc.

(e) *Token reinforcers* include rewards such as points, play money, or tickets that can be accumulated and redeemed for tangible rewards (Callahan, Clark, & Kellough, 2002).

Canters' Assertive Discipline

Students need to understand that rules for classroom behavior are essential to achieving their educational goals. Canter and Canter's *assertive discipline model* (1992) emphasizes the importance of reinforcing appropriate behavior and the consequences for inappropriate behavior. Their model focuses on the following four points:

(a) The teachers has the right to expect appropriate student behavior.

(b) The teacher should plan appropriate limits for acceptable behavior.

(c) The teacher should clearly state the expectations and rules for behavior.

(d) The teacher should identify and implement a behavior management system of positive consequences for good student behaviors and negative consequences for inappropriate behaviors.

The Canter model advocates a standardized set of rules and consequences throughout the school, with procedures for the first, second, and third times that a student fails to comply with the rules. Rewards are established for students and classes that comply with the rules on a regular basis. For example, students who comply with the rules can be allowed to play a computer game.

Dreikurs' Logical Consequences Approach

Dreikurs' *logical consequences approach* emphasizes the following strategies for classroom management:

(a) The teacher should be firm and fair; students should participate in establishing and implementing class rules.

(b) Students should understand the rules and be aware of the logical consequences for misbehavior. For example, the logical consequence of a student's deliberately damaging computer equipment would be for him or her to pay for it.

(c) Students are held responsible for other students' behavior. For example, students try to influence other students to behave appropriately in the classroom.

(d) Students should encourage respect for themselves and others; they should make other students feel welcome in the class.

(e) The teacher should address and reinforce students' goals of belonging, status, and recognition.

(f) The teacher recognizes but avoids reinforcing students' desire to seek power, attention, and revenge (Dreikurs, Grunwald, & Pepper, 1982).

Glasser's Reality Therapy Model

William Glasser (1986) developed a model based on *reality therapy*, which advocates that inappropriate behavior stems from the present situation rather than the past. This model emphasizes that teachers can lead students to make appropriate choices about their behavior. Glasser advocates holding class meetings devoted to setting class rules, standards for students' behavior, and the consequences for misbehavior. He stresses that students who attend quality schools should enjoy learning and feel a sense of belonging and empowerment (Kellough & Kellough, 1999).

Kounin's Ripple Effect

Kounin's classic study of orderly and disorderly classrooms (1970) found that classroom order resulted from the teacher's efforts to prevent misbehavior rather than to use specific disciplinary techniques after students acted inappropriately. Kounin also identified the *ripple effect*, or the effect of a teacher's response to one student's misbehavior on other students in the classroom. His research revealed that effective teachers constantly monitored their students' behavior and displayed *withitness*, a term he used to describe "eyes in the back of your head," or their awareness of everything that occurs in the classroom.

Teachers use the following strategies to achieve withitness (Kellough & Kellough, 1999):

(a) Watching the entire class constantly, even when working individually with students.

(b) Moving around the classroom frequently and establishing eye contact with each student about once a minute.

(c) Involving all students in the lesson, including unresponsive students; calling on students randomly; and checking on individual students' progress.

(d) Spending no more than 30 seconds attending to one student or group of students.

(e) Avoiding turning one's back to the class, especially when writing on the board.

(f) Being alert to potential misbehavior and redirecting students' attention before their behavior gets out of control.

(g) When two or more incidents of misbehavior occur at the same time, addressing the most serious infraction first, while addressing the other situation(s) nonverbally (e.g., frowning or pointing).

CLASSROOM MANAGEMENT STRATEGIES

Planning, organization, and consistency are the keys to effective classroom management. The following basic strategies are essential for successful classroom management:

(a) Plan classroom management strategies

(b) Organize the physical environment

(c) Clearly communicate classroom rules

(d) Establish and reinforce classroom procedures

(e) Develop a positive learning environment

(f) Keep students attentive and on task

Plan Classroom Management Strategies

Novice teachers should remember the *five P's of planning*—Proper Planning Prevents Poor Performance. Wong & Wong (1998) stress the importance of planning by stating in their popular book, *The First Days of School*, "If you do not have a plan, you are planning to fail" (p. 141).

A teacher should prepare for the first day of school long before the school year begins. The planning stage of classroom management begins when a new teacher makes an effort to learn as much about the school as possible, including the facilities, support services, district and school policies, procedures, students, and resources. New teachers should obtain as much information as possible well in advance by networking with administrators, department chairs, and other teachers; obtaining and studying district and school student handbooks, employee manuals, and Web sites; and examining departmental curricular materials such as course syllabi, textbooks, and other resources. In addition, new teachers should visit special education, counseling, and other key departments to introduce themselves and obtain necessary information about student services, including those for students with special needs.

Business teachers who are fortunate to have their own classrooms or computer labs should organize their materials and arrange the room well before the start of school. Teachers without their own designated classrooms generally have the use of a desk, computer, and file cabinet that can be set up and organized in advance. A new business teacher needs to know the location and procedures for obtaining and using office supplies, copying machine, computer equipment and supplies, audiovisual equipment, desk copies of textbooks, and teachers' manuals to accompany each textbook.

Effective teachers develop a written plan for classroom management by establishing clearly written rules and procedures, consequences, and rewards for appropriate behavior. The classroom management plan should be prepared, along with all course materials, syllabi, and other resources, well before the first day of school.

Organize the Physical Environment

Effective teachers prevent misbehavior by having their classrooms well organized (Wong & Wong, 1998). Well-organized classrooms promote efficiency in teaching and learning, while poorly organized classrooms create confusion, waste time, and foster misbehavior.

The physical environment of a classroom or lab should be organized in a way that maximizes learning and minimizes disruptions (Lyle, 2001). A sufficient number of tables or desks, chairs, computers, textbooks, and handouts should be in each class-room before the first day of school. Lessons, materials, and assignments should be prepared and organized in advance and ready for the students before class begins.

The furniture in a classroom or technology lab should be placed where the teacher can easily observe all the students and the students can easily see the teacher. Students' desks usually face the teacher, although technology labs are often an exception. Com-puter desks or tables in a lab may be arranged in various configurations, including an inverted U-shape with students facing the wall, in order for the teacher to observe the students' computer screens. Swivel-type chairs allow the students to turn easily to face the front of the room when the teacher addresses them. Conventional classrooms without computers may be arranged in various configurations, including placing tables and chairs in groups or pods to facilitate group work or learning centers. The teacher's desk may be placed either at the front or the back of the classroom, depending on the type of class and the arrangement of students' desks. If the students' tables or desks in the computer lab are arranged horizontally in rows with the students facing the front of the room, the teacher's desk may be placed in the back of the room to facilitate observation of students' computer screens. A chair and small table or desk can be placed at the front of the room for the teacher's use when addressing the class.

Curricular materials and classroom supplies such as computer paper should be kept in an easily accessible location. Toxic materials such as printer or copier toner, glue, correction fluid, and cleaning supplies should be stored in a locked cabinet to comply with OSHA (the federal Occupational Safety and Health Administration) require-ments. OSHA also requires that Materials Safety Data Sheets (MSDS) be stored in an easily accessible location (Rader & Kurth, 1999). These sheets, which contain safety information about toxicity and antidotes for chemical products, may be obtained from the manufacturers.

Clearly Communicate Classroom Rules

The teacher should provide students with a brief written list of rules that they are expected to follow in the classroom or lab. These rules are general or specific behavioral standards that regulate students' conduct. All classroom and lab rules should be consistent with school policies. To increase students' acceptance of the rules, the teacher can involve the class in a discussion of the reasons for the rules and their advantages to the students.

To set a positive tone, rules should focus on positive rather than negative behaviors and should be stated in positive rather than negative terms (Eby, Herrell, & Hicks, 2002). Because students have difficulty remembering a long list of items, the rules for a classroom or lab should be stated briefly and include no more than five to seven rules. The list of rules should address behaviors that are observable and enforceable (Burden & Byrd, 1994).

Examples of ineffective and effective rules for a technology lab are shown in Table I. The ineffective example on the left side of Table I contains eight rules that convey a negative tone. The improved version on the right projects a positive tone and condenses the previous list to three basic rules that students can easily remember; the bulleted items listed under the three rules are presented as explanations.

The teacher should display the list of rules in a prominent place, with a large typeface that students can easily see. The use of attractive artwork and color can enhance the appearance of the rules displayed. Rules that regulate students' behavior

Table 1. Examples of Ineffective and Effective Rules for the Technology Lab

Ineffective Lab Rules	Effective Lab Rules

1. Don't leave a messy workstation.
2. Food and drink are prohibited.
3. Don't leave the folders around the room.
4. Inappropriate language is prohibited.
5. Hats are never allowed in the lab.
6. Don't be tardy.
7. Don't talk while the teacher is speaking.
8. Don't interrupt without permission.
	1. Respect the environment.
	  - Keep workstations clean and neat.
	  - Return folders to the file box.
	  - Keep food/drink out of the lab.
	2. Respect Coronado High School rules.
	  - Use polite language.
	  - Dress appropriately.
	  - Arrive on time.
	3. Respect others.
	  - Be quiet when the teacher is speaking.
	  - Raise your hand if you want to speak.

in a technology lab and specify appropriate use of hardware and software can be written in the form of an agreement or contract for students and parents to sign.

On the first day of class the teacher should identify and explain each of the rules in a positive way, including providing examples of desirable behaviors. The students should recognize and discuss the advantages of obeying the rules and the consequences of rule infractions (Burden & Byrd, 1994). The tone of the discussion should be as positive as possible, with an emphasis on consideration for others rather than punitive measures.

Students tend to forget the rules unless they are taught and reinforced on a regular basis. During the first week of school, the teacher should briefly review the rules each day. For the next few weeks, the rules should be reviewed at least once a week. The teacher should avoid reminding the class of the rules when a student breaks one; rule infractions should always be addressed discretely rather than by calling attention to a student's misbehavior in front of the class.

Establish and Reinforce Classroom Procedures

Procedures are specified ways to accomplish various tasks and other classroom routines (Burden & Byrd, 1994). Classroom procedures may range in complexity from simple routines such as where students should sit and how they should turn in their work, to complicated instructions for operating computers in the lab. Procedures also include actions that students should take in the event of fire drills or other emergencies.

Classrooms without clearly established procedures for daily tasks are typically noisy, confused, and undisciplined. Business teachers should establish procedures for all routine tasks such as taking the roll, passing out papers, and collecting papers as efficiently as possible. Efficient procedures allow students to avoid wasting time on unproductive activities and spend as much time as possible on instructional tasks. Students who are wasting time waiting for instructions on what to do are likely to engage in misconduct. Classroom procedures allow work to be accomplished in a smooth and organized manner without confusion. For example, students should know where to sit, where the day's assignment is located, and how to begin the assignment without being told what to do.

On the first day of class the teacher should begin by establishing a routine for seating arrangements. Some teachers allow students to sit where they choose, while other teachers assign seats. Assigned seats have a number of advantages, including minimizing interaction between students, reducing the classroom noise level, and preventing unmotivated or disruptive students from sitting together in the back of the room. Students can quickly find their assigned seats if the teacher hands them a card identifying their assigned seat number or a copy of a completed seating chart as they enter the room. A seating chart allows the teacher to take the roll very rapidly and facilitates learning students' names.

Basic classroom procedures include how students should indicate that they want to speak, that they need help, that they are finished with an assignment, or that they want to go to the rest room. Classroom procedures also include what materials to bring to class, where to find handouts and classroom supplies, what to do after being tardy or absent, and how to behave in group assignments. Procedures should also be established for finding and completing special assignments such as make-up work, extra credit, and individualized assignments for students with special needs.

On the first day of school, the teacher should introduce the students to the basic classroom procedures and rehearse the procedures until the students know them thoroughly (Wong & Wong, 1998). The time spent teaching students classroom procedures is not wasted and will actually save a great deal of time throughout the year. Procedures should be reinforced by repetition and by praising students for performing them correctly.

Develop a Positive Learning Environment

A good relationship between the teacher and students creates a positive learning environment. Students who like their teacher put forth their best effort to succeed because they want to please the teacher. In contrast, a poor relationship between a teacher and students creates a negative classroom climate that fosters inattention, poor motivation to learn, and misbehavior.

Classroom climate is the mood or feeling between the teacher and the students (Burden & Byrd, 1994). A negative classroom climate is cold, adversarial, and unpleasant. In contrast, a positive classroom climate is warm, caring, and supportive. A positive classroom climate is essential to a positive environment for learning (Jacobsen, Eggen, & Kauchak, 2002).

Business teachers can develop positive relationships with their students by earning their respect and trust. Teachers develop credibility with their students by exhibiting characteristics such as fairness, impartiality, and integrity. Teachers must take the first step toward developing rapport with students by liking, respecting, and trusting them.

Teachers communicate their attitude towards students by their tone of voice, choice of words, nonverbal behavior, and actions. No matter what the circumstances, teachers should never lose their temper, shout, make sarcastic remarks, demean, or embarrass students. Teachers should demonstrate their interest and concern for students by learning their names as soon as possible, getting to know them personally, joking with them, expressing interest in their personal activities such as sports, cheerfully helping them, complimenting them for their successes, tactfully correcting them when they make mistakes, and promptly grading and returning their tests and homework assignments. Group rapport can be developed by encouraging students to work together in teams, providing and supporting group activities, and recognizing group accomplishments.

Keep Students Attentive and on Task

Incidents of misbehavior often occur when students are bored or have nothing to do. Providing a variety of instructional methods and materials prevents monotony and maintains student interest (Gabler & Schroeder, 2003). Students enjoy being involved in the learning process by participating in class projects that add depth and provide relevance to the curriculum. Lessons should employ a variety of teaching methods such as demonstration, lecture and discussion, cooperative learning, computer-assisted instruction, games, and discovery learning. Instructional strategies can be varied by occasionally inviting guest speakers, showing videos, and taking students on field trips. Overheads, PowerPoint presentations, and handouts can be enlivened with the use of color, clip art, animation, and music.

A teacher's personality, voice, and style of delivery also affect students' attention. To maintain students' interest, a teacher should speak enthusiastically rather than in a monotone, move around the room, and use appropriate gestures and facial expressions. Students appreciate the use of humor, anecdotes, and examples to enliven the course content.

Lessons should be presented at a good pace, with students constantly engaged in various learning activities and not wasting time. *Transitional activities* (supplementary activities) should be provided for students who complete their assignments early. When students are kept busy and interested, they have little or no time to engage in misbehavior.

The teacher should constantly monitor individual students and frequently ask them questions to determine if they are paying attention and if they understand the lesson. The teacher should call on students randomly rather than in a predictable pattern such as horizontally across the rows of desks, as students pay more attention if they think the teacher is likely to ask them a question at any time. Questioning techniques are also an important component of student evaluation, as discussed in Chapter 7.

STUDENT MISBEHAVIOR

Student misbehavior includes rule infractions such as interrupting others, speaking out of turn, lying, cheating, tardiness, truancy, defiance, sleeping in class, throwing objects, failing to follow directions, using inappropriate language, failing to complete homework or other assignments, refusing to participate in group activities, and abusing school property (Burden & Byrd, 1994). More serious infractions include stealing, assaulting other students, using illegal drugs, and bringing weapons to school. Infractions of schools' acceptable use policies for computers include inappropriate use of the Internet, posting prohibited or inappropriate material on school Web sites, illegally copying or downloading software, "hacking" or breaking into confidential files such as student records or personnel data, plagiarizing materials obtained from the Internet, or using school computers to perpetrate crimes such as credit card fraud (Rader, 2002).

Causes of Student Misbehavior

Student misbehavior occurs for a variety of reasons that may be categorized as physiological, environmental, and psychosocial (Evans, Evans, & Schmid, 1989). Physiological reasons include physical and health-related factors such as illness, neurological disorders, lack of sleep, vision or hearing problems, and substance abuse. Environmental causes include adverse conditions in the home or school environment that affect students' behavior. Adverse conditions in the home may include problems such as lack of basic needs such as food, shelter, and clothing; child abuse, parental substance abuse, or lack of parental support; and family crises such as separation, divorce, parental death, or incarceration. Adverse conditions in the school environment may include ineffective teachers or administrators, poor classroom management, and a negative classroom climate. Psychosocial causes may include emotional problems, developmental disorders, or learning disabilities. Other psychosocial causes may include individual attitudes, values, and motivation. These causes are influenced by factors such as students' self-esteem, peer pressure, expectations, and need for attention.

Responses to Student Misbehavior

As previously discussed, most incidents of student misbehavior can be prevented by effective classroom management. However, when students do misbehave, the teacher should respond by using an intervention strategy that is appropriate for the particular situation, depending on its severity. Mild misconduct such as being off task or whispering to another student may be ignored if the teacher thinks the incident will be short-lived. If the misconduct continues for longer than a moment or two, the teacher should use the *teacher look* technique, or stern stare, to extinguish the behavior (Weinstein, 1996). If the student disregards the teacher look, the next step is to address the student by name to get his or her attention. If the student continues the misbehavior, the teacher should call the student's name and remind the student of the correct task or procedure that he or she should be following. The reminder should be stated as positively as possible; for example, a teacher should say, "Bob, do you need help with your spreadsheet?" rather than "Bob, you should be working on your spreadsheet instead of talking to Mary." The teacher's intervention response should be made as quickly and quietly as possible, to avoid interrupting the flow of the lesson. The teacher can use other nonverbal behaviors such as proximity or standing next to the student, frowning, or putting a finger to the lips to extinguish mild misbehaviors such as inattentiveness or talking to another student.

Misbehavior that disrupts the class—for example, talking loudly out of turn, interrupting or arguing with the teacher, or clowning around—should never be ignored, as this type of behavior tends to be contagious and is likely to escalate. The teacher should warn the student, and if the behavior continues, immediately enforce the consequences—for example, giving the student a detention (Kellough & Kellough, 1999).

Teachers should never respond to student misbehavior by losing their temper. Other inappropriate responses to misbehavior include yelling at students, threatening students, corporal (physical) punishment, punishing the entire class, ridiculing a student, giving extra assignments as punishment, or harshly reprimanding a student in front of the class (Burden & Byrd, 1994). Teachers who use any of these inappropriate responses will lose the respect of the class as well as the support of the administration.

Major problems such as fighting, violence, or illegal acts should be handled by immediately calling a security guard, law enforcement officer, or administrator to remove the offending student from the classroom. For safety reasons, a teacher should not attempt to break up fights or deal with any type of violence or weapons. Teachers should familiarize themselves with the school's safety procedures and follow them in case of a fire drill, lockdown, or other emergency.

SUMMARY
Good classroom management is essential for effective teaching and learning. Effective classroom management occurs when a teacher plans classroom management strategies, organizes the physical environment, clearly communicates classroom rules, establishes and reinforces classroom procedures, develops a positive learning environment, and keeps students attentive and on task. Business teachers can deal appropriately with student misconduct by understanding the causes of student misbehavior and using appropriate intervention strategies that are consistent with school policies.

REFERENCES
Becker, W., Engelmann, S., & Thomas, D. (1975). *Teaching 1: Classroom management.* Champaign, IL: Research Press.

Burden, P. R., & Byrd, D. M. (1994). *Methods for effective teaching.* Needham Heights, MA: Allyn and Bacon.

Callahan, J. F., Clark, L. H., & Kellough, R. D. (2002). *Teaching in the middle and secondary schools* (7th ed.). Upper Saddle River, NJ: Merrill/Prentice-Hall.

Canter, L., & Canter, M. (1992). *Assertive discipline: Positive behavior management for today's schools* (Rev. ed.). Santa Monica, CA: Lee Canter & Associates.

Cruickshank, D. R., Bainer, D., & Metcalf, K. (1995). *The act of teaching.* New York: McGraw-Hill.

Dreikurs, R., Grunwald, B. B., & Pepper, F. C. (1982). *Maintaining sanity in the classroom: Classroom management techniques* (2nd ed.). New York: Harper & Row.

Eby, J. W., Herrell, A. L., & Hicks, J. (2002). *Reflective planning, teaching, and evaluation: K-12* (3rd ed.). Upper Saddle River, NJ: Merrill/Prentice-Hall.

Evans, W. H., Evans, S. S., & Schmid, R. E. (1989). *Behavior and instructional management: An ecological approach.* Boston: Allyn & Bacon.

Gabler, I. C., & Schroeder, M. (2003). *Constructivist methods for the secondary classroom.* Boston: Allyn and Bacon.

Glasser, W. (1986). *Control theory in the classroom.* New York: Harper & Row.

Jacobsen, D. A., Eggen, P., & Kauchak, D. (2002). *Methods for teaching: Promoting student learning* (6th ed.). Upper Saddle River, NJ: Merrill/Prentice-Hall.

Kellough, R. D., & Kellough, N. G. (1999). *Secondary school teaching: A guide to methods and resources: Planning for competence.* Upper Saddle River, NJ: Merrill/ Prentice-Hall.

Kounin, J. S. (1970). *Discipline and group management in classrooms.* New York: Holt, Rinehart & Winston.

Lyle, C. (2001). Classroom management theory and practice. In B. J. Brown (Ed.), *Management of the business classroom* (Yearbook No. 39, pp. 167-183). Reston, VA: National Business Education Association.

Rader, M. H. (2002). Strategies for teaching Internet ethics. *Delta Pi Epsilon Journal, 44*(2), 73-79.

Rader, M. H., & Kurth, L. A. Federal workplace laws: Are business work experience programs in compliance? (1999). *Business Education Forum 53*(6), 26-29.

Skinner, B. F. (1971). *Beyond freedom and dignity.* New York: Knopf.

Wang, M. C., Haertel, G. D., & Walberg, H. J. (1993). What helps students learn? *Educational Leadership, 51*(4), 74-79.

Weinstein, C. S. (1996). *Secondary classroom management: Lessons from research and practice.* New York: McGraw-Hill.

Wong, H. K., & Wong, R. T. (1998). *How to be an effective teacher: The first days of school.* Mountain View, CA: Harry K. Wong Publications.

Evaluating and Assessing Student Performance

Marcia L. Bush
Mission Valley Regional
Occupational Program
Fremont, California

Donna Henderson
Central County Occupational Center
Metropolitan Education District
San Jose, California

The primary focus of this chapter is student assessment and evaluation at the classroom level. The chapter discusses the process of evaluation as an integral part of classroom assessment, tests used by teachers, performance-based assessments, and tools for evaluation. Examples for using the data gathered from the components of evaluation and assessment are included. Suggestions to assist the teacher in developing an assessment plan that provides a framework for teaching and learning are presented throughout the chapter.

THE PROCESS OF EVALUATION AND ASSESSMENT

The role of assessment is to educate students and improve their performance (Wiggins & McTighe, 1998). From every assessment situation, teachers can gain important and useful information, which assists them in making informed decisions about curriculum and instruction, and ultimately in improving student learning (Falk, 2000). As instruction occurs, teachers need information to evaluate whether their teaching strategies are working. Teachers also need information about the comprehension level of their individual students, so they can identify the next steps in instruction. In addition, students need feedback to monitor their own success in learning and to know where they may need additional instruction.

Definition of Terms

The terms "evaluation" and "assessment" are frequently used interchangeably (Carr & Harris, 2001; Popham, 2001; Wiggins & McTighe, 1998). Currently in education, *assessment* is the more comprehensive term, used to include the processes of quantifying, describing, judging, gathering data, or giving feedback about performance. For the purposes of this chapter, *evaluation* is defined as the judgment that is involved with placing a value on or assigning worth to a response, product, or performance. Assessment is addressed in the broader sense, with evaluation as an integral part of the entire process.

Relationship to Objectives, Course Competencies, and Standards

Assessment as an activity does not function in isolation, but must be closely connected to the curriculum, instructional goals, and standards. To be effective, assessment must be deliberately aligned with both curriculum and instruction. *Alignment* is defined by Wahlstrom (1999, p. 271) as "the process of assuring a match between the written, the taught, and the tested curricula."

The first step in the classroom process for a classroom teacher is to set broad goals for what students will learn. The next step is to adopt standards that define and outline what students should know and be able to achieve. In the realm of education, *standards* are usually used in reference to a "degree or level of requirement, excellence or attainment" (*American Heritage Dictionary*, 2000). *Content standards* specify what the student should know or do; *performance standards* specify how much students should know or to what degree they should be able to do something. The following statement is an example of a content standard for the use of technology in business communication: "Use technology to enhance the effectiveness of communication" (National Business Education Association [NBEA], 2001, p. 41). This statement is an example of a Level 3 (high school) performance expectation: The student should "demonstrate ability to use voice input and voice recognition tools" (NBEA, 2001, p. 42). After standards are defined, teachers need to develop assessments to measure progress, design curricula and materials to help students meet the standards, and then report student progress in meeting the standards.

Assessment of Academic, Business Content, and Workplace Skills

Applying multiple measures toward an accurate assessment of skills is particularly important in business education, as business subjects focus on the attainment of demonstrable skills and competencies needed for employment. To succeed in today's increasingly competitive economy, employers seek not only technically proficient employees, but also employees who are able to "think and reason effectively, to solve complex problems, to work with multidimensional data and sophisticated representations, to make judgments about the accuracy of masses of information, to collaborate in diverse teams, and to demonstrate self-motivation" (National Research Council, 2001, p. 22).

To prepare students for careers in today's economy, teachers need to assess more than business content and skill levels. Academic proficiency in essential skills such as English and math are needed for job success, and "soft skills" such as teamwork, effective communication, and initiative are in demand by today's employers. To develop these skills, a teacher in an entrepreneurship class might assign a team project that integrates communication skills, prerequisite writing skills, and subject content expertise by asking students to design a small business, including a business plan, a product, a personnel plan, and an advertising plan. For a further evaluation activity, the team could present the project to the class, using demonstration software such as PowerPoint.

Multiple Measures

Because no one assessment measure or test can gauge everything, teachers need to prepare multiple measures and use varied types of assessments to obtain the most complete picture of a student's progress. These could include written quizzes or tests, performance tests, skill demonstrations, oral presentations, projects, case studies, and portfolios. For example, a teacher in a spreadsheet software class can give students many opportunities to demonstrate their learning. Quizzes on individual skill topics, completion of end-of-chapter assignments, exercises combining multiple spreadsheet skills, demonstrations on how to perform a skill, and integrated projects incorporating realistic business or personal applications will provide a more comprehensive assessment picture for the teacher, as well as multiple opportunities for students to exhibit their knowledge and skills.

METHODS OF ASSESSMENT

Assessment in the classroom may be conducted either formally or informally. A student who is being *formally* assessed knows that he or she is being evaluated. The student might be performing a task, completing a project, or demonstrating a skill. The teacher can observe the student perform specific tasks or evaluate the quality of a finished product. When a student is being *informally* assessed, the student may not be aware that the assessment is taking place. Informal assessment includes techniques such as evaluating the students' interactions with other students, observing their computer screens, or orally questioning them.

Formative Assessment

Some types of assessment are used in a *formative* manner, to shape and guide the learning process and to give feedback along the way, so that the learner can improve his or her understanding or skill. Examples of formative assessment include checks for understanding, self-assessments, and demonstrations. For example, at the end of a lesson on the mail-merge feature of Word, a teacher could orally check for understanding by asking questions to determine whether the students have grasped the basic concepts. When a teacher demonstrates a mail-merge, he or she could ask students to respond with the appropriate next step. These formative assessments help the teacher to decide whether to spend more time on review or to assign a practice mail-merge assignment. Table 1 illustrates some sample activities and characteristics of formative assessment.

Table 1. Characteristics of Formative Assessment			
Sample Activities	**Time**	**Material Tested**	**Purpose**
• Pre-test • Written quiz • Oral quiz • Self-assessment • Checklist • Skill demonstration	• Given at frequent intervals, usually after small amounts of information • Given before or during instruction	• Tests specific skills • Ideally tests every concept and/or objective taught	• Determines specific skills, concepts, and objectives which student has mastered • Provides immediate feedback to student • Identifies specific weaknesses in on-going instruction
Note. Adapted from *Performance Assessment for Science Teachers* by Dr. Hugh Baird © Copyright 1997 by Dr. Hugh Baird. Production of this manual was funded by the Utah State Office of Education.			

Summative Assessment

Other assessments are used in a *summative* fashion, as benchmarks to recap or summarize the learning that has taken place. Summative assessments are frequently used as grades at the end of a project or a class. Examples of assessment used in this way would be a midterm, a final test, a term paper, or a portfolio. At the end of major sections in an accounting course, the teacher may want to document student understanding and progress by giving a midterm. A teacher may assign a portfolio due at the end of a unit on job preparation that displays the resume, letter of application, reference letters, and other work samples that provide evidence of the learning experience to the teacher as well as to a prospective employer. Table 2 illustrates some samples and characteristics of summative assessment.

TESTS

Tests, another component of the assessment process, offer a wide range of choices to the classroom teacher. Tests can be obtained from many commercial sources, including publishers, textbook authors, professional associations, industry certification groups, and nonprofit or for-profit testing businesses. Tests are available for industry certification, as well as for measuring the efficacy of industry standards, job readiness, subject-matter content, and skill level. Commercial tests offer advantages such as convenience of use, predetermined reliability and validity, professional testing and measurement expertise, ease of scoring, and credibility. Disadvantages may include the lack of alignment with content standards being used in a particular course or program, the potentially high cost, and the generic nature of the tests.

Table 2. Characteristics of Summative Assessment

Sample Activities	Time	Material Tested	Purpose
• Checklist • Unit test • Midterm • Final • Portfolio • Oral presentation • Term paper	• Given infre-quently throughout the year, usu-ally at the end of a large amount of instruction • Given after instruction is completed	• Tests general concepts and skills • Samples from among con-cepts, skills and/or objec-tives that were taught	• Used to deter-mine student grades and report them • Determines course effec-tiveness • Used to revise or redesign a course

Note. Adapted from *Performance Assessment for Science Teachers* by Dr. Hugh Baird © Copyright 1997 by Dr. Hugh Baird. Production of this manual was funded by the Utah State Office of Education.

Teacher-Made Tests

Classroom teachers know best what they have taught in their classrooms, and in many cases, prefer to construct their own tests. Teacher-made tests are advantageous because they can be tailored to specific curricula or specific needs for information about students, and they are relatively inexpensive to administer and correct. In addition, teacher-made tests can provide information on small units of instruction not covered by standardized tests. Teacher-made tests are generally criterion-referenced (tests are corrected against certain standards or criterion) and are designed to measure students' mastery of the material being taught. To avoid problems of validity and reliability, teachers need opportunities for training in the development and use of tests. Some educational software comes with test generators that randomly select appropriate questions for quizzes or tests based on the material covered and can be customized to fit the teachers' needs.

Industry Certification Tests

A recent development in the educational arena is the use of competency-based tests using industry standards and resulting in industry recognition of accepted software and hardware skill levels. The information technology industry has expanded and changed so rapidly that companies have begun to include curriculum development for training materials as part of their product development and market-support programs. Standardized testing is a method of evaluating the skills leading to industry certifica-tion. Some of the more popular certifications include Cisco Certified Network Associ-ate, Microsoft Certified Professional, Microsoft Certified Systems Engineer, Microsoft Office Specialist (MOS), A+ (for computer service technicians), Oracle Database Administration, and Sun Developer series. These tests are generally administered for a fee at an independent testing site. Schools are often official test sites. Teachers who are preparing their students to take these tests can find a great variety of information available on the Web sites of the specific industry companies or test sponsors.

Job-Readiness Tests

Job-readiness tests are available from professional organizations, publishers, and state employment services. These tests seek to validate employability skills often referred to as "soft skills," basic skills such as reading and writing, or both. For example, a popular but somewhat expensive assessment called WorkKeys (2002), produced by the American College Testing Program (ACT), measures and documents attainment of employability skills for students in secondary and postsecondary career and technical programs. The National Occupational Competency Testing Institute (NOCTI) has developed job-ready assessments for a wide range of occupational clusters as well as a workplace readiness assessment. NOCTI assessments are developed by experts from industry, based on national standards, nationally validated, and frequently reviewed and revised (National Occupational Competency Testing Institute, 2001). Sample tests include accounting, administrative assisting, advertising design, business information processing, and computer technology. Teachers who prepare students for careers may want to use these job-readiness tests to ascertain whether their students are adequately prepared to enter the workforce.

Textbook Publishers' Tests

Textbook publishers provide an abundance of tests predominantly for content and skill testing of material in their textbooks. These tests correlate highly with the textbook material and are often provided at little or no cost to teachers who use the publisher's textbooks. Teachers should use care when selecting textbooks to ensure that the textbooks are aligned with the course and content standards and the curriculum. If the textbooks are appropriately selected, then the accompanying tests are a convenient and suitable assessment tool for the classroom.

PERFORMANCE-BASED ASSESSMENTS

All tests are assessments, but not all assessments are tests. Tests are indirect ways of predicting what students might be able to do in an actual situation where they have to apply what they know. *Performance-based assessment* as used in this chapter refers to a classroom setting where students are given the opportunity to actually demonstrate how they would apply their knowledge, skills, and abilities in a given context. Wiggins (1998) maintains that conventional test questions do not replicate the kinds of challenges that adults face in the workplace, in civic affairs, or in their personal lives. Wiggins also describes standards for *authentic assessment*. An assessment task, problem, or project is authentic if it

    (a) *is realistic.* The tasks replicate real-world situations.

    (b) *requires judgment and innovation.* The student must solve unstructured problems, and the solution involves more than following a set routine or procedure.

(c) *asks the student to "do" the subject.* The student must carry out an exploration and work within the discipline.

Properly constructed performance-based assessments, including written response items, case studies, demonstrations, projects, portfolios, and presentations, can provide challenges that are more authentic for students. A student must draw upon his/her learning, not just in a single course but also across the curriculum, and apply it in a new way. Suggestions for developing these performance-based assessments are illustrated by the *National Standards for Business Education* (NBEA, 2001), a compilation of achievement standards and performance expectations.

Written Response Items

A written response item requires students to respond in writing to a prompt or situation that is presented to them. Students must generate, develop, and express their ideas to create the answer rather than choosing the correct answer as in a multiple-choice test item.

Written response items can be either short or long. Longer items are also called *scenarios* and present a "job-like" problem or authentic situation that the student responds to in writing. A structure for preparing written response items is presented as part of the development of the Assessments in Career Education (ACE) and Career-Technical Assessment Program (C-TAP) by WestEd (O'Neill & Stansbury, 2000). The structure includes an item name, prompt, and instructions.

One of the Level 3 (high school) performance expectations for an NBEA Information Technology achievement standard is to select operating systems, environments, and utilities appropriate for specific hardware, software, and tasks. A short written response item is shown in Table 3.

Table 3. Structure of a Short Written Response Item – Information Technology Standard

Item Name: **A New Computer System**

Prompt: You are the manager of a small computer repair business with four employees, and you have been given the responsibility to develop a proposal for a new computer system to meet the needs of the business.

Instructions: Identify at least four critical functions and the specific hardware and software needed to effectively process the information for this business.

Case Studies

Case studies are often used as an effective strategy for business education instruction. Students are called upon to think critically and articulate both verbal and written responses to demonstrate comprehension of how concepts are applied. For example, a case study assessing what students know about building teams could present a detailed workplace situation or scenario within a company setting. The student is asked to analyze and synthesize all the evidence of team building presented in the case and prepare a written and/or oral response.

Demonstrations

Demonstrations are another instructional strategy used by business educators that can also be developed as a performance-based assessment. Students are asked to demonstrate what they know and can do. For example, a student in a high school marketing class could demonstrate closing a sale.

Projects

A project is a cumulative assessment, meaning that it is done over time rather than being completed in one class session. The key criterion to qualify the project as an assessment measure is that students are doing independent work and creating a product, performance, or event that is original. One example of a project idea to assess an NBEA Information Technology standard is shown in Table 4.

Table 4. Sample Project Idea

Computer Software FAQ Page: Investigate the typical computer software questions asked by beginning users and develop a FAQ screen for a class Web site.

Note. Adapted from O'Neill and Stansbury, *Developing a Standards-Based Assessment System: The ACE/C-TAP Example.* San Francisco: West (2000).

Students need clearly stated requirements and guidelines. The first step might be to describe the project topic, idea, or purpose. A list of ideas can be generated by the teacher or by the students. Project requirements (O'Neill & Stansbury, 2000) include planning, research and development, and producing and presenting the final product. Students could develop their own written project plan based on the requirements, as outlined in Table 5.

Ideas for other projects include the following examples:

- Office information manual for a local business
- Membership campaign materials and computerized membership system for a campus organization

- Business survey reporting types of hardware and software being used
- Newsletter service
- Design and production of a student course catalog

Table 5. Written Project Plan
Project idea/topic: A brief overview of the focus of the project
Project purpose and goals: Stated in specific, measurable terms and including the standards-related knowledge and skills
Process for completing the project: Major steps
Resources needed to complete the project
Evidence of progress that will be collected during project development
Timeline for completion
Note. Career-Technical Assessment Program: 1999 Student Guidebook. WestEd (1999).

Portfolios

Portfolios can serve a variety of assessment purposes, reflecting multiple standards. They can be used formatively, as a current picture at any given time, or summatively to document learning over time. An example of possible required contents for a portfolio is shown in Table 6 (Bush & Timms, 2000, p. 115).

The work samples included in the portfolio are actual student performance products. Work samples for an NBEA Information Technology standard could include the following projects:

- A Web page designed by a student for a Junior Achievement enterprise

- A brochure designed for the school in a desktop publishing class

- Financial reports prepared for an FBLA chapter using advanced features of a spreadsheet

Each work sample can be accompanied by a short summary (half-page memo) prepared by the student to describe the work, identify the skills demonstrated, and explain what was learned as the work sample was completed (O'Neill & Stansbury, 2000).

Table 6. Portfolio Contents
Introduction (Student introduces himself/herself and the portfolio contents.) Table of contents Letter of introduction
Career Development Package (The pieces presented here demonstrate readiness to transition to the next level.) Résumé Employment or college application Letter of recommendation
Work Samples (These are samples that a student might share with a prospective employer.) Four examples and descriptions of work, demonstrating mastery of important career-technical standards
Writing Sample (A student documents his or her ability to communicate in writing.) A writing sample demonstrating investigative, analytical, and writing abilities
Supervised Practical Experience Evaluation (This is optional but useful if the student has done an internship or participated in work-based learning under the direction of a workplace supervisor.) Documentation of a student's practical or work experience, demonstrating workplace readiness
Note. Adapted from Career-Technical Assessment Program: 1999 Student Guidebook. WestEd (1999).

Each teacher can develop a portfolio structure that best serves the purposes of the students in a particular class or program. The portfolio experience has direct carryover to the workplace. A portfolio is a ready reference in the job application process and is used by many working professionals to showcase their actual experience in a given field. In some schools, portfolios are now a graduation requirement. As an example, Anzar High School in San Juan Bautista, California, has established graduation by exhibition where students compile a portfolio throughout high school and present the evidence of their knowledge, skills, and abilities in required subjects through the contents of the portfolio, accompanied by a presentation for both teachers and business/community representatives.

Presentations

Having the students actually present their work is a natural extension of the use of case studies, projects, or portfolios, because in each case students may be called upon to do a presentation. For example, the student might present his or her analysis of the case or share the results of a long-term project.

Presentations provide an opportunity for students to showcase their skills, as well as demonstrate their ability to communicate orally and visually. The ability to deliver presentations that are appropriate for the particular situation and audience is valued in the workplace. Delivering a presentation is an authentic, performance-based task or assessment.

One or more of the performance-based assessments presented in this section should be among the multiple measures of every teacher's comprehensive assessment plan. In addition to determining which performance assessments will be used and developing the guidelines and requirements, special tools are needed to evaluate the particular performances. Several of those tools, including rubrics, are discussed in the next section.

TOOLS FOR EVALUATION

In the process of making a judgment about a variety of student performances, teachers need to employ a number of ways to communicate to others how the particular value was assigned. This communication is essential to inform students, parents, and other stakeholders about how the student is doing compared to the desired expectations or objectives. In addition, as pointed out by Popham (2001), these results are valuable in making decisions about how and what to teach as well as to evaluate the effectiveness of instruction. The use of one or more tools for evaluation such as checklists, rubrics, or scoring guides usually leads to the assignment of a grade.

Checklists

Checklists contain the details (usually a list of numbered or bulleted items) of what a teacher expects students to address, display, or submit in final form. A checklist can be an organizer for the student. A checklist can vary from a very simple list to a complex display of individual points for many components of a comprehensive project or presentation. For example, checklists might be used in the following situations:

- To check proper keyboarding posture/technique—hand position, distance from the keyboard, and eyes on the copy. A checklist should include all the components of posture and technique that the teacher would be looking for when observing the student in the proper position at the computer, as shown in Table 7.

- To check the presence or absence of contents—parts of a resume, business letter, or report. A checklist should contain all the critical parts, as shown in Table 8 for a sample business letter checklist.

- To check off points made in an oral presentation—used in business during the interview process, as shown in Table 9.

- To check off key ideas developed in a writing sample.

Table 7. Computer Applications Technique Checklist

Date: _____   Name: _____   Period: _____

Computer Applications Technique Check

Yes   No

___   ___   **Eyes** (Eyes always on textbook or screen, not looking at hands)

___   ___   **Hands/Fingers** (Fingers curved hugging home row)

___   ___   **Posture** (Sitting straight in chair and feet flat on the floor, legs not crossed)

___   ___   **Wrists/Arms** (Wrists up, not touching the table or wrists higher than or or even with knuckles)

___   ___   **Keys** (Fingers reaching and striking the correct key properly; the enter key and the backspace key are hit with the right pinky without lifting the hand from home row)

Note. Developed by Michelle Crary, Desert Vista High School, Phoenix, Arizona (by permission).

A writing sample could be an assessment for two *National Standards* (NBEA, 2001): (a) the NBEA Communication Standard—"Compose and produce a variety of business messages and reports using correct style, format, and content," (p.38), and/or (b) the NBEA Information Technology Standard—"Explain how information technologies meet human needs and improve quality of life" (p.82).

For example, a writing sample checklist for a short report on how information technologies meet human needs and improve quality of life is shown in Table 10.

Rubrics or Scoring Guides

A *rubric* is a scoring guide that provides information about how students are progressing (Bush & Timms, 2000; Stiggins, 2001; Wiggins, 1998). A checklist often is the starting point for rubric development. A rubric can be used for both formative and summative evaluation and is widely accepted for use with the performance-based assessments discussed earlier in the chapter.

Table 8. Business Letter Checklist

Business Letter Checklist

Yes	No	
___	___	2-inch top margin
___	___	Date (month spelled out with a 4-digit year)
___	___	Quadruple space after the date
___	___	Receiver's name and address
___	___	Double space after the receiver's address
___	___	Salutation – open punctuation
___	___	Double space after salutation
___	___	Body single-spaced
___	___	Paragraphs aligned left
___	___	New paragraph identified by double space
___	___	Double space after the body
___	___	Complimentary close – open punctuation
___	___	Quadruple space after complimentary close
___	___	Writer's name
___	___	Single space
___	___	Writer's position and/or company, if applicable
___	___	Double space between elements such as enclosure, notation

Note. Developed by Michelle Crary, Desert Vista High School, Phoenix, Arizona (by permission).

A rubric clearly identifies what is expected, as well as indicates what has been achieved. The rubric also provides information about what might be done to improve the product or performance. The language of the rubric gives a word picture describing the characteristics and level of a student's performance. More than that, the rubric "language" becomes a common denominator for discussion of student learning with colleagues within a subject area, with teachers across a campus, with community

Table 9. Mock Interview Checklist

Name of person being interviewed: _____

Did the student:

Introduce himself/herself and state the position he/she is applying for?   Yes   No

Look you in the eye and offer a firm handshake?   Yes   No

Wait until he/she was told to be seated?   Yes   No

Interview Questions:

	1	2	3	4	5
Relax and tell me about yourself.	□ Has nothing to tell	□ Has little to tell (name, age, grade, & school)	□ Talks about himself/herself at school & extracurricular activities he/she is involved in	□ Talks about accomplishments, but they are not aligned with job description	□ Talks about accomplishments, and they are aligned with job description
Tell me about your education and/or qualifications.	□ Has nothing to tell	□ Has little to tell (name, age, grade, & school)	□ Tells about his/her class schedule	□ Tells his/her class schedule and what he/she has learned in each class	□ Explains how his/her education has helped him/her prepare for the position

	Has nothing to tell	Has little to tell, but mentions accomplishments	Tells you about the accomplishment and what he/she learned from it	Tells about the accomplishment, how he/she learned that accomplishment, and what he/she learned from it	Tells about the accomplishment, how he/she learned that accomplishment, and what he/she learned from it, and aligns it with the job description
Give me an example of one of your accomplishments. What did you learn from it?	☐ Has nothing to tell	☐ Has little to tell, but mentions accomplishments	☐ Tells you about the accomplishment and what he/she learned from it	☐ Tells about the accomplishment, how he/she learned that accomplishment, and what he/she learned from it	☐ Tells about the accomplishment, how he/she learned that accomplishment, and what he/she learned from it, and aligns it with the job description
Give me an example of a problem you faced and how you solved it.	☐ Has nothing to tell	☐ Tells a problem he/she had but not how it was solved	☐ Tells a problem he/she had and how he/she solved it	☐ Tells you a problem he/she encountered, options he/she had and how the problem was solved	☐ Tells an example as a story, defining the problem, identifying options, explaining how he/she handled obstacles and solved the problem

Did the student:

Ask at least one question?   Yes   No

Thank you for your time?   Yes   No

Note. Developed by Michelle Crary, Desert Vista High School, Phoenix, Arizona (with permission).

stakeholders and business partners, and perhaps most importantly with students. In his work and study of rubrics in practice, Marzano (2000) believes that assigning a rubric score to represent performance is more accurate than assigning points. He encourages teachers to conceptualize student progress in terms of a rubric, rather than by accumulating points.

A teacher can develop a rubric by following these steps (Bush & Timms, 2000):

(1) *Start with a standard and performance expectations (criteria).* The tie to standards provides the answer to the question, "What should a student know and be able to do?"

(2) *Identify the criteria to be used as a basis for judging the performance.*

The beginning development of the rubric is illustrated in Table 11.

(3) *Provide a definition for the criteria.* The next step is to define or characterize the expected performance in terms of its achievement of the standard, as shown in Table 12.

(4) *Set a scale or rating system.* Use three to five levels of numbers or words to evaluate or judge the performance, as in the following examples:

	(a)	Advanced	Proficient	Basic	
or	(b)	4	3	2	1
or	(c)	Exemplary	Proficient	Progressing	Not Meeting Expectations

When all four steps are completed, the result will be a rubric containing standards, performance expectations, criteria for judging performance, and a scale or rating system, as shown in Table 13.

This integrated project incorporates the subject matter content of entrepreneurship, the academic skills of writing and researching, the use of technology, and the employability soft skills of teamwork, communication, and responsibility. The rubric shown in Table 14 can be used both as a guideline for the teams as well as a tool for evaluating the final project.

Many resources and references are available for rubric models or templates that can be adapted for individual use. For example, the teach-nology.com Web site that includes worksheets, teaching tips, and rubrics also has a rubric generator that can

Table 10. Sample Checklist for a Short Report

Short Report Format		Content	
Unbound style		Introduction	
1" Margins		Technologies identified	
Double spaced		Meeting of human needs analyzed	
Pages numbered		Quality of life improvements summarized	
		Conclusion	
		Recommendations	

Table 11. Rubric Development Steps 1-2

Communication Standard:
Compose and produce a variety of business messages and reports

Criteria	Organization	Content	Format

Table 12. Rubric Development Step 3

Organization	Presents information in logical, interesting sequence.
Content	Introduces topic and develops analysis with specific examples to reach logical conclusions and suitable recommendations.
Format	Uses correct placement of all report parts and contains no typographical errors.

build an assortment of general-use rubrics quickly and easily. The following Web sites provide excellent resources for rubrics:

- http://teach-nology.com/
- http://school.discovery.com/schrockguide/assess.html
- http://edweb.sdsu.edu/webquest/rubrics/weblessons.htm
- http://www.4teachers.org/projectbased/checklist_1999.shtml
- http://www.odyssey.on.ca/%7Eelaine.coxon/welcome.htm

Grades

The traditional reason for using tests and other summative evaluation tools is to be able to report the student's readiness to move to the next step, level, or course in an articulated sequence. Grades or the process of assigning grades should be a part of the effective communication that takes place between student and teacher. Consider the following five steps suggested by Stiggins (2001):

(1) Examine the overall achievement expectations.

(2) Develop a plan that identifies each of the assessment measures to be used.

(3) Develop and administer the actual assessments.

(4) Determine how the pieces fit together (relative weights of individual measures).

(5) Assign a grade.

Stiggins (2001) cautions that the "set of five letter grades cannot shoulder the responsibility for being both (1) our primary way of sharing information about student achievement, and (2) our primary means of motivation" (p. 411-412). The evolving practice with grading and using tools to determine grades is to move away from thinking of assigning a grade as the endpoint. Instead the grade is a step on a continuum, a part of the ongoing communication that takes place within an overall assessment plan. The student and the teacher must have a clear understanding of each step along the way and be mutually accountable for reporting the results.

USING EVALUATION AND ASSESSMENT DATA

Jamentz (2001) points out that educators must not only learn to analyze data, but also become skilled at reporting and using this evidence to make decisions. According to Wahlstrom (1999), data tasks fall into four areas that include collecting, organizing, analyzing, and using data.

Data Collection and Organization

Teachers at all levels must plan for data collection. The plan should detail what data will be collected, the sources of that data, how it will be gathered, and how it will be organized. According to Wahlstrom (1999), teachers should collect outcome or performance data that indicates what students have achieved. Possible data sources include many of the assessment measures presented in this chapter; examples are classroom observation results, quizzes, student assignments, test results, and information from performance-based assessments.

In the current standards-based, data-driven environment, the use of technology to organize the data is a must. The spreadsheet, grade book program, or relational database all offer a range of possibilities for the teacher to be able to collect, organize, and display achievement data for each and every student. A student record is no longer

Table 13. Rubric Development Steps 1-2-3-4

	Advanced	Proficient	Basic
Organization	Presents information in logical, interesting sequence.	Presents information in logical sequence.	Presents information out of sequence.
Content	Introduces topic and develops analysis with specific examples to reach logical conclusions and suitable recommendations.	Introduces topic and develops analysis with some examples to reach conclusions and recommendations.	Introduces topic, analysis may be limited or lack examples, and conclusions or recommendations may be missing.
Format	Uses all report elements, correctly placed, and contains no typographical errors.	Uses most report elements (correctly placed), and contains no typographical errors.	Contains placement and typographical errors that interfere with readability and presentation.

a single line in a grade book; now it is a data point in a huge network with information available for random access.

Data Analysis

Fox (2001, p. 14) contends that without data, instruction becomes a series of well-intentioned but essentially "random acts of teaching." Data supports decisions about what students know and can do, provides a basis for diagnosing student needs, and gives information necessary to plan appropriate instruction.

The process of data analysis can involve posing questions and determining factors to analyze, as illustrated in Table 15. This data analysis will in turn drive the collection and organization of data.

Data Reporting

Using technology, the data can be collected, processed, and displayed in many forms and formats. Displays such as charts, graphs, and tables provide visual pictures that can be used to communicate stories of student success, as well as student and program needs. Teachers should "celebrate" their students' successes and share the stories on a regular basis with students, parents, administrators, business and industry partners, and community representatives.

Table 14. Project Rubric Example

Project and Presentation Scoring Rubric (Total Points = 300)

Name: Date:

Title of Project: Block:

	Exemplary (100)	Accomplished (80)	Proficient (70)	Emerging (60)	Not Addressed (50)
Relevant to the Audience	Steps are consistent and repeatable.	Steps follow and relate to each other logically.	Some details unclear that might hinder training. Information is fairly organized.	Difficult to follow steps. Steps do not match action performed.	Steps make little or no sense.
Well Written	Writing is done in grammatically correct English; it has no spelling or punctuation errors; it can be easily used by others, regardless of background or ability.	Writing is done in grammatically correct English; it has no spelling or punctuation errors; it is clear and concise.	Writing is done in grammatically correct English; it has no spelling or grammatical errors. Some details are unclear and may inhibit learning.	Writing has some grammar and punctuation errors (4). Details are sketchy or unclear, making replication unlikely.	Details that would allow replication *not* provided. Five or more grammar and punctuation errors.
Presentation	Design for project is superior and complete. All elements are turned in on time.	Design for project is good and complete. All elements are turned in on time.	Design for project is too ordinary or dull. All elements are turned in on time.	Design for project showed minimal effort. All elements in on time.	Design is cluttered and confusing. Elements of project missing.

Table 15. Analyzing Student Performance		
Assessment Measure	**Data Analysis Questions**	**Factors to Analyze**
Paper/Pencil Tests	Did students consistently perform poorly on any of the test questions? How did the performance of students on this test compare to performance on other tests given in the course?	Did the test measure higher-level thinking and not just recall? Does the test appropriately measure the standards it was designed to measure?
Performance-based Assessments	What number and percentage of the students met the performance expectation? Is there quality in student achievement on this test?	Is there a plan about what to do to help students who did not perform well? Were the materials and resources necessary for success available?

SUMMARY

Evaluating and assessing student performance is an essential component in the process of teaching and learning. Teachers should have an overall assessment plan that is made up of multiple measures that are aligned with overall goals, objectives, curriculum, and instruction. The multiple measures are both formative and summative and include tests as well as performance-based assessments. In the process, a variety of evaluation tools are used to provide feedback for both teacher and student. The data gathered, organized, interpreted, and analyzed are used to report on student achievement to a variety of audiences and to give valuable information for the continuous improvement of the teaching process.

The assessment plan in action becomes an indicator of the teacher as a professional in meeting the National Association for Business Teacher Education (NABTE) Business Teacher Education Achievement Standard: "The business teacher assesses student progress to alter and enhance the learning environment to optimize student success" (National Association for Business Teacher Education, 1997).

REFERENCES

American heritage dictionary of the English language, (4th ed.). (2000). Boston: Houghton Mifflin Company. Retrieved March 12, 2002, from http://www.bartleby.com/61

Baird, H. (1997). *Performance assessment for science teachers.* Salt Lake City, UT: Utah State Office of Education.

Bush, M., & Timms, M. (2000). Alternative assessment. In J. Rucker (Ed.), *Assessment in business education* (Yearbook No. 38, pp. 103-120). Reston, VA: National Business Education Association.

Carr, J. F., & Harris, D. E. (2001). *Succeeding with standards: Linking curriculum, assessment, and action planning.* Alexandria, VA: Association for Supervision and Curriculum Development.

Falk, B. (2000). *The heart of the matter: Using standards and assessment to learn.* Portsmouth, NH: Heinemann.

Fox, D. (2001). No more random acts of teaching. *Leadership, 31,* 14-17.

Jamentz, K. (2001). Beyond data mania. *Leadership, 31,* 8-12.

Marzano, R. J. (2000). *Transforming classroom grading.* Alexandria, VA: Association for Supervision and Curriculum Development.

National Association for Business Teacher Education. (1997). *Business teacher education curriculum guide & program standards.* Reston, VA: Author

National Business Education Association. (2001). *National standards for business education: What America's students should know and be able to do in business.* Reston, VA: Author.

National Occupational Competency Testing Institute. (2001). *Catalog of assessments.* Big Rapids, MI: Author

National Research Council, Center for Education. (2001). *Knowing what students know: The science and design of educational assessment.* (2001). Retrieved March 12, 2002, from http://books.nap.edu/books/0309072727/html/index.html

O'Neill, K., & Stansbury, K. (2000). *Developing a standards-based assessment system: A handbook.* San Francisco: WestEd.

Popham, W. J. (2001). *The truth about testing: An educator's call to action.* Alexandria, VA: Association for Supervision and Curriculum Development.

Stiggins, R. J. (2001). *Student-involved classroom assessment.* Upper Saddle River, NJ: Prentice-Hall, Inc.

Wahlstrom, D. (1999). *Using data to improve student achievement.* Suffolk: Successline, Inc.

WestEd. (1999). *Career-technical assessment program: 1999 student guidebook.* San Francisco:

Wiggins, G. (1998). *Educative assessment: Designing assessments to inform and improve student performance.* San Francisco: Jossey-Bass, Inc.

Wiggins, G., & McTighe, J. (1998). *Understanding by design.* Alexandria, VA: Association for Supervision and Curriculum Development.

WorkKeys. (2002). Retrieved November 4, 2002, from http://www.act.org/wys.index.htmlorkke

Input Technologies

Margaret J. Erthal	Al S. Roane	Kim Larsh
Illinois State University	South-Western/Thomson	Mesa Public Schools
Normal, Illinois	Cincinnati, Ohio	Mesa, Arizona

A variety of techniques allow people to input data into a computer, including keyboards, voice and handwriting recognition, and touch screens. Input technology refers to a process in which a person interacts with a computer. This interaction may take the form of entering data, accessing a database, manipulating existing data, or retrieving information from the World Wide Web. Keyboarding is only one example of an input technology. This chapter discusses strategies for teaching keyboarding, including keyboarding instruction and assessment, keyboarding software, and keyboarding for children and for students with special needs. The chapter also introduces speech- and handwriting-recognition instruction.

TEACHING KEYBOARDING

A vast body of research and knowledge on teaching keyboarding exists. In 1878 Frank McGurrin taught himself to keyboard using all of his fingers without looking at the keys; thus the first instance of the "all-finger method" occurred. In 1889 Bates Torey published a manual describing the touch system (Bartholome, 1996). World War I increased the need for trained typists so that directives and orders would not be misinterpreted, and touch typing became popular. After the war ended, keyboarding evolved with much research devoted to teaching the touch system, developing speed and accuracy, applying learning theories, and analyzing the role of techniques (West, 1974, 1983).

Keyboarding is a *psychomotor skill* that is characterized by coordination and actions relating to fine motor skills. Keyboarding focuses on the manipulation of the computer keyboard by touch (Bartholome, 1996; Erthal, 1998). Information technology performance standards described in the *National Standards for Business Education* (2001) include developing proper input techniques (keyboarding) and developing input technology skills at acceptable speed and accuracy levels.

Initial Instruction

Both operant and classical conditioning play a role in learning to keyboard. *Operant conditioning* relies on reinforcement and is used during the early learning stages. For example, when a learner makes a correct response, that action is recognized and rewarded. *Classical conditioning* relies on the stimulus-response model and occurs during higher stroking speeds. In keyboarding, classical conditioning attempts to associate a visual stimulus with a specific response. The learner is presented with a *stimulus* (letter) and makes a *response* (strikes a key). An important component of stimulus-response theory is knowledge of results. If learners perceive that their response is correct, the next time they are presented with that stimulus, they should make the same response. Knowledge of results dictates closeness in time. If learners do not receive immediate feedback, they will not know if the response to a stimulus was appropriate. This learning process is referred to as *Contiguity* = **S**timulus + **R**esults + **K**nowledge of **R**esults (West, 1974).

The usual method of instruction is to teach the home row keys in one day and then teach two new keys the next lesson. A review lesson is normally presented every fifth or sixth lesson.

When first learning the keyboard, neophytes vocalize the letters. Anything that intervenes between the stimulus and the response to inhibit keystroking is called a *mediator*. Keyboarding teachers should discourage mediators, which should be eliminated in order to touch keyboard. Elimination methods include decreasing the interval between the stimulus and response by calling out letters, urging students to key faster, and setting individual goals.

During the initial stages of psychomotor learning, a student learns, develops, and refines kinesthesis. *Kinesthesis* is the sensation of motion and position in muscles and joints (Cratty, 1973; McLean, 1994; Singer, 1975; West, 1983). For example, kinesthesis allows people, with their eyes closed, to touch their noses or feed themselves without missing their mouths. Kinesthesis, which is often referred to as "the feel of the motion," is the principle that enables students to make the appropriate responses at the keyboard. Visual feedback is important when developing and refining kinesthesis. In the beginning stages of keyboard instruction, learners need to watch their fingers make the reach to a new key location and then back to the home row. Insisting that students not look at the keyboard is detrimental to skill development (West, 1974). Even experienced keyboarders glance down at the keyboard from time to time. A study by Hayes and Reeve (1980) found that visual feedback produced the best overall performance while copying paragraph material for speed and accuracy. McLean and Pulak (1995) found similar results in their study of visual access and keyboard performance.

Motivation plays a vital role in all learning and particularly in keyboard learning. *Intrinsic motivation*, which comes from within, is preferred over *extrinsic motivation*, which is external, as intrinsic motivation is learner-defined and learner-centered. Examples of motivators pertinent to keyboard learning are encouragement, praise, competition, incentives, and goal setting; however, success at the task is the most powerful of all motivators (West, 1983). Motivation allows learners to overcome plateaus and experience greater success. Transfer of learning is also tied to motivation. *Transfer* is the extent to which a task in one environment resembles a task in another environment. For transfer to occur, the tasks must be similar; and learners must see the similarity. Learners are more likely to succeed if they are motivated and challenged by the task.

Techniques
The techniques displayed during the early stages of learning are indicators of future keyboarding success. Just as an athlete must display good form, the learner must exhibit proper techniques. Correct techniques become the most important element when developing keyboarding skills (White, 1998). Learners must be reminded to sit up straight with both feet flat on the floor, to keep wrists low and fingers curved, to use a *ballistic* (quick and snappy) stroking motion, and to keep their eyes on the copy. Instructors should model and reinforce good techniques and be watchful for improper keyboarding techniques, which increase the chances of repetitive stress injuries. "Resters" rest their hands on the edge of the desk or wrist pad while keying, "leaners" keyboard while placing their arms on the desk, and "loungers" sit in a slumped position (Arp & Brundick, 1996). A learner who insists on using poor techniques is unlikely to excel at keyboarding.

Students need feedback to identify their progress, and feedback on techniques is particularly important. The teacher typically walks around the room while the students are practicing and offers commentary, such as, "Your wrists and fingers are correctly positioned," or "Please sit up straight." Because furniture affects posture, the teacher also should observe chair and desk height in relation to the student's size. Labs often contain furniture that was not designed for computer equipment, and students may be either reaching up to the keyboard or bending over it.

Practice
The sequence of instruction in keyboarding textbooks is based on principles of psychomotor skill development. Practice exercises focus on new keys and machine parts, such as the "Enter" key or the space bar. The teacher should not permit learners to skip these drills. Practice is of two types: spaced and massed. *Spaced practice*, which is spread out over time, is especially useful in the early stages of learning. In the early

weeks of keyboarding, learners' muscles are tense. Therefore, they need periods of rest between instruction and practice. Learners should engage in *massed practice*, or practice all at once, only when they have the ability to key for longer periods of time without undue muscle stress. Massed practice is appropriate for assignments requiring 20 or more minutes to complete. The quality of attention that the learner gives to the task is more important than the duration of practice or the number of times a task is practiced (Cratty, 1973).

Speed Building

Learners must develop and practice any skill in order to master it. For example, a pianist practices daily in order to improve and achieve success, and the same rigor is necessary for keyboarders. Learners move through three stages while acquiring keyboarding skills: cognitive or pre-letter-level stage, associative or letter-level stage, and autonomous or chained-response stage (West, 1974). The *cognitive stage* of keyboard learning consists of learning the steps that make up the different movements for the various keystrokes. During the *associative stage*, responses become smoother, mediators begin to disappear, motions are less hesitant, and the learner exhibits less delay between keystrokes. The *autonomous stage* is characterized by kinesthetic cues; for example, while keying "**and**" the "**a**" is the stimulus for the "**n**" and the "**n**" serves as the stimulus for the "**d**." To build speed, the learner must be "forced" to key faster. Speed-forcing drills are necessary for students to move beyond 40 words a minute (West, 1974). These drills should be of short duration, thirty seconds to one minute, with the overall time less than five minutes. Permitting students to key at a slow and easy rate will not build speed; the teacher should assign stimulating and purposeful repetition to build speed (Olinzock, 1998; West, 1974).

Accuracy Development

Debate over how to improve students' accuracy has existed for many years. West (1974) suggested that learners should correct errors as soon as they are knowingly made. One technique is to have them key a number of alphabetic sentences, circle the errors, and then analyze the errors, looking for patterns and repetitions. Next the student is assigned drills loaded with the error combinations in an attempt to provide practice and eliminate the errors. Error correction drills are questionable, because stroking errors occur at random (McLean, 1994; West, 1983). Accuracy is a matter of "finding" the "right speed," which is usually one to two words a minute below what is comfortably keyed. As an unfamiliar word is encountered, keystroking slows down and the learner reverts to vocalization. Even experienced keyboarders resort to vocalization and then speed up again. For example, as an individual keys in "zeppelin" or "quizzical" at normal speed, he or she will automatically slow down until the word is completed. If accuracy drills are used, the teacher can assign *response differentiation drills*, which concentrate on adjacent letters (b and v; m and n) and opposite hand letters (i and e; t and y). However, the learner must concentrate on what he or she is keying for the drills to have any effect. The teacher should emphasize techniques, speed, and accuracy, in that order, and separate speed practice from accuracy practice (West, 1974).

KEYBOARDING ASSESSMENT

Keyboarding assessment should be based on the goals and objectives of the course. If the goal is to learn touch keyboarding, then students should be evaluated on their ability to key with reasonable speed and accuracy without looking at the keyboard. If students are enrolled in a one-semester keyboarding/formatting course, then evaluation generally includes keying of documents, such as letters, memos, tables, and reports.

Evaluation Criteria

The objectives of the course should be the basis for assessment. For example, if the course objectives are to attain a specific speed level with acceptable accuracy, then those objectives become the evaluation criteria. If the objective of the course is to locate information and prepare reports with acceptable levels of speed and accuracy, then a major portion of the grade should be based on the final product—the report and its contents. Instructors' manuals that accompany keyboarding texts and instructional software generally provide guidelines for weighting various components, such as techniques, timed writings (timings), and formatting. These manuals typically include speed charts with accuracy levels that change every few weeks as students improve their keying skills.

Straight-copy timings. Straight-copy timed writings are usually the basis for evaluation of keyboarding throughout the course. The teacher initially gives practice timings to familiarize students with the procedure and process of taking timings. One-minute timings are generally given initially, then three-minute timings, and then five-minute timings at the end of the course. Five-minute timings are the standard that replicates a real-world environment, because people usually do not key longer than five minutes before stopping for one reason or another (West, 1974, 1983). When grading a timed writing, a teacher should separate speed and accuracy, with each component receiving a grade. Teachers should avoid collecting and averaging all timings over the duration of the course. A psychomotor skill is product-oriented; and although a teacher is concerned with the process, the final product is most important (McLean, 1994; West, 1983). A reasonable strategy for assessing speed is to collect the best three or four timings during the grading period.

Various straight-copy grading schemes have surfaced over the years. One method is *error cut-off* where after the "nth" error, any further material is not accepted. For example, if a student makes "n" errors in the first line and no more errors, nothing past the first line would be counted. *Net words per minute* penalize a student for each uncorrected error. The penalty may be as high as 10 words a minute, which can result in a negative speed. Net words per minute put a strain on students, who keep track mentally of their errors and give up when they exceed the limit. *Gross words per minute* considers all words keyed and views accuracy separately; this grading scheme is the preferred choice. While gross words per minute separates speed and accuracy, the teacher should set a limit on the number of errors, in addition to a minimum speed level.

Application tests. Keyboarding applications are cognitive, not manipulative tasks (West, 1974) that require the student to produce a document such as a letter, table, or report within a specified period of time. The grade for an application test is based on the time needed to complete the activity, as well as on accuracy. No correlation between straight copy timings and application tests exists because application tests measure decision-making factors such as margin setting, line spacing, and tabulation. A rule of thumb, however, is that application speed is about half that of straight copy speed.

Common evaluation methods include production words a minute, points, and the norm-based approach (McLean, 1994; West 1983). *Production words a minute* take into account formatting requirements such as setting margins and tabs. Students are given a set amount of time to key the task and make formatting decisions. Often a student has adequate keying speed and accuracy but takes too long in the decision-making portion of the task. Points are often assigned to a task; for example, 5 points for a memo, 15 points for a letter, and 25 points for a report. The problem with this approach is that points are arbitrarily assigned. The *norm-based* approach takes into account speed and the types of errors—major or minor errors. A *major error* might be keying the wrong sentence or using incorrect margins, while a minor error might be failing to underline or italicize the title of a book. The previously described methods require the teacher to keep track of the time from start to finish. In the *work approach*, the students raise their hands when finished, and the teacher records the time. The *time approach* allows each student the same amount of time for completion. Obviously, the longer the time, the greater the chance for making errors. Therefore, having each student signal when finished is a more equitable approach.

KEYBOARDING SOFTWARE

State-of-the-art computer hardware and software have changed how business educators deliver and manage keyboarding instruction. Integrated software programs provide teachers with an opportunity to expand traditional keyboarding and computer instruction to include spreadsheet, database, Web page design, speech recognition, and presentation software applications. The use of software also creates the need for teaching new types of documents commonly used in the workplace, such as e-mail, charts, graphs, and newsletters.

Students are entering the keyboarding classroom with various skill levels. Having software that permits individualization is important to meet this broad range of skill ability. Keyboarding software allows students who have had no prior keyboard training to begin learning the keys, while students who enter with some level of skill can start with skill-building lessons. Keyboarding software can introduce the keyboard and numeric keypad, improve students' speed and accuracy scores, and administer timed writings. Tutorial software can prescribe learning activities for students based on individual performances and keep track of student progress and achievement records. These prescriptive and record keeping features facilitate management of the instructional process and eliminate many time-consuming tasks for teachers and students.

Effective instructional software includes illustrations of key locations and reach patterns. These illustrations help students learn the location of keys and the appropriate reach from the home row position. Drill copy used for learning should quickly move from "nonsense" drills into the keying of actual words. Word length, however, should be kept at the three- to five-stroke level so that students develop fluent keystroking.

As students key, the teacher should encourage them to watch the computer screen while it illustrates the reach and direction of new keys. Students should look at their keyboards to locate the new keys and practice the proper reaches. Next, the students should key additional lines by touch, with their eyes on the computer screen, without watching their fingers. Some keyboarding software includes a "lock-and-flash" feature for use when a student is learning a new key (MicroType Multimedia User's Guide, 1999). If the student keys an incorrect key in the drill practice, the keyboard locks and flashes the correct key. As students are keying their drill practice from the computer screen, they can immediately see if the result is correct. A student must strike the correct key before continuing.

Some keyboarding software records which lessons and lesson parts the students have completed, as well as the speeds and lines keyed in the skill-building activities. If a student does not complete a lesson during a given class period, the software prompts the student to continue where he or she left off when returning to the program. Once students have completed a lesson, they should go to the open or blank screen and re-key the skill-building drill lines from the corresponding textbook lesson for additional practice and reinforcement. This activity helps students practice keeping their eyes on the copy instead of on the computer screen. If the software has a timer in the open or blank screen, students can also time themselves for speed in the early lessons.

Keyboarding software should be user-friendly and allow students to navigate with ease throughout the program. All of the lessons should use the same navigation techniques. Once students have worked through a few of the lessons, they should have mastered most features of the software.

Skill Development and Software

Neither speed nor accuracy can be taught or learned directly. Keyboarding software should not emphasize speed and accuracy too early in beginning keyboarding, as these skills are eventual outgrowths of proper technique. Research verifies that correct technique is critical in early keyboard learning (Robinson, Erickson, Crawford, Beaumont, & Ownby, 1979). The sequence of emphasis in teaching/learning a skill is (1) technique or good form; (2) speed; and (3) control (accuracy). During initial keyboard learning, software timings that emphasize speed goals are not recommended because they divert student attention from the main goal of developing good keystroking technique patterns. For the same reason, software tutorials should not focus on accuracy when students are learning the keyboard. Furthermore, "early" accuracy emphasis, penalties, and error limitations represent a negative approach to skill development, because students are likely to become frustrated and discouraged (Robinson, 1979). Typical keyboarding lesson exercises are ideal for skill building, as they are designed to motivate the student through individualized goal setting. The instructor should use these features of the software for motivational, diagnostic, and goal-setting purposes, not for grading (KeyboardingPro User's Guide, 2000; MicroType Multimedia User's Guide, 1999).

Good skill-building software allows students to complete practice drills and take timed and paced writings under various conditions. For example, students can choose to take a speed or accuracy timed writing for a variable or fixed length period. After students complete the timed writing, the software calculates the speed and identifies any errors for accuracy writings; this feature eliminates the need for manual checking of timed writings. Some products can identify use/non-use of the backspace/delete key and even offer a "locking" feature to prevent its use in correcting errors.

Software can generate a comprehensive report revealing the results, along with detailed diagnostics. The diagnostic report generated by the software identifies errors that need improving, such as finger, row, key reach, and miscellaneous (e.g., transposed letter, extra letters, opposite hand, double letter, omitted letter, home row, adjacent key, direct reach, shift key, and spacing). Students then go to the drill practice section of the software and practice prescribed drills in any area that needs improving.

Some software can check students' document production work. The checker can verify the keystrokes of most documents, including tabs and hard returns, but not formatting. For example, checking software can determine whether or not a student used the tab key, but not where the tab stop is placed. These programs can check the accuracy of the keystrokes in report headings, but not whether they are appropriately centered or underlined. However, these features save the teacher the time-consuming task of proofreading a student's work; the teacher needs only to check it for appearance.

Record Keeping Features

Some keyboarding software programs include teacher utilities that provide options to adapt record keeping for class needs. For example, the teacher can change a particular student's demographic information or change the class preferences for variables such as timing length, number of errors per minute, or use of the backspace to correct errors.

Keeping track of students' performance can be a very time consuming task. Some keyboarding software packages keep cumulative records of lesson and summary reports. The reports also provide detail about the students' progress, performance, and completion. Summary reports may also include the number of lessons completed and any speed and accuracy results. Student reports and class reports are important features of keyboarding software.

Checking software may provide the following reports: lesson reports, activity checklists, summary reports, timed-writing results, and performance graphs. The reports include such information as the speed, number of errors made, and total keying time. They should also include the "pass" and the number of edits for each document. Each time a document is started from the beginning, it counts as a pass. If a student opens and edits an existing document, the software considers the document an edit when it is checked (CheckPro 2002 for Microsoft Word 2002 User's Guide, 2003).

KEYBOARDING FOR CHILDREN

Children now interact with computers at an early age, as computers are now used in many schools at all grade levels. Although computers are present in more than half of all homes (Information Technology Research and Development, 2000), all children have not yet learned how to touch keyboard. Jennings (2001) determined that 11 % of elementary schools and 51 % of middle schools nationwide offer keyboarding. Research indicates that the earliest age that children can acquire touch keyboarding skill is age 8 or 9, or about the third grade (Bartholome, 1996; Elementary/Middle School Keyboarding, 1992; Hoot, 1986; McLean, 1994; Russell, 1994).

Keyboarding Benefits for Children

The basic premise of teaching touch keyboarding is to allow children to obtain a usable, necessary skill that will serve them throughout their school days, careers, and lives. Numerous studies have documented the many benefits that accrue to children who can touch keyboard (Bartholome, 1996; Hoot, 1986; McLean, 1994; Myers & Spindler-Virgin, 1989; Russell, 1994). General benefits include (1) being able to work faster and more efficiently; (2) reinforcing effective writing and editing skills; (3) participating more actively in the learning process; (4) developing enthusiasm about writing, and spending more time on writing, and developing fluency in writing; (5) improving reading and writing scores; and (6) improving performance in all subjects. Specific objectives of teaching keyboarding to children include enabling them to enter data into the computer, to search for information on the Internet, and to key an assignment.

Methods and Resources for Children

Touch keyboarding requires hand-eye coordination, good control of fine motor muscles, and adequate hand size (Erthal, 1998). Introducing touch keyboarding before these traits are present is questionable. When children begin using the computer, they should learn where the home row keys are located, using the right index finger for "**Y**" and "**N**," the right little finger for the enter and backspace keys, and the left little finger for the tab key. Once they learn the keyboard, children need practice and reinforcement if they are to retain this skill (Balajhy, 1987). A student's persistence is a factor in successfully learning touch keyboarding.

Teaching children keyboarding requires different methods from teaching middle school students, high school students, or adults. First, lessons should be no more than 30 minutes in length and offered daily until the children learn the entire keyboard.

(Elementary/Middle School Keyboarding, 1992). Second, children need continuous practice and reinforcement in order to retain this new skill (Bartholome, 1996). Third, a teacher should not evaluate children's keyboarding outcomes in terms of speed and accuracy; correct techniques should be the focal point of instruction (Diffley, 1995).

Alternative or smaller keyboards are available for students who are too young to manipulate a normal-sized keyboard. Resources for teaching children keyboarding include textbooks specifically designed for that age level and software for drill and practice. Some publishers offer a combination of textbooks and software that complement each other. Probably the most important ingredient is a qualified keyboarding teacher, as software alone cannot produce a student with good keyboarding skills. (McLean, 1994; Russell, 1994). This person can offer advice on techniques, help develop skills, and most of all provide motivation to a young learner. With the guidance of a qualified instructor, keyboarding software allows children to progress at their own speeds, provides for individual differences, and offers another vehicle for drill and practice.

KEYBOARDING FOR STUDENTS WITH SPECIAL NEEDS

Because a typical class may include a variety of aptitudes within the student population, business teachers must be prepared to teach keyboarding for students with special needs. A teacher must be aware of these students' special requirements, such as shortened assignments, seating preferences, extended test-taking time, special equipment, and other required resources. Evans and Henry (1989) suggest strategies for working with students with special needs in the keyboarding classroom. These strategies include recognizing individual learning styles and needs, adapting the classroom to accommodate the student, working with resource people, obtaining appropriate instructional materials, and providing for individualized evaluation.

MacArthur (1996) conducted a study to review specific ways in which computers can support and augment the writing process for students with learning disabilities. He concluded that students with special needs need keyboarding instruction if they use word-processing software to facilitate writing skills. MacArthur suggested the use of word-prediction software and word banks for these students. *Word-prediction software* predicts the intended word as the user keys a word. *Word banks* collect all words keyed in and allow the user to choose a word from the displayed list.

Special keyboarding textbooks and software are available from publishers for keyboarding students who can use only one hand, who have missing digits, or who have limited vision. Adaptive keyboards are also available for students with one hand. For example, The BAT one-handed keyboard (2002) is a fully functioning keyboard that is suited to students with physical or visual disabilities. Software allows customization of the BAT keyboard device. The Half-QWERTY keyboard is another device that presents half a keyboard with full-sized keys. Software is also available that can be used with a full-sized keyboard (Matias, MacKenzie & Burton, 1994).

Assistance for students with special needs is often included within the operating system of a computer. Windows-based computers include an accessibility menu with features that affect the keyboard, sound, display, and mouse; StickyKeys is used for Shift, Ctrl, or Alt keys by pressing one key at a time; FilterKeys ignores brief or repeated keystrokes or slows down the repeat rate; ToggleKeys sounds a tone if Caps Lock, Num Lock, or Scroll Lock are depressed; SoundSentry uses a visual warning when a sound is made; ShowSounds displays captions for speech and sounds; HighContrast uses colors and fonts for easier reading; and MouseKeys controls the pointer with the numeric keypad. Other adaptations for students with physical disabilities include plastic key guards, miniature keyboards, and infrared pointing devices (Types of Assistive Technology, 2002).

NEW INPUT TECHNOLOGIES

Speech and handwriting recognition are the next generation of input devices, and students need to be prepared with skills for the future. A mere novelty just a few short years ago, speech and handwriting recognition technologies are now readily available throughout the U.S. To be competitive in the workplace and in the schools of tomorrow, students need to learn speech and handwriting recognition skills today.

Teaching speech and handwriting recognition reinforces back-to-basic skills along with business education competencies. These input devices increase productivity, improve communication and computer skills, and reduce the risks of repetitive stress injuries such as carpal tunnel syndrome.

Speech Recognition

Speech recognition is an alternative to traditional input methods that outperforms all previous options and increases productivity. Improvements in speech recognition products in recent years have resulted in easier implementation, use, and accuracy. Speaking clearly and naturally to a computer and learning the proper commands requires only a few hours of practice. This short practice period produces the equivalent of three semesters of intense keyboarding practice, with students achieving speeds up to 110-170 words per minute (Barksdale, 2002a), with an accuracy rate rivaling that of a skilled typist. Prerequisite skills for speech recognition users include knowledge of computer concepts, proofreading, editing, and document formatting.

Most states have started speech recognition "train-the-trainer" programs that help business educators implement this latest technology. At least one state has asked each business education teacher to start a speech recognition program for all students no later than the 2004 school year (Washington State OSPI, 2002). This mandate is aligned with the *National Standards for Business Education* (2001).

Appropriate hardware is critical for teaching speech recognition effectively. A basic minimum configuration includes a computer with a Pentium III processor, 128 MB of RAM, and 300 MB of hard drive space. Software choices include Dragon

NaturallySpeaking 6 (http://www.speakingsolutions.com), Microsoft Office XP Speech Recognition (http://www.microsoft.com), and IBM ViaVoice 9 (http://www-3.ibm.com/software/speech). Regardless of the software selected, students must have a high-quality noise cancellation headset. Some major manufacturers of noise cancellation headsets include Plantronics (http://www.plantronics.com/north_america/en_US/index_flash.jhtml), Andrea (http://www.andreaelectronics.com), and Telex (http://www.computeraudio.telex.com).

In most schools only modest lab accommodations are needed to teach speech recognition effectively. Absolute silence is not required for speech recognition accuracy. With the improvement of speech recognition headsets over the past few years, dictation is now possible in fairly noisy environments. Labs often have as many as 30 to 35 students speaking at the same time without interfering with one another. To become proficient with speech recognition software, students need to learn the following categories of skills: (1) setting up the speech system; (2) enunciating clearly; (3) correcting speech recognition errors immediately; (4) training speech recognition errors permanently; (5) spelling aloud; (6) correcting capitalization; (7) dictating symbols, special characters, and numbers; (8) navigating, selecting, deleting, or moving text; and (9) formatting documents by voice (Barksdale, 2002b). These skills are easily taught in five to fifteen, 55-minute class periods, depending on the age of the students. After learning these skills, students commonly achieve a voice typing speed of 110-170 words per minute and an accuracy rate of 95 % or above after learning these skills (K. Zahner, personal communication, March 8, 2002).

Handwriting Recognition
Handwriting recognition is an innovation that uses a digital pen on a tablet PC to replace the mouse and the keyboard. This technology is designed to replace the desktop or laptop PC with a new type of computer that is more powerful, user-friendly, and accessible. Tablet PCs are accurate and easy to use; they are especially useful for people who cannot or do not want to key. Tablet PC users indicate that the pen is faster than the mouse for editing purposes. A tablet PC allows users to write with a pencil-like device, and the output appears directly on the computer screen. Students need to use readable penmanship and can screen write with either cursive or printed letters. Writing instantly turns to text and appears as if the words had been keyed or spoken. Handwriting recognition is a very convenient tool when speech recognition is impractical to use. Students can learn the basics of handwriting recognition in only about 45 minutes (Barksdale, 2001).

SUMMARY
Because keyboards are the standard method of entering information into a computer, learning to touch keyboard is one of the most important skills a person can learn. A qualified teacher is essential in order for keyboarding students to learn to interact effectively and efficiently with the computer. Keyboarding instruction involves teaching the keyboard, correct techniques, speed building, accuracy, and document

formatting. After students learn the keyboard, they must practice regularly to retain the skill. Keyboarding instruction can be augmented with software tutorials that provide individualized instruction. Keyboarding software can assist the teacher in diagnosing keyboarding errors, grading papers, and record keeping. Keyboarding teachers must be prepared to teach students with special needs, who may need to use special adaptive equipment. Speech recognition software, which transforms the spoken word into text at higher rates of speed than keyboarding, is now being taught. Handwriting recognition is becoming a popular input device as well.

REFERENCES

Andrea. (2002). Retrieved February 1, 2002, from http://www.andreaelectronics.com/HMA.htm

Arp, L., & Brundick, E. (1996). The importance of proper keyboarding techniques in reducing computer-related repetitive stress injuries. *Organizational Systems Research Association, 14*(2), 3-18.

Balajhy, E. (1987). Keyboarding and the language arts. *The Printout, 41*(1), 86-87.

Barksdale, K. (2001). Handwriting recognition and tablet PCs: Why keyboarding instruction will fizzle in this decade. Retrieved July 1, 2002, from http://speakingsolutions.com/handwriting/index.html

Barksdale, K. (2002a). It's not just keyboarding anymore. Retrieved July 1, 2002, from http://speakingsolutions.com/news/art12.html

Barksdale, K. (2002b). Speech recognition: How do we teach it? *Business Education Forum, 56*(3), 52-55.

Bartholome, L. (1996). Typewriting/keyboarding instruction in elementary schools. Report from Business Information Systems and Education Department, Utah State University. Retrieved June, 1998, from http://www.bus.usu.edu/bise/faculty/lwb/typewrit.htm

BAT One Handed Keyboard by Infogrip, Inc. (2002). Retrieved January 5, 2002, from http://www.nanopac.com/Keyboard.htm

CheckPro 2002 for Microsoft Word 2002 user's guide. (2003). Mason, OH: South-Western/Thomson Learning, Inc.

Cratty, B. (1973). *Movement behavior and motor learning* (2nd ed.). Philadelphia: Lea & Febiger.

Diffley, J. (1995). A technological edge—elementary keyboarding. *The Kansas Business Teacher,* 3-4.

Dragon NaturallySpeaking 6.0. (2002). Retrieved February 1, 2002, from http://www.speakingsolutions.com

Elementary/middle school keyboarding strategies guide. (1992). Reston, VA: National Business Education Association.

Erickson, L. (1993). *Basic keyboarding guide for teachers.* Cincinnati, OH: South-Western Publishing Co.

Erthal, M. (1998). Who should teach keyboarding and when should it be taught? *Business Education Forum, 53*(1), 36-37.

Evans, C., & Henry, J. (1989). Keyboarding for the special needs student. *Business Education Forum, 43*(7), 23-25.

Hayes, V., & Reeve, T. (1980). Role of visual feedback for response guidance and response confirmation in typewriting. *Perceptual and Motor Skills, 50,* 1047-4056.

Hoot, J. (1986). Keyboarding instruction in the early grades: Must or mistake? *Childhood Education, 63*(2), 95-101.

IBM ViaVoice 9. (2002). Retrieved February 1, 2002, from http://www-3.ibm.com/software/speech

Jennings, S. (2001). National keyboarding trends. *Business Education Forum, 55*(3), 46-48.

Information technology research and development: Information technology for the 21st century. (2000). Retrieved February 1, 2002, from http://www.whitehousegov/WH/New/html/20000121_2.html

KeyboardingPro user's guide. (2000). Cincinnati, OH: South-Western/Thomson Learning, Inc.

MacArthur, C. (1996). Using technology to enhance the writing process of students with learning disabilities. *Journal of Learning Disabilities, 29*(4), 344-354.

Matias, E., MacKenzie, I., & Burton, W. (1994). Half-QWERTY: Typing with one hand using your two-handed skills. Paper presented at the Conference on Human Factors in Computing Systems, New York.

McLean, G., & Pulak, T. (1995). The myth of touch keystroking. *Business Education Forum, 49*(3), 28-30.

McLean, G. (1994). *Teaching keyboarding.* Little Rock, AR: Delta Pi Epsilon.

Microsoft. (2002). Speech recognition in Office XP. Retrieved February 1, 2002, from http://www.microsoft.com/office/evaluation/indepth/speech.asp

MicroType multimedia user's guide. (1999). Cincinnati, OH: South-Western Educational Publishing.

Myers, S., & Spindler-Virgin, R. (1989). Time to teach keyboarding? *The Writing Notebook, 7*(2), 26-27.

National Business Education Association. (2001). *National standards for business education: What America's students should know and be able to do in business* (2nd ed.). Reston, VA: Author.

Olinzock, A. (1998). Computer skill building: The answer to keyboarding instruction? *Business Education Forum, 52*(3), 24-26.

Plantronics. (2002). Retrieved February 1, 2002, from http://www.plantronics.com/north_america/en_US/index_flash.jhtml

Robinson, J., Erickson, L., Crawford, T., Beaumont, L., & Ownby, A. (1979). *Typewriting learning and instruction.* Cincinnati, OH: South-Western Publishing Co.

Russell, R. (1994). Teaching keyboarding to elementary children. In A. McEntee (Ed.), *Expanding horizons in business education: Elementary and middle level education* (Yearbook No. 32, pp. 1-6). Reston, VA: National Business Education Association.

Singer, R. (1975). *Motor learning and human performance* (2nd ed.). New York: MacMillan Publishers.

Telex. (2002). Retrieved February 1, 2002, from http://www.computeraudio.telex.com

Types of assistive technology. (2002). Retrieved February 1, 2002, from http://www.microsoft.com/enable/at/types.htm

Washington State Office of Superintendent of Public Instruction. (2002). Retrieved February 1, 2002, from http://www.k12.wa.us/curriculuminstruct/

West, L. (1983). *Acquisition of typewriting skills* (2nd ed.). Indianapolis, IN: Bobbs-Merrill.

West, L. (1974). *Implications of research for teaching typewriting* (2nd ed.). Delta Pi Epsilon Research Bulletin No. 4. Little Rock, AR: Delta Pi Epsilon.

White, C. (1998). Beginning keyboarding for elementary schools: A third grade instructional design. *Delaware Business Journal, 13,* 13-18.

Information Technology

George A. Mundrake
Ball State University
Muncie, Indiana

Information technology is an important part of the business education curriculum at all levels. Courses in information technology are offered at the middle school through college/university levels. These courses have evolved from an early emphasis on "how-to" and hands-on experiences, to a later emphasis on understanding concepts and ways to use technology to solve problems. The business world in recent years has added certification programs, adding emphasis to the need for skills and knowledge of information technology.

This chapter discusses changes in the information technology curriculum, describes the basis for those changes, and outlines ways in which information technology is taught at various educational levels. The chapter lists strategies for teaching information technology concepts, skills, and knowledge at various educational levels and in the courses that are typically included as part of information technology programs.

CHANGES IN THE INFORMATION TECHNOLOGY CURRICULUM

What should be taught in courses on information technology? The answer to this question drives the choices that determine the content of these courses and how to teach them. As technology has advanced, courses in information technology have changed. The approach to curriculum development has evolved from software mastery (the "software is content" approach) to software solutions (the information systems approach).

Both educators and students have had to adapt to the pace of change. New technology has allowed educators to "raise the bar" for expected student outcomes. Faster processors, built-in help files, self-paced tutorials, user-friendly software with a wider variety of business applications and more standardized features are common in most applications. These enhancements allow students to learn software faster and give teachers more opportunities to expand the curriculum and take it to higher-level uses, such as problem solving and theoretical and creative applications for computers.

Articulation, duplication, and overlap of course content and coverage at all educational levels must be considered in course design and delivery. As content has moved into elementary grade levels in the forms of keyboarding and the use of computers for interactive lessons, educators must address the trickle-down effect of new content throughout the curriculum and raise levels of expected student outcomes.

A Question of Tool or Content

Information technology may be viewed either as a tool or as content. The trend for courses to bear the name "information technology," implies the use of technology as a tool. This trend is not surprising since, in the past, teachers spent much of their class time teaching the details of how to use the tool. Because details were necessary to perform simple tasks and operations, they became the content. As software became more user-friendly, the trend in teaching shifted to the problem-solving approach. This approach included teaching how and when to select from the varieties of software (and functions within the software) to perform tasks more efficiently.

Business computer technologies as a tool extend to all functional and organizational areas of business, including the primary function of providing a basis for decision making. The act of arranging, processing, organizing, and communicating raw data in a manner that transforms it to useful information facilitates decision making. Management information systems instructors treat information technology as a management tool (Harder, 2001) and emphasize processes and procedures. Information technology is regarded as a tool for management. Further, business technology courses have become an integral part of the middle school curriculum, providing ways for students to enhance their work and life skills and use their newly developed business skills in and out of school. Increasingly, elementary students are using information technology tools in their classrooms as aids to learning (Andelora, 2001).

High School Curriculum

High school information technology offerings vary among states and school districts. The National Business Education Association's *National Standards for Business Education* (NBEA, 2001) outlined in detail standards for four educational levels from elementary through two-year postsecondary/community college or technical college. These standards included all areas of business: accounting, business law, career development, communication, computation, economics and personal finance, entrepreneurship, information technology, international business, management, and marketing.

The emphasis on information technology as a tool is clear. Technology use is embraced in all sections of the standards.

As the standards movement became an important force in education at all levels, state departments of education provided guidelines or standards for the business education curriculum. The Indiana Department of Education and many other state departments of education provided standards documents for business educators that included course descriptions, course objectives, performance expectations, content grids, and other curriculum information (Indiana DOE, 2002). Courses for information technology include keyboarding and document formatting, computer applications, as well as advanced applications classes in desktop publishing, database management, Web page design, programming, and networking and systems management.

College Curriculum

College information technology courses usually include an introductory information systems or a core course. This course provides an overview of computer hardware and software, the systems development cycle, classification and use of software among functional areas of business, social issues about computing, and computer applications using word processing, spreadsheet, Internet, database, and/or presentation graphics software.

Administrators often are concerned about a lack of consistency in the content of information technology courses among schools. However, Stephens and O'Hara (2001) concluded from their research that this concern is unwarranted. They compared course syllabi to determine the commonality of topics in information technology courses and identified a core of five topics for the courses. Courses may have different titles, but the content tends to be similar among schools accredited by the International Association for Management Education (AACSB). Common among these courses is a mix of information technology (software skills) and management information systems (conceptual knowledge). Courses for two-year majors and minors in information technology are often designed for more hands-on applications to prepare graduates for positions that require problem solving skills using technology. Some schools use internships, job site shadowing, and workplace visitations as part of their programs.

Advanced information technology courses include classes in application of desktop publishing, multimedia, networking, and database administration software; programming in business-related languages, including those used for Internet development; and Web design. These courses usually have a prerequisite of the basic concepts course and keyboarding and are designed for in-depth study of theory and application.

Industry Certification

Several software vendors offer certification programs and "partnership" agreements with private training firms and schools. The programs offer certificates based on completion of courses and/or experiential work and the passing of examinations.

Microsoft Corporation (Microsoft, 2002) offers several certification programs. According to CDi Communications, Inc. (2002), Microsoft's MOS (Microsoft Office Specialist) is one of the most popular types of certification programs, with more than 9,000 "IQcenters" worldwide. This certification is offered through secondary schools, vocational schools, continuing education programs, private business colleges, community/junior colleges, and some universities. Increasing numbers of schools offer Microsoft's MCSA (Microsoft Certified System Administrator) certification for networks and system administration. Others offer Microsoft certifications for MCP (Microsoft Certified Professional), MCP+I (Internet applications), MCP+SB (Site Building), MCSD (Microsoft Certified Solutions Developer), and MCT (Microsoft Certified Trainer).

In addition to Microsoft, other vendors offer certification or user/training groups, including Corel Corporation (Corel Corporation, 2002)—WordPerfect, PageMill, and Corel Draw; Adobe (Adobe Corporation, 2002)—PageMaker desktop publishing and software solution network training; IBM/Lotus (Lotus Corporation, 2002)—CLS (Certified Lotus Specialist) Spreadsheet and IBM Solutions; and Quark Corporation (Quark, Inc., 2002)—DMS (Digital Media Specialist) for Quark XPress DTP and digital media. Web sites for these certification programs outline the requirements for certification and usually provide tutorials, partnership lists, and knowledge bases for end users and trainers.

STRATEGIES FOR TEACHING INFORMATION TECHNOLOGY

Lambrecht (1999) exhorted teachers to examine their assumptions about how students learn to use software. An important aspect of learning is the ability to transfer knowledge from the learning setting to business settings and to be able to continue to learn new software as versions change. An instructor must examine all strategies for teaching and learning with both of Lambrecht's objectives in mind. Students must learn to use the hardware and software, but they must also learn strategies for continuing to learn after they leave the classroom. Lynch (2002) found that contextual teaching and learning and authentic assessment are critical for acquiring knowledge and learning skills.

Schmidt and Kirby (1995) examined ways to emphasize critical thinking, reasoning, and problem solving, i.e., higher order skills, in technology-based courses. They advocated approaches that (1) emphasize critical thinking, (2) aid students to develop higher order thinking and skills, and (3) foster the ability to work cooperatively with others. Students must demonstrate that they can learn on their own, solve problems, make decisions, reason through diverse and complex situations, evaluate their own and others' work, and work in teams. The challenge to teachers is to meet the needs of students in developing the higher order skills demanded in the workplace.

Strategies for teaching information technology vary among courses and content. Hands-on courses for computer software applications have several common or generic strategies. As the applications become more specialized, as in desktop publishing and multimedia, the selection of samples, problems, and student learning activities also become more specialized.

Generic Strategies

Common teaching strategies span all information technology classes and include the following items:

- Specify the objectives. Give students an overview of each lesson and let them know what is expected of them.

- Introduce the software by exploring its possible uses. This introduction can occur in small group discussions. Students may be urged to leave computers off until terms and uses are explored.

- Demonstrate the software features, menus, toolbars, and special purpose functions unique to the software.

- Sequence instruction from simple to complex and build upon tasks in a logical manner.

- If a problem occurs, take the opportunity to troubleshoot solutions with students.

- Emphasize that software usually has two or more ways to accomplish the same task. This knowledge will be valuable for troubleshooting and higher level critical thinking activities, including the use of shortcut keys and display of nonstandard toolbars to perform tasks more efficiently.

- Use tutorials after a brief introduction. Most tutorials provided by textbooks are self-paced and well written; however, they tend to start with a file. Ask students to make adjustments in a step-by-step manner and print a document. Supplement tutorials with thought problems and exercises that require that the students "start from scratch." Frequently use quizzes, exercises, and activities that give students feedback as a means of formative evaluation, as discussed in Chapter 7. Formative evaluation provides data and information that can be used to improve instruction and learning (Fulkert, 2000).

- Use a variety of assessment tools, including summative evaluation, as discussed in Chapter 7, to make evaluation more reliable and valid and provide for differences in student learning styles.

- Prepare and use self-timed PowerPoint quizzes (about 20 seconds per frame). Have students grade their own quizzes with answers on duplicate slides after the self-timed quiz is complete. Discuss the questions and answers. Provide students with expectations for projects and describe the method of grading. Develop and use rubrics and evaluation checklists to increase reliability and validity of assessment on projects, as discussed in Chapter 7.

- Integrate examples from other disciplines and courses taken by students to make applications relevant to their fields of study.

- Have alternative plans for lesson delivery in case of technology failures, such as network crashes, software failure, or projection problems. Divide class time into smaller segments and use student-centered activities.

- Use small group and cooperative learning activities when possible. For optimum performance, the instructor should select heterogeneous groups rather than letting students form their own groups (Caton, 1995).

Word Processing

Word processing is the most widely used commercial application software and is used in all work environments. Vendors allocate tremendous resources to make their products useful for almost anyone. Many features of the software are only occasionally employed for personal use by casual end users; however, learning these features increases productivity in the work environment.

Beginning a word processing unit may require some stage setting activities. Often students enter a class and advise their teacher that they have already had a word processing class. A diagnostic test or hands-on problem may be used to dispel some students' beliefs that they "know it all" and to emphasize the additive effect of learning about word processing.

Some teaching strategies for word processing include the following suggestions:

- Take the time to use those activities that enable students to define terms that are specific to word processing. Use end-of-chapter quizzes or questions or online tutorials. Do not consider terminology to be "low-level" learning. Vocabulary mastery is also helpful in more advanced applications.

- Supplement tutorials with case problems and constructivist-approach (problem solving) assignments to reinforce concepts and build skills.

- Use reproduction assignments (give a sample document and have students replicate it) that allow students to problem solve by selecting and using the necessary word processing functions.

- Use "rewrite" assignments to incorporate communication skills, proofreading, and computer skills. Require students to revise a document that uses all of these skills.

- Have students do their written assignments using word processing software.

- Use fill-in-the-blank assignments for multipage manuscripts about information technology terms and concepts or have students write paragraphs for given subheadings.

Spreadsheet Software

Extensive use of spreadsheet software in all functional business areas allows teachers a wide variety of activities and opportunities. However, applications in marketing, accounting, management, and other business functions pose a dilemma if students do not have a conceptual understanding of the application. Therefore, beginning spreadsheet instruction should concentrate on those applications that are familiar, such as a personal budget, loan calculation and repayment schedules, checkbook balancing, and other relatively simple applications that incorporate basics of spreadsheet use.

Other teaching strategies to consider include the following ideas:

- Early on, encourage students to become accustomed to using Help files available with software.

- Cluster concepts such as cell formatting and number display, and provide a brief introduction and/or demonstration of the concepts before students begin tutorials.

- Have students take time to plan and sketch out spreadsheets that they are creating "from scratch" and anticipate the results of calculations before they start the spreadsheet.

- Encourage the use of system tools such as the calculator to check formula calculations *after* they have entered formulas.

- In columns that require a formula in an assignment, give the formula algebraically or algorithmically to avoid having students merely entering numbers.

- Encourage students to "let the computer do the work" by insisting that they use formulas and absolute values wherever possible.

- After a spreadsheet is completed, pose questions as part of the feedback phase about other ways the spreadsheet could have been completed to get the same results. For example, students should be able to think critically about their use of formulas: Could they have used an "If" statement in more than one way? Could they have asked whether a value or label was "equal to" or "not equal to" another value or label, using "If" statements in different ways? Their evaluation of ways to solve problems in a spreadsheet is an important part of learning how to use the software effectively.

- Develop applications that draw from other areas of study, such as using the Internet to look up monetary exchange rates for a currency conversion spread-sheet, or getting stock quotes to track a stock.

- Have students duplicate tables from business magazines or newspapers.

- Collect samples of misleading tables and charts to illustrate the importance of proper scaling and data ranges.

- Integrate charts and graphs created in spreadsheet software into word processing documents or presentations.

Database

Database software is usually introduced as a part of information technology classes. Some schools offer more in-depth classes, combining theory and application for different file management and database systems. If database software is not available, general concepts can be taught by using the data table features of spreadsheet software. Strategies for teaching database software include the following suggestions:

- Begin database instruction with a simple explanation of how data is handled manually, as many students have not worked with manual filing systems and may not understand the basic concept of databases.

- Explain how computers store data and how computers build databases from bits, bytes (characters), fields, records, and files. If they understand the components of files and databases, students will begin to understand how databases work. Invite guest speakers, such as database administrators from businesses, or have students visit companies and present their own reports about the use of databases in business firms.

- Integrate the Internet into learning about database management by having students search for descriptions of different kinds of database software.

- At each workstation, have each student create a common database table or layout of student information about classmates (name, hobbies, sports, etc.) and have students rotate to input their information. Show students the importance of database protocols (some students will use all caps or only lower case). Query the file and make on-screen reports and printed reports.

- Clip advertisements of automobiles from local newspapers and have students develop a database of used cars with make, model, color, prices, and features. Have the group input the information, query the database, and print reports.

- Use library search systems to illustrate very large database files and search techniques.

- Use sports data to create a database about the school's sports teams.

- Have students search for products from online vendors and auction sites that combine text and graphic forms of databases.

Graphics and Presentation Graphics

Software uses for graphics include scanning, photo editing, drawing, and painting applications. Scanning software also may include features for optical character recognition (OCR) and form scanning software for business forms. Presentation graphics such as PowerPoint allow users to chain together slides into a linear (slide to slide) or nonlinear (branching) show. Both forms of graphics software may act as ancillary software for other applications such as word processing, desktop publishing, and multimedia. Scanned images and text can be inserted into documents, used for Web pages, or added to animated files using Graphic Interchange Format (GIF) animation software. In addition, single frames of PowerPoint presentations can be used as graphics in other documents by saving each frame as a graphics file.

Some teaching strategies for graphics and presentation graphics include the following suggestions:

- Explore the toolboxes, toolbars, and pull-down menus of various software draw and paint graphics programs such as Adobe Photoshop, Corel Draw, and Microsoft Paint. Start out with simple draw/paint software such as Microsoft Paint (which comes with Windows). The drawings can be imported or placed into most word processing, desktop publishing, and presentation graphics software.

- Teach students file-size economy when scanning images. Keep the size of files small by changing resolution, scaling, cropping, choosing grayscale, and/or limiting the number of colors.

- Introduce the PowerPoint slide master feature, which allows students to develop a format for a series of presentation slides with a "master" that is then applied to all subsequent slides. The concept of using a master slide should be introduced early to avoid the need to change fonts and backgrounds of presentation slides.

- Use search assignments on the Internet for sites that include multimedia and presentation design tips.

- Divide the class into small groups and ask students to analyze their class as a potential audience. What kind of presentation would be most suitable for the class as an audience? Each group can report its opinions orally. This exercise stresses the importance of matching presentations to their intended audience, an important skill for effective presentations in business.

- Use small groups to develop a presentation in smaller sections or units. The group will decide on fonts and backgrounds, create a master file or template, create the units, and merge the file into one large presentation. Provide rubrics or check lists for group or individual projects, as discussed in Chapter 7.

- Assign a presentation about the ethical use of copyrighted materials taken from the Internet.

- Assign a presentation that branches or hyperlinks to Internet sites, other programs or files, other presentations, and within the same presentation (menus).

- Assign a presentation that has students address design steps, tools, and techniques for development of a presentation.

Internet Software

At a beginning level, teaching students how to use the Internet effectively usually involves learning general theory about how the Internet works and classifying different types of software used to access the Internet. In a unit about Internet use, students learn general concepts and terminology and how to use Web browsers, search engines, e-mail, and file transfer programs. Web site design and development are usually in a separate, more advanced course. Some strategies for teaching Internet software include the following ideas:

- Integrate hardware and software concepts by having students search for hardware or software prices and specifications on the Internet.

- Develop business questions for students to answer through Internet searches, such as, names of corporate executives, company product lines, and accounting information.

- Integrate the Internet with lessons on finance by using available financial calculators online.

- Have students track stock prices or develop mock portfolios using spreadsheet and Internet software.

- Have students access sites around the world, such as regional stock markets, foreign companies, and governments.

- Use small groups to compare company Web sites and develop criteria for what makes a good site. Have students rank and/or report on strengths and weaknesses of the sites.

- Use the browser's view codes features and discuss the HTML codes as an introduction to Web development.

- Develop a small unit on the maintenance of a desktop computer's Internet software including cache cleaning, removal of temporary Internet files, update procedures, and virus checking.

- Use small groups to develop and refine keywords for searches. Give the group a list of items that have more than one meaning or use in different constructs.

STRATEGIES FOR TEACHING INTERMEDIATE AND ADVANCED INFORMATION TECHNOLOGY

Intermediate and advanced information technology classes build upon previous courses and experiences. However, some advanced courses such as desktop publishing, the World Wide Web, and multimedia attract students from disciplines other than business. Prerequisite courses may be kept to a minimum to accommodate their needs; therefore, these courses should be designed on a stand-alone basis with minimal prerequisites.

Desktop Publishing

Desktop publishing (DTP) classes offer students a creative and challenging application of the computer. Publication design choices, font and layout selections, and unique software packages characterize typical desktop publishing topics. Hardware and software requirements for DTP need attention as part of the course content. Emphasis on scanners, laser printers, modems or LAN (Local Area Network) cards for Internet access, hard drives, Zip or Jaz drives, digitizing tablets, and digital photography equipment should be included in the course, along with the software needed for these devices.

In addition to hardware and software, students must learn terms, concepts, and problem solving related to publishing and printing. These concepts should be introduced before learning electronic pasteboard software (QuarkXPress, PageMaker, MS Publisher, or other desktop software) because many of the menus use the terminology and concepts of printing and publishing.

Desktop publishing is rapidly becoming electronic publishing. New features of most programs have "save as" features to convert files to HTML or Portable Document

Format (PDF) formats. Word processing software has evolved by adding many DTP and multimedia features, and spreadsheet software has added many database features. Trends in DTP software include addition of Web, draw and paint, table, photo-editing, and hyperlink features that must be addressed in our classes.

Some other teaching strategies for consideration are the following items:

- Use design portfolio assignments so students can find and identify examples of desktop publishing design.

- Give a small group a list of design features (tint screens, dropped caps, bleeds, etc.) and resources (old newspapers and magazines) and have them find examples of each.

- Have students find and prepare a report about hardware, software, fonts, and other desktop-related items found on the Internet. Have students save the file in word processing, so they can later place the text into a desktop publishing file.

- Use multitasking and have students import special characters (dingbats, wingdings, and Webdings) as graphics in the character map feature of Windows. These features may be used as watermarks or as other design features in a publication.

- Have students use Word art, Autoshapes, and other features of word processing and place or paste them into DTP files.

- Use the Windows Paint accessory and have students draw a graphic and place it into a DTP project.

- Use scanning software to scan an image and place the file into a project, and use photo-editing features of the DTP software to create stylized graphics. Invite local printers or graphic artists as guest speakers and ask them to critique students' projects. If possible, arrange a field trip to a printing company so students can observe and discuss techniques used in design and printing.

- Create business forms using DTP software and save them as PDF files for Internet use. Use Adobe Acrobat (a free download) to view the files.

- Include projects to teach layout and execution of portrait and landscape flyers, two- and three-fold flyers, business cards, letterhead, certificates, logos, posters (tiling), nametags, table place markers, package design, technical bulletins, programs, menus, maps, signs, product information, instruction booklets, and other business applications.

- Be flexible. Allow students to do projects that interest them, and that they may be able to use for personal reasons, such as clubs or teams.

Web Design and Development

Internet software includes browsers, search engines, development tools (to create and edit Web pages), FTPs (File Transfer Programs), sound and video capture software, and nonlinear digital editing software, e-commerce development software, animation software, and programming languages such as C++, Java, HTML, and Visual BASIC. In Web design classes, as in multimedia and networking classes, some of the software concepts overlap in different software packages, such as scanning, GIF animation software, sound recording and editing, and concepts related to graphics file extensions and Internet usage.

Teaching strategies include the following ideas:

- Create units that emphasize the concept or application being taught, such as recording and editing sound, working with still and motion graphics, using animation, creating and using navigation and buttons. This tactic will help to group students by task and to allocate computer resources.

- Have students create different types of Web pages or sites including personal, informational, and commercial Web sites.

- Set up a Web site for student organizations as a project. Use small groups and have each group visit and critique the design of a Web site.

- Use small groups to design and create a Web site; have each group "beta" test the other group's site and suggest improvements.

- Use online tutorials and help files to determine scripting needed for some advanced tasks (hit counters, site searches, scrollable text blocks, and input of end user information).

Computer Networking

Networking classes require an in-depth understanding of networking theory, computer hardware, systems and LAN software, and cabling systems or topologies. Peer-to-peer operating systems such as Windows NT and XP and client-server networks using a dedicated file server computer have made knowledge of connectivity and networking important concepts for students to understand.

A major problem with delivery of networking courses is having a venue for actual network setup. Older machines may be used for students to cable and network two or more machines into a network. In larger classes, it may be necessary to rotate students through the hands-on part of the course or work in small groups. Some other teaching strategies may include the following suggestions:

- Have students prepare interview questions and visit a company that has a LAN. They should report on the topology, technical aspects of the network, and network administration features.

- Invite guest speakers from local companies, including network administrators, software specialists, and vendors, to discuss their work.

- Use the Internet to find available network hardware and software used in creating a network.

- Prepare a presentation to management to promote a networking project.

- Compare various features of software for network administration, including login scripting, security matters, speed, and efficiency.

- Have students develop a proposal for a LAN for management, including hardware and software requirements, benefits and cost analysis, and network administration plans.

Multimedia

Multimedia classes encompass a wide variety of software types, including presentation graphics, scanning, authoring, animation, video capture and editing, sound recording and editing, and photo editing. Multimedia software tends to be expensive and require state-of-the-art equipment for effective use. However, classes can rotate software and workstations either through small groups or by using a LAN . With a scanner, photo-editing software, video capture cards, video editing software, and scan converters, an instructor can design a workstation that students can use to create a presentation and store it on videotape.

Knowledge of hardware is important in multimedia classes for troubleshooting and upgrading a system. In addition to computer hardware, instruction about analog equipment, such as VHS video cameras and TV monitors must be included in order to convert analog media to digital or computer media.

Some activities and strategies for teaching multimedia delivery include the following practices:

- Break down components of the class into smaller units, such as multimedia hardware and software, design tools and techniques, sound applications, still graphics, motion video, navigation, hyperlinks, multimedia and the Internet, and animation. Using a unit approach allows for more flexibility and use of computing resources.

- Develop situation cards and use them for small group brainstorming. Give a situation such as this: "You have a videotape of a speaker and you want to create a digital video clip for a presentation. What hardware, software, and other equipment would you need to complete this task?" Alternatively, give each group a situation card and ask them to brainstorm on what hardware, software, special equipment, and cables would be needed. The situations may include having a videotape of a speech for which you want to digitize a clip to include in a presentation, taking sound from a cassette tape and putting it into a presentation, or similar situations where analog and digital media must be incorporated. Situation cards can be adapted for many scenarios.

- Use small groups and rotations to demonstrate applications on equipment such as scanners, video capture equipment, and computers to videotape output devices.

- Use a major project to allow students to bring together units. As a final project have students develop a presentation that includes still and motion graphics, sound, and navigation buttons on a topic of their choice. Examples of topics may include the profile of a company, a product sales promotion, an informational presentation about an event or student organization, a training presentation about a business-related topic, or a charity campaign.

- Allow students to work in small groups or teams when setting up complex tasks such as video capture.

- Follow a "least common denominator" approach to multimedia. Files are created in many different formats, and equipment capabilities vary dramatically. Students should learn to use files and file extensions that are mainstream (AVI, WAV, GIF, JPG, MPG) to avoid the need for special downloads of media players and other multimedia software that may not be available to most users. This approach will minimize presentation failure when used on another system.

- Encourage students to create separate folders for each project and save the files to that folder to avoid linking problems. Often students save video clips, images, sound files, or other multimedia components on a different device such as a hard drive or Zip disk and on different workstations. Most multimedia software links these to the particular machine where the presentation was created. When the presentation is run on another machine, the links are likely to fail.

- Capture analog still and moving video and incorporate the picture or clip into a presentation.

- Use Internet access to demonstrate and reinforce discussion on multimedia terminology, hardware, software, and techniques.

- Take advantage of shareware when possible to reduce costs and allow students to evaluate software. Have students download and evaluate software for functional areas of multimedia software.

- Use small group demonstrations for scanning instruction, and provide instruction sheets for specialized software.

- Because many software applications are available for multimedia, encourage students to utilize online help and other self-directed software aids.

SUMMARY

The information technology curriculum for all educational levels has evolved over the last several years. At early levels, students learn how to use the tools of technology for school and personal use. At more advanced levels, problem solving and creativity are emphasized as students learn to use sophisticated tools for business applications.

Teaching strategies for information technology courses range from generic strategies that apply to all software packages and all hardware configurations to strategies that lend themselves to helping students to learn how to use more sophisticated, complex applications. For desktop publishing, multimedia, and Web design courses, a constructivist approach is wise. Students must learn how to solve problems and apply their knowledge to the types of problems they will face in the workplace. They must learn that technology will change very rapidly, and that their ability to solve problems and find help for a software application or hardware problem are critical to their success. This chapter has presented strategies and techniques for instruction to help students to build those skills.

REFERENCES

Adobe Corporation. (2002). Adobe Solutions Network. Retrieved May 21, 2002, from http//www.adobe.com/training.html

Andelora, S. (2001). Shaping the elementary and middle school business education curriculum. In B. Brown (Ed.), *Management of the business classroom.* (Yearbook No. 39, pp. 112-124). Reston, VA: National Business Education Association.

Caton, J. (1996). Extending the use of cooperative learning. In H. Perreault, (Ed.), *Classroom strategies: The methodology of business education.* (Yearbook No. 34, pp. 117-130). Reston, VA: National Business Education Association.

CDi Communications, Inc. (2002). Retrieved June 14, 2002, from http://www.computer-certification-training.com/html/mous_certification.html

Corel Corporation. (2002). Training and Certification Program. Retrieved May 21, 2002 from http//www.corel.com/CertificationPrograms/index

Fulkert, R. (2000). Authentic assessment. In J. Rucker (Ed.), *Assessment in business education.* (Yearbook No. 38, pp. 71-90). Reston, VA: National Business Education Association.

Harder, J. (2001, October). A consensus of experts: The standards at a glance. *Business Education Forum, 56*(1), 12.

Indiana Department of Education. (2002). Standards. Retrieved May 21, 2002, from http//www.doe.state.in.us/octe/bme/standards%20welcome.htm

Lambrecht, J. (1999, January/February). Teaching technology-related skills. *Journal of Education for Business, 74*(3), 144-151.

Lotus Corporation. (2002). Certification. Retrieved May 20, 2002, from http//www.lotus.com/services/education/

Lynch, R. (2000). *New directions for high school career and technical education in the 21st century* (Information Series No. 384). Columbus, OH: Clearinghouse on Adult, Career, and Vocational Education, Center on Education and Training for Employment. (ED444037).

Microsoft Corporation. (2002). Training and Certification. Retrieved May 21, 2002, from http//www.microsoft.com/traincert/mcp/default.asp

National Business Education Association. (2001). *National standards for business education: What America's students should know and be able to do in business.* Reston, VA: Author

Quark, Inc. (2002). Quark Digital Media System Certification Training. Retrieved May 20, 2002, from http//www.quark.com/service/learning/quarkxpress/

Schmidt, B., & Kirby, M. (1995). Technology and the development of critical thinking skills. In N. Groneman (Ed.), *Technology in the classroom.* (Yearbook No. 33, pp. 32-39). Reston, VA: National Business Education Association.

Stephens, C., & O'Hara, M. (2001, March/April). The core information technology course at AACSB-accredited schools: Consistency or chaos? *Journal of Education for Business, 76*(4), 181-184.

Communication

Bobbye J. Davis
Southeastern Louisiana University
Hammond, Louisiana

Clarice P. Brantley
Innovative Training Team
Pensacola, Florida

Communication permeates every facet of life: education, employment, and personal relationships. The importance of being able to communicate effectively applies to all disciplines. In the business arena, employers rate communication as the number one attribute for recruits (*Job Market*, 2002). Personal and work-related associations begin and develop through communication-based interactions. Thus, business educators need to provide opportunities for students to develop communication expertise.

This chapter addresses course objectives and instructional levels in its focus on four communication areas: essentials, form/mode, social communication, and employment. Specific teaching strategies, resources, and suggested evaluations provide additional tools for classroom use.

COMMUNICATION COURSE OBJECTIVES AND INSTRUCTIONAL LEVELS

The *National Standards for Business Education* (National Business Education Association, 2001) identifies specific communication objectives at four levels of performance: elementary, middle/junior high, secondary, and postsecondary levels. This chapter relates to communication at the secondary and postsecondary levels.

Frequently, a course entitled "Business English" appears in the curriculum of the English department rather than among business course offerings. "Business Communication" often appears in postsecondary course catalogs, while only intermittently making the list of secondary course offerings. According to the *National Standards*, grammar, writing, listening, and speaking skills should be reinforced and incorporated into the area of communication at all levels.

When communication is offered as a separate course in a secondary school business curriculum, a plan similar to the one used in Nebraska may serve as a guide. The URL for the Nebraska Web site is http://www.nde.state.ne.us/BUSED/bused/curric/appcomm.htm.

For information about business communication at the collegiate level, contact the Association for Business Communication at http://www.businesscommunication.org/ or at Baruch College/Communication Studies, Box B8-240, One Bernard Baruch Way, New York, NY 10010. The Association for Business Communication publishes *The Journal of Business Communication*, *Business Communication Quarterly*, and numerous special publications on business communication. This organization also sponsors annual conferences on business communication at the international, national, and regional levels.

When business communication is not offered as a separate course, business educators should include vital communication concepts in every business subject. An even stronger recommendation is given in the *National Standards* (2001), that " . . . communication standards should not be limited to one course; they should be integrated throughout the curriculum" (p. 36).

COMMUNICATION ESSENTIALS

Communication essentials include speaking, signaling (nonverbal communication), listening, writing, and reading. To develop these essential skills, students need to have opportunities to practice them in every business class (Dittmar, 2000). Business teachers should search for and integrate appropriate communication teaching strategies that relate to and reinforce the specific course content (Schepf, 2002). For example, when discussing a case or conducting a mock trial in business law, essential communication skills apply as they would in a stand-alone business communication class.

Speaking

People spend many hours each day communicating on the telephone or in person with customers, coworkers, and supervisors. Spoken communication is often impromptu or unplanned and cannot be edited or retracted easily. Signaling, inflection, and immediate feedback enhance understanding of spoken communication. Planned responses require careful preparation, thought, and practice.

Both spontaneous and planned teaching strategies help to develop spoken communication skills (Swanson, 1987). Students responding to teachers' questions, greeting and introducing visitors, placing and receiving telephone calls, and interviewing for jobs provide opportunities for unplanned spoken communication. When given time to plan, prepare, revise, and rehearse, placing telephone calls and interviewing can also be planned spoken communication. In addition, students could react to an in-class video in two or three sentences; introduce classmates at the beginning of a semester; interview a local celebrity and obtain specific information; read, critique, and report on a newspaper or journal article; and research an approved topic for a three- to five-minute presentation (Davis, 1999).

Unplanned teaching strategies are generally used for practice and not formally evaluated, though students should receive some feedback on their efforts. Planned presentations should be evaluated with various assessments that have been explained to the students. Campbell, Mothersbaugh, Brammer, and Taylor (2001) suggest that instrument components should be adapted and values adjusted depending on the activity. These components include, but are not limited to, the following functions:

- Accomplish the objective

- Include an adequate outline

- Supply documentation

- Use appropriate delivery (extemporaneous, textual, memorized, or a combination)

- Incorporate effective presentation aids

- Exhibit good speaking techniques (grammar, word choice, tone, etc.)

- Encourage audience participation when appropriate

Optimist International and Toastmasters International offer instructional materials and encourage student involvement in spoken competitions. Educators may contact Optimist International at http://www.optimist.org or 4494 Lindell Boulevard, St. Louis, Missouri 63108; and Toastmasters International at http://www.toastmasters.org or P. O. Box 9052, Mission Viejo, CA 92690.

Signaling
Speakers convey messages with more than words; body language and other signaling also help to persuade and inform audiences (Long, 1998). Nonverbal communication occurs either intentionally or unintentionally and can be easily misinterpreted. Individuals often interpret signals involuntarily and without conscious thought. Students should become aware of signaling categories that vary within and among cultures:

- Body language includes posture, eye contact, facial expressions, grooming, and gestures. Body language exists in all actions and even in nonactions.

- Space incorporates person-to-person distances, work-related arrangements, and bodily contact.

- Time perceptions differ widely among countries and cultures.

Students need chances to practice and interpret appropriate signaling. Students may view and note examples of nonverbal communication in videotapes, movies, or television programs. Additionally, students might pantomime actions and ask others in the class to identify the intended message; they might role play situations in which nonverbal communication by the listener can either encourage or distract speakers; and they can research and prepare spoken and/or written reports on signaling differences among various cultures.

Evaluating appropriate signaling is best accomplished by judging it as one component of a larger spoken report.

Similarly, within a written report, document appearance can be considered as one component of signaling. Misuse of headings and inappropriate margins are examples of negative signaling in a business report.

Listening

One of the most needed and least practiced of all the communication skills is listening. According to Lehman and DuFrene (2002), "Listening commonly consumes more of business employees' time than reading, writing, and speaking combined" (p. 54). Students can apply these tips to improve listening proficiencies:

- Observe signals that may reinforce the words in a message.

- Practice active listening; concentrate on content and provide suitable feedback (verbal and/or nonverbal).

- Maintain an open mind; eliminate preconceived ideas about the speaker and focus on the message.

- Avoid the temptation to interrupt; ask questions at an opportune time.

- Record notes in outline format; avoid writing verbatim.

- Resist both environmental and mental distractions.

- Use *lag time* (the difference in speech speed and thought speed) to review what has been said or to anticipate what the speaker will say next.

Teaching strategies to develop and strengthen listening competencies include the following practices:

- Lead students in identifying factors that influence listening, using techniques such as group discussions, brainstorming sessions, role playing, and simulation.

- Give directions one time only. Call upon specific students to explain or repeat the directions if necessary.

- Play pre-recorded background noises such as phones ringing, doors slamming, and people talking. Give directions while the tape plays to illustrate environmental effects on listening. Students write information, repeat instructions or information, and/or follow directions. Conduct a discussion on the effects of noise on listening.

- Interview employees and prepare an inventory of listening situations in business.

- Keep a log of time spent listening over a given period and record the purposes for listening.

- Ask each student to complain about something that really bothers him or her. The next student then offers a statement of limited agreement, paraphrases the statement, identifies feelings that might lie behind the statement, or offers justification for the complaint.

Listening evaluation may be conducted by the teacher by having students recall information and respond in written or spoken form. Evaluation may also be self-directed, when students complete printed or electronic inventories. Locate electronic inventories through online searches using the keywords "listening self-evaluation." One valuable site is http://www.positive-way.com/listenin.htm.

Writing

Many hiring professionals believe the ability to write well can move employees up the corporate ladder (Karr, 2001; NBEA, 2001). Writing tends to be the most difficult form of communication, since writing lacks the advantage of spontaneous feedback or signaling as aids to understanding.

One of the most worthwhile teaching strategies is to have individuals or groups critique and revise sample documents (Gdovin, 2001). The documents should include both effective and ineffective messages. Additional strategies for the teaching of writing consist of the following practices:

- Incorporate revision beginning with the first writing assignment.

- Use proofreading exercises for evaluating students' abilities to detect errors in punctuation and word usage.

- Individualize instruction for students who lack command of English mechanics.

- Use current issues/topics in the news for writing assignments.

- Motivate students by giving timely feedback either online or in person.

To assist students as they develop writing skills, ask students to follow the tips given below:

- Write frequently with a positive attitude.

- Determine and record the purpose of the message.

- Outline key ideas and prepare a draft.

- Verify content correctness.

- Revise, revise, revise!

Table 1. The 3x4 Writing Plan

I. Plan a Message	II. Compose a Draft	III. Complete the Message
1. Identify the Objective	1. Choose Words	1. Proofread
2. Visualize the Audience	2. Construct Sentences	2. Edit
3. Gather Supporting Data	3. Assemble Paragraphs	3. Revise
4. Organize the Data	4. Sequence Paragraphs	4. Finalize

Note. From *Effective Communication for Colleges*, 9th edition, by Brantley, C., & Miller, M. © 2002. Reprinted with permission of South-Western Educational Publishing a division of Thomson Learning.

When students prepare entire documents or messages, one writing approach is the 3 x 4 plan, as shown in Table 1 (Brantley & Miller, 2002).

The 3 x 4 plan applies to all spoken and written documents including electronic messages.

Evaluating written documents tends to be subjective. The process is difficult for instructors to complete and even more difficult for students to accept. Therefore, instructors must establish with students the evaluation criteria for written documents. To address the subjective issue, instructors may develop an evaluative *rubric* (a grading plan that identifies what students should learn and the criteria for measuring the performance levels). A rubric given to students ahead of time becomes a guideline for a written assignment, a guide for peer review, and an aid for revision. Ultimately, the rubric becomes a tool for assigning grades (Sibert, Krejci, Schoenrock, & Sydow, 2001).

Reading

Information is exploding in print and online. The increased availability of reading material mandates efficient reading skills for anyone who handles information on a regular basis. According to Mindell (2001), the four types of reading are *scanning* (a quick sort), *skimming* (a quick sort with evaluation), *prereading* (a search for central structure—the thesis statement), and *deep reading* (a careful reading of every sentence and every idea). Like any other skill, reading can be developed and improved with practice. One improvement plan is the SQ3R approach:

- Survey

- Question

- Read and Underline

- Recite and Write

- Review

To implement the SQ3R approach, select a two- to three-page article in a recent periodical and guide the students through each step as they read. Students may select a longer business-related article and proceed through the SQ3R steps as a follow-up group activity. A detailed explanation for SQ3R is available at http://www.iss.stthomas .edu/studyguides/texred2.htm.

Additional strategies for the teaching of reading are as follows:

- Select a multiple chapter book (not a textbook). Group students determined by the number of chapters in the book. Within a group, each student reads and reports on one chapter in the book. This procedure requires less time than having each student read the entire book and promotes reading and oral communication skills.

- Collect typical written business documents (insurance forms, reports, manuals, etc.); students read the documents and answer instructor-prepared questions to detect major points.

- Develop vocabulary preview sheets, especially in courses with technical terms. Divide the sheet into three columns. Column 1 contains the correct spelling; Column 2 shows phonetic pronunciation; and Column 3 identifies definitions and sample usages. The teacher or the student may develop Column 3.

- Ask students to maintain reading logs for specified times. Students write summaries at assigned intervals.

The evaluation of reading skills is not in the realm of business teachers' usual responsibilities. Business-related reading, however, should result in student progress in content areas and prepare them for work-related reading tasks in the future. Because reading is an essential skill, business teachers who engage with the process of reading, training, and evaluation improve students' capabilities significantly.

Two providers of additional resource materials that complement essential communication skills (speaking, signaling, listening, writing, and reading) are International Paper Company and the Newspaper Association of America Foundation. Educators can write to the International Paper Company, 400 Atlantic Street, Stamford, CT 06921 and request a set of the *Power of the Printed Word* series. If the local newspaper does not sponsor a Newspaper in Education (NIE) program, educators may contact the Newspaper Association of America Foundation, 1921 Gallows Road, Suite 600, Vienna, VA 22182-3900.

COMMUNICATION FORM/MODE
Writers must analyze the communication situation before selecting the message form and determining the transmission mode.

Message Form
When choosing the message form to use in developing messages, writers should review these questions:

- Permanency—Is a permanent record needed?

- Message complexity—How difficult would the message be for the audience to understand?

- Type of feedback—Is an immediate response needed? Is a written or spoken response required? Will one answer be adequate or will the discussion be ongoing?

- Audience size and location—Is the message for one person only or for a widely dispersed audience?

Transmission Mode

When deciding how messages will be transmitted, writers should consider these variables:

- Intended receivers—Will the message go to varied audiences or specialized audiences?

- Privacy—Does the message contain confidential or highly sensitive information?

- Timeliness—Is immediate or delayed feedback required?

- Cost—Do time and privacy justify a faster but potentially more expensive delivery method?

Teaching strategies include developing scenarios that require students to determine the most appropriate message form and transmission mode. For example, an invitation to a reception for someone recently promoted to an upper level management position requires a printed message using the U.S. Postal Service. However, when a reporter needs to verify the spelling of names, the message form is spoken and the transmission mode is the telephone. Because students will become employees who will represent a business to the public, they need occasions to practice and develop their telephone techniques (*Teaching Students*, 1996). The following suggestions provide practice and discussion points:

- Answer the telephone promptly, preferably on the first ring.

- Develop a friendly and cheerful greeting; identify yourself.

- Create a positive image for the company and yourself through your voice: tone, volume, and articulation.

- Record and transmit information completely and accurately.

- Demonstrate interest in the other person; repeat names and include courteous words in the conversation such as "please," "thank you," and "you're welcome."

- Maintain professionalism; avoid personal phone calls at work.

Students can learn good telephone techniques when given correct instruction and chances to practice. According to Okula (1998), telephone skills can transfer to effective voice messaging, because the same skills apply to creating voice mail messages. Also, the techniques will ensure that cell phone calls are successfully sent and received (Everett, 2002).

While the telephone is the most widely used equipment to deliver spoken communication, technology also provides methods of transmitting the written word through such tools as fax machines and e-mail. For example, a manager soliciting volunteers to assist in a fund-raising event is an appropriate scenario for using e-mail. The message is transmitted quickly, efficiently, and inexpensively to a wide audience; and message recipients can respond easily.

Whenever e-mail is the transmission mode, the sender should observe electronic etiquette known as *netiquette*. The following netiquette guidelines are suggested:

- Use the same grammar and punctuation rules as though the message were being mailed. Using all capital letters is often interpreted as shouting. Using all lowercase letters is indicative of the "I'm-too-lazy-to-care syndrome."

- Consider e-mail a permanent record that can easily be forwarded to others; therefore, send only messages appropriate for family or future employers to read.

- Include a descriptive subject line; otherwise, the message may be considered "junk mail."

- Open the message with a suitable greeting, similar to the greeting used in face-to-face conversation.

- Compose concise messages related to the subject line. One advantage of e-mail is its brevity.

- Consider using a more formal tone when communicating with international receivers. Use humor sparingly, since humor is not universally understood.

- Include a signature line in case the message is separated from the header.

- Observe a "send later" choice if the message might create an emotional response.

- Proofread the message before clicking the "Send" button.

As e-mail is increasingly used, netiquette guidelines will continue to develop. Having and showing consideration for other people forms the basis for netiquette (and etiquette).

Teaching strategies focus on creating scenarios and case studies for students to use in determining the most efficient and effective message form and transmission mode. Students also can retrieve and discuss online publications related to emerging communication technologies, telephone techniques, and netiquette.

Evaluation techniques include using a checklist to assess student performance during role playing scenarios of incoming and outgoing telephone calls. E-mail messages written by students can be evaluated with a checklist that includes netiquette guidelines.

SOCIAL COMMUNICATION

Communication skills should be integrated throughout the curriculum. According to the *National Standards for Business Education* (2001), students should be given opportunities to apply basic social communication skills in personal and professional situations. Selected social skills include making ethical decisions, participating in group situations and meetings, and developing leadership abilities.

Ethics

Goree (1999) quotes Justice Potter Stewart, who defines ethics as "knowing the difference between what you have a right to do and what is right to do." Arnold, Schmidt, and Wells (1996) suggest that students at every educational level should study ethics and practice ethical decision making. Therefore, students need models for decision making.

Goree (2002) describes the ACT model from the Center for American and International Law for use in deciding ethical issues. The model consists of three steps:

- **A** – Alternatives. What choices are available for making this decision? List at least three options available for each situation.

- **C** – Consequences. What is expected to happen for each alternative? Label each alternative as having either positive or negative consequences.

- **T** – Telling. Answer the question, "How will I feel explaining this situation to my supervisor? My family? My friends? A police officer? A news reporter?"

Making ethical decisions may not be easy, but having a model to follow encourages students to consider many alternatives and effects. Therefore, teaching strategies include students locating and discussing additional models from print and electronic sources. Given case studies and scenarios, individual students or student groups can select and apply a model to the situation. Even though debate will ensue, ultimately individuals must decide whether an action is ethical or unethical.

Examples of ethical decision making in communication may involve technology usage; for example, forwarding an e-mail message without the consent of the originator is both unethical and illegal (Lewis & McGrew, 2000). Honoring confidentiality is another ethical issue, whether a message is received by e-mail, fax, telephone, or traditional letter format. Choosing precise and accurate details when constructing resumes also reflects ethical communication (Lampe & Schneider, 2000).

Ethical decision making is basically nonevaluative; however, teachers can observe and assess how well students apply the chosen model to given situations. Teachers may also document student participation in small or large group discussions.

Teaching resources are available from the Center for American and International Law, Suite 212, 1778 North Plano Road, Richardson, TX 75081

Group Dynamics
Communication tasks present multiple opportunities for cooperative learning (working in teams or groups), which is an essential workplace skill (Worley & Dyrud, 2001). Since many employers include teamwork skills among employment criteria, educators should use group activities to maximize individual learning, enhance collaborative learning, improve decision-making techniques, and develop group member roles. According to Bovee and Thill (2000), "The combined knowledge and skills of team members can lead to high performance and good decisions" (p. 46).

Educators may pre-assign students to teams based on assessments, such as personality profiles or career interest inventories. Teams may be randomly assigned by counting off every five students. Ideally, no more than seven students should be assigned to a group. To alleviate tied votes when decisions are made, form groups with an odd number of members. However the members are assigned, be sure that gender and ethnicities are reflected in the group.

Teaching strategies that work well with teams include the following activities:

- Brainstorming and making decisions on ethical issues

- Evaluating peer writing and speaking efforts

- Analyzing and revising written materials, such as changing negative statements to positive statements

- Collecting and reporting on current events

- Designing and preparing visuals for reports

Both team members and the instructor can participate in the evaluation process (Crews & North, 2000). Evaluations of both individual members and group efforts are best done by using prepared score sheets or checklists. Recommended checklists may be found in *Best Practices in Business Instruction* (Tucker, 2001).

Meetings
Throughout their lives students may be involved in meetings, both face-to-face and virtual; therefore, they need opportunities to plan and conduct meetings. All the

essential communication skills (listening, speaking, reading, signaling, and writing) are used in meeting processes. Fry (NBEA, 1997) states that successful meetings require three phases: planning, implementation, and follow-up.

The planning phase involves determining the purpose, identifying the participants, preparing the agenda, and determining the location. The planning phase is more complex for virtual meetings because participants might live in different time zones; speak different languages; receive advance materials in various formats, such as computer files or fax; access the meeting through different technologies; and possess varying levels of skill in handling technology.

In the implementation phase, a roll call is even more important in virtual meetings than in a face-to-face setting to ensure that all participants are online and that all equipment is operational. In all meetings, use *Robert's Rules of Order* (2000) to govern activities. Each member is encouraged to participate.

Visuals enhance face-to-face and virtual meetings. In creating visuals, especially PowerPoint slides, observe the following guidelines (Lehman, 2000):

- Use landscape rather than portrait orientation.

- Maintain 10 percent white space for borders.

- Select a light background with dark print. For digital projection, do the opposite.

- Observe the 6 x 6 rule—no more than six words per line and no more than six lines per slide.

- Choose at least 36-point type.

- Use lowercase and uppercase letters.

The final phase includes distributing the minutes in a timely manner and monitoring follow-up activities. After a meeting, encourage participants to share comments, questions, and ideas at a virtual site, through e-mail, or with telephone conversations. When the meeting includes a Web or slide presentation, notify participants how to access and review the saved presentation. A follow-up review may be necessary to clarify points; also, absentees can access the presentation.

Additional information on conducting virtual meetings is available online at the following URL: www.ddiworld.com/inthenews.

Leadership

According to Reynolds (1993), "The first people-skill essential to modern day leadership is communication ability" (p. 53). Participating in groups allows students to develop leadership skills as they perform various roles. Student organizations in business education enhance leadership development when members participate in activities, serve as officers, and enter competitive events. Teacher support of curriculum-based organizations assures student participation at the local, state, and national levels.

Teaching strategies hinge on providing practice materials and role-playing situations where students can hone their leadership skills. Practice materials include preparing and following agendas for mock meetings and completing sample competitive event tests. Role-playing situations involve students' assuming roles in mock meetings where parliamentary procedure is followed. Students also can visit civic organizations, such as Rotary, Kiwanis, Civitan, Business and Professional Women, and Lions, to observe adults in leadership roles.

Evaluation tools similar to those used in group assessment are valid in the leadership area. Both members and leaders should be evaluated by peers and by instructors.

EMPLOYMENT COMMUNICATION

Exciting, practical, and rewarding outcomes for learners and instructors occur after concluding a successful job search process. The process often culminates in employment offers for students and satisfaction for instructors. The search consists of several components: conducting self-assessment, identifying potential employers, developing a resume, composing application letters, completing application forms, participating in interviews, and composing various follow-up messages.

At the beginning of the study or job search, each student should obtain an expandable file to contain job search documents, information, and diskettes. In later years when students change jobs or careers, the saved materials can be updated. Additionally, job seekers will find the portfolio useful when samples of their work are kept in the folder and can be shared with interviewers.

Self-Assessment

Materials available from school libraries, from publishers, and on the Internet assist students in conducting self-assessments. These tools help students to recognize their own strengths. Students' abilities and career interests should match employers' needs. After assessing skills and abilities, students can determine potential employers in the geographic area of employment.

Potential Employers

Students identify potential employers from newspaper ads, library materials, people (friends, relatives, and teachers), placement offices or career centers, chambers of commerce, employment agencies, and the Internet. From a list of potential employers, students can then target firms that best meet their interests and abilities. Students should customize their resumes for each selected firm.

Resumes

Because students will lack experience in developing resumes, teachers should assist them in selecting formats, paper, font styles, and wording. Listing the strongest area first and maintaining absolute accuracy and honesty are points teachers should emphasize with the students. If students construct an initial high-quality resume, they can revise the content in later years when changing jobs and/or careers.

Since the Internet is used increasingly for individual job searches and for employer identification of employees, students will need to adapt their traditional resumes to scannable formats. Students may conduct a keyword search for scannable resumes and locate examples on the Internet. Sample resumes are also in printed sources, such as those shown by Smith (1999) and Barksdale & Rutter (2000). Mailing a hard copy of an electronically transmitted resume is recommended because data can be lost or distorted in cyberspace.

Application Letters

Because resumes are sent with an application (cover) letter, composing these letters is the next step in the job search process. Application letters emphasize three points: identifying the position applied for, mentioning strong points (avoid repeating exact information from the resume), and asking for an interview. The application letter should be addressed to a specific person within a firm.

Application Forms

Most employers require potential employees to complete an application form. Teachers should caution students to complete every blank space on the form either with information or N/A (not applicable). In addition to neatness and completeness, the information provided must be honest and accurate.

Interviews

Students should prepare not only for face-to-face interviews, but also for telephone interviews. Employers are increasingly using telephone interviews as a screening device. The following tips are helpful in any interview:

- Use the resume as a reference tool.

- Project enthusiasm, courtesy, and clarity through voice quality.

- Follow the interviewer's lead to pace the interview.

- Repeat unexpected questions to allow time to think of a response.

- Emphasize the match between individual qualities and a company's needs.

In a face-to-face interview, grooming and body language convey preparation and suitability for the position. Both in-class and out-of-class practice can build interview confidence and preparedness.

Follow-Up Messages

A thank-you letter should be written immediately after every interview. Other follow-up messages include an acceptance, a refusal, or an inquiry letter. A sample resignation letter should be included in the portfolio as an example to follow when career changes are made.

The primary teaching strategy is developing the employment portfolio that can be maintained throughout the students' careers. A portfolio may contain an up-to-date resume, samples of original work, relevant class projects, academic transcripts, recommendation letters, and commendation messages. Other strategies include the following items:

- Ask impromptu interview questions to various members of a class; e.g., "What is your greatest strength?" "Tell me about a problem you had and how you solved it." "What can you offer this company?" Impromptu questions provide opportunities for building spoken communication skills and interview confidence.

- Conduct mock interviews. This practice can be between the teacher and one student, between two students, or between a guest interviewer and student. Mock interviews can be taped and replayed for discussion and evaluation.

- Invite guest speakers from employment agencies or human resource departments. Speakers may discuss job search skills, including interview tips, illegal interview questions, personal appearance, and other relevant topics.

- Locate and discuss Web sites that are related to employment. Students may search with keywords such as "scannable resumes," "interview techniques," and "cover letters."

The portfolio provides the basis for evaluating the employment communication process. Students and teachers should cooperatively develop a rubric to use in assessing the portfolio.

SUMMARY

Communication is an essential tool that serves as a foundation for success in educational endeavors, career growth, and personal relationships. Essential communication skills (speaking, signaling, listening, writing, and reading) are the building blocks for developing and refining communication proficiency.

As technology further integrates with business, decisions must be made about selecting the most suitable message form and transmission mode. Factors to consider include cost, privacy, timeliness, permanency, message complexity, type of feedback, audience size, and receiver location. When a telephone call or an e-mail message is the chosen transmission mode, students need to be aware of acceptable protocol.

Since people do not live and work in isolation, they must use communication to function in society. As students study and discuss social communication issues, such as ethics, group dynamics, and leadership, they prepare for life beyond the school arena. Using ethical decision-making models in a classroom setting can provide the basis for making ethical decisions in later life. When given opportunities to investigate social communication issues as members of a group, students experience training in teamwork. Employers continue to expect effective teamwork from their employees. Group participation also may lead to students' developing leadership skills—another trait employers seek.

Building an employment portfolio is an ongoing project. A portfolio should be updated frequently and used throughout the work life of the student. All communication skills, especially employment communication, should be integrated and reinforced in every business course.

REFERENCES

Arnold, V., Schmidt, J., & Wells, R. (1996, Fall). Ethics instruction in the classrooms of business educators. *The Delta Pi Epsilon Journal, 38,* 185.

Barksdale, K., & Rutter, M. (2000). *Online resume and job search.* Cincinnati, OH: South-Western/Thomson Learning.

Bovee, C., & Thill, J. (2000). *Business communication today.* Upper Saddle River, NJ: Prentice Hall.

Brantley, C., & Miller, M. (2002). *Effective communication for colleges* (9th ed.). Cincinnati, OH: South-Western/Thomson Learning.

Campbell, K., Mothersbaugh, D., Brammer, C., & Taylor, T. (2001, December). Peer versus self-assessment of oral business presentation performance. *Business Communication Quarterly, 64,* 23-42.

Crews, T., & North, A. (2000, June). Team evaluation: Part 2. *Instructional strategies: An applied research series, 16,* 1-4.

Davis, B. (1999). Strategies for improving oral communication skills. *Business Education Forum, 54* (2), 34-36.

Dittmar, E. (2000). Integrating high-level communication competencies into business courses. *Business Education Forum, 54 (4)*, 33-34.

Everett, D. (2002). Technology and effective communication. In A. Remp (Ed.). *Technology, methodology, and business education* (Yearbook No. 40, pp. 236-237). Reston, VA: National Business Education Association.

Gdovin, S. (2001, November/December). Top ten tips for writing to learn in all disciplines. *Teaching and Learning News, 11*, 7.

Goree, K. (1999, May-June). Ethics: It's just good business. *The Balance Sheet.* Retrieved January 25, 2002, from http://www.balancesheet.swep.com

Goree, K. (2002, January-February). Ethics: It's just good business. *The Balance Sheet.* Retrieved January 24, 2002, from http://www.balancesheet.swep.com

Job market for the class of 2002. (2002). *Planning Job Choices: 2002*, 20-26. Bethlehem, PA: National Association of Colleges and Employers.

Karr, S. (2001, June). Learning business writing online. *Financial Executive, 17*, 64-65.

Lampe, M., & Schneider, G. (2000, Fall). Teaching ethics in the information systems curriculum: A pragmatic, values-based approach. *Journal of Business and Training Education, 9*, 117-133.

Lehman, C. (2000). *Creating dynamic multimedia presentations using Microsoft PowerPoint.* Cincinnati, OH: South-Western/Thomson Learning.

Lehman, C., & DuFrene, D. (2002). *Business communication* (13th ed.). Cincinnati, OH: South-Western/Thomson Learning.

Lewis, S., & McGrew, L. (2000). Teaching the perils of e-mail. *Business Education Forum, 54 (3)*, 26-27.

Long, T. (1998, April). *"Date with an angel": A non-verbal communication teaching tip.* Saratoga Springs, New York: Eastern Communication Association. (ERIC Document Reproduction Service No. ED425481).

Mindell, P. (2001, December). Power reading in the digital age. *Executive Update.* Retrieved January 2, 2002, from http://www.gwsae.org/executiveupdate/2001/December/

National Business Education Association. (1996). Teaching students the unwritten rules: Business etiquette. *Keying In, 6 (3)*, 1-7.

National Business Education Association. (1997). How to conduct a successful meeting. *Keying In, 7 (4)*.

National Business Education Association. (2001). *National standards for business education: What America's students should know and be able to do in business* (2nd ed.). Reston, VA: Author.

National Business Education Association. (2001). What business wants. *Keying In, 12 (2)*, 1-8.

Okula, S. (1998). New etiquette for evolving technologies: Using e-mail and voice mail effectively. *Business Education Forum, 53 (1)*, 6-9, 51.

Reynolds, F. (1993). What does business have to say about leadership? In M. Bush & H. Taylor (Eds.), *Developing leadership in business education* (Yearbook No. 31, p. 53). Reston, VA: National Business Education Association.

Robert, H. (2000). *Robert's Rules of Order, Newly Revised* (10th ed.). Cambridge, MA: Perseus Publishing.

Schepf, G. (2002). *Real world projects.* Retrieved January 26, 2002, from http://www.irvingisd.net/schepf/real_world_projects.htm

Sibert, B., Krejci, D., Schoenrock, R., & Sydow, S. (2001). Learning from Nebraska's assessment system. *Business Education Forum, 56 (2)*, 46-50.

Smith, R. (1999). *Electronic resumes & online networking.* Franklin Lakes, NJ: Career Press.

Swanson, J. (1987). Incorporating oral presentations in the business classroom. *Instructional Strategies: An Applied Research Series, 3*, 1-4.

Tucker, S. (2001). Collaborative teamwork in the classroom. In D. Briggs (Coordinator), *Best practices in business instruction* (pp. 18-24). Little Rock, AR: Delta Pi Epsilon.

Worley, R., & Dyrud, M. (2001, December). Managing student groups. *Business Communication Quarterly, 64 (4)*, 105.

Accounting and Business Computation

Carol Blaszczynski
California State University, Los Angeles
Los Angeles, California

Accounting and business computation are building blocks in the business education curriculum. Not only are these courses necessary to education *for* business, but also they are critical to education *about* business—one aim of which is to prepare students for their roles as discerning consumers, investors, and citizens. This chapter discusses accounting course contents and objectives, presents strategies for teaching and activities for learning accounting, outlines business computation course content and objectives, suggests strategies for teaching and activities for learning business computation, and identifies practical resources for teaching accounting and business computation.

ACCOUNTING COURSE CONTENT AND OBJECTIVES

This section discusses the levels at which accounting is taught, the objectives of instruction at each level, and the role of accounting skills in various jobs. Five achievement standards for accounting have been promoted by the National Business Education Association (NBEA) (2001). These standards address the accounting cycle, the accounting process, financial statements, special applications, and the interpretation and use of data. More specifically, accounting students should be able to (a) "complete and explain the purpose of the various steps in the accounting cycle (NBEA, 2001, p. 2); (b) "apply generally accepted accounting principles (GAAP) to determine the value of assets, liabilities, and owner's equity" (NBEA, 2001, p. 3); (c) use both manual and computerized accounting systems for financial statement preparation, interpretation, and analysis for manufacturing, merchandising, and service businesses; (d) apply correct accounting principles to income taxation, payroll, various ownership forms, and managerial systems; and (e) use principles of planning and control to assess organizational performance and use present-value concepts and differential analysis for decision making.

Levels at Which Accounting Is Taught

Accounting is taught at the secondary, postsecondary/community college, and university levels. At the secondary level, courses are offered in recordkeeping, book-keeping, and accounting. *Recordkeeping* is a course designed to give students entry-level skills in routine recording activities, such as keeping records for budget, credit, cash receipts, banking, petty cash, retail sales, accounts payable and receivable, and payroll. The next level, *bookkeeping*, covers the recording, classifying, and summarizing of accounting tasks (Schrag & Poland, 1987). This course emphasizes the "how" of recording data. *Accounting* goes beyond addressing the recording, classifying, and summarizing of financial-related information to incorporate accounting information analysis and interpretation. Due to decreasing accounting student enrollments at the secondary level, Accounting I and II are often taught simultaneously in the same classroom. Computerized accounting or automated accounting may be integrated in the accounting course or taught as a separate semester course. Articulation with area two-year colleges is encouraged through advanced standing or articulation agreements.

Most two-year colleges offer courses in financial accounting and more specialized courses such as taxation, payroll accounting, and cost accounting. Students may elect to complete a certificate program or an associate's degree.

The university level offers courses, certificates, and majors or minors in accounting. Students may specialize in financial accounting, managerial or cost accounting, governmental accounting, taxation, auditing, or accounting information systems.

Objectives of Instruction at Each Level

At the secondary level, accounting instructional objectives include introduction of the accounting cycle and the preparation of financial statements such as the balance sheet, income statement, and statement of retained earnings. Bittner (2002) suggests an updated secondary level accounting curriculum consisting of four courses. The first course would teach financial accounting, including reports analysis, financial state-ments, and the accounts themselves, covering the accounting cycle for a sole propri-etorship. The second course would focus upon accounting for corporations. The third accounting course would be devoted to line items in individual financial statements and the issues surrounding those particular line items. The fourth course, which would be optional, would serve as an introduction to computerized accounting.

At the community college level, instruction is geared toward preparing students for additional study in business and for advanced courses in accounting. In addition, entrepreneurs and other business people are part of the target audience for accounting courses. Supervisors, managers, and entrepreneurs study accounting to facilitate the reading of cost reports and financial statements to determine if they are meeting their budgets or how their businesses are performing.

At the university level most business majors complete introductory courses in financial and managerial accounting. Nonaccounting business majors study accounting to gain the background necessary to make financial business decisions and to act as entrepreneurs.

Accounting majors then complete a sequence of various courses, depending upon each student's specialization.

Role of Accounting Skills in Various Jobs
Students who enroll in accounting in high school may work part-time as participants in a business cooperative education program. Upon graduation from high school, students may qualify for entry-level accounting clerk positions in local business and other organizations. Students with an associate's degree in accounting may seek positions as entry-level or higher-level accounting clerks in many organizations. Walendowski (2000) identified a community college-level accounting assistant program as a stopgap for accounting positions midway between that of bookkeeper and management accountant. Students with a bachelor's degree in accounting may work for industry, for the government, or for nonprofit organizations. In addition, they may sit for the Certified Public Accountant (CPA) or the Certified Management Accountant (CMA) examinations. Specializations are available such as the Certified Fraud Examiner (CFE), Certified Internal Auditor (CIA), and Certified Financial Manager (CFM) designations. In addition, students may pursue certification in database reporting software such as Oracle.

STRATEGIES FOR TEACHING AND ACTIVITIES FOR LEARNING ACCOUNTING
Many strategies may be used to teach accounting. Cunningham (1999) recommends using a variety of active learning experiences in accounting instruction. Among these strategies are incorporating the user approach versus the preparer approach, writing to learn accounting, speaking about accounting, collaborating/working in groups or teams, participating in professional student organizations, and service learning. Recommended learning activities are integrated among the corresponding instructional strategy sections.

Incorporating the User Approach Versus the Preparer Approach
Traditionally, accounting instruction followed the *preparer approach*, which emphasized the (a) teaching of debits and credits and (b) preparing of financial statements. Within the past decade, the *user approach* to accounting instruction has become popular. For example, some leading accounting researchers (Pincus, 1997) believe that for postsecondary nonaccounting majors the emphasis on debits and credits, as well as on the preparation of financial statements, is ill-advised; such instruction is thought to

take away from the instructional time required to cultivate understanding needed by managers and other users (nonpreparers) of accounting information. Albrecht and Sack (2000) suggested that introductory accounting focus more on analysis than on financial statement preparation.

Few studies have been conducted about the user approach and its effect on student performance in intermediate-level accounting courses. Bernardi and Bean (1999) found that prior instruction in the user approach, while not giving students a disadvantage in the pivotal intermediate-level courses, did not appear to hinder course performance as evidenced by the course grade earned by students. Vangermeersch (1997) asserted that emphasis on debits and credits is imperative. Of course, the instructional approach adopted by institutions dictates course content and topic sequencing and may raise articulation issues as students continue their accounting education.

Teaching the Accounting Cycle
Learners should understand the accounting cycle before technology is introduced. If students fail to understand the fundamentals of the accounting cycle, the introduction of the technology may serve to confound the lack of mastery. Boyd, Boyd, and Boyd (2000) recommended using a visual approach to introducing the steps of the accounting cycle. Providing a handout for students, even if it is as simple as a flowchart, allows students to refer to the steps when completing homework and project assignments.

One community college instructor avoids introducing the term *debits* and *credits* at the beginning of the first course in accounting, preferring to use *left* and *right* instead (S. Aoto, personal communication, February 6, 2002). Her experience has shown that using the technical terms tends to confuse students until they become familiar with what is happening with the various accounts. When students have gained understanding of accounts, the terms debit and credit are introduced and quickly become meaningful.

As an example, one way to reinforce accounting cycle concepts is to ask students to trace all the accounts that are affected by the purchase of a $3,600 computer for cash. From the initial invoice document through the closing entries, students can analyze the impact one purchase can have on the bottom line, as shown in Table 1.

Using Computers in Teaching/Learning Accounting
Information systems and accounting are irrevocably intertwined, because accounting is an information system used by organizations and individuals. At all three levels—secondary, two-year/community college, and university—students may go to the computer lab to complete assignments, because gaining access to electronic classrooms may be difficult.

Table 1. Transaction Summary for Month Ended December 31						
	Balance Sheet Accounts			Income Statement Accounts		
Account	Cash	+Other Assets	=Liabilities	+Equity	+Revenues	-Expenses
Cash	-3,000					
Computer Equipment		3,000				
Accumulated Depreciation		-100				
Depreciation Expense						-100

Accounting students must demonstrate facility with software for spreadsheets, word processing, database technology, and references for the computerized Certified Public Accountant Examination slated to debut in 2004. Software facility will be necessary for the simulation section of the exam, which is weighted at 20% (Accounting Institute Seminars, 2002).

Software selection is vital in the accounting classroom. An instructor may select a fairly simple package for beginning accounting classes such as Peachtree or QuickBooks. At a more sophisticated level Microsoft Great Plains Dynamics, MAS 90, Oracle, or SAP may be employed, particularly if enterprise resource-planning packages are part of the curriculum. Enterprise resource planning is "an information system model that enables an organization to automate and integrate its key business processes" (Hall, 2001, p. 35). Leaders in the ERP system market include Baan, J. D. Edwards & Co., PeopleSoft Inc., Oracle, and SAP (Hall, 2001). In the auditing area, auditing software packages such as Audit Command Language (ACL) and Interactive Data Extraction & Analysis (IDEA) can be used when covering computer-aided auditing techniques (CATT).

Microsoft Excel provides a sound launching pad for presenting financial statement and transaction analysis. Many textbooks and workbooks contain exercises and problems that use Excel or other computer applications. Instructors should, of course, demonstrate the use of any software package included with the textbook or other course materials. Devoting class time to the demonstration of software shows students the usefulness and the ease with which software can be employed.

The AICPA published a list of the top ten technologies affecting the accounting profession (American Institute of Certified Public Accountants, 2002). Listed in order of importance, these technologies include (1) security technologies, (2) XML (Extensible Markup Language), (3) communication technologies (bandwidth, in particular), (4) mobile technologies, (5) wireless technologies (including wireless networks), (6) electronic authentication, (7) encryption, (8) electronic authorization, (9) remote connectivity tools, and (10) database technologies.

Demonstrations of various technologies can be helpful as a supplement to textbook knowledge. A number of ready-made technology demonstrations that are appropriate for accounting classes are available on the Internet. For example, to reinforce Web-based and Web-enabled applications, an instructor can demonstrate how messages are transmitted over the Internet through VisualRoute, a visual routing package, at http://www.visualware.com/visualroute/index.html. A world map display and efficiency information that can stimulate class discussions are included. Lucent Technologies' Bell-Labs provides a text-to-speech synthesis demonstration that can be shown to students at http://www.bell-labs.com/lucent.com/search/text-to-speech/.

XBRL (eXtensible Business Reporting Language) is believed to be the new standard for financial reporting (Zarowin & Harding, 2000). The American Institute of Certified Public Accountants (AICPA) Web site hosts the official XBRL Web site at www.xbrl.org. At the university level both XBRL, SAP, and Oracle courses are offered to provide students with cutting-edge accounting technology skills.

Students can analyze the information in annual reports to improve their analytical abilities, as well as to promote the use of real data. Annual report data can be obtained online at the Web site of the Public Register's Online Annual Report Service, www.annualreportservice.com, or at an individual organization's Web site. Annual reports from Australian and European organizations can be found at www.carol.co.uk/. Students can evaluate the effectiveness and accuracy of the visual aids that appear in an annual report. Groups of students can make oral presentations with visual examples, perhaps prepared in PowerPoint, to illustrate the effectiveness or ineffectiveness of the data displays. Annual reports can be used for other assignments as well (Pasewark, 1997).

Accounting Ethics/Writing to Learn Accounting

Events such as the Enron scandal have heightened interest in ethics among accounting professionals. Students can research the various codes of ethics of professional accounting organizations such as the American Institute for Certified Public Accountants (AICPA) at www.aicpa.org, the Institute of Management Accountants (IMA) at www.imanet.org, and the Association of Certified Fraud Examiners at www.cfenet.com/home.asp. Students can be presented with scenarios that include ethical considerations and engage in debates about the various actions and their consequences. A model for ethical decision making may serve as the framework for discussion (Goree, 2002).

Ethical issues can be explored by using case studies. The Delta Pi Epsilon publication *Case Studies for Effective Business Instruction* (1999) includes cases about accounting and ethics that can be used at any instructional level—secondary, two-year college, and university levels. Additional ethics case studies are available from the Illinois CPA Society at www.icpas.org/icpas/consumer/ethics-casestudies.asp. If an instructor is using WebCT or Blackboard, students may engage in a threaded discussion about accounting ethics. A professional ethics research project is described at the *Balance Sheet* Web site, www.swep.com/swepstuff/balancesheet/archives/1101/1101-ethics.html. Case studies can be used as a vehicle to improve the writing skills of students, as well as to pinpoint ethical issues and behavior.

Writing across the curriculum has been in place for many years in educational institutions. *Writing to learn accounting* can be helpful to both students and instructors (Riordan, Riordan, & Sullivan, 2000). A common type of assignment asks students to write a letter to a friend describing a certain concept. For example, a writing to learn accounting activity that could be employed in the classroom would use the following situation:

> A friend does not understand the concept of "cooking the books." Write a letter explaining the expression, using examples from recent events that have had an important impact on organizations such as Enron and Adelphia. Background information can be gathered online from various Web sites such as the AICPA, the *Wall Street Journal Online*, and other business sites.

Speaking About Accounting

Many employers of accounting students comment upon the need for students to develop speaking and presentation skills. Such skills should be developed in every accounting class, not solely in a business communication course. In addition, accounting students at all levels can participate in department-sponsored Toastmaster's International clubs. If no such organization is available on campus, students may elect to join a Toastmaster's club in the community. Information about Toastmaster's clubs is found at www.toastmasters.org/find/default.asp.

Collaborating/Working in Groups

The ability to collaborate with others is increasingly required in the workplace. As an alternative to listening to a lecture, groups of students may cooperate to solve problems. If the instructor elects to require students to work in teams, a module on team dynamics should be presented prior to beginning the effort. McConnell and Sasse (1999) provide an anticipatory case for managing teams and team projects. One method that may be employed is to ask students to first try to solve problems individually. Students then can work in groups to reinforce individualized learning. Group work provides each student with an opportunity to discuss the problem and to use the appropriate vocabulary without the anxiety produced by situations that require speaking before the entire class. Students can learn from one another—not just the correct answer, but the steps that were taken to solve the problem as well as the thinking or analysis that occurred.

The following problem is an example for students to analyze:

> A book was purchased for $15. A week later the book was sold to a friend for $25. Selling the book was a mistake, and the book was purchased back from a friend for $35. Another friend wanted the book to complete a collection and purchased it for $45. What was the amount of profit or loss from trading the book?

Students can be asked to solve the problem either individually; or within a group. Students should be able to explain the logic they used to solve the problem, and each group can be called upon to discuss the solution and the procedures used to arrive at the solution.

Participating in Professional Student Organizations

Beta Alpha Psi (www.bap.org), established in 1919, is the national honors fraternity for accounting and business information professionals. Collegiate-level chapters prepare students for the realities of professional accounting work and provide networking opportunities with accounting practitioners. Active student participation in Beta Alpha Psi promotes the development of leadership and communication skills. At the secondary level, Future Business Leaders of America (FBLA) offers competitive events in accounting (see Chapter 19). The student organizations FBLA and Phi Beta Lambda (PBL) both hold competitive events in accounting. FBLA has events for Accounting I and Accounting II, while PBL holds events in Accounting Principles and Accounting for Professionals (http://www.fbla-pbl.org/).

Service Learning

Service learning (volunteerism) projects may be used as an adjunct to classroom learning (Cruz, 2001). For example, an instructor may offer students the option to volunteer a minimum number of hours in the community at nonprofit organizations performing accounting-related work. Those students unable to participate in the service learning experience may complete a case project or another project as an alternative. One activity that has been used at the university level is the Volunteer Income Tax Assistance or VITA—a program accounting majors may elect to complete. After the completion of 14 hours of income tax training, trainees receive a certificate from the IRS and are eligible to prepare income tax returns for eligible community members (typically the elderly and low-income individuals) under the supervision of a faculty sponsor or an IRS agent. Student participation in the VITA program develops interpersonal communication skills necessary for working with clients (Basile, 1998; Gabriel, 2000; Mayberry, 1995; Quinn, Garrer, Marshall, & Smith, 1995).

BUSINESS COMPUTATION COURSE CONTENT AND OBJECTIVES

This section addresses the levels at which the business computation course is taught, the objectives of instruction at each level, the role of business computation in various occupations, and the trend toward online course delivery.

Levels at Which Business Computation Is Taught

Some high schools offer courses in business mathematics or business computation. The most frequent level at which business computation is taught, however, is at the two-year college level. Typically, the course title is business mathematics or mathematics for business, and the course may be a prerequisite to the study of accounting and finance. Business computation courses may be housed in either a business or mathematics departments.

Objectives of Instruction at Each Level

Instruction in business computation is designed to go beyond merely performing accurate calculations. In addition, students should be equipped to make good decisions, solve mathematics-based problems, and perform data analysis and interpretation (National Business Education Association, 2001). Six computation standards have been specified by NBEA (2001). These standards address (a) mathematical foundations—solving problems by applying foundational mathematics operations; (b) number relationships and operations—solving problems that involve decimals, whole numbers, fractions, percents, averages, ratios, and proportions; (c) patterns, functions and algebra—solving problems via algebraic operations; (d) measurements—solving problems using common international measurement standards such as the metric system and foreign currency conversions; (e) statistics and probability—using common statistical tools for analyzing and interpreting data, and (f) problem-solving applications—employing mathematical procedures in the analysis and solution of business problems. Business computation mastery is fundamental for many occupations. As Sells (1974, 1992) asserted, mathematics is the critical filter that prepares students for gainful employment. Students who are unable to master mathematics may be unable to obtain well-paying positions.

Trend Toward Online Course Delivery

Increasingly, postsecondary courses in business mathematics are offered online. Much of the subject matter may be considered appropriate for drill and practice and tutorial presentations; as a result, online delivery may be a natural fit. On the other hand, students need to be highly motivated to complete online courses successfully. Many students benefit from having an instructor who can point out errors in logic and computation as soon as they occur and provide the positive reinforcement necessary for the student to persist. Meeting with a live instructor perhaps two to three times a week not only adds structure, but also provides distributed practice necessary for building business computation skill.

STRATEGIES FOR TEACHING AND ACTIVITIES FOR LEARNING BUSINESS COMPUTATION

Various strategies may be employed in the teaching of business computation. The strategies presented in this section include recognizing mathematics anxiety/avoidance behaviors, overcoming computation illiteracy, integrating business computation into other courses, estimating answers and cultivating number sense, teaching 10-key calculator or graphing calculator skills, incorporating international aspects of business computation, using metric conversion calculators, using foreign currency conversion calculators, teaching discounts and percentage rates, writing to learn business computation, using computers in teaching/learning business computation, and collaborating/ working in groups. Recommended learning activities are integrated among the corresponding instructional strategy sections.

Recognizing Mathematics Anxiety/Avoidance Behaviors

The incidence of mathematics anxiety and mathematics avoidance behaviors has been well publicized in the media (Drew, 1996; Tobias, 1993). *Mathematics anxiety* describes the feelings that ensue when people uncomfortable with mathematics encounter math classes and problems. *Mathematics avoidance*, on the other hand, is considered to be a behavior (Tobias, 1993) and is demonstrated by students postponing a required math course again and again, or habitually registering for a math course and dropping it in the early part of the term.

Overcoming Computation Illiteracy

Computation illiteracy is a complex phenomenon that may be caused by many factors. Sometimes known as *innumeracy*, computation illiteracy may be surmounted by the following instructional practices: communicating about mathematics through reading, writing, listening, and speaking about mathematics; valuing the study of mathematics; setting expectation of high achievement rather than accepting the false notion that it is difficult to excel in mathematics; serving as a model for students when approaching mathematics problems; and acknowledging and reducing the incidence of negative mathematics behaviors such as math anxiety and avoidance (Blaszczynski, 2001).

Integrating Business Computation into Other Courses

The integration of business computation into other courses is critical for subject matter mastery. Most people do not solve problems just for intellectual stimulation. Because most problems are generated from practical or business applications, problem solving should be emphasized in such areas using real world scenarios (Bittner, 2000). Business computation skills may be applied in accounting, economics, information systems, marketing, operations management, and consumer education courses. Such applications reinforce the business computation skill set and lend credibility to the study of business computation.

Estimating Answers and Cultivating Number Sense

The National Business Education Association Standards delineate the importance of estimating answers (NBEA, 2001). Asking students to estimate answers before solving a problem aids in error detection and promotes the development of number sense (Blaszczynski, 1992).

Teaching Graphing Calculator Skills

In addition to developing number sense and estimating answers, students may need to use computational aids, such as calculators and 10-key devices to verify the accuracy of calculations. Instructors should not assume that students know how to use a calculator or 10-key. In fact, before instruction begins, an instructor should review how to use such devices to ensure that students are not making errors due to incorrect input of data and to lower the frustration levels of students who may be experiencing mathematics anxiety compounded by computer anxiety.

Incorporating International Aspects of Business Computation

International aspects of accounting and business computation should not be ignored. The influence of culture on accounting is particularly germane for students (Scott, 1990, 1996). Blaszczynski and James (2001) studied the mastery of international business mathematics expressions by students and found that students were not adept at understanding and using such expressions for the writing of dates, times, and numbers. Classroom examples, homework problems, and test items should include international mathematics expressions to increase student facility and knowledge of global aspects of business mathematics and accounting.

Using Metric Conversion Calculators

As stated in the *National Standards for Business Education* (NBEA, 2001), business computation involves measurements. The standard promotes the use of common international measurement standards when solving business computation problems.

Metric conversion calculators are available on the World Wide Web (Christmann, 2000). Some of the metric conversion Web sites provide students with a visual frame of reference for a particular measurement (U. S. Metric Association, 2001). Online conversion calculators are available on various Internet sites; for example, www.sciencemadesimple.com/conversions.html. Furthermore, hands-on activities that allow students to work with the measurements in a realistic fashion can assist them in mastery of metric measurements. Instructors can bring to class items that include both United States and metric measurement units, such as measuring cups, rulers, and tape measures so that students can work with both metric and the U.S. measurement systems and visualize how the measurements compare.

Using Foreign Currency Conversion Calculators

Foreign currency converters are available on the Internet at sites such as www.oanda.com and www.x-rates.com/calculator.html. Currency converters allow students to access the current exchange rate and perform the mechanics of the calculations quickly and accurately when the correct amount is entered.

Students can research a dream vacation to another country and estimate the expenses for the entire trip, including airfare, lodging, and per diem expenses. Students can convert the total cost of the vacation into the currency of the country they plan to visit using online currency conversion calculators. In addition, they can calculate the metric equivalent of the number of miles they will travel using the metric equivalents by using an online metric conversion calculator at www.webflyer.com/travel/milemarker/. Airport codes are available at many Web sites, such as www.orbitz.com. Average daily temperature can be calculated using the online tools. Students can present their findings in a short memo or short presentation to the class.

Teaching Discounts and Percentage Rates
One common weakness among students involves discounts and percentage rates. Percentage rates are also a major area of weakness for the general public. Reviewing fractions before beginning this instructional module increases student understanding. Furthermore, using examples to which students can relate helps students to grasp the mathematics more readily.

As an example, one instructional activity for discounted purchases involves the following scenario:

Today's newspaper featured a sale of the student's favorite brand of jeans. The regular price of the jeans is $39; however, the advertised sales price is one-third off the original price. (a) Calculate the price of the jeans. The jeans purchase was postponed. A week later the jeans are on sale for an additional 25% reduction from the original price. (b) Calculate the reduced purchase price of the jeans. (c) What percentage was the original purchase price discounted?

Writing to Learn Business Computation
Writing activities may be assigned to students to promote the learning of business computation. As is true for accounting, students need to learn the language of business computation. Many times the inability to use the terminology or vocabulary correctly is a stumbling block for student learning. A sample story that could be used to explain the distinction between proper and improper fractions is shown in Table 2.

Using Computers in Teaching/Learning Business Computation
Once the mechanics of business computation have been mastered, the instructor can use Microsoft Excel as a platform to demonstrate how to solve various problems. The concept of order of operations is necessary for effective spreadsheet use and should be reviewed before students use spreadsheets. Online math tutorials such as *Algebra Solutions*, located at www.gomath.com/algebra.html, are useful for student review of basic mathematical operations and provide prompt knowledge of results.

> ## Table 2. Example of Using Writing to Learn Business Computation, "Fractionally Speaking."
>
> "Hi! What is your name?"
>
> "I'm 5/3; I'm an improper fraction. What is your name?"
>
> "I'm 4/5. I am a proper fraction."
>
> Another fraction joined these two fractions. "I don't know you. My name is 3/3"
>
> "Huh," said 4/5. "You're improper, too!"
>
> "As my name suggests, 3/3 equals one, since I have a numerator and a denominator that are equal to one another."
>
> "That may be true," uttered 5/3, "but I am larger than you are—I'm bigger than one."
>
> "As a matter of fact," said 3/3, "improper is just a term for us. It is not necessarily bad. It simply means that we can be written another way. We have two names."
>
> "What are you talking about? I don't understand you," said 4/5.
>
> "Some improper fractions can be written as mixed numbers. We can be written as a whole number and a fraction. For example, 5/3 can be written as 1 2/3. That is, one whole and 2/3 besides! Other improper fractions are equal to one, such as 3/3, because their numerators and denominators are equal."
>
> "I see," said the proper fraction. "You have two ways you can be written to communicate better with people. Depending upon the situation, one way may be easier than the other."

This particular tutorial contains mini-lessons about decimal number operations, unit conversions, rules for fractions, decimal, fractions, and percentage, and percentage word problems that may be helpful to business computations students needing a refresher.

Collaborating/Working in Groups

Collaborating and teaming are instructional strategies that may be used to enhance business computation skills as well as accounting knowledge. In addition to providing interaction among students, a benefit to the instructor is the reduction in the number of papers to grade.

Participating in Professional Student Organizations

FBLA holds a competitive event in business computations for secondary students. PBL members are eligible to compete in the area of quantitative methods (see Chapter 19).

PRACTICAL RESOURCES FOR TEACHING ACCOUNTING AND BUSINESS COMPUTATION

Resources for teaching accounting and business computation, such as simulations and practice sets, Web sites, software programs, free and inexpensive resources, and games are presented in this section.

Simulations and Practice Sets

Students can experience the elements of the accounting cycle by completing manual or computerized simulations and practice sets. A *practice set* is a business simulation that allows students to complete the steps of the accounting cycle just as an employee would. Practice sets/simulations provide students with an opportunity to integrate classroom knowledge with current business practices (Swanson, Ross, & Hanson, 1984). Bittner (2000) provides suggestions for creating a practice set from problems that appear early in the textbook. One advantage of such an approach is that it prepares students for the traditional culminating practice set activity.

Most accounting textbooks include CDs that contain problems or practice sets. An effective teaching strategy involves requiring students to complete the problems in a group and administer an audit test (also in a group) to assess learning. The role of the instructor is to act as an information resource while students work on simulations and practice sets.

Web Sites

Table 3 contains a list of major Web sites that can be used in accounting and business computation instruction.

Instructors may obtain information about the accounting profession and examples of teaching strategies from the Web sites of many organizations. Students can access organizational sites, not only for current information, but also when researching careers.

Free and Inexpensive Resources

Many teaching materials are available on the Internet in a downloadable format. For example, accounting instructors can use free accounting worksheets from www.bboinc.com/ (Do a site search for free samples/accounting worksheets.), as well as a unit on understanding taxes that was prepared by the Internal Revenue Service. Taxation materials can be found at www.irs.ustreas.gov. In addition, a teaching resources manual includes a video from the Understanding Taxes program. Free mathematics worksheets are available at www.sssoftware.com/freeworksheets. The *Money for Life* program written by the U. S. Treasury Department reinforces mathematics concepts. A 91-page booklet can be downloaded from www.savingsbonds.gov/sav/savlearn.htm. Other materials that reinforce business mathematics concepts focus upon personal financial literacy and are accessible from www.jumpstartcoalition.org.

Table 3. Web Sites for Teaching Accounting and Business Computation

Site	Location
Accounting Education Using Computers & Multimedia (AECM) listserv	pacioli.Loyola.edu/aecm/
Accounting Information Systems Educator Association	www.ais-educ.com
Accounting Monopoly	www.geocities.com/CollegePark/Quad/ 5687/monopoly.html
Accounting Syllabi	www.apsu.edu/clarkr
American Accounting Association	www.accounting.rutgers.edu/raw/aaa
American Institute of Certified Public Accountants	www.aicpa.org
American Society of Women Accountants	www.aswa.org
Business Computation Teaching Materials	www.nbea.org/curfbes.html (Click on the Materials computations link, then click on Teaching URLs)
Century 21 Accounting Internet Activities Home Page	accounting.swpco.com/
Education Alliance Network (EAN) for Faculty Using Great Plains	www.greatplains.com/partners/ean
Financial Accounting Standards Board (FASB)	www.fasb.org
Gazillionaire Game	www.gazillionaire.com/edu.html
Glencoe Teacher Site: Games for the Classroom	www.glencoe.com/sec/accounting/ teacher/games/index.htm
Government Accounting Standards Board (GASB)	www.gasb.org
Great Ideas for Teaching Accounting	www.swcollege.com/ (Do a site search for teaching accounting)
Income Tax Database	www.quicken.com/taxes/
Income Tax Information	www.1040.com
IRS Digital Daily	www.irs.ustreas.gov/prod.voer.html

Site	Location
International Accounting Standards Committee	www.iasc.org.uk/cmt/0001.asp
Online Resource for Accounting	www.accountingnet.com
Securities and Exchange Commission	www.sec.gov
Tax Forms	www.irs.ustreas.gov/forms_pubs/index.html
Tax-related Sites	www.taxsites.com
Teaching Business Education Newsletter	www.teachbused.com
Virtual Stock Exchange	www.virtualstockexchange.com
Yahoo Finance	finance.yahoo.com

Games

Well-planned and implemented games motivate students to learn. The sampling of games that follows can get students interested in accounting and computational concepts:

(1) *Deck of cards* (illustrates the probability concept) A deck of cards may be used to teach statistical concepts (Knapp, 1996). For example, probability concepts can be illustrated by asking the following questions:

- What is the probability of drawing a red card? The answer is .50, because a deck of 52 cards includes 26 red cards.

- What is the probability of drawing a 10? The answer is 4/52 or .077.

- What is the probability of drawing a face card? The answer is 12/52 or .231.

Various games can be used in the classroom to reinforce the learning of both accounting and business computation skills. For example, students can play the game "Jeopardy Pursuit" to reinforce concepts in accounting, such as account classifications, debits and credits, and financial statement analyses. This game can be used to review terminology for both business computation and accounting. The instructor should discuss the rules of the game with students before play begins (Blaszczynski, 1999).

(2) *Jeopardy Pursuit* (illustrates computational skills) Select the number of team members based upon class size. If only four teams are formed, each team can meet in a separate corner of the classroom to build team cohesiveness. Students respond to questions without referring to notes or books. The teacher should encourage team

members to collaborate by discussing possible responses before announcing the answer. Answers must begin with "What is" to remain true to the rules of classic Jeopardy. Team No. 1 begins the game by selecting the first category. If it does not respond with the correct answer within 30 seconds, Team No. 2 has 15 seconds to give a response. If Team No. 2 is unable to respond with the correct answer, play advances to Team No. 3. Team No. 3 must respond within 10 seconds. If Team No. 3's response is incorrect, play advances to Team No. 4; its response must be made within 5 seconds.

If Team No. 1 supplies the correct answer, it receives the category points and maintains control of the category selection. If another team answers the question, that team receives the category points. However, play advances to Team No. 2. In this manner, the game is truly a pursuit.

Instructors can modify the game by asking for more details. A verbal prompt such as "Can you provide an example?" may be used to take advantage of the teachable moment. Daily double questions and the inclusion of a "Final Jeopardy" round of play are optional. The winning team may be awarded a small prize such as bonus points or candy bars. Game materials may include transparencies, a PowerPoint presentation, or simply writing on the board.

(3) *M & M's* (illustrates statistical concepts) Statistical concepts may be learned by providing each student with a small bag of M&Ms. Assign students to groups of four or five. Each student records the number of each color of M&Ms found in the bag on a form that is provided to the group. A sample form that may be used for this activity is shown in Table 4. After each student has entered the data for the bag of M&Ms on the group form, ask the group members to calculate the measures of central tendency—the mean, median, and the mode—for the group data. Each group should prepare a frequency distribution for the group and a table and graph of the group's distribution of candy colors. If computers are available, students can prepare the visuals using computer software. Students should communicate the group frequency distribution to the instructor, who combines the information and provides the merged data to the class. Students can prepare a short memo report with an embedded table or graph about the distribution of candy colors for their groups.

(4) *Class Polls* (measures of central tendency—mean, median, and mode) Before major sporting events, the teacher can conduct a class poll to determine what the class members believe will be the outcome. This activity may also be used for major awards shows such as the Academy Awards. The class can calculate the measures of central tendency from the data.

SUMMARY

Accounting and business computation are pivotal components of the business curriculum that provide a foundation for the study of business. This chapter presents a discussion of the levels at which accounting and business computation are taught,

Table 4. M&M Activity Form							
M&M Color	**Name**	**Name**	**Name**	**Name**	**Mean**	**Mode**	**Median**
Red							
Orange							
Yellow							
Brown							
Blue							
Green							
Total							

course content, and course objectives. Incorporating active strategies for teaching and learning accounting and business computation such as writing to learn/ethics, speaking, collaborating/working in groups or teams, participating in professional student organizations, service learning, and using computers, enhances student mastery of course content. A number of practical resources for teaching accounting and business computation are identified, including simulations and practice sets, Web sites, software programs, free and inexpensive resources, and games. The judicious use of these instructional strategies and resources helps to create a learning environment that promotes active and deep learning.

REFERENCES

Albrecht, W. S., & Sack, R. J. (2000). *Accounting education: Charting the course through a perilous future.* Accounting Education Series, Vol. No. 16. Sarasota, FL: American Accounting Association.

Accounting Institute Seminars. (2002). CPA exam changes. Retrieved August 1, 2002, from http://www.ais-cpa.com/changes.html

American Institute for Certified Public Accountants. (2002). Top ten technologies. Retrieved August 1, 2002, from http://www.toptentechs.com/techs/

Basile, A. (1998). VITA: A hands-on learning experience for accounting students. *Business Education Forum, 52*(4), 22-24.

Bernardi, R. A., & Bean, D. F. (1999). Preparer versus introductory sequence: The impact on performance in Intermediate Accounting I. *Journal of Accounting Education, 17*(2-3), 141-156.

Bittner, J. (2000). Using real-world scenarios in accounting classes. *Business Education Forum, 54*(4), 27-29.

Bittner, J. (2002). Revamping high school accounting courses. *Business Education Forum, 56*(3), 32-33, 60.

Blaszczynski, C. (1992). Student empowerment through math. *The California Business Teacher, 6*(1), 16-17.

Blaszczynski, C. (1999). A motivating review activity: What is jeopardy pursuit? *Delaware Business Journal, 15,* 49-52.

Blaszczynski, C. (2001). Stamping out business mathematics illiteracy. *The Delta Pi Epsilon Journal, 43*(1), 1-5.

Blaszczynski, C., & James, M. (2001). International business mathematics expressions. *Journal for Global Business Education* 1, 1-11.

Boyd, D. T., Boyd, S. C., & Boyd, W. L. (2000). Changes in accounting education: Improving principles content for better understanding. *Journal of Education for Business, 76*(1), 36-42.

Christmann, E. P. (2000). Converting with confidence. *Science Scope, 23*(8), 42-44.

Cruz, A. M. (2001). Using service learning to motivate and engage accounting students. *Business Education Forum, 56*(2), 34-35.

Cunningham, B. E. (1999). Energizing your teaching: A view from deep in the trenches. *Issues in Accounting Education, 14*(2), 307-321.

Delta Pi Epsilon. (1999). *Case studies for effective business instruction.* D. McAlister-Kizzier (ed.). Little Rock, AR: Author.

Drew, D. E. (1996). *Aptitude revisited: Rethinking math and science education for America's next century.* Baltimore: The John Hopkins Press.

Gabriel, L. T. (2000). Clients, community, and tax assistance. *New Accountant, 15*(5), 7-11.

Goree, K. (2002). The ACT model for ethical decision-making. *Balance Sheet Online.* Retrieved July 30, 2002, from http://www.swep.com/swepstuff/balancesheet/archives/0102/0102-ethics.html

Hall, J. A. (2001). *Accounting information systems, 3e.* Mason, OH: South-Western College Publishing.

Knapp, T. R. (1996). *Learning statistics through playing cards.* Thousand Oaks, CA: Sage Publications.

Mayberry, R. C. (1995). VITA: A "win-win" program. *New Accountant, 10*(5), 6-7, 33.

McConnell, C. A., & Sasse, C. M. (1999). An anticipatory case for managing teams and team projects. *Issues in Accounting Education, 14*(1), 41-54.

National Business Education Association. (2001). *National standards for business education: What America's students should know and be able to do in business.* Reston, VA: Author.

Pasewark, W. R. (1997). Integrating corporate annual reports into the accounting curriculum. *Accounting Education, 2*(1), 79-94.

Pincus, K. V. (1997). Is teaching debits and credits essential in elementary accounting? *Issues in Accounting Education, 12*(2), 575-579.

Quinn, J. D., Garrer, R. M., Marshall, P. D., & Smith, K. J. (1995). Revitalizing VITA to address AECC position statement no. 1 objectives. *Journal of Accounting Education, 13*(4), 479-497.

Riordan, D. A., Riordan, M. P., & Sullivan, M. C. (2000). Writing across the accounting curriculum: An experiment. *Business Communication Quarterly, 63*(3), 49-59.

Schrag, A., & Poland, R. P. (1987). *A system for teaching business education.* New York: McGraw-Hill Book Company.

Scott, J. C. (1990). Accounting around the world. *Business Education Forum, 45*(3),19-21.

Scott, J. C. (1996). Culture and accounting—not so strange bedfellows. *Business Education Forum, 50*(4), 36-38.

Sells, L. (1974/1992). Mathematics—a critical filter. In M. Wilson (Ed.), *Options for girls. A door to the future: An anthology on science and math education* (pp. 79-82). Austin, TX: Foundation for Women's Resources.

Swanson, R. M., Ross, K. E., & Hanson, R. D. (1984). *Accounting: Learning and instruction.* Cincinnati, OH: South-Western Publishing Co.

Tobias, S. (1993). *Overcoming math anxiety.* (Rev. ed.). New York: W. W. Norton & Company, Inc.

U.S. Metric Association. (2001). Antoine frame-of-reference method. . . familiar-item examples. Retrieved November 5, 2001, from http://lamar.colostate.edu/~hillger/frame.htm

Vangermeersch, R. G. (1997). Dropping debits and credits in elementary accounting: A huge disservice to students. *Issues in Accounting Education, 12*(1), 581-583

Walendowski, G. (2000). Accounting education at community colleges: Preparing for the future. *Business Education Forum, 55*(2), 32-34.

Zarowin, S., & Harding, W. (2000). Finally, business talks the same language. *Journal of Accountancy, 19*(2), 24-31.

Business Foundations and Management

Betty J. Brown
Ball State University
Muncie, Indiana

Basic business/economic education is a broad area of business education that provides students with knowledge and skills that they need to be better consumers, producers/entrepreneurs, employees, and citizens. A foundation course in basic business/economic education (which may have titles such as "Introduction to Business," "Business Concepts," or "Business Foundations") and a management course are two elective courses taught at both the secondary and postsecondary levels. In this chapter the foundation course is identified as "business foundations," although the course may have different titles in different states and schools. The business foundations course offers an opportunity for business educators to assist all students to develop skills and knowledge for their own personal business affairs and to develop consumer skills and knowledge. They have opportunities to learn about the economic system and explore careers in all areas of business. The course acquaints students with functional areas of business, such as management, production/operations, marketing, finance, economics, international business, and business ethics.

A management course gives students an opportunity to learn about and develop the abilities they will need to manage their own businesses or to work as managers for a business. They develop their knowledge of the basic management functions of planning, organizing, leading, and controlling. They explore careers in management and the "foundation" skills that are essential for success in management, such as decision-making; ethical choice making; communication, analytical, and human relations skills.

This chapter discusses course content for both business foundations and management and describes instructional strategies and resources for teachers of those courses. Challenges in helping students to attain the knowledge and skills to meet the objectives of these courses are discussed, as well as ways of assessing student achievement in the courses.

THE BUSINESS FOUNDATIONS COURSE

The introductory course for basic business/economic education provides students with a survey of the field of business. The course has three major focuses: career exploration, consumer education, and economic education. Consumer and personal economics, as well as societal economics, are important components. Clow (2001) defined basic business and economic education as having two components: basic economics and basic business. This definition applies economic concepts and thinking processes to the individual's role as consumer, investor, wage earner, entrepreneur, and business leader. The introductory course has both of these components.

Business Foundations has one overall objective—economic literacy. All individuals must be able to handle their personal business affairs. To do so, they must understand their economic system, the myriad of opportunities the economic system offers them, and the skills and knowledge needed to operate effectively in all of their economic roles.

National Standards

The *National Standards for Business Education* (NBEA, 2001) includes standards for economics and personal finance. The performance expectations listed for Level 2 (grades 7-9) describe the knowledge and skills that are important components of a business foundations course. The performances link basic economic concepts and personal financial literacy and define the content of a business foundations course.

Study of Business in an Economic System

In business foundations, students learn about the role that individuals and business firms play in an economic system. Economic systems are increasingly linked globally, as business firms in all countries have economic ties to many other countries. The business foundations course introduces students to the interdependence of basic types of economic systems as a result of a global economy. More importantly, one of the objectives of the course is to help them understand how these concepts affect the role of business and consumers.

The Consumer Role

A major portion of a typical business foundations course provides students with knowledge and skills to manage their own personal finances. Students learn how they can manage their money better and how they can make better use of banking services, credit, investment services, insurance, and other consumer services provided by business firms. They also learn what information is available to them from many sources to help them manage their personal finances and how to access that information.

A business foundations course includes units of study on consumer choices and decision making. Students learn about services offered by business firms to consumers. Because students enrolled in a business foundations course are typically 14 or 15 years of age, consumer skills are especially important to them. They are an economic force as teenagers, accounting for about $160 billion in consumer spending each year (Kissinger, 2002). Mandell (2000) has assessed the personal financial literacy of high school seniors over three years and has found that they lack the basic knowledge and skills necessary to be competent consumers of many goods and services. The business foundations course can assist students to develop the financial literacy they will need as consumers.

Decision Making

All individuals, companies, cities, states, and economic systems share a common problem: scarcity. The scarcity of resources relative to wants necessitates that all persons, whether as individuals or as groups, must make choices. Much of the content of the business foundations course deals with how individuals or groups can make better choices. A decision-making model helps students to understand the process of how to make a choice. Brown and Clow (2002) identified a five-step process that can be used as a teaching tool to assist students in making decisions:

1. Identify the problem—what causes an individual to choose?

2. List the alternatives—what are possible actions for an individual?

3. Determine the pros and cons (opportunity costs) of each alternative—weigh the advantages and disadvantages of each; consider one's values and goals in the process.

4. Make a decision based on the information available—given the alternatives and the pros and cons of each, which is the "best" choice?

5. Evaluate the decision—at a later time, decide whether the choice has been satisfactory and whether the same choice should be made again.

For example, how does an individual decide what vehicle to buy? A first step is to identify some models that are attractive. Next, the task is to gather information about each one. Consumer magazines and Web sites provide information and advice; vehicle sales agencies provide literature, and the Internet has a number of sites where prices can be checked on various makes and models. After gathering all the information, an individual can choose the best vehicle for his or her needs. Later, after driving the vehicle, evaluate the decision to decide whether it was the best choice. The decision-

Table 1. Decision-Making Model

Assume you have saved $500. Using a decision-making model, list four places you could put your money for safekeeping (examples below are piggy bank at home, savings account at local bank, money market account at local bank, and certificate of deposit at local bank). Then identify criteria for savings (examples are return on savings, safety of money, availability when needed, and whether or not the alternative requires a large deposit). Evaluate each alternative using the four criteria. Put a plus sign (+) for each criterion the alternative meets; put a minus sign (-) if the alternative does not meet a criterion. The alternative with the most pluses is the "best" alternative.

Alternatives	Criteria			
	Return on Savings	Safety of Money	Availability When Needed	Large Deposit Required
Piggy Bank at Home				
Savings Account at Local Bank				
Money Market Account at Local Bank				
Certificate of Deposit at Local Bank				

making process applies to decisions of all types. Town councils, business firms, state governments, the federal government, and all other entities must decide how to use their scarce resources to make choices. They use this process, often without thinking about the steps. Table 1 illustrates an activity for which students can use a decision-making process.

As each topic in the business foundations course is introduced, a decision-making model can be used. When students learn about basic economic concepts, for example, they can apply the model to a decision a state government must make, such as choosing how to spend tax dollars. For individuals, the model can be applied to decisions about ethical behavior in a situation or sources of credit for consumers. Teachers can use this decision-making model as a tool throughout the course.

INSTRUCTIONAL STRATEGIES FOR BUSINESS FOUNDATIONS

Instructional strategies for a business foundations course may require some experimentation. No two classes are the same, and individuals in each class learn in different ways. A teacher must have a wide array of teaching strategies to fit different classes and different individuals. Students learn by doing, and they learn more readily if the material is relevant to their own experiences and is reinforced by activities. These concepts are part of constructivist theory for learning. In their work about constructivist classrooms, Gagnon and Collay (2001) identified six basic events in the classroom that teachers can arrange to foster student learning: (1) the content (the knowledge or skills to be learned); (2) groupings of students and the materials provided for learning; (3) the bridge of students' prior knowledge to the new subject matter; (4) questions that stimulate student thinking and sharing of information; (5) the artifacts of learning (ways students can present what they have learned); and (6) student reflections about their learning. Mandell (2000) also found that interactive learning enhanced student learning and application of personal finance concepts.

The business foundations course may first appear to be a collection of different topics not closely related. However, the topics do fit a pattern—they revolve around consumers, their personal finances, and their role in their economic world. Reinforcement of learning helps students understand the relationships and patterns that exist in what they learn. Some concepts may need repeated explanation, supported by several activities in which students apply and reinforce their knowledge and skills. If the teacher provides opportunities for students to see how the concepts apply to their own lives, students will see the value of their study.

Strategies for teaching the business foundations course can be classified in various ways, but one method is to group them as large-group, small-group, and individual strategies. Cochrane (2001) described a teaching strategy as "the most effective classroom management tool." Using a variety of teaching strategies enables the teacher in a business foundations course to engage students in their learning, providing opportunities for them to participate actively in group projects, research, simulations, surveys, field trips, and hands-on learning.

Large-Group Strategies

These strategies for a business foundations course are an efficient way to organize the content that students need to master. Some teacher-centered strategies are efficient and effective ways to present basic concepts. The course includes extensive new vocabulary and concepts. To "set the stage" for learning activities, a mini-lecture is a good choice. Used with visual aids or handouts, a mini-lecture gives students foundational material that they can use with activities. The technique becomes more effective when students are invited to ask questions or are provided with handouts that require them to "fill in" missing information during the presentation. Although the lecture is frequently criticized as a method of teaching, it can be effective when employed appropriately and not overused.

Short question-and-answer sessions help students check their knowledge of basic principles and concepts. A teacher can select questions at the end of a section in the textbook for this purpose or write similar questions. The questions provide frequent checks of the content and are good tools for checking student understanding.

A higher-level instructional strategy, discussion, requires students to listen to others, react to comments, and think about whether they agree or disagree. Students may not find it easy to discuss; too often the "discussion" becomes only questions and answers. In discussions, the teacher's role is to keep students focused on the discussion topic, encourage all students to participate, ask for clarification when students' ideas are unclear, and provide summaries of major ideas at various points in the discussion.

Brainstorming encourages students to think and contribute ideas. Students must understand how brainstorming differs from questioning and discussion. After they have listed as many ideas as they can, the students then evaluate all ideas to decide which are feasible and which are not practical. For example, students can brainstorm with a question such as this one: "What are some ways a small town could raise enough money to renovate a civic center?" All answers are acceptable in brainstorming. "Have a bake sale, add a tax to services, or apply for funding from the state" would be "acceptable" answers for brainstorming. After evaluating each idea, students can identify which responses are realistic and promising.

Guest speakers and field trips are traditional learning tools for business teachers. These choices bring realistic information to students in a business foundations course. If students have some information about the business firm ahead of time, they can collect questions they want the guest to answer to ensure a more successful visit. If students cannot visit a local business on a field trip, someone from that business firm can come to the classroom and share information, perhaps sharing videotapes of activities at the company.

Small-Group Strategies

These strategies include activities such as small-group discussions and activities, cooperative learning activities, committees, panel groups, and role-playing groups. Groups of students can complete activities in class, but they should also explore the business community. Questions for discussion or problems for students to solve may come from a textbook, situations in the local business community, newspapers, magazines, or pamphlets. Research projects for small groups can require students to go to the library, visit companies in the business community, or talk with family and friends to collect information. For example, when they study banking services, students can use a structured interview (an interview guide is prepared by the class ahead of time) to collect information from family, friends, and neighbors about the banking services they use and banking locations they visit.

Marzano, Paynter, Pickering, and Gaddy (2001) described cooperative learning as one of the most popular small-group strategies. Informal groups, such as pair-and-share or turn-to-your-neighbor, are good strategies to check students' understanding of new content, clarify an assignment, review a skill, check homework, or provide closure for an activity. Formal groups work well with extended assignments over several days or even weeks. Students will be interdependent in a formal group and must use their social skills to work effectively and meet the objectives for their projects.

Individual Strategies

These strategies can involve research projects with newspapers, magazines, pamphlets, brochures, and the Internet to supplement textbook content. The wealth of material in these resources allows students to find up-to-date information easily and quickly. The teacher can build activities around information that students collect. Students visit Web sites and conduct research to report to the class. For example, students might visit a site such as Cable News Network's financial news site (http://money.cnn/com/tools/) and use calculators on that site to complete an assignment to find the best rates for credit cards, bank loans, or other financial assistance. Research ideas for small groups can be assigned to individuals if it is not feasible for students to work as a group.

CHALLENGES IN TEACHING BUSINESS FOUNDATIONS

The average reading level of a textbook for a business foundations course is a 7th- or 8th-grade. Even so, some students will have problems reading and comprehending text materials. At the beginning of the course, teachers can help students to use the textbook more effectively by showing them how it is organized and what reading tools are available in the text. If students can approach the text material with definite objectives in mind, they will more readily understand it.

The business foundations course introduces students to a vocabulary unique to business. Audio and visual materials can help students with reading problems, when used as supplements to text material. Tapes, computer-based materials, and oral presentations can be used to introduce content. The text can be supplemented with handouts, individual learning packets, and teacher-prepared materials. Visual representations help students to understand relationships and concepts. Students can prepare graphic organizers, for example, creating flowcharts that diagram ideas related to a key word to further understanding of a concept in their reading (Riggs & Gil-Garcia, 2001).

A business foundations instructor can also teach students an approach to reading assignments in the text. The SQ3R Reading Method (Graves, Watts-Taffe, & Graves, 1999) helps students to survey the reading assignment before reading it; to develop a few key questions that they answer as they read; and then to read, reflect, and review what they have read and answer their questions. For example, if students were to read part of an introductory chapter in the textbook (an overview of the business world), they first would skim the text. They should note how the chapter is divided into sections and determine what the section and paragraph headings tell them. They then examine the review questions at the end of each section so they can answer those questions as they read. As they read, they can reflect on and review the content and answer the questions. This method is just one example of ways in which students can approach a reading assignment. If they know how to read the content with more meaning, they can more easily acquire the basic concepts that will make it possible for them to engage in learning activities profitably.

Consumers who lack basic math skills have difficulty managing their money, so math is an important skill to review in a business foundations course. Computing the value of a discount or deciding the "best buy" can be frustrating if one does not understand the computations. As a part of developing their consumer skills, students may need practice in basic mathematics for consumers. The problems should be simple and realistic. Using round numbers is helpful when students calculate interest rates, credit costs, budget figures, and everyday computations, such as the amount of tip to leave in a restaurant. Students may lack skill in figuring percentages or computing fractions and need a review session. Textbooks provide review activities and may have supplemental mathematics materials for the teacher (Math Skills Review, 1997).

Probably the greatest challenge for the teacher of business foundations is the problem of motivation. Stimulating the interest of all students in the class can be challenging. Other difficulties, such as reading and comprehension problems, personal or family problems, or apathy about education in general may affect students. A teacher can try to motivate them by providing a variety of activities, matching learning activities to learning styles, and making activities relevant to everyday life.

Course content relevant to the business world can spark student interest. A major component of the business foundations course focuses on understanding our economic world. Students should know about such policies as equal opportunity employment, diversity, family leave, discrimination, safety and ergonomics in the workplace, and training. As a guide for teachers in addressing diversity policies, Jones (1999) identified core dimensions of diversity and cited examples of companies operating effective diversity programs for employees. Ball (1997) also reported a number of types of diversity programs used by business organizations. Business foundations textbooks provide information and activities about such programs and policies to help students to understand their role and importance in the business world.

RESOURCES FOR BUSINESS FOUNDATIONS

Students learn best in business foundations when they can be actively involved and can participate in activities based in the local community. If students can apply what they know about their community in their study, their work is more meaningful. For example, when they study business organizations, they can survey their own business community and see how local businesses are organized. If they map a section of their local business community, they can use the map as a springboard for discussing community businesses, new businesses that are needed, and ways in which firms meet consumer and business demands. Students can discuss zoning laws, land use in the community, and the impact of government on business in their community.

Teachers can find a wealth of teaching ideas in various resource materials. Kagan (1994) described a variety of cooperative learning activities and techniques. Cooperative learning activities, case problems, business activities, simulations, and communication and math review activities engage students actively in their learning.

Many Web sites provide teaching ideas and information for ordering materials. Free and low-cost government publications are available on many topics in business foundations, particularly consumer-related topics. The Web site for the Federal Consumer Information Center at www.pueblo.gsa.gov/specpubs.htm lists free and inexpensive materials. Most Federal agencies have educational materials for teachers. The Federal Reserve System and all of its district banks have Web sites that list resources for teachers. The Insurance Education Foundation provides materials for teaching insurance. Consumer Credit Counseling Services provides information on managing credit. The Better Business Bureau offices in most major cities have their own Web sites. Using a search engine to find business resources for teachers yields materials ranging from lesson plans to interactive sites that lead students through a simulation, game, or survey on the topic they are studying.

Table 2 lists a sampling of Web sites that are valuable resources for business foundations, teachers, and students.

Table 2. Some Internet Resources for Teachers and Students	
www.bbb.org	National Better Business Bureau site
www.ftc.gov	U.S. Federal Trade Commission site
www.fda.gov	U.S. Food and Drug Administration site
www.usda.gov	U.S. Department of Agriculture site
www.metlife.com	Topics on life choices and opportunities under "Marketing Life"
www.Edmunds.com	New and used car buyer's guide
www.miningco.com	Selective listing of thousands of Web sites, including business, careers/education, and news/issues
www.consumerlawpage.com	Articles on consumer issues
www.iii.org	Insurance Information Institute site with online consumer brochures on insurance issues
www.stretcher.com	Tips for stretching consumer dollars
www.federalreserve.gov	Publications and education resources—links to sites for all Federal Reserve Banks
www.ief.org	Insurance Education Foundation site (A quarterly lesson plan; provides kits for teaching about insurance on request)

www.ncee.net	National Council on Economic Education provides online lesson plans sorted by title, grade, standard, concept, or type (Economics Minute or Millionaire Minute)
www.themint.org	A Web site with activities and quizzes for students and lesson plans for teachers about the business world
http://school.aol.com/teachers/ lesson plans/	Lesson plans and student and teacher resources
www.nfcc.org	National Foundation for Credit Counseling site with consumer services for handling credit problems
www.consumerworld.org	Links to over 2,000 useful consumer sites

ASSESSMENT STRATEGIES FOR BUSINESS FOUNDATIONS

Assessment of student learning in a business foundations course should include a variety of tools and methods. Class activities that engage students in their learning should be assessed for student achievement. Zeliff and Shultz (1998) described three forms of assessment: traditional, alternative, and performance assessment. Assessment in business foundations should include all three forms.

Quizzes and tests are traditional assessment tools. Written quizzes and tests efficiently measure whether students have learned the "fundamentals" of course content. The published quizzes and tests furnished with a textbook are useful for this purpose. When students participate in group and cooperative activities, use alternative assessment tools such as self-evaluation and peer evaluation. Some topics in a business foundations course lend themselves to activities in which students create a product; both the process and product can be assessed.

When students work in small groups, they can assess the contributions of their fellow students to the project or product, as well as their own contributions to the project. A student can produce a poster, a written paragraph, a script, a graph, a written reflection on work, or an oral presentation, all of which can be assessed for determining grades. Rubrics are a useful tool for reporting assessments to students. Schrock (2002) has published a guide for rubrics for classroom assessment at http://school.discovery.com/schrockguide/assess.html and includes examples of rubrics for various types of learning activities.

THE BUSINESS MANAGEMENT COURSE

The business management course typically enrolls students who are juniors or seniors. Some students may already have plans to enroll in a business administration program at the postsecondary level or to become owners or employees in a business field. Others want to explore the field of management but have no plans to become managers. The course can serve a general education objective of helping all students to learn about the business environment, the interrelationships of consumers and business, and how their basic and academic skills fit the business world. It can serve as a career objective for students who plan employment or advanced study in business management, introducing them to the functional areas of business. With this foundation in management, their further study of business will be more meaningful. The Policies Commission for Business and Economic Education (1995), in presenting an evolving vision of education for and about business, stated that courses such as management "are critical to developing comprehensive business understandings," teaching students about business and preparing them for business.

Business management enables students to integrate knowledge from other business subjects, such as business foundations, business law, and economics. A basic responsibility of company managers is to create a climate that enables workers to do their best work, produce quality products and services at competitive costs, and provide the consumer with value. The business management course gives students an appreciation of that responsibility and introduces them to various specialized fields in business management.

National Standards
The organization of a business management course varies according to the characteristics of the students and their abilities, educational plans, and career goals. The *National Standards for Business Education* (2001) identified these objectives for business management:

- Illustrate how the functions of management are implemented.

- Compare and contrast the basic tenets of management theories.

- Develop and use general managerial skills.

- Define, develop, and apply a code of ethics to various issues confronted by businesses.

- Describe human resource functions and their importance to an organization's successful operation.

- Analyze financial data influenced by internal and external factors in order to make long-term and short-term management decisions.

- Identify various organizational structures and identify advantages and disadvantages of each.

- Identify, describe, and analyze the impact of government regulations and community involvement on business management decisions.

- Describe the role of organized labor and its influences on government and business.

- Apply generally accepted operations management principles and procedures to the design of an operation plan.

The Management Process

Management may be defined as the process of deciding how best to use a business' resources to produce goods or provide services. Persons employed as managers are the collective decision-making body of a business firm. Those individual managers are charged with balancing the demands of owners, shareholders, labor, government, regulatory agencies, and the public while providing goods and services competitively. In addition, management must be aware of the social responsibility of the business firm. To be a "good citizen," a company must be concerned with community issues, environmental concerns, workplace diversity, fair and equitable treatment of all employees, and regional and national concerns that affect the business and the community.

Textbooks for business management emphasize the functions of management and explore the organization, policies, procedures, and human relationships in a business firm. Unlike other basic business/economic education courses, business management does not emphasize personal financial skills. Instead, it focuses on giving a student the knowledge and skills for business management or further study in that field.

An Economic Framework

An economic framework for business management should be established initially in the course. To introduce students to the concept of an economic system, the teacher might use the course might use a story such as this one:

> You are a survivor of a shipwreck, and you and your fellow travelers were able to swim ashore with only the clothing you were wearing. Later in the day, some wreckage drifted ashore, and you recovered a few tools and some food and water. The island you are on has a few trees and little evidence of food. You decide to use the tools and scarce resources that you can find for survival. What tasks must you immediately confront? The problem facing you is similar to problems faced in an economic system: Since you have limited resources, how can you produce all the goods and services that people want? How will you organize to produce those goods and services? What roles will people fill? Who will be in charge? How will the goods and services you produce be distributed among you and your fellow travelers?

Students can build on this introduction and examine business systems and functions in our economy. Web sites for many companies furnish information about management functions and the role of managers and can be used for activities. Other activities might require student writing, Internet research, interpreting charts and graphs, researching specific companies, planning for a new business, analyzing company financial reports and case studies, and analyzing differences between domestic and international business activity. For example, students might read a recent news report about a company's financial problems and identify probable causes. Small groups can develop a plan for a new business firm in the community and identify major tasks to be undertaken. Company financial reports are available on Web sites. Students can access those reports and analyze the data. Is the company profitable? What comparative data are reported, and how does one quarter or year compare with earlier time periods? Students can participate in role-playing to demonstrate behaviors required when they move to another company in a management role. They can study a procedure such as telecommuting or outsourcing and identify advantages and disadvantages to business firms who adopt those practices.

Students must understand the concepts of private property; government-business relationships; political, ethical, and legal concerns; the profit motive, competition and the role of prices; freedom of contract; and how an economic system answers the basic economic questions (Gregory, 2002):

- What will be produced?

- How will these products and services be produced?

- For whom will the products and services be produced?

After students understand the fundamental economic concepts that determine the environment in which businesses operate, they can explore the responsibilities of a business firm in a market economy. The basic function of a business is to provide the goods and services that consumers want and are willing to buy. Those goods and services must be offered at a price that will attract a sufficient number of buyers to enable the firm to realize a reasonable profit. In order to remain competitive, a business manager is required to innovate—to produce new goods and services or introduce new processes for creating its products. In order to stay in business, the business firm must generate a profit for the owners and generate a fair return on investments in the business.

Management Functions

A business management course includes the study of business areas, such as production/operations, marketing/distribution, finances/accounting, human resources, business in a global economy, and service functions. Managers must plan, organize, lead, and measure performance and then refine plans to meet the company objectives.

Managers must address the needs of the firm, as well as be concerned with providing a safe work environment, meeting government regulations, and accepting the social and ethical responsibilities of the firm. The business management course introduces students to all of these roles.

In recent years, business firms have been expected to be more attentive to their roles as "good citizens." This philosophical base adds to the responsibilities of management, so students should explore the social and ethical responsibilities of business. Managers must lead others in the company so that they are productive and effective. How can workers be motivated to contribute at a high level to the objectives of the firm? Studies have shown that pay is only one motivator. Good working conditions, an atmosphere conducive to cooperation among workers, and a feeling that they are critical to the success of the firm are important motivational factors (Hiam, 1999). These aspects of business management are important areas for students to explore.

Communication with workers is critical. Thus, students who study business management must know that they need good oral and written communication skills. Much of a manager's communication will be focused on changing the minds of others or persuading them to accept new ideas or procedures or challenges. Effective managers often think of themselves as leaders rather than directors.

Rue and Byars (2001) encouraged a business management teacher to address the concept of manager as leader and include these topics in the course:

- Diversity in the workplace—what is fair and equitable for all workers, regardless of their differences?

- Job satisfaction—what factors contribute to a worker's motivation to meet the objectives of the firm?

- Technology in the workplace—how has technology changed the workplace, and what concerns does the infusion of technology raise?

- Ethical behaviors and practices—what is ethical in given situations, particularly on the part of management?

- Global economy—what must management be aware of as companies move into a global market? How do customs and protocol in different countries affect relationships with business and consumers in those countries? Which local companies trade in foreign markets? Students may be surprised to find that global markets affect their local business community. They can discuss whether a global economy is "good" and examine decisions that management must make about trading in foreign markets.

INSTRUCTIONAL STRATEGIES FOR BUSINESS MANAGEMENT

As students read, conduct research, visit with businesspersons, and explore their business community, they can bring their ideas to class for discussion and questioning. They can read supplemental materials, such as business publications, and complete projects that use those materials. Class discussions can be focused on news about businesses in the local community. Students can search the Internet, and they can use classroom resources such as newspapers, business magazines, and other supplementary materials, including *Business Week, U.S. News and World Report, Fortune, the Wall Street Journal,* and others.

An article from *U.S. News and World Report* (Hobson, 2001) had this headline: "Retailers sell more, earn less." Students can read articles such as this one and analyze the information. They might answer the following questions: What factors have increased sales? Are companies attempting to decrease inventories? What consumers are they appealing to? Why have earnings dropped?

Students and teachers, with the permission of school administration, can set up and manage a business within the school throughout the term. Management students have successfully operated school banks, school stores, and other school-based businesses as class projects. Students should be involved in all aspects of the project including planning, financing, day-to-day operations, accounting, marketing, and reporting results in a suitable form.

Because human relations and communication skills are important to business managers, teams of students can complete projects that emphasize these skills. The projects should reinforce the concept that managers are involved in leading other people to carry out the tasks for day-to-day operations of a company. Students can research a topic and present their findings in any form they choose, such as role-playing, an illustrated presentation (handouts, presentation by computer, or overhead transparencies), or panel presentation/discussion. For example, a panel of students could discuss the article on "retailers sell more, earn less" with the class.

Case problems illustrate the role of business management. Students can solve problems in a logical manner by applying a problem-solving model (Brown & Clow, 2002). They must determine the problem, get the facts, examine alternative solutions, select the best solution, and evaluate it later. Here is an example of a case, written by the author, that requires students to think about the role of management:

The Union City Corporation manufactures small home appliances. The company is located in a town in a Midwestern state and has existed for more than 50 years. Many of its skilled employees and supervisors have been with the company for years. The company buildings are old and in need of renovation. Most of the production equipment should be replaced with modern electronic equipment. Sales have fallen off during the past seven quarters, and profits show a decline for that period.

The labor force is unionized. The work force has been stable, with a low turnover rate, probably because most of the workers have lived in the area for a long time, own their own homes, and have raised their children there. The community is heavily dependent on the company as a main source of employment.

The company directors are considering closing the plant, since this plant is only a small part of the corporation's total operations. A major argument against modernizing the present facilities is the large capital outlay that would be required. A recent market analysis showed a decreasing demand for the appliances produced at this plant. The chief argument against closing the plant is that it would have a devastating economic impact on the employees and the community.

Students should consider questions such as these as they analyze the case:

- What alternatives are open to corporate management?

- What responsibilities does the corporation have to the community to keep the plant open, despite declining profits?

- What could the local community do to save the plant? What is the responsibility of local government? The local town council or Chamber of Commerce? Citizens in the community?

- What is the "best" solution for the company?

With a case study such as this one, students think of business operations from the viewpoint of managers, employees, and the community, as well as customers and owners.

CHALLENGES IN TEACHING BUSINESS MANAGEMENT

As in other basic business/economic education courses, the students have varied backgrounds in business. Some may have had work experience that motivates them to explore business management as a possible career field. Others may have little experience that contributes to their understanding of course content. A teacher must find ways to engage students, regardless of their background, experience, or prior knowledge.

Teachers without managerial experience may find the course content challenging. Actual business experience is one of the best ways to enhance the content of the course. Part-time or summer work experience enriches preparation and builds a teacher's confidence. Explore the local business community for ideas for activities for the course.

Ask local managers to provide experiences, advice, materials, and personal involvement. They can share their management experiences when they visit the classroom. Students can find many Internet resources, provided by business firms, trade associations, or professional organizations, that reinforce content. Web sites provide help for teachers in planning and presenting projects, such as preparing a business plan.

RESOURCES FOR BUSINESS MANAGEMENT

If a teacher must prepare case studies, simulations, projects, and similar activities for a course, the preparation can be a daunting task. However, free and inexpensive resources from business firms, professional associations, nonprofit organizations, and other teachers provide information and content for those activities. Clark-Madison (2002) edits a newsletter, available to subscribers, that provides case studies on managing people at work. Each issue includes a case study with solutions from a panel of experts. A recent case study addressed potential employee burnout, provided a list of alternative actions, and discussed the panel members' recommended solution.

Simulated investment projects allow students to have hands-on experience in investing funds in stock. At the beginning of the term, they "invest" in selected stocks; and then they track the investments and research the company or companies throughout the term. At the end of the term, they can discuss what they have learned about market fluctuations. Centers and State Councils of the National Council on Economic Education (www.ncee.net) work with teachers using the Stock Market Game, available from the Securities Industry Foundation for Economic Education. This simulation teaches students economic principles and the fundamentals of a market economy. The National Council on Economic Education (2002) also publishes a manual of lesson plans and assessment activities to assist a teacher in using the simulation.

The National Council Web site (www.econedlink.org/datalinks/index.htm) leads a reader to a variety of resources, including data on key economic indicators for the most recent week. This site lists rates for inflation, unemployment, and productivity, as well as figures on the spending, public debt, balance of trade, money supply, international trade, and exchange rates for foreign currency. The site describes other sites where students can study the rates and figures in depth.

Numerous Web sites provide information about business firms. Many large firms include links from their consumer-oriented sites to their business reports. Table 3 lists two examples of corporate Web sites that students may consult (Levi Strauss and McDonald's). Students can search the Internet for additional sites for companies in the news. The table also lists other sites for students and teachers, including some sites that provide lesson plans with supplemental materials.

ASSESSMENT IN BUSINESS MANAGEMENT

Evaluation of student accomplishments can be based on a variety of activities and performances. Written tests are one component, measuring student mastery of text

Table 3. Some Internet Resources for Teachers and Students	
www.standardandpoors.com	Standard and Poor's site has information on U.S. companies; resource center includes answers to frequently asked questions about investments.
www.amanet.org	American Management Association site includes articles on current management topics.
www.shrm.org	Society for Human Resources Management site publishes news about human resources, a tip of the day, and links to sites about human resources materials.
www.informs.org	Institute for Operations Research and the Management Sciences site has a link for students and teachers that offers free career videos for middle and high school students.
www.businessweek.com	Online version of *Business Week* magazine has current news about businesses around the world.
www.business2.com	Free online newsletter covers general topics in business; links to prominent companies and business leaders, e-commerce, and careers sites.
www.wsj.com	*Wall Street Journal* site has news items about businesses in the U.S. and worldwide.
www.levistrauss.com	News and financial data about Levi Strauss corporation is available.
www.mcdonalds.com	McDonald's site publishes quarterly financial data on the corporation, as well as information about policies on diversity, social responsibility, and franchising.
www.ncee.net	Site has lesson plans, teacher and student resources, and links for economic data.
www.school.aol.com/teachers/	Site has lesson plans organized by subject and by grade level.
www.nytimes.com/learning/	A Web site for teachers from the *New York Times*; contains lesson plans related to articles in the *New York Times*; the related articles can be retrieved online.
Note: Students may access the Web sites of other major U.S. businesses for information.	

content and discussions. Students can be evaluated on their work on projects and activities in the business community where they learn about business firms. They can demonstrate their knowledge through presentations to the class and by conducting discussions. The teacher and students can evaluate their presentations of what they have learned by using rubrics (Zeliff & Schultz, 1998). Several authors (Bush & Timms, 2000; Fulker, 2000; Zeliff, 2000) have published examples of instruments for assessment of processes and products that result from engaging students in a wide variety of learning activities.

Table 4 shows an example of a rubric for evaluating student participation in a case study project. If students were asked to work in small groups to analyze the situation of the Union City Corporation presented earlier in this chapter, this rubric would evaluate their work. The case listed four questions that students were to consider. This rubric assesses their understanding of the case and their ability to answer the questions.

Table 4. Project Participation Rubric

Category	1 Excellent	2 Commendable	3 Acceptable	4 Marginal or Unacceptable	Score in Points
Completeness	All major points covered thoroughly	Most major points covered thoroughly	Some major points covered adequately	Points not covered or not covered adequately	
Correctness	Information especially clear, accurate, and reflective	Information mostly clear, accurate, and reflective	Information sometimes clear and correct; more accuracy needed	Information not clear and/or accurate	
Analysis	Correct analysis of all questions	Correct analysis of most questions	Some questions analyzed correctly	Questions not analyzed and/or addressed inadequately	
Solution and Rationale	Viable solution presented and clear, convincing rationale presented	Viable solution presented; good rationale for solution presented	Solution partially viable; rationale could be stronger	Viable solution and/or rationale not presented	
				Total Points	

SUMMARY

The business foundations course provides the groundwork for economic understanding and assists students in developing personal financial literacy. A business management course provides students with an understanding of how business firms operate in our economic system and preparation for further study or work in business management. Keys for success in teaching both of these courses are activities—activities that directly involve students actively in their learning and that reinforce the course content in ways that students see relevance to their own lives and future careers. Instructional strategies provide opportunities for students to work in large groups, in small groups, or individually to apply what they have learned in case studies, projects, cooperative learning activities, and other strategies for learning.

This chapter has presented instructional strategies, resources, and assessment tools for teachers and students. Numerous Web sites provide lesson plans and materials for teachers and information and activities for students. Both business foundations and business management present challenges to teachers; but a wealth of information and activities is available from businesses and organizations that develop and distribute learning activities, lesson plans, and other resources. These resources can supplement and reinforce concepts presented in the courses and make teaching and learning more enjoyable and rewarding.

REFERENCES

Ball, S. (1997). Workforce diversity: Implications for business educators. *The Delta Pi Epsilon Journal, 39*(3), 125-138.

Brown, B., & Clow, J. (2002). *Introduction to business*. New York: Glencoe/McGraw-Hill.

Bush, M., & Timms, M. (2000). Rubric- and portfolio-based assessment: Focusing on student progress. In J. Rucker (Ed.), *Assessment in business education.* (Yearbook No. 38, pp. 71-90). Reston, VA: National Business Education Association.

Clark-Madison, M. (Ed.). (2002). *Managing people at work.* Addison, IL: Professional Training Associates.

Clow, J. (2001). The basic business and economic education curriculum. In B. Brown (Ed.), *Management of the business classroom* (Yearbook No. 39, pp. 10-23). Reston, VA: National Business Education Association.

Cochrane, D. (2001). Setting the stage for successful learning. In B. Brown (Ed.), *Management of the business classroom* (Yearbook No. 39, pp. 154-166). Reston, VA: National Business Education Association.

Fulkert, R. (2000). Authentic Assessment. In J. Rucker (Ed.), *Assessment in business education.* (Yearbook No. 38, pp. 71-90). Reston, VA: National Business Education Association.

Gagnon, G., & Collay, M. (2001). *Designing for learning: Six elements in constructivist classrooms.* Thousand Oaks, CA: Corwin Press.

Graves, M., Watts-Taffe, S, & Graves, B. (1999). *Essentials of elementary reading.* Boston: Allyn & Bacon.

Gregory, P. (2002). *Essentials of economics* (5th ed.). Boston: Pearson Education, Inc.

Hiam, A. (1999). *Streetwise motivating and rewarding employees*. Avon, MA: Adams Media Corporation.

Hobson, K. (2001, December 24). Sell more, earn less. *U.S. News and World Report, 131,* 35.

Jones, C. (1999). Fostering a diverse workforce for today's global marketplace. In P. Gallo Villee & M. Curran (Eds.), *The 21ˢᵗ century: Meeting the challenges to business education* (Yearbook No. 37, pp. 128-141). Reston, VA: National Business Education Association.

Kagan, S. (1994). *Cooperative learning*. San Clemente, CA: Kagan Cooperative Learning.

Kissinger, M. (2002). *Teen spending soars*. Milwaukee,WI: Scripps Howard News Service. Retrieved December 26, 2001, from http://www.abcnews.com

Mandell, L. (2000). *Improving financial literacy: What schools and parents can and cannot do*. Washington, DC: Jump$tart Coalition for Personal Financial Literacy.

Marzano, R., Norford, J., Paynter, D., Pickering, D., and Gaddy, B. (2001). *A handbook for classroom instruction that works*. Alexandria, VA: Association for Supervision and Curriculum Development.

Math Skills Review. (1997). New York: Glencoe/McGraw-Hill.

National Business Education Association. (2001). *National standards for business education: What America's students should know and be able to do in business*. Reston, VA: Author.

National Council on Economic Education. (2002). *Learning from the market: Integrating the stock market game across the curriculum*. Retrieved July 25, 2002, from http://store.ncee.net/learfrommar.html

Policies Commission for Business and Economic Education. (1995). *The evolving vision of education for and about business* (Statement No. 57). Cincinnati, OH: South-Western Educational Publishing.

Riggs, E., & Gil-Garcia. (2001). *Helping middle and high school readers: teaching and learning strategies across the curriculum*. Arlington, VA: Educational Research Service.

Rue, L., & Byars, L. (2001). *Business management: Real-world applications and connections*. New York: Glencoe/McGraw-Hill.

Schrock, K. (n.d.). *Teacher helpers: Assessment and rubric information*. Retrieved July 22, 2002, from http://school.discovery.com/schrockguide/assess.html

Zeliff, N. (2000). Alternative assessment. In J. Rucker (Ed.), *Assessment in business education*. (Yearbook No. 38, pp. 71-90). Reston, VA: National Business Education Association.

Zeliff, N., & Schultz, K. (1998). *Authentic assessment in action: Preparing for the business workplace*. Little Rock, AR: Delta Pi Epsilon.

Economics and Personal Finance

Roger L. Luft
Eastern Illinois University
Charleston, Illinois

Economic and financial decisions affect all aspects of life for every individual. Purchasing an automobile, selecting insurance, renting or purchasing a home, and choosing investments are all topics that consumers must consider.

This chapter addresses the content of economics and personal finance and discusses standards for instructional development. The chapter also offers teaching suggestions and resources for business teachers to help students understand concepts that are necessary for lifelong learning.

THE IMPORTANCE OF ECONOMICS AND PERSONAL FINANCE

Economics and personal finance are business education topics that are often shared by other curricular areas. Economics is often taught as a social studies course, and personal finance is sometimes taught in family and consumer sciences. Both economics and personal finance have enjoyed a recent resurgence in the business education curriculum. The *No Child Left Behind Act,* signed into law January 2002 (U.S. Department of Education) addressed economics and personal finance when it stated the following:

> Innovative Assistance Programs - Funds made available to local educational agencies under section 5112 shall be used for innovative assistance programs, which may include any of the following: Activities to promote consumer, economic, and personal finance education, such as disseminating information on and encouraging use of the best practices for teaching

the basic principles of economics and promoting the concept of achieving financial literacy through the teaching of personal financial management skills (including the basic principles involved with earning, spending, saving, and investing) (p. 60).

The National Council on Economic Education (1999) commissioned research of adults and parallel research of students in grades 9 through 13, which revealed that high school students scored an average of 48% on their understanding of economic concepts. Other research conducted for The Jump$tart Coalition for Personal Financial Literacy (Duguay & Strang, 2002) illustrated similar problems with personal finance literacy that are prevalent in the United States. When given a test for personal finance literacy, students in grade 12 answered 50.2% of the questions correctly. That score was a decrease from previous surveys given in 2000 and 1997 when high school seniors scored 51.9 and 57.3% respectively.

Not only are test scores on economics and personal finance declining in the United States, but also the rate at which citizens save their income is decreasing. U. S. citizens now save only about 2 to 2.5% of their disposable income. Financial illiteracy has affected the nonbusiness bankruptcy rate in the United States, which increased steadily until 1996 and 1997, when it spiraled suddenly upward and continues to remain high (American Bankruptcy Institute, 2002).

COURSE CONTENT FOR ECONOMICS

Business educators can provide the expertise to assist in the battle against financial illiteracy. Most business teachers have completed at least two economics courses in college, including one course in macroeconomics and one in microeconomics. Those who enjoyed these courses may remember a teacher who made the content come to life. Today's business teachers need to present the basics of economics and personal finance in ways that emphasize the importance and relevance of those topics to every student's life.

The Basics of Economics

Economics is typically described as the study of how a society attempts to solve the human problem of unlimited wants and the environmental dilemma of scarce resources (Luft, 2001). At the secondary level, the subject is sometimes referred to as *consumer economics*; such courses focus on the economic problems of individuals—for example, why individuals decide to eat at a restaurant and go to a movie, rather than eating at home and watching the season's final episode of a television show.

Basic to the content of economics is decision making relative to wants, needs, and scarcity. Human nature causes individuals to have wants, even though they do not need to own the desired good or service. Because human wants and needs are endless, scarcity of goods and services often occurs.

The factors of production include land, labor (human resources), capital, and entrepreneurship. From those four factors comes the concept of specialization and answers to the following economic questions: What should be produced? How will production occur? How much should be produced? And who will be the recipients?

Economic systems around the world are linked more closely than ever before, and students should learn about interdependence among economies, or how one system affects another. Students also need to learn about different types of economic systems and how economic systems help to determine standards of living, trade between countries, and concepts such as trade agreements and embargos.

Economic Units of Instruction

An economics course typically begins with a unit explaining why economics is important and that economic decisions are a part of everyone's life. The previous example of choosing to go out to dinner or staying home is a decision with economic consequences. A model that can be used to teach students to make wise decisions is presented in a typical unit on business foundations and management.

Economics instruction includes a unit on supply and demand. Students should understand why shortages or surpluses occur and how prices are determined. They also need to realize that profit is necessary for businesses to continue to operate and to understand the influence of competition and the role of competition on economic decision making.

As consumers, students should understand how production decisions are made, why products are imported from other countries, and why products are exported to other countries. The balance of payments and balance of trade are also important concepts. Students should be able to discern between arguments for increasing versus lifting trade embargos against other countries. Because global travel is becoming commonplace, economics now includes the study of foreign currencies, foreign exchange, and exchange rates.

Economics includes units on labor and management relations and the reasons why some people earn more than others. Students need to understand why and how governments influence economies. Topics such as taxes, governmental controls, and public and private goods are also important issues.

National Standards for Business Education

The *National Standards for Business Education* (National Business Education Association, 2001) addresses the general economic concepts of allocation of resources, economic systems, economic institutions and incentives, markets and prices, market structures, productivity, the role of government, international economic concepts, and aggregate supply and aggregate demand. Each of the concept areas includes a standard such as, "Assess opportunity costs and trade-offs involved in making choices about how to use scarce economic resources" (NBEA, p. 56). Performance expectations are described for each of four levels of instruction, which include Level 1, elementary school; Level 2, middle/junior high school; Level 3, secondary school; and, Level 4, two-year postsecondary/community college or technical college. The *National Standards for Business Education* is an excellent framework from which to develop an economics curriculum.

NCEE Economic Content Standards

Economic content standards have also been developed by the National Council on Economic Education (n.d.). Each of the standards is based on important economic concepts and includes a rationale, practical applications of the concepts, and benchmarks to measure achievement in grades 4, 8, and 12. Also included are assessment exercises. Table 1, an excerpt from the *NCEE Standards*, illustrates how the content standards are structured.

This example depicts a sample of the publication titled *Voluntary National Content Standards in Economics* published by the National Council on Economic Education (n.d.). These standards serve as the basis for curriculum development and are available on the NCEE Web site, as shown in Table 2, which appears later in the chapter.

Table 1. Excerpt from NCEE Standards	
Content Standard 1	
Students will understand that... productive resources are limited. Therefore, people cannot have all the goods and services they want; as a result, they must choose some things and give up others.	**Students will be able to use this knowledge to...** identify what they gain and what they give up when they make choices.
Students face many choices every day. Is watching TV the best use of their time? Is working at a fast-food restaurant better than the best alternative job or some other use of their time? Identifying and systematically comparing alternatives enables people to make more informed decisions and to avoid unforeseen consequences of choices they or others make.	
Benchmarks	
At the completion of Grade 4, students will know that... people make choices because they can't have everything they want.	**Students will use this knowledge to...** identify some choices they have made and explain why they had to make a choice.

At the completion of Grade 8, students will know the Grade 4 benchmarks for this standard, and also that...	Students will use this knowledge to...
scarcity is the condition of not being able to have all of the goods and services that one wants. It exists because human wants for goods and services exceed the quantity of goods and services that can be produced using all available resources.	work in groups representing a scout troop that has volunteered to assist at a local nursing home on Saturday morning. The nursing home has a list of 30 possible projects, all of which it would like completed. Explain why all 30 projects cannot be completed on a Saturday morning.
At the completion of Grade 12, students will know the Grade 4 and Grade 8 benchmarks for this standard, and also that... choices made by individuals, firms, or government officials often have long-run unintended consequences that can partially or entirely offset the initial effects of the decision.	**Students will use this knowledge to...** explain how a high school senior's decision to work 20 hours per week during the school year could reduce her lifetime income. Also, explain how an increase in the legal minimum wage aimed at improving the financial condition of some low-income families could reduce the income of some minimum wage earners.

Note. From the National Council on Economic Education (NCEE), *Voluntary National Content Standards in Economics*, available at http://www.economics america.org/standards/cs1.html (By permission).

COURSE CONTENT FOR PERSONAL FINANCE

Personal finance may be taught either as a separate course or as part of another course, such as introduction to business. Personal finance courses are increasing in popularity, and many resources for teaching personal finance are available. Many of the strategies that are used for teaching economics can be applied with equal success to teaching personal finance.

Standards for Personal Finance

Personal finance has a separate set of standards. The *National Standards for Business Education* (NBEA, 2001) includes standards for personal finance in the broad content areas of personal decision making, earning a living, managing finances and budgeting, saving and investing, buying goods and services, banking, using credit, and protecting against risk. An example of the standard for using credit is "Analyze factors that affect the choice of credit, the cost of credit, and the legal aspects of using credit" (NBEA, p. 66). As with economics, performance expectations are outlined for all four levels of instruction.

The Jump$tart Coalition for Personal Financial Literacy (2002) published the second edition of *National Standards in Personal Finance*, which is designed for grades K through 12. These standards are also appropriate for postsecondary and adult instruction. The personal finance standards are structured similarly to the economics standards. Jump$tart specifies the standards and benchmarks appropriate for grades 4, 8, and 12. Personal finance standards outline what students should know and provide examples for assessing the learning. The grade 8 benchmarks build upon what is specified for grade 4, and the grade 12 benchmarks also include the standards for grades 4 and 8. These standards offer a logical sequence of broad instructional areas that can be used to create units of instruction.

Personal Finance Units of Instruction

The *National Standards in Personal Finance* (Jump$tart, 2002) include the general content areas of income, money management, spending and credit, and saving and investing. From those general content areas, more specific units of instruction may be developed.

For example, topics of instruction within units related to "income" include sources of income and how educational choices and skills affect income. Students should be introduced to economic conditions and how economic cycles influence employment and income. Other related topics include the role of government in taxation of income, social security, and benefits.

For "money management," the units of instruction include the economic concepts of needs and wants and opportunity cost. Students should learn how to establish budgets and be introduced to computer software that can assist them in planning and managing their budgets. Additional topics are insurance and other ways to manage risk, financial information for money-management decisions, and the importance of wills and other legal documents. The money management unit should prepare students to develop a basic financial plan for earning, spending, saving, and investing.

"Spending and credit" topics should include consumer decision making and comparison shopping. A realistic activity is for students to "shop" for a new or used automobile. This unit should introduce students to Web sites that contain information on MSRP (manufacturers' suggested retail price), dealer invoice prices, and specific information on the auto of their choice. A helpful Web site for that activity is http://www.edmunds.com, which is a source for pricing information about automobiles. Before assigning such a project, teachers should become familiar with the Web site and its terminology.

Additional topics that might relate to the car buying activity include how to pay for the purchase. Students need to understand the cost of credit and the consequences of failure to maintain adequate records of their spending. Bankruptcy is a topic also closely related to credit and spending. A credit unit should include consumer credit protection and what consumers should do if they encounter credit difficulties such as lost or stolen credit cards.

A unit on saving and investing includes advantages of beginning a saving and investing plan early in life to maximize the advantage of compounding interest. Students also need to understand the time value of money. A simple software package developed by Financial Players Center, which is listed in Table 2, includes a calculator that students can use to enter necessary data and calculate time value formulas. When calculators are used, students should be aware of the concepts and process used to perform the calculations. Students should be introduced to the "rule of 72" when calculating interest. Units of instruction should also include saving and investing vehicles such as stocks, bonds, and mutual funds and the importance of diversification. Students should learn about income-sheltering savings plans such as 401(k), 403(b), and other employer-sponsored programs. Many economic concepts can be introduced in a unit on "saving and investing." For example, supply and demand can be discussed in relation to purchasing stock. The teacher also should introduce students to the role of government in regulating the financial industry.

Adams (2000) outlined a consumer finance framework that included topics or units for foundational, intermediate, and advanced content levels. The foundational level includes an introductory unit and other units on cash management and credit management. Intermediate units include taxes, housing, and insurance needs. Advanced financial topics include investing, retirement, and estate planning. These concepts are essential for teaching personal finance at the secondary and postsecondary levels.

TEACHING STRATEGIES
No single instructional strategy works best for teaching economics or personal finance, as both areas are suitable for a myriad of instructional strategies. Teachers should be proficient in the use of many instructional methods and should be aware of instructional resources that are appropriate to facilitate effective instruction.

Because much of the content for economics and personal finance is conducive to similar teaching strategies that are discussed in this section, teachers should use methods and strategies that encourage and enhance decision-making skills in both areas. Active learning that involves students and encourages critical thinking is essential. Using a variety of methods to teach each topic can help all students to be successful.

Case Analysis
Students can more readily understand the concepts that are being taught when they can relate these concepts to *case studies* that present real-life situations. Case problems can vary from short and straight forward to long and more complex. Many textbooks and other resource materials provide cases to illustrate the topics that are being discussed and suggest solutions to these cases.

A Delta Pi Epsilon publication titled *Case Studies for Effective Business Instruction* (McAlister-Kizzier, 1999) contains 74 ready-to-use cases for several areas of business education. Teachers can develop additional cases by following these guidelines:

1. Make the situation realistic.

2. Write an introduction that provides salient facts about what the case includes.

3. Follow the introduction with a logical problem.

4. Include all of the information necessary to complete the analysis.

5. Include charts, tables, figures, or diagrams if appropriate.

6. Disguise the organization if it is based on a real business to prevent students from recognizing it.

7. Have the completed case study reviewed by someone else, including someone in the business about whom the case was developed.

8. Revise the case after it has been tested with students.

The following example illustrates a short case study:

> Jean and Ed have been thinking seriously about purchasing a new home. They have been living in a two-bedroom apartment in rural Nebraska for the past five years and have managed to save $10,000 that they will use for the down payment on a new home. They are concerned because they have heard economic reports that indicate the country is on the verge of a recession. They do not fully understand all of the ramifications a recession has on interest rates, home prices, employment, and other economic factors. Jean and Ed need your help. Your job is to develop a list of all the economic concerns that might affect a home purchase when an economic recession approaches. Prepare a report that will answer the questions and concerns that Jean and Ed might have to consider.

Case analysis is an excellent way to promote active learning. This technique is a logical complement to teaching methods such as guided discussion, questioning, and collaborative learning. The previous case may include either questions for students to answer or may be open-ended. Appropriate questions about case problems encourage students to think and develop critical decision-making skills.

Proper questioning techniques lead to the discussion of important concepts. Open-ended questions are effective because they encourage students to "think on their feet," as they would be expected to do in business situations. An example using the case study previously outlined could be "Jerry, what might be the reasons for a difference in the economic situations in Nebraska and Washington State?" If Jerry is unable to answer the question, the teacher can follow up with other leading or probing questions.

Teachers typically wait about one second for an answer before calling on another student and one second after a student responds before probing the response, rephrasing the question, redirecting to another student, or providing the answer (Wilen, Ishler, Hutchison, & Kindsvatter, 2000). The teacher should allow students several seconds to formulate an answer before they respond.

Games and Simulations

Games and simulations are terms that are often used interchangeably. *Simulations* may or may not include competition among students, or winners and losers. *Games* frequently involve competition, as in a classroom version of a television game show that can be used to review for an exam.

Games and simulations are very effective strategies for motivating students toward participation and involvement. Most games and simulations require a high degree of decision making for students to complete the activity. Students learn more when they are excited about the activity.

Computer games and simulations have become very popular. Technology allows games and simulations to be completed individually or as a group activity. Economics and personal finance have benefited greatly from computer simulations and games, and many of these resources are available on the Internet.

A simulation example that has been popular for many years is *The Stock Market Game*™developed by the Securities Industry Foundation for Economic Education. This popular teaching tool combines a stock trading simulation with a classroom curriculum that teaches economics and personal finance, while also building skills such as math and communication. This activity, which is available on the Internet and in paper format, is listed as a resource in Table 2. This simulation provides teacher support materials, and it is correlated to the economics standards. This simulation, when combined with use of the *Classroom Edition of the Wall Street Journal* (see Table 2), offers tremendous teaching/learning activities and opportunities in both economics and personal finance courses.

Nominal Group Process

The *nominal group process* includes structured group participation that involves the knowledge, experience, and feelings of everyone in the group. The primary reason to use this instructional technique is to enhance group decision making, stimulate critical thinking, and guide the group members in their generation of ideas (Miller, 1990).

Any group size can be used for the nominal group process. The process requires written participation and assures that everyone will have an opportunity to be involved. A teacher should allow ample time for the process to be completed, especially with more complex situations. The following problem situation gives students an opportunity to discuss many economic and personal finance concepts:

1. Present the problem to the students in a written format. Assume that an economic and personal finance situation has arisen in class. For example, a student's parent has been investigating the purchase of a new Ford Thunderbird and discovered that the demand for the car is so high that most dealers are able to sell the vehicle for about 25% above the MSRP. The situation should be written in problem format and presented to the students.

2. All students should be asked to write their solutions to the dilemma without assistance from their classmates. Each student is then asked to present one solution from his or her list, and the teacher writes the solutions on the board.

3. Discuss each solution that has been presented and allow students an opportunity to present their thoughts. Additional solutions may be added to the list. Some solutions will not be acceptable and can be eliminated after discussion.

4. All students should rank the solutions in writing, based on their own opinions. The teacher then collects the ranking sheets and records the rankings for the class to see. Any concerns that the students might have should be discussed at this time.

5. Ask the students to rank the list again and then prepare a final ranked listing of solutions.

Peer Instruction
Peer instruction is an alternative partnership approach to teaching, in which students serve as tutors, coaches, or models for other students. This strategy is particularly effective when the learning capacities of students vary widely. Students who have a difficult time grasping concepts can benefit from assistance from other students.

Peer instruction helps develop social skills and self-esteem for students who are involved in the tutoring arrangement. This instructional method allows the teacher to be available to students who need additional attention from the teacher. Peer tutoring is also a way for teachers to increase the effectiveness of individualized instruction time for students. Teachers who use peer teaching find that students receive more individualized instruction, learn at an accelerated rate, take more responsibility for their learning, and are more involved with creating a positive classroom environment (McNeil, 1994).

Traditional Instructional Methods and Strategies

Traditional instructional methods and strategies for teaching economics and personal finance include lectures, field trips, interviews, panel discussions, and buzz sessions.

Lecture is an effective method to introduce new topics or ideas. Lectures must be carefully planned and organized and include materials that are designed especially for the audience. To maintain students' interest, lectures should be kept short and supplemented with dynamic visuals.

Field trips are very appropriate for many topics of instruction. For example, imagine the excitement that could be created if students have an opportunity to visit a large trading room of an investment company. Field trips to a business site should be followed by a written report, oral report, or a class discussion.

An *interview* is a strategy in which one or two resource persons visit the class and respond to questions from one or two students. Interviews can be used to give students an opportunity to gain social interaction skills and to learn more about a selected topic. Questions should be prepared in advance, and the visiting respondents should know what is expected of them. For example, an insurance agent might visit the class and be interviewed about automobile insurance, a topic that would interest most students.

Panel discussions use a group of three to six resource people to present a variety of information or viewpoints to students. Students or the teacher may facilitate the panel. For example, a topic could be interest rates and purchasing power, with the panel consisting of bankers and other businesspeople.

Buzz sessions facilitate involvement by all students with the class divided into several small groups that meet simultaneously to discuss an assigned topic or to perform a task that is given to them. After sufficient time, one person from each group presents the results of their discussion. Those results might naturally lead to large group discussions, especially when groups of students disagree.

RESOURCES

Numerous resource materials have been developed in recent years to support teaching and learning in economics and personal finance. Many of the printed resources are supported with computer software or online instructional materials. Some of the popular resources and Web sites are discussed and/or listed in this section.

National Council on Economic Education (NCEE)

This organization was founded in 1949 with the mission to help all students develop economic ways of thinking and problem solving that they can use in their lives as consumers, savers, investors, members of the workforce, responsible citizens, and effective participants in a global economy. The NCEE offers a vast array of services and materials that are available to business educators. A network of affiliated state and regional Councils on Economic Education with affiliated university/college-based Centers for Economic Education provide numerous instructional materials, classes, and workshops for economic teachers.

Jump$tart Coalition for Personal Financial Literacy

Jump$tart is an organization that seeks to improve the personal financial literacy of young adults. Jump$tart has identified personal finance standards for grades K through 12, promotes the teaching of personal finance, and maintains a clearinghouse of educational materials for personal finance instruction.

Security Industry Foundation for Economic Education (SIFEE)

This organization is affiliated with the Securities Industry Association and was formed to promote public understanding of the stock market and the securities industry. The primary activity of SIFEE is *The Stock Market Game™*, which has been used for years by many teachers. *The Stock Market Game™*(SMG) program combines a ten-week stock trading simulation and an extensive classroom curriculum portfolio designed to teach basic economics and other subjects. The activity is available in print as well as on the Internet.

Junior Achievement (JA)

Best known for its after-school entrepreneurial program, Junior Achievement has been actively developing programs for elementary through secondary instruction. Two of the popular high school programs include JA Economics and JA Personal Finance. Many of the concepts and skills taught in the JA materials are related to the previously discussed standards.

The Wall Street Journal Classroom Edition

This resource covers a wide variety of topics and concepts every month and is designed to help teachers address the *National Standards for Business Education* and implement the *Voluntary National Content Standards in Economics*. The monthly publication contains activities for students that make the study of economics and personal finance more timely and relevant.

YoungBiz

The mission of YoungBiz is to empower youth with entrepreneurial, business, and financial skills through innovative education and real-world experience. YoungBiz has several in-school and after-school programs. Programs for teachers include training workshops for teaching business, entrepreneurship, and personal finance. While the emphasis of YoungBiz is entrepreneurship, personal finance materials and programs are also available. Economic skills can also be developed through teaching entrepreneurship.

Financial Players Center

Mathematical concepts that are taught in economics and personal finance are often dependent upon an understanding of the time value of money. Financial Players Center has developed software that simplifies calculations and helps students to grasp these concepts.

Table 2 can can serve as a resource for teaching economics and personal finance.

Table 2. Web Sites for Teaching Economics and Personal Finance	
Web Address	**Site Description**
www.ncee.net	The National Council on Economic Education publishes economics materials for all grades beginning with kindergarten.
www.fte.org	The Foundation for Teaching Economics offers lesson plans and curriculum design materials, including online courses for teachers and students.
www.nice.emich.edu	The National Institute for Consumer Education is at Eastern Michigan University and serves as a clearinghouse in economics, personal finance, and consumer education.
www.jumpstartcoalition.org	The Jump$tart Coalition for Personal Financial Literacy is a clearinghouse and source of hundreds of instructional materials.
www.wsjclassroomedition.com	*The Wall Street Journal Classroom Edition* is a monthly publication designed specifically for teaching economic concepts in the classroom.
www.smgww.org	The Stock Market Game™ sponsored by the Securities Industry Foundation for Economic Education teaches about economics and the securities industry through the use of a simulation.
www.ja.org	Junior Achievement has K-12 programs to educate young people to value free enterprise, business, and economics.
www.youngbiz.com	YoungBiz publishes materials as well as conducts workshops and training for students and teachers to learn entrepreneurial, business, and financial skills.
www.financialplayerscenter.com	Financial Players Center offers a simplified software package that allows students to learn and under-stand the time value of money concepts.

www.aba.com	The American Bankers Association site has many opportunities to learn about saving that are designed for children, parents, teachers, and bankers.
www.irs.gov	The IRS site has important information on how federal, state, and local taxes work, specifically under "individuals" and then under "TAX Interactive" to find a teacher's toolkit.
www.nyse.com	The New York Stock Exchange provides information on how the exchange works, company information, real-time information, and live Web cam shots of the exchange.
www.nasdaq.com	The National Association of Security Dealers site has information on the over-the-counter market.
www.amex.com	The American Stock Exchange site has several education links to learn about the different investment vehicles available via AMEX.
www.usinfo.state.gov/topical/econ	This U.S. Department of State site has a wealth of information on international economics topics, including an archive of electronic journals.
www.federalreserve.gov	The Federal Reserve Board site has information about the Fed and discusses several economic concepts. It has many publications and educational resources, including an interactive learning tool.
www.fl2010.org	Financial Literacy 2010 provides teaching guides for high school teachers at no cost, including links to other useful sites.

SUMMARY

Economics and personal finance are subjects that students will use throughout their lifetime. This chapter discusses the importance of economics and personal finance, the topics included in the economics and personal finance curriculum, including critical standards for business education, and offers appropriate teaching strategies for both areas. Instructional strategies emphasize the need for experiential learning and active involvement by students in the teaching/learning process. These strategies include case analysis, games and simulations, nominal group process, and peer instruction. Traditional approaches for instruction include lecture, field trips, interviews, panel discussions, and buzz sessions.

Appropriate usage of instructional strategies and support materials create a positive learning environment. Resources that enhance instruction are important to the teaching/learning process. A list and descriptions of organizations that produce materials for teaching economics and personal finance are included. Various Web sites include games and simulations that bring active learning to the curriculum and at the same time challenge the student to learn about life situations.

REFERENCES

Adams, E. (2000). Consumer finance: A teaching framework including strategies, activities, and resources, part 1. *Instructional Strategies: An Applied Research Series*, 16(3, Pt.1).

American Bankruptcy Institute. (2002). U. S. bankruptcy filing statistics. Retrieved May 20, 2002, from http://www.abiworld.org/stats/newstatsfront.html

Duguay, D., & Strang, L. (2002, April). From bad to worse: Financial literacy drops further among 12th graders—Jump$tart urges states to apply newly available funds towards innovative personal finance education programs. Retrieved May 20, 2002, from http://www.jumpstart.org/upload/news.cfm?recordid=99

Jump$tart Coalition for Personal Financial Literacy. (2002). *National standards in personal finance: With benchmarks, applications and glossary for K-12 classrooms* (2nd ed.). Washington, DC: Author.

Luft, R. L. (2001). Economics. In B. Kaliski (Ed.), *Encyclopedia of business and finance* (Vol. 1, pp. 267- 272). New York: Macmillan Reference USA.

McAlister-Kizzier, D. (1999). *Case studies for effective business instruction*. Little Rock, AR: Delta Pi Epsilon.

McNeil, M. (1994). Creating powerful partnerships through partner learning. In J. S. Thousand, R. A. Villa, & A. I. Nevin (Eds.), *Creativity and collaborative learning: A practical guide to empowering students and teachers* (pp. 243-259). Baltimore: Paul H. Brooks Publishing Co.

Miller, W. R. (1990). *Instructors and their jobs*. Homewood, IL: American Technical Publishers, Inc.

National Business Education Association. (2001). *National standards for business education: What America's students should know and be able to do in business* (2nd ed.). Reston, VA: Author.

National Council on Economic Education. (n.d.). *Voluntary national content standards in economics*. Retrieved May 21, 2002, from http://www.economicsamerica.org/standards/index.html

National Council on Economic Education. (1999). *Literacy survey: Results from the standards in economics survey*. Retrieved May 20, 2002, from http://www.ncee.net/cel/results.html

U.S. Department of Education. (2002). *No Child Left Behind Act*, Title V, Promoting Informed Parental Choice and Innovative Programs; Subpart 3, Local Innovative Education Programs; Section 5131, Local Uses of Funds, (a), (11). Retrieved May 28, 2002, from http://www.ed.gov/legislation/ESEA02/pg60.html

Wilen, W., Ishler, M., Hutchison, J., & Kindsvatter, R. (2000). *Dynamics of effective teaching* (4th ed.). New York: Longman.

Business Law

Paul Sukys
North Central State College
Mansfield, Ohio

The law and business are inseparable partners in an ongoing relationship that affects all aspects of the economy. This chapter provides an overview of the complex relationship between law and business. Its topics explain the need to study business law, explore some recent trends in the law that affect business, outline the content of a course in business law, suggest some methods for integrating legal issues into the overall business curriculum, and present several techniques for creatively engaging students in the study of the law.

STUDYING BUSINESS LAW

Like many areas of commerce, the legal aspects of conducting business cannot be viewed in isolation. Every entrepreneur in the United States, from the local merchant running a neighborhood grocery store to the CEO of a multinational corporation, must keep an eye focused on the law. The law, like many aspects of society, is in a constant state of growth and change. Fortunately, the growth and change experienced by the law is often unhurried and usually, though not always, predictable. If merchants know what areas of the law directly affect their businesses and remain alert, they generally can keep abreast of developments. Today, the smart entrepreneur will keep his or her eye on three key areas of legal growth and development. These areas include trends in litigation, patterns in governmental regulation, and the direction of technology.

Trends in Litigation

The process of bringing a civil lawsuit into a court of law is known as *litigation* (Oran & Tosti, 2000). The litigation process has always been an important component of the legal system. The process is designed to give people who believe that they have been wronged the opportunity to seek some sort of compensation. The court system creates a balance by permitting those individuals who have been implicated in wrong-doing to have their day in court. Recently, however, the system has been criticized for various problems such as substantial delays, costly proceedings, and the fact that many decisions appear to be unjust. In addition, the considerable volume of many court calendars discourages a number of litigants. For instance, the number of lawsuits initiated in this country has climbed from approximately 10,000 in 1940 to more than 200,000 about 45 years later (Gerstl, 2000).

Some people bypass the courts and use one of the many *alternative dispute resolution (ADR)* methods that are now available (Mulligan & Hutson, 1996; Oran & Tosti, 2000). The National Business Education Association has recognized this growth in the popularity of ADR and has included performance expectations related to ADR in the Business Law content area of the latest edition of the *National Standards for Business Education* (NBEA, 2001). ADR techniques include mediation, arbitration, early neutral evaluation, summary jury trials, private civil trials, and ADR contract clauses. *Mediation* involves using an objective third party, generally a professional *mediator,* to listen to both sides of a disagreement and then to offer advice and direction on how to resolve that disagreement. The job of the mediator is to bring the parties together by urging them to compromise (Oran & Tosti, 2000). Arbitration is similar to mediation. The difference is that in *arbitration* the objective third party actually decides how to resolve the disagreement. The objective third party is referred to as an *arbitrator* (Oran & Tosti, 2000). Sometimes the parties to a contract will agree in advance to use arbitration should a disagreement arise. This technique is referred to as *compulsory arbitration.* Such an approach is often used in employment cases, especially when a union negotiated contract is involved (Friedman & Strickler, 1997).

Four relatively new ADR techniques include early neutral evaluation, summary jury trials, private civil trials, and ADR contract clauses. *Early neutral evaluation (ENE)* involves the use of an unbiased reviewer who examines the facts in a case and renders an opinion on each party's legal rights and duties. The evaluator may also determine the most appropriate award in a case (King, 1998). A *summary jury trial* is a short trial that is conducted before real jurors who decide the case. To be effective, a summary jury trial generally is conducted within a single day before a relatively limited number of jurors. The verdict rendered by the jury may be either advisory or binding. The process is a valuable alternative because it reveals how real jurors might evaluate the merits of a case which helps the litigants decide if they want to go forward or settle out of court (Meagher, 1998; Oran & Tosti, 2000).

In a *private civil trial,* the entire case is presented before real jurors and a judge, often one who is retired. The trial is then conducted following the rules of evidence and procedure that would be used in an official trial. The results are just as binding as they would be in an official trial. The advantage to this procedure is that the parties can sidestep the lengthy court calendar and select a date and time that is mutually agreeable (Cox, 1998). Unlike the other techniques discussed thus far, each of which is used after a dispute has occurred, *ADR contract clauses* are written before any difficulties arise. Generally, the parties decide to use an ADR contract clause because they have entered a long and involved agreement. The ADR clause means that the parties have agreed to use an ADR technique should a dispute arise (Doan, 1998).

Patterns of Government Regulation

The government sometimes adjusts its procedures after seeing how new techniques work in the private sector. This pattern has occurred in the area of alternate dispute resolution. Seeing not only the need for an adjustment in its own methods, but also the success of using ADR programs outside official channels, the government now offers certain alternate dispute resolution practices. Two of these practices include settlement week and negotiated rule making. *Settlement week* occurs when a court sets aside a specific time period, usually a one-week period once or twice a year, during which the usual routine of the court is suspended. During that week, the court is involved only in negotiating settlements of actions pending on the calendar. Prior to settlement week, attorneys submit a list of pending cases that they would like to present during settlement week. Volunteer mediators hear the cases and render decisions. Generally, such decisions must be approved by the presiding judge (Krueger, 1998).

Another ADR technique instituted by the government is known as *negotiated rule making,* or *reg-neg.* This process involves governmental agencies that are contemplating a change in regulations. Under reg-neg procedures, rather than simply imposing the rules, the agency compiles a working team of representatives from all segments of society that will be affected by the new regulations. An independent leader is also chosen to act as chair of the team. The team then draws up the new or revised regulations as a free exchange of ideas. The final result of this negotiation process should be a set of rules and regulations that are acceptable to everyone on the team. (Mone, 1998).

Directions in Technology

Innovations that frequently occur every day in science and technology often affect the legal aspects of business. No technological area is more susceptible to such rapid changes than computer technology. Advances in computer technology have had far-reaching effects on the way that people conduct business in the United States and around the globe. The use of the Internet to buy and sell goods, a process generally referred to as *e-commerce,* has changed the face of commerce in the modern age (Towle & Nielander). E-commerce is discussed in Chapter 15, Entrepreneurship and E-Commerce. The latest edition of the *National Standards for Business Education* includes an extensive series of performance expectations on e-commerce within the business law content area (NBEA, 2001).

PLANNING A COURSE IN BUSINESS LAW

Despite the latest developments in litigation, governmental regulation, and technological advancements, many traditional concepts must still be covered as a foundation for a course in business law. Some of the essential ideas, concepts, and principles identified in the *National Standards for Business Education* include procedural law, contract law, the law of sales, employment law, and the law of business organizations (NBEA, 2001).

Procedural Law

The use of alternative dispute resolution methods has not eliminated the traditional litigation system. Therefore, business people must be acquainted with the structure and the operation of the court system in the United States. The federal system includes three levels. At the foundation are the *district courts*, which serve as the trial courts of that system. The federal system also consists of two appellate levels, the *court of appeals* and the *United States Supreme Court*. An *appellate court* reviews the decisions rendered by the lower courts to determine whether those courts made errors of law in their proceedings (Schneeman, 1995). Business students must also have some knowledge about the litigation process. For example, a businessperson should be aware of the difference between a civil action and a criminal prosecution. A *civil action* involves a lawsuit between parties, the object of which is generally to uphold a right or compensate an injured party as compensation for a loss; in a *criminal case*, the government prosecutes someone accused of a crime (Oran & Tosti, 2000).

Contract Law and the Law of Sales

Areas of civil law that frequently affect business people include contract law and the law of sales. Business students must have knowledge of contract law because contractual relationships are essential to the carrying out of commercial activities. Entrepreneurs should understand that a *contract* is a legally binding agreement and consists of certain definable elements. These elements include genuine agreement resulting from mutual consent between parties with the required competence, supported by consideration to perform a legal action (Handler, 1994)

Business people should be able to analyze a real-life situation to determine whether a contract has formed, whether either party has breached the contract; and, if such a breach exists, to determine what remedy might be appropriate to compensate for the breach. When analyzing a contract, a businessperson must determine the proper law to apply to the contract in question. Contracts involving the sale of goods are governed by rules that are somewhat different from those that govern other types of contracts, such as contracts involving services. *Goods* are items of moveable personal property such as appliances, clothing, and food. Contracts for the sale of goods are covered by Article 2 of the Uniform Commercial Code (UCC). This area of the law is generally referred to as the *law of sales*. While some of the same principles that affect other contracts apply to the sales of goods, many are different (Frey & Frey, 2001; Oran & Tosti, 2000).

Employment Law

In most states, the generally accepted principle of employment law is the doctrine of at-will employment, which holds that an employer can discharge an employee at any time for any reason with or without notice. This principle is based on the idea that both the employer and employee should be free to work with and for whomever they please. In reality, this doctrine frequently puts some workers at the mercy of the employer. Consequently, the doctrine has recently seen some revision. Some of the factors contributing to this change have been the development of antidiscrimination laws and the advent of the doctrine of wrongful discharge (Rothstein & Liebman, 1998).

Federal legislation also has played a key role in curtailing discrimination in the workplace. Perhaps the most crucial antidiscrimination law is the Civil Rights Act of 1964 that prohibits discrimination based on five protected characteristics. These characteristics are race, color, creed, gender, and national origin. The law prohibits such discrimination in education, voting, public accommodations, and employment. Employment is covered by Title VII of the act. Under this title, the Equal Employment Opportunity Commission was established to hear complaints related to violations of the statute (Rothstein & Liebman, 1998). Another key antidiscrimination statute is the Age Discrimination in Employment Act that prohibits discrimination in hiring, promoting, and discharging employees based on age. This act specifically protects workers aged 40 and over (Rothstein & Liebman, 1998). Grounds for a wrongful discharge lawsuit include public policy, implied contract, and implied covenant of good faith and fair dealing. *Public policy* is a legal doctrine that says that no one should be permitted to harm the public at large. The courts have used the doctrine to hold that a firing that hurts the public at large will not be permitted. Thus, an employer who discharges an employee under such circumstances would be liable for wrongful discharge. For example, if an employer fires an employee for refusing to commit a crime on behalf of the employer, such as the illegal disposal of hazardous waste, under public policy that employer would be liable for wrongful discharge (Rothstein & Liebman, 1998).

Wrongful discharge can also occur when the discharge violates an implied contract between the employer and the employee. An *implied contract* can arise when an employer says or does something that leads an employee to believe legitimately that his or her employment is not subject to the employment-at-will doctrine. Such statements can be found not only in oral declarations made by the employer but also in employee handbooks, rulebooks, and manuals, especially those that are written by the employer and are clearly intended to set down the conditions and regulations of employment (Rothstein & Liebman, 1998). A few states have recognized the existence of an *implied covenant of good faith and fair dealing* in all employment relationships, regardless of whether or not anything is said or written about fair treatment (Rothstein & Liebman, 1998).

The Law of Business Organizations

Every businessperson should be acquainted with each type of business association that is available within his or her state. Learning the advantages and disadvantages of each type or organization also helps the entrepreneur understand which of the forms is best suited for certain types of businesses. This knowledge is especially important today because of the growing number of business associations that are available. Business law students should understand the differences, advantages, and disadvantages among various forms of business organizations, including sole proprietorships, general partnerships, limited partnerships, corporations, limited liability companies, and franchises.

INTEGRATING BUSINESS LAW WITHIN THE BUSINESS CURRICULUM

Business law courses are taught at the secondary, two-year college, and university levels. In addition, the law of business associations offers many opportunities to integrate law with other areas of the business curriculum. The existence of such opportunities is due to the fact that the law of business associations must itself involve a wide variety of other legal subjects such as contract law and employment law. This variety provides business teachers with a number of ways to integrate law into management, economics, marketing, and international business courses that are taught at both secondary and collegiate levels.

Business Law and Business Management

Business governance is one of the key issues found within the study of the law and management. The issue involves the question of whose interests should be foremost in the mind of business managers as they make their business decisions. For instance, according to one school of thought, the short-term investment interests of the shareholders should come first. Lately such a view has been losing support in the United States. Another theory places the emphasis on the responsibilities of businesses to many diverse groups, including employees, customers, and noncustomers (Drucker, 2002).

The rules of law and the principles of management suggest different solutions or different approaches to this dilemma. For example, the law has dealt with this issue primarily in the corporate arena and has provided a standard, the business judgment rule, by which directors can passively avoid liability (Schneeman, 1993). In contrast to the legal standard, some of the principles of business management demand that business managers actively consider the effects that a business decision will have on those involved in that decision, including all stakeholders—the people who have placed trust in the business (Mondy, Sharplin, & Premeaux, 1991).

Business Law and Economics

Business law and economics also overlap in a variety of ways. As in the intersection of law and management, the intersection of law and economics can often be seen in the area business associations, where the law provides guidelines for managers who want to avoid liability. The study of management provides procedures for making business decisions, while the study of economics provides a system for determining the allocation of resources. Specifically, an understanding of economics can answer three key questions for managers. Those questions are (a) What goods and services should a business provide? (b) What techniques should be used to provide those goods and services? (c) What part of the market should the business attempt to service? (Schiller, 1999). Understanding the law also helps managers make sound economic decisions because the law gives concrete guidance to abstract economic principles. Although economics tends to be theoretical and general, the law tends to be concrete and specific (Friedman, 2000).

Business Law and the Rest of the Curriculum

Business law can be easily assimilated into other areas in the business curriculum. A study of the law clearly overlaps with courses in marketing and international business. In marketing, for example, one of the key topics involves understanding the nature of the distribution channels. Examining this topic, however, requires knowledge of both marketing and the legal aspects of distribution channels. Thus, a marketing course must cover not only a study of how to choose, design, and control channels but also how to detect the legal complications involved in the use of those channels. Legal issues involve an examination of the legality of certain tactics such as exclusive dealing practices, tying agreements, exclusive-territory programs, and the refusal to deal with certain wholesalers or retailers (Etzel, Walker, & Stanton, 1997). Similarly, a course in international business should include how to plan for the international market. However, such a study cannot be separated from a serious look at the external and internal influences of the law. Thus, a course in international business must include an examination of the trade agreements and treaties that exist between the United States and other nations, as well as the legal systems within those countries (Etzel et al., 1997).

TEACHING BUSINESS LAW

Because business law involves such a large quantity of information, a business law instructor may be tempted to fall back upon the traditional lecture method to disseminate that information. Certainly, the lecture method has its advantages. It can be an efficient and effective way for a teacher to make certain that all of the necessary topics are covered. The danger of relying exclusively on the lecture method is that although the students are introduced to all the topics, they learn none of those topics in depth. Consequently, a business law teacher should look for as many different ways of reaching the students as possible. Fortunately, business law lends itself easily to a wide variety of methods, including mock trials and mock hearings, legal debates, case analysis teamwork, news analysis teamwork, and Internet research projects.

Mock Trials and Mock Hearings

Mock trials and mock hearings can be among the most educational and most enjoyable of all alternative teaching techniques. Such trials and hearings permit students to see how the law applies to real-life situations and to use legal reasoning and research methods in the developments of a case. As a result, students become engaged with the material and learn much more about the law than they do when they face only daily lectures. The creation of a mock trial or a mock hearing exercise begins with the development of a fact pattern that illustrates one or more of the legal principles taught in a business law classroom. The fact patterns may be fashioned on a real case or on a hypothetical situation. Many business law textbooks offer sample fact patterns that can be used in these exercises, and some offer a complete mock trial package.

One serious shortcoming of mock trials is that only a limited number of students can participate as attorneys in the law firms. This limitation is unfortunate because most of the learning that goes on during a mock trial exercise occurs as the students research the law, apply the law to their fact pattern, fashion their arguments, and then deliver those arguments during trial. The mock hearing can be used as a solution to this problem. Like the preparation for a mock trial, preparation for a mock hearing begins with the fashioning of a fact pattern. The difference is that the mock hearing fact pattern involves one side filing a motion with the court. The most popular motion to file is a summary judgment motion. A *summary judgment motion* asks the court for an immediate judgment without going to trial because no dispute exists as to the facts; and, as a matter of law, the party who filed the motion is entitled to a judgment.

Preparation for and running a mock trial or a mock hearing requires a great deal of planning on the part of the instructor. The first step must be to ensure that the students are thoroughly versed in the legal principles that will be the focal point of the exercise. Students should be given at least three days of class time to prepare their cases. However, the more time that can be spared the better. The instructor must also factor in the extra time that some "law firms" will have to prepare because their hearing or trial is scheduled later in the semester. The teacher should also remember that the "law firms" that schedule their trial or hearing later in the semester also have the advantage of seeing how the other groups perform. Such an advantage should be factored into the grading process.

Choosing which students will play each role in a mock trial is one of the most difficult parts of the mock trial exercise. Typically, the instructor is tempted to team the best students with one another to insure at least one stellar performance. Instructors are also frequently inclined to give the most productive students key roles as attorneys in the case. Both approaches, however, can deprive many students of a valuable educational opportunity. For this reason, a better approach is for the students to volunteer for their respective positions in the trial or to have the positions assigned by a random lottery. This entire problem can be avoided, however, if the instructor opts for a mock hearing exercise instead of a mock trial because in a mock hearing, each student assumes the role of an attorney.

In a mock hearing, the class is divided into law firms of three to five students each. The instructor, or a willing colleague, takes the role of the judge. The only other job that needs to be filled in the mock hearing is the role of the bailiff, who can be chosen from among those students not presenting their cases on that particular day. The mock hearing begins with a presentation by the party that has brought the motion before the court. The judge can have the law firm present the facts, the nature of the motion, and the legal arguments that they believe will compel the judge to grant their motion. Students representing the other law firm then present opposing arguments. The judge can provide controversy by asking questions, challenging points of law, and compelling the students to defend their positions. Moreover, the assignment can be designed to require each student to play some speaking role in the hearing. Generally, one hearing can be covered in a single 50-minute class period. At the end of class, the judge calls for a recess. The judge should not render an opinion until the next class or at a later debriefing session to encourage the students to discuss the case after the hearing is completed.

Grading can be based on either an individual or a team basis. If grading is based on an individual basis, the instructor may want to require each student to prepare a written report on the issues argued before the court and on their personal assessment of how well the law firm did its job. If grading is done on a team basis, the teacher may evaluate the team presentation on whether the facts were presented properly, whether the legal points were clear and accurate, whether the arguments were persuasive, whether the team members responded well to the judge's questions, and whether each team member participated in the hearing itself. Should the instructor act as the judge, each hearing should be videotaped so that the instructor can freely play the role of the judge without having to worry about grading until later. The tape can also be a valuable debriefing tool for the students to view at a later time. Both law firms should supply the instructor with a written legal brief outlining the facts, the issues, and the legal rationale that they intend to present at the hearing.

Legal Debates
A study of business law also lends itself easily to the debate format. Legal debates can be fashioned much like the mock hearings, which require a fact pattern illustrating one or more of the legal principles taught in the business law classroom. The fact pattern can be fashioned to accomplish two objectives. One objective is to demonstrate two or more different ways to interpret the legality of the activities of the characters in the fact pattern. The second objective is to explore the advisability of preserving or changing the actual legal principle in question. For example, a fact pattern that involves an employee's claim of wrongful discharge could be used to explore whether a particular discharge really was wrongful and to debate the advisability of replacing the employment-at-will doctrine with a standard based on good faith and fair dealing.

Case Analysis Teamwork

Students can also benefit from teamwork in short case analysis exercises. This technique is used to give students a feel for how the principles of business law work in the real world. In addition, case analysis tests the students' understanding of legal principles by showing them how those principles work in a variety of settings. Generally, case analysis exercises involve four to five short fact patterns that illustrate the operation of a legal principle. Most patterns end in a question asking the students to determine the legal principle illustrated by the pattern or to decide which of the characters is liable. Such fact patterns are often available at the end of each chapter in many business law textbooks and in the student study guides and instructor manuals that accompany most textbooks.

Certainly students can decipher such case analysis exercises individually. However, the students often learn a great deal from one another when they work in small teams of three to five, as they attempt to understand the problem and look for its solution. For this reason, the instructor should give the fact patterns to the students at the end of a class period, so that they can have the time between classes to work on the cases independently. In this way, the students do not spend valuable class time simply reading the cases. Instead, they come to class armed with a knowledge of each case and prepared to discuss the issue with their teammates. Responses to the case analysis exercises can be handled in one of two ways. Either each student can turn in his or her own answers, or the entire team can return one set of answers.

News Analysis Teamwork

A similar technique, the news analysis exercise, works in much the same way. The difference is that in the news analysis approach, actual articles from newspapers, newsletters, and news magazines are used instead of cases. The advantage to this approach is that the students see how the law operates in the real world and develop an appreciation for the relevance and the practical side of business law. A disadvantage to this technique is that news stories rarely come packaged well enough to use in the classroom and may, therefore, require some editing. Also, unless the instructor uses the same stories over the span of several years, which somewhat defeats the purpose of demonstrating relevance, he or she has no guarantee that appropriate stories will appear in the news on time each semester.

The teacher can use the same procedure for news analysis exercises as that suggested for the case analysis exercises. As a variation on this approach, the instructor can require students to read newspapers and news magazines each week with the objective of developing a portfolio of news stories about general law and business law. The students can use the stories that they have collected as the basis for their teamwork sessions. To keep the stories current and to prevent portfolios from being handed down from one generation of students to the next, the instructor can require that all the news articles be dated after the start of the term.

Internet Research Projects

The Internet provides a wide range of possibilities for research projects. Virtually every area of the law is represented on a variety of Web sites. The following list represents a few of the possible types of assignments that can be fashioned for students using the Internet:

- The most recent news releases from the federal courts are found at http://www.uscourts.gov, a Web site maintained by the Administrative Office of the United States Courts. Students can access the Web site and prepare an oral or written report about a recent news release.

- Also located at http://www.uscourts.gov is *The Third Branch*, a newsletter published by the federal courts. Students can access the Web site and prepare an oral or written report about a recent article appearing in the newsletter.

- Students can access http://www.gama.com, the Web site of the Global Arbitration and Mediation Association and prepare an oral or written report on ADR.

- QuickForm Contracts maintains a Web site at http://www.quickforms.com, which can be accessed for help in drafting a contract. Students can access the Web site and draft a contract based on a hypothetical fact pattern. (Note: A fee is charged for using the forms on the site.)

- A list of resources on contracts is available from the WWW Virtual Law Library at http://www.law.indiana.edu/v-lib/. Students can select the topic "Contracts" for a wealth of information for reports on various aspects of contract law.

- Students can access http://www4.law.cornell.edu/uscode/42/ch21.html and prepare an oral or written report on the Civil Rights Act as it relates to employment.

- Students can access http://www.sbaonline.sba.gov/, the Web site of the Small Business Administration (SBA), and prepare an oral or written report on how to start a business.

As noted above, these assignments represent only a small sampling of the sites available for business law research on the Internet. Instructors may also consult the latest editions of most business law textbooks, many of which now include assignments tailored for the Internet.

SUMMARY

The study of business cannot be separated from a study of the law. In many ways the two disciplines overlap and intertwine with one another. Both business and the law must respond to changes in society and in the workplace. Recently, the law has responded to several challenges in such areas as alternate dispute resolution, government regulation, and computer technology. Despite these innovations, many traditional topics still form the foundation of business law. These topics include litigation, contract law, the law of sales, employment law, and the law of business associations. Because of its diverse nature, the law can be integrated into courses such as management, economics, marketing, and international business. The business law instructor can take advantage of a wide variety of different teaching techniques for creatively engaging students in the study of the law. These techniques included mock trials, mock hearings, legal debates, case analysis exercises, news analysis exercises, and Internet research.

REFERENCES

Cox, D. A. (1998). Overview of ADR: What is it? Private judging. In *The appropriate use of ADR in your practice.* (pp. 1e.1–1e.18). Columbus, OH: OSBA/CLE Institute.

Doan, J. N. (1998). The corporate forum and ADR: Use and drafting of ADR clauses. In *The appropriate use of ADR in your practice.* (pp. 2a.1-2a.3). Columbus, OH: OSBA/CLE Institute.

Drucker, P. F. (2002). *Managing in the Next Society.* New York: St. Martin's Press.

Etzel, M. J., Walker, B. J., & Stanton, W. J. (1997). *Marketing.* New York: McGraw-Hill.

Frey, M. A., & Frey, P. H. (2001). *Essentials of contract law.* Albany, NY: West Legal Studies/Thomson Learning.

Friedman, D. D. (2000). *Law's order: What economics has to do with the law and why it matters.* Princeton, NJ: Princeton University Press.

Friedman, J., & Strickler, G. (1997). *The law of employment discrimination.* Westbury, NY: Foundation Press.

Gerstl, H. N. (2000). *How to cut your legal bills in half: A guide to reclaiming America's promise: Affordable justice for all.* Monterey, CA: Millennium Publishing Group.

Handler, J. G. (1994). *Ballantine's law dictionary.* Legal Assistant Edition. Albany, NY: Delmar Publishers, Inc. and Lawyers Cooperative Publishing.

King, F. E. (1998). Overview of ADR: What is it? Early neutral evaluation. In *The appropriate use of ADR in your practice* (pp. 1c1–1c.2). Columbus, OH: OSBA/CLE Institute.

Krueger, E. H. (1998). The use of ADR in the courts: Settlement week. In *The appropriate use of ADR in your practice.* (pp. e.1–1e.18). Columbus, OH: OSBA/CLE Institute.

Meagher, J. M. (1998). Overview of ADR: What is it? Summary jury trial. In *The appropriate use of ADR in your practice.* (pp. 1d.1–1c.8). Columbus, OH: OSBA/CLE Institute.

Mondy, R. W., Sharplin, A., & Premeaux, S. R. (1991). *Management, concepts, practices, and skills.* Boston: Allyn and Bacon.

Mone, M. L. (1998). How government agencies use ADR: Negotiated-rule making. In *The appropriate use of ADR in your practice,* (pp. 4a.1-4a.19). Columbus, OH: OSBA/CLE Institute.

Mulligan, T. P., & Hutson, J. W. (1996). An overview of ADR. In *ADR for litigators: Strategies & tactics.* (pp. 1.1-1.8). Columbus, OH: OSBA/CLE Institute.

National Business Education Association. (2001). *National standards for business education: What America's students should know and be able to do in business* (2nd ed.). Reston, VA: Author.

Oran, D., & Tosti, M. (2000). *Oran's & Tosti's dictionary of the law.* Albany, NY: Thomson Learning.

Rothstein, M. A., & Liebman, L. (1998). *Employment law: Cases and materials.* New York: Foundation Press.

Schiller, B. Rd. (1999). *Essentials of economics.* New York: Irwin/McGraw-Hill.

Schneeman, A. (1993). *The law of corporations, partnerships, and sole proprietorships.* Albany, NY: Lawyers Cooperative.

Schneeman, A. (1995). *Paralegals in American law.* Albany, NY: Thomson Legal Publishers, Inc.

Towle, H. K., & Nielander, T. E. (1999). Electronic commerce: Selected issues in contracting. In *Computer law: Issues in the new millennium.* (pp. 2.1–2.20). Columbus, OH: OSBA/CLE Institute.

Entrepreneurship and E-Commerce

James W. Bovinet
Winona State University
Winona, Minnesota

Judith A. Bovinet
Winona State University
Winona, Minnesota

John P. Manzer
Indiana University–Purdue
University Ft. Wayne
Ft. Wayne, Indiana

Entrepreneurship education demonstrates to students how the activities of an entrepreneur are integrated into the business world. Business in the United States is changing rapidly, and much of that change is a direct result of the growth of the Internet. E-commerce continues to increase geometrically, and this expansion has opened up many opportunities for entrepreneurs everywhere. Entrepreneurship education introduces students to these opportunities, familiarizes them with the characteristics of entrepreneurs, and helps them to understand the role and importance of entrepreneurship in society.

This chapter discusses the nature and role of entrepreneurship in the economy and suggests learning activities for entrepreneurship education programs. The chapter also introduces business practices on the Internet, discusses how e-commerce affects the role of entrepreneurs in the economy, and suggests related resources and student activities.

ENTREPRENEURSHIP EDUCATION PROGRAMS AND STANDARDS

Entrepreneurship is taught at various levels of education, from creating awareness at the elementary level to developing business start-up skills at the postsecondary level. At the secondary level, entrepreneurship is taught as a separate course or as part of another course such as basic business, marketing, or economics. E-commerce is also taught as a separate course or as part of another course, typically entrepreneurship or marketing. Whether entrepreneurship or e-commerce are taught separately or within another business course, the basic concepts and instructional strategies are similar (Clodfelter, 2002).

The *National Standards for Business Education* (National Business Education Association, 2001) provides a basis for teaching entrepreneurship at various levels. Entrepreneurship integrates the basic functions of business, including management, marketing, accounting, and finance, as well as economics and the legal environment of business. The *National Standards* (NBEA, 2001) addresses the following concepts that are necessary for entrepreneurship education: entrepreneurs and entrepreneurship opportunities, marketing, economics, finance, accounting, management, global markets, legal issues, and business plans.

DEFINITION OF AN ENTREPRENEUR

An *entrepreneur* is an individual who identifies a business opportunity or need, establishes a business based on that opportunity, and operates and maintains that business (NBEA, 2001). Because the business world is constantly changing, entrepreneurs analyze the process of change in order to discover opportunities such as consumer needs for new product or services that are not being fulfilled.

Entrepreneurs take advantage of new wealth-creating opportunities that constantly arise from economic, social, and technological changes. Creating opportunity from change has always been part of the culture in the United States. Today, an entrepreneurial renaissance is transforming the business world. Entrepreneurs develop innovations to take advantage of such opportunities and then create companies to bring the innovations to market (National Commission on Entrepreneurship, 2000).

Successful entrepreneurs analyze current economic trends and seek information from many sources such as the Internet, journals, and trade in an attempt to garner as much knowledge as possible before deciding on a business venture (Francis & Banning, 2001). However, students should understand that entrepreneurs must be willing to take significant, calculated, and personal risks in building their companies. Although the profit motive is important, entrepreneurship occurs primarily because imaginative individuals desire success through innovation (Douglas, 2002).

Rapidly evolving business opportunities throughout the world provide many opportunities for today's entrepreneurs. Although radio took 38 years to reach 50 million listeners, the Internet is expected to reach 50 million users in five years (Acs, 1999). This rapid change is providing many opportunities for success in e-commerce.

ENTREPRENEURSHIP EDUCATION

Entrepreneurship education is an ideal way for business teachers to help students meet the challenges of the new century's economy. Students become enthusiastic when they perceive that the skills they are learning will be useful in any career they choose— whether or not they own their own businesses (Ries, 2000).

Although entrepreneurship education should be a lifelong learning process (Ashmore, 2001), entrepreneurship is often a recent addition to school curricula. At the elementary and middle school level, entrepreneurship education programs focus on the basics of the U.S. economy, career opportunities, and the need to master basic skills such as math, English, speech, economics, and personal finance. These skills are the building blocks of success in a free-enterprise system. At the secondary level, entrepreneurship primarily focuses on concepts necessary for owning a small business. Advanced secondary and postsecondary students integrate previously learned business skills such as management, marketing, accounting, and finance and develop a business plan for starting a specific company.

INSTRUCTIONAL STRATEGIES FOR ENTREPRENEURSHIP

A foundation in economics is essential to entrepreneurship. The basic concepts of economics are identified by the National Business Education Association and the National Council on Economic Education, as discussed in Chapter 13. The concepts of scarcity, opportunity cost, productive resources, market system, costs of production, supply and demand, and marginal analysis need to be taught or reviewed in order to convey entrepreneurial concepts and issues effectively. Teachers should introduce or reinforce economic concepts throughout all units of instruction. A list of Internet resources for entrepreneurial education is shown in Table 1.

Scherrer (2002) provides guidelines for the development of a rationale and objectives for an entrepreneurship course: the course should be designed to give students realistic entrepreneurial experiences and apply the skills and competencies they learn to

Table 1. Internet Resources

Center for Entrepreneurial Leadership – Clearinghouse on Entrepreneurship Education	http://www.celcee.edu/
Centre for Entrepreneurship Education and Development	http://www.ceed.ednet.ns.ca/
The Consortium for Entrepreneurship Education	www.entre-ed.org
Enterprise Ambassador USA	www.fgse.nova.edu/eausa
Entrepreneurship Education on the Web – St. Louis University	http://eweb.slu.edu/Default.htm
Glencoe/McGraw-Hill Educational Publishing	www.glencoe.com/home.html
Journal of Entrepreneurship Education	http://www.alliedacademies.org/entrepreneurship/jee.html
The Kauffman Center for Entrepreneurial Leadership	www.emkf.org/index.cfm

KidsWay Inc.	www.kidsway.com
Lifelong Learning for Entrepreneurship Education Professionals	http://www.lleep.net/
The National Foundation for Teaching Entrepreneurship	www.nfte.com
REAL Enterprises	www.realenterprises.org
South-Western Educational Publishing	www.swep.com
U.S. Small Business Administration	http://www.sba.gov

realistic projects. Junior Achievement provides many entrepreneurship learning activities for students at the middle and high school levels. Current events assignments, personal assessments, student interviews, panel discussions, demographic analysis, marketing plans, biographies, franchise analysis, games, and case studies are all appropriate learning strategies for entrepreneurship.

Current Events Assignments

A current events assignment is a learning activity that generates a high level of student interest in entrepreneurship. Using newspapers as a resource, students document the contributions of entrepreneurs. This assignment requires students to have regular access to a daily newspaper, either in a traditional format or on the Internet. The *Wall Street Journal Classroom Edition* or *Online Edition* is an ideal resource, supplemented by a local newspaper. Students read, analyze, and synthesize information related to entrepreneurship and prepare a written report in the form of a journal summary and a short oral report to the class. This assignment allows students to learn about the numerous contributions of entrepreneurs to the economy in terms of new and improved business services, employment opportunities, and resources for economic growth and productivity. Students can participate in this activity in small groups or as individuals. This activity provides an opportunity for students to discover the importance of risk assessment and identify acceptable levels of risk.

Assessment of this activity can involve English and speech teachers to evaluate students' efforts. Students can answer a short essay assignment about what they believe are important recent contributions of entrepreneurs. An additional element of this activity is for students to develop a profile of successful entrepreneurs based upon their readings. The NBEA *National Standards* category "Characteristics of an Entrepreneur" can be the basis for helping students identify their own personality traits from their newspaper journal entries.

Personal Assessments

A related activity is for students to assess their own personalities as future entrepreneurs as perceived by friends, teachers, and families. Students can have the option of reporting the results to the class for feedback. Although students should be aware that personalities develop and change over time, they may draw preliminary conclusions about their own potential as entrepreneurs.

Students need to be aware that entrepreneurs are involved in all sizes of businesses, both large and small. The teacher can provide reinforcement by citing examples of entrepreneurs in the local community, as well as nationally recognized entrepreneurs, such as Bill Gates or the late Sam Walton (Scherrer, 2002). Another research activity is for students to develop a personal list of the costs and benefits of starting a business. Some students may have already been engaged as entrepreneurs and may be willing to share their experiences with the class. Parents or friends who own a local business may be invited to visit the class to share their experiences. These activities permit students to develop a complete picture of the life of a business owner and realize how much time, dedication, and energy are required to start a business.

Student Interviews

The skills and knowledge of successful entrepreneurs can be tapped to help students understand how businesses operate. In small groups of up to four, students can interview local business owners and ask them to identify specific management skills that are needed to run a business. Students might also ask owners to rank their responses. Student findings can be presented in the form of a short written report. Students' reports can serve as a basis for a class discussion on entrepreneurial management strategies, including how to avoid common mistakes made by managers of small businesses.

Panel Discussions

An important question is how entrepreneurs select the type of product or service they sell. A related question is how they change the product and service mix in order to increase their profits. These are excellent research questions for a small group activity involving students serving on a discussion panel. Another panel variation involves student teams interviewing local business owners to determine how they began marketing their products and services.

Demographic Analysis

The ability to identify important demographic trends is essential for entrepreneurial success. Students can maintain a journal with entries from magazines and newspaper articles and collect radio and television reports on important demographic trends. In preparation for this activity, the teacher should review the demographics and discuss how they help the entrepreneur to market particular goods and services. Based on their research, students can develop lists of products and services they believe would be affected, in terms of either a growing potential market or a declining market. The assignment can include identifying specific new types of products and services that might be created by these possible demographic trends.

Marketing Plans

Marketing and product development are additional areas for students to explore from the perspective of an entrepreneur. Students can develop a marketing plan for a new product, including determining a marketing budget. In addition, they can create a series of radio and print advertisements appropriate for a new business.

Students also can identify new ways to sell existing products and services and incorporate them in their marketing plans. For example, students can begin with a list of ten products and list three alternative uses for each product. They can prepare answers to the following questions: How could this alternative use be communicated to potential customers? What types of advertising are used to communicate to potential customers? What types of advertising themes could be used? Are the alternative uses offensive in any way to current users of the product? Students could complete this activity in small groups and report their findings to the entire class.

Biographies

Another related learning activity is for students to discuss biographies of famous entrepreneurs in small groups and present group reports to the entire class. Students can highlight the characteristics of these entrepreneurs that contributed to the success of their ventures. Based on these biographies, students can create bulletin board displays in the classroom or nearby hallways. These assignments can develop students' appreciation of the personal qualities and business knowledge that lead to the achievement of successful entrepreneurs.

Franchise Analysis

Students need to understand that entrepreneurs use various forms of business organizations to accomplish their goals. Franchises are one of the most frequently used methods of business organization used by entrepreneurs. A franchise involves product or service distribution that is governed by contract. Franchises have a number of important advantages, including the opportunity for expertise in the marketing and distribution of a particular group of products and services that the purchaser of the franchise may not have. Second, the franchises may have specialized management systems that minimize costs and maximize revenues. Third, the franchises can provide programs, assistance, and name recognition for the business. However, franchises do limit the owner's ability to do what he or she wants with the business. For example, a franchise may be required to buy supplies from particular suppliers and follow certain restrictive policies and procedures when operating the business.

Students can research selected franchises available in their communities. This assignment involves requesting information from various national or regional franchises. Students can compare various franchises in terms of required start-up capital, background requirements, location factors, start-up timelines, and other pertinent factors. Beginning with the 20 top franchises featured annually by *Entrepreneur Magazine*, students can identify the products and services sold by these franchises, some common advertising themes, and what they believe to be the future of each franchise, both locally and nationally. This activity can also provide material for a classroom or hallway bulletin board display.

Games

Business simulation games can develop entrepreneurial skills such as risk assessment and strategic planning. Organizations such as Junior Achievement and the Stock Market Foundation offer simulations in these areas, as discussed in Chapter 13.

Case Studies

Case studies are an excellent closure activity after students complete a unit of instruction. A short case is appropriate for high school students to use when answering case analysis questions. The following example illustrates a typical case study:

> Dick Freeland, an ironworker in Iowa 35 years ago, needed a second job and began washing dishes and waiting on tables at a local Pizza Hut restaurant, which was a relatively unknown company at the time. He now owns more than 44 Pizza Hut Restaurants in 19 counties in Indiana and Ohio and also owns 3 Kentucky Fried Chicken franchises. At age 65, he is now facing an organizational decision regarding his successor. He has searched for a leader to replace him and he is waiting six months to make a final decision on his replacement. One aspect of Dick Freeland's business is the successful culture he has established over the years, as he owns 14 of the top 20 Pizza Hut restaurants in sales volume among the 7,700 restaurants within the chain nationally, and the top three restaurants are his. His culture is based upon the fact that the customer is number one, followed by the employees, and then third, the stockholders. He learned the importance of treating people well from his father, who was a clergyman. He believes that the effectiveness of his management teams is one of the major factors in his success. Team members are impressed by Dick's ability to listen and delegate effectively. Following through is another part of this culture, which recognizes that just saying you intend to do something is not enough—you have to get it done. Dick Freeland's successful ventures started because he was willing to work harder for less pay to learn the business that he now owns.

> 1. How would you describe his business philosophy?

> 2. Why might he wish to work so hard at a second job?

> 3. Why are employees probably more important than stockholders?

> 4. Is his management team important to him?

> 5. Why are well-treated employees important?

This short case can provide the basis for a class discussion or small group activity.

Business Plans

Advanced secondary and postsecondary students should learn to develop a viable business plan specifically targeted to their product or service idea. Because no business plan is acceptable for every situation, each business plan must be customized for a particular project. An outline for a student business plan is illustrated in Table 2.

Table 2. Outline for Student Business Plan	
1. Cover Letter	a. Actual letter to precede loan information b. Introduce principals, give general description of business mission and goals, and give reason for desiring loan (if necessary)
2. Cover Sheet	a. Name, address, and phone number of business b. Name of principals (Who will own business? Who will manage business? etc.) c. Table of contents (List the items in the business plan.)
3. The Business	a. Business description (What business will you be in? What are you going to sell?) b. Potential market and target customer (marketing plan, strategic marketing, etc.) c. Number and skill of competitors and cumulative draw in location d. Proposed business location description (advantages, disadvantages) e. Legal form of business (sole proprietorship, partnership, corporation) f. Personnel plans (employees, management, etc.)

4. Statement of Image-Building Strategy	a. Company profile (the mission "beyond sales"):
	  (1) Strategic plan for image building and community relations
	  (2) Crisis management plan
	  (3) Company philanthropic mission
	  (4) Publicity techniques
	b. Company advertising and promotion plan:
	  (1) Strategic plan for creating awareness of business
	  (2) Advertising techniques (media, direct mail, cable TV, etc.)
	  (3) Promotional techniques (point-of-purchase, demos, coupons, etc.)
	  (4) Budgetary concerns

5. Financial Data	a. Sources and application of funding (Doing what with capital?) b. Capital equipment list (if necessary) c. Break-even analysis d. Finishing costs (remodeling, redecoration, ADA requirements, etc.) e. Working capital requirements (fixed costs for 3-6 months) f. Pro forma income statements (by month for 1st year, by quarter for 2nd year) g. Pro forma cash flow statement (by month, for 1st year, by quarter for 2nd year) h. Pro forma balance sheet
6. Supporting Documents	a. Résumés of principals b. Personal financial statements c. Letters of reference for principals d. Letters of intent (to sell, to buy, to extend credit, etc.) e. Copies of leases, contracts, and other necessary legal documents f. Other supporting information (trademarks, copyright, patents, etc.)

The teacher can add or delete from this outline according to the various classroom projects that are required. A grading rubric can be adapted from the final outline, as a checklist to determine if each student and/or student team has included all the necessary items in their business plans. Following this checklist, instructors should compare business plan sections among the students and comment on the effectiveness of their written presentations. For additional information about the development of appropriate rubrics, see Chapter 7.

E-COMMERCE

Combining entrepreneurship with e-commerce provides a synergistic approach that can enlighten and motivate students. *E-commerce* is any process that a business entity conducts over a computer-mediated network. E-commerce can be conducted between businesses (business-to-business or B2B), between businesses and consumers (Internet), and within a business (intranets) (Hisrich & Peters, 2002). The consumer e-commerce market has grown exponentially, with an increase from $9.2 billion in 1999 to more than an estimated $120 billion in 2003.

E-Tail

E-tail is retail business conducted on the Internet. The act of shopping is a social phenomenon, involving human interaction that is not available on the Web. The key to successful e-tail is consumers' willingness to purchase goods and services at a distance, without tangible feedback (touching the merchandise) or human contact (salespeople, expert advice, etc.). During the early growth of e-commerce, e-tail was expected to hold a distinct advantage over standard "brick and mortar" establishments. E-tail businesses could avoid building or renting costly stores that come burdened with rent, utility bills, and maintenance expenses. Most importantly, Internet businesses can avoid hiring a sales force to deal personally with customers. Labor is inherently the most expensive part of a retail operation (wages, payroll taxes, and especially benefits), and the turnover in this industry sector (retailing) is historically very high.

In cyberspace, a store never closes (time utility). The market or selling area has no geographic limitation–the world is the marketplace (place utility). E-commerce enterprises can function in an inexpensive warehouse space with vast shelving. For these reasons, retailers have recognized the potential of the Internet, as observed by Berman (2001):

> Economists get dizzy thinking about all this. . . . Add a few servers, a dozen more Web pages, a couple more customer-service reps. . . . This kind of growth . . . defies conventional valuation and make[s] the usual measure of retailing–same-store sales, sales per square foot–seem like Roman numerals, or the abacus, relics of another age. (p.169)

The reality has become something quite different. The malls are still packed, where traditional outlet shoppers can touch and evaluate the merchandise first hand. Shopping in a traditional setting allows an immediate purchase, with the instant gratification that spurs so many American activities.

E-tail is expected to continue to increase dramatically. Nearly one-third of adults over age 18 shop online, and the demographics are skewed toward high-income and high-education brackets (Brown, 2001). This target market is highly lucrative and relatively simple to reach.

With a few exceptions such as Amazon and eBay, which are online-only retailers, customers seem to like the combination of "bricks" (bricks-and-mortar, traditional retail outlets) and "clicks" (online e-tail sites) in the same business. Often, shoppers will peruse products at a mall and then order them over the Internet. In addition, many customers prefer the ease of ordering online and then returning any products to a brick-and-mortar location. A successful business plan typically incorporates a synergy between the "bricks" and "clicks" side of the same business (Greenfield, 1999).

Advantages/disadvantages of online retailing. Advantages of online retailing are numerous. Capital investment is much lower, and multiple stores may be unnecessary. Internet customers can usually be charged before inventory bills are paid by the e-tailer; this procedure creates a positive cash flow for the business. Stores are open around the clock without the ensuing labor expenses. The shopping experience can be customized, as e-tailers have the ability to contact individual customers and ask them about their products or services and what changes the customers would like to see. E-tailing facilitates the addition of new product and services. Businesses can expand geographically in the United States or even begin exporting to international customers.

E-tailing also has a number of disadvantages. Because comparison shopping is fast and easy on the Internet, competition is great and profit margins are low or nonexistent. Some search engines provide price comparison shopping for customers with a mouse click. Building customer relationships is especially critical when doing business on the Internet. Successful e-tailers attempt to maximize all forms of customer contact (e-mail, telephone, conventional mail, etc.), and every one of these activities increases labor expenses and impacts the bottom line of the firm. Shipping and delivery costs tend to increase with added Web use. In addition, returns are historically higher on the Internet than in traditional stores or with the use of catalogs. These expenses add inventory costs and cut profit margins.

Building an efficient Web site is challenging. The creation of a site often depends on hiring outside consulting assistance. In addition, the constant changing and reworking that are required to keep a site up-to-date, as well as attractive, add a further expenses (Evans, 2001).

Finally, credit card abuse has been a major problem, and many customers are wary about the security of online purchasing. Although security problems are gradually being solved, many people still view nontraditional merchandising as a threat to the security of their credit cards and bank accounts (Evans, 2001).

Basic operations of e-commerce. The Internet encompasses two basic operations for e-commerce entrepreneurs. The *front end* is comprised of the Web site itself and its components including search capabilities, speed, shopping cart, secure payment, customer contacts to the business, feedback to the customer, etc. The *back end* represents the integration of distribution (inventory storage, delivery, etc.) with the sales activities.

Most business mistakes made in the early days of e-commerce resulted from ignoring the importance of the back end. A well-designed and functioning Web site is useless if the warehouse and delivery activities are unable to deliver the product in a timely and accurate fashion. Delivery problems have led to the downfall and bankruptcy of many relatively new businesses.

Factors affecting an entrepreneur's decision to go online are listed below:

a. The entrepreneur needs to have the skills to create an efficient Web site or the capital to have one designed.

b. The products considered for the business should be easily and economically delivered (for instance, food has continually proven to be a difficult e-business).

c. The product should be attractive to a large segment of the population (making sure the target market is of sufficient size to warrant the investment in a Web site).

d. The business should be prepared to ship out of its geographic area (and consider opening its vistas to international markets as well).

e. An e-business should represent significant cost reductions over a similar brick-and-mortar operation (lower overhead costs).

f. The e-businessperson needs to be able to attract visitors to the site and maintain their interest long enough for a possible sale.

g. The Web site must never be allowed to become predictable or outdated. Constant change and improvement is the rule of e-commerce.

Class Web Site

A low-cost method of introducing e-commerce and entrepreneurship to a group of students is to allow them to create a class Web site, if computer access is available at the school. This activity should be interdisciplinary in order to teach the business connections between accounting, Web design, marketing, finance, management, etc. This activity is ideal for a Junior Achievement project, as discussed in Chapter 13. If the development of a Web site is not feasible, assigned projects can include evaluating the effectiveness of existing e-commerce Web sites. Guidelines for assessing a Web site are illustrated in Table 3.

Every teacher should be aware of the acceptable use policy (AUP) for the school district, the individual school, and the computer lab. Concerns that are commonly

Table 3. Guidelines for Assessing a Web Site	
1. Overall Look	A site should be clean, simple, and attractive. Underwhelm the user. White space is less intimidating than excessive copy.
2. Home Page	Think billboard. Tell visitors exactly who you are and what you do right up front – simply, clearly, and immediately.
3. Message	Give visitors a reason to stay. What is in it for surfers if they stay? What makes your site different from others in the same industry? Consider using contests, rewards, and incentives.
4. Speed	Use graphics judiciously. Try to keep each page and all its components under 20 KB. Graphics consume bandwidth–reduce dimensions and use compression software to squeeze out extra bytes.

5. Text Legibility	A simple font on a light background is usually best. Use large fonts. Older people are heavy Web users and appreciate readability. Separate wide blocks of text into columns. Leave plenty of white space.
6. Copy Quality	Use short headings at the beginning of each paragraph. Keep paragraphs and sentences short. Talk directly to the customer. Fill your site with regularly updated content.
7. Navigation	Make the site easy to navigate. Include a link to the home page on every page of the site. Use a navigation bar.
8. Contact Form	Collect only as much information as necessary. Tell customers what the information will be used for. Make sure that your site is safe and tell your customers why it is safe.
9. Testimonials	Prominently list testimonials from good customers.
10. Mistakes	No broken links, missing graphics, or anything that does not run correctly. Check the site constantly with all the popular browsers.
11. Customer Service	Focus on customer service and relationship building. Give customers a way to contact you. Follow up on all sales (e-mail confirmation, at least). List the phone number prominently.

addressed include acceptable content, the use of appropriate manners on the Internet ("netiquette"), and parental permission and contact guidelines. Many school districts do not permit school-sponsored Web sites to be used for commercial purposes. School policies should be posted and taught to the students.

The technology aspect of e-commerce should not be overemphasized, as a general course in entrepreneurship should not be taught as a computer class. Time constraints and other necessary projects limit the time devoted to a Web development project. Some students who already possess advanced computer skills may be willing to assist with development of the class Web site. A separate course in e-commerce, however, can include a major emphasis on Web site development.

SUMMARY
All students, regardless of their occupational plans, benefit from a basic understanding of entrepreneurial activities and how these activities affect our economy. Entrepreneurship courses integrate all the functions of a business such as accounting, management, marketing, and finance that the managers of successful small business must address. Entrepreneurs start new businesses that take advantage of opportunities that arise from economic, social, and technological changes.

Entrepreneurship education programs should introduce or review basic economic concepts. Appropriate learning strategies for entrepreneurship include current events assignments, personal assessments, student interviews, panel discussions, demographic analysis, marketing plans, biographies, franchise analysis, games, case studies, and business plans.

Combining entrepreneurship with e-commerce can enlighten and motivate students. E-commerce has increased dramatically in recent years and provides a vast opportunity for entrepreneurs. E-commerce can be taught separately or as part of an entrepreneurship, marketing, or other business course. Students can develop a class Web site as a project for learning about e-commerce. Teachers are responsible for ensuring that students and projects comply with the acceptable use policy of the school.

REFERENCES
Acs, Z. J. (Ed.). (1999). *Are small firms important?* Boston: Kluwer Academic Publishers.
Ashmore, C. (2001). *Building an entrepreneurial culture.* Columbus, OH: The Consortium for Entrepreneurship Education. Retrieved August 1, 2002, from http://www.entre-ed.org/index.htm
Berman, D. K. (2000, June 12). Shop online: Pick up at the store. *BusinessWeek,* 169.
Brown, J. (2001, December 24). Shoppers are beating a path to the Web. *BusinessWeek,* 124.
Clodfelter, R. (2002). Entrepreneurship and creating the online business. In A. Remp (Ed.), *Technology, methodoloy, and business education* (Yearbook No. 40, pp.196-210). Reston, VA: National Business Education Association.
Douglas, E. J. (2002, Spring). Self-employment as a career choice. *Entrepreneurship: Theory and Practice, 26*(3), 81-91.
Evans, J. R. (2001, Fall). The emerging role of the Internet in marketing education: From traditional teaching to technology-based education. *Marketing Education Review,* 1-19. Retrieved August 1, 2002, from http://cbpa.louisville.edu/mer/JREmer.pdf
Francis, D.H., & Banning, K. (2001, Spring). Who wants to be an entrepreneur? *Journal of the Academy of Business Education, 2*(1), 5-11.
Greenfield, K. T. (1999, December 27). Clicks and bricks. *Time, 154*(26), 88-90.
Hisrich, R. D., & Peters, M. P. (2002). *Entrepreneurship.* New York: McGraw-Hill.
National Business Education Association. (2001). *National standards for business education: What America's students should know and be able to do in business* (2nd ed.). Reston, VA: Author.
National Commission on Entrepreneurship (NCE). (2000). *Embracing innovation: Entrepreneurship and American economic growth.* Retrieved August 1, 2002, from http://www.NCOE.org/research/whitepap.pdf
Ries, E. (2000). Owning their education. *Techniques, 75,* 26-32.
Scherrer, B. (2002). Making entrepreneurship come alive in the classroom: How to develop a national award-winning entrepreneurship program. *Business Education Forum, 56*(3), 40-42.

International Business

Les R. Dlabay
Lake Forest College
Lake Forest, Illinois

The presence of the global marketplace and the subsequent need for international business education are evident in the products Americans buy, in the companies where people work, and in the cross-cultural interactions that occur daily. Because economic interdependence is now commonplace, students must be prepared to live and work in a system that facilitates global business activities. This chapter presents an overview of global trends and topics, along with resources and instructional activities for international business units and courses.

GLOBAL BUSINESS TRENDS

Globalization is commonly viewed as the process of expanding business activities in order to gain a worldwide perspective. Organizations attempt to use a standardized approach to business and marketing activities that extends across different cultures and levels of economic development (Dlabay, 1998), and therein lies the challenge. The growth of globalization occurs in a context of change: changing political environments, expanding regional integration, advancing technology and information systems, and the increasing cultural homogeneity created by the global reach of Western products and brands.

Changing Political Environments

While most visible in Eastern Europe, emerging political freedoms have set a new tone for global business relationships. Similar political and economic directions are also evident in Africa, Asia, and Latin America. As ideologies evolve and economies move from central planning models to market economies, they create new opportunities for foreign investment and entrepreneurial efforts.

Expanding Regional Integration

Although globalization maintains center stage in most international trade discussions, regional economic integration is also taking hold. Trade agreements and organizations connect nations in close proximity. The North American Free Trade Agreement (NAFTA), the European Union, and the Mercosur in South America laid the groundwork for this movement. More recently, emerging markets in Central America, the Caribbean, and Africa have created trading blocs to compete in the world economy (Hill, 2003).

Advancing Technology and Information Systems

Throughout history, innovations have enhanced the quantity and quality of international trade. Improved worldwide telecommunications systems, freight containerization, and overnight delivery services have expanded global activities. Today e-commerce has opened up global opportunities to organizations previously restricted by geographic, financial, or political constraints (Dlabay, 2001).

Increasing Cultural Homogeneity

The expansion of global companies, products, and brands has occurred in all regions of the world. Cultural homogeneity will likely intensify as the Internet makes products and brands as easily available in Egypt and Thailand as in Houston and Miami. Many observers are concerned with the loss of cultural identity associated with global business expansion. Younger generations tend to prefer modern ideas, products, and activities more than traditional aspects of their culture.

INTERNATIONAL BUSINESS CONTENT

For an organization to be a successful international presence, education in global issues should be a prerequisite. "Business educators have primary responsibility for providing the necessary business-related education and training for full participation in the global economy" (Policies Commission for Business and Economic Education, 1992). This mandate has created the foundation for the international business curriculum.

Several studies have identified the content and competencies forming the foundation for international business instruction. Javalgi et al. (1997) categorized several areas of international business competence, such as identifiying business opportunities, conducting international business transactions, appraising diverse cultures, and communicating in global settings. Zeliff, Herbers, Meyers, and Sly (1999) identified 80 international business competencies that might be addressed when implementing global instruction.

These and other investigations are synthesized in the *National Standards for Business Education* chapter entitled, "The Role of International Business in Business Education" (National Business Education Association, 2001). This curriculum guide outlines a comprehensive set of performance standards for teaching international business. These standards focus on the following areas: international trade foundations, global business environment, international business communication, global business ethics, organizational structures, trade relations, international management, international marketing, and international finance.

International Trade Foundations

Business transactions between companies in different countries are based on two economic principles—absolute advantage and comparative advantage. *Absolute advantage* exists when a country can produce a good or service at a lower cost than other countries. This situation may occur as a result of an abundance of natural resources or raw materials in a country. When a *comparative advantage* exists, a country specializes in the production of a good or service that it is relatively more efficient in providing.

Products bought by a company or government from businesses in other countries are called *imports.* From the point of view of the seller, *exports* are products sold to companies or governments in other countries.

A common measure of a country's international business activity is b*alance of trade*—the difference between the value of a country's exports and imports. Balance of trade does not include all international business transactions, just imports and exports. In contrast, *balance of payments* measures the total flow of money coming into a country minus the total flow of money going out. Included in this economic measurement are exports, imports, investments, tourist spending, and financial assistance (Dlabay & Scott, 2001).

Global Business Environment

Geographic, economic, cultural, and political factors create the foundation for exporting activities and global business activities. Location, climate, terrain, waterways, natural resources, and other geographic factors are fundamental to understanding international trade relations. Due to topography, products commonly transported by truck or train in some countries may require oxen or other traditional transportation modes in other countries. Various studies reveal a need for expanded emphasis on geography instruction in all educational settings (Hise, Davidow, & Troy, 2000).

The level of economic development reflects a country's ability to create wealth and to participate in international trade. An *industrialized country* has a high level of industrialization with advanced technology, a highly educated population, and a well-established infrastructure. A *less-developed country (LDC)* is a country with little economic wealth and an emphasis on agriculture or mining. Between these extremes are *developing countries*—nations characterized by improving educational systems, increasing technology, and expanding industries (Dlabay & Scott, 2001).

In addition to concerns about geography and level of development, culture— traditions, language, family relationships, education, and religion—must be considered when developing business strategies. Behaviors such as using an improper gesture, giving an inappropriate gift, or negotiating in an offensive manner can damage business relationships.

Legal and political concerns also present challenges to businesses that market worldwide. Global companies commonly face trade barriers such as tariffs, import quotas, and packaging regulations. These legal restrictions, along with political instability, can result in higher operating costs and lost international sales. Enforcement of intellectual property protections can also create difficulties when distributing products covered by brand names, copyrights, patents, and trademarks. For example, counterfeit t-shirts with characters owned by Disney or other companies are commonly sold in many areas of the world.

International Business Communication

Greeting methods, formal titles, nonverbal interactions, and negotiation styles are some of the common issues encountered when communicating across cultures. Facilitating mutually beneficial global business transactions, implementing improved technology, encouraging cooperative ventures, and cultivating economic development in emerging markets can be achieved through effective international business communication (Scott, 1999).

Global Business Ethics

Culture and political environments can frequently influence business practices. Aggressive companies based in Europe and Asia commonly use payoffs to gain access to new markets. While some countries may consider this payment a normal business expense, U.S. companies that cooperate with such a system might face fines or prison sentences. Government regulation of business practices such as safety, environmental pollution, and advertising vary widely throughout the world (Amin, 1996).

Organizational Structures

Forms of business ownership and entrepreneurial opportunities differ widely around the world. International companies may use various business modes in different countries (Dlabay & Scott, 2001). For example, cereal brands such as Cheerios, Lucky Charms, and Trix with the name "Nestle" printed on the box instead of the familiar "General Mills" label are not marketed in the United States. However, in Latin America, Europe, and the Middle East, these packages are a common sight. Cereal Partners Worldwide (CPW) is a joint venture that combines the popular products of General Mills with the brand name and distribution system of Nestle.

A *joint venture* is an agreement between two or more companies (frequently from different countries) to share a business project. The main benefit of a joint venture is the sharing of raw materials, shipping facilities, management skills, technology, or production facilities. Joint venture arrangements, sometimes called *strategic partnerships* or *strategic alliances*, are frequently used for manufacturing.

Management contracting involves a company selling only its management skills. Hotels, hospitals, and information technology organizations may use this method. *Contract manufacturing* occurs when a company in a foreign country produces an item for another company. This relationship allows a business to enter a foreign market without investing in production facilities (Dlabay & Scott, 2001).

Licensing is selling the right to use some intangible property (production process, trademark, or brand name) for a fee or royalty. A *franchise* is the right to use a company name or business process in a specific way. Franchising and licensing both involve a royalty payment for the right to use a process or identifiable name. Licensing usually involves a manufacturing process, while franchising commonly involves selling a product or service.

As companies increase their global commitments, funds may be used to buy real estate or other resources in other countries, commonly called *foreign direct investment (FDI)*. The *wholly owned subsidiary,* which is an independent company owned by a parent company, is also a type of FDI. Multinational companies frequently have wholly owned subsidiaries in various countries that are the result of foreign direct investment. Previously U.S.-owned businesses such as Burger King, Pillsbury, and Green Giant are now owned by foreign companies (Dlabay & Scott, 2001).

International Trade Relations
Trade relations among countries are affected by strategic trade alliances such as NAFTA, that seek to promote free trade among countries. Tariffs, quotas, and various laws restrict trade between countries (National Standards for Business Education, 2001).

International Management
Managerial practices and styles differ widely from one country to another. Human resource management issues include child labor practices and laws, compensation, benefits, labor-management practices, health and safety issues, environmental concerns, employee relocation, and career paths (National Standards for Business Education, 2001).

International Marketing
When a company does business in another country, it must decide whether to use a "standardized" product or a "customized" product. While some products such as cameras, computers, or motor vehicles can be sold almost the same throughout the world, others must be adapted. For example, the McDonald's menu is revised in different parts of the world based on tastes, customs, and religious beliefs. In the Philippines and other countries, Tide detergent is sold in three forms—powder, liquid, and bar. The detergent bar is used for clothes washed by hand in areas without washing machines (Dlabay & Scott, 2001).

International Finance

Foreign exchange is the process of converting the currency of one country into the currency of another country. The e*xchange rate* is the amount of currency of one country that can be traded for one unit of the currency of another country. Currency exchange rates among countries are affected by three main factors: a nation's balance of payments; economic conditions, such as inflation and interest rates; and political stability (Dlabay & Scott, 2001).

CURRICULUM IMPLEMENTATION PATTERNS

The international business curriculum may consist of integrated instructional units or specialized international courses. At the high school level, international business units often are integrated into other business courses such as basic business, marketing, keyboarding, computer applications, and cooperative office education. Some high schools offer a semester course in international business. At the two-year or four-year college level, international business concepts are often integrated into other courses such as management, marketing, and business communication. In many colleges and universities, specialized international courses are included in the business curriculum, which may include a comprehensive international business program.

Integrated Instructional Units

Most people have either traveled to other countries or know someone who has traveled. These experiences can provide a foundation for instruction. Inviting guest speakers, integrating videos, planning a foreign vacation, and exchanging e-mail messages with people in other countries can enhance the international climate of a course (Glenn, 2002). Other teaching ideas are available in *Creative Teaching Ideas for International Business* (National Business Education Association & International Society for Business Education, 1996). This resource book offers ready-to-use assignments for various international business topics.

In an accounting course, a starting point might be the study of recordkeeping practices in other countries, along with a discussion of currency exchange rates. Online research as a source of information and a discussion of global stock exchanges would also be appropriate.

In a business communication course, students should develop an awareness of cultural differences in dress, greetings, and business hours around the world. For example, while shaking hands is appropriate in many countries, other types of greetings may include bowing or hugging. A business communication class might include a discussion of cross-cultural negotiation styles.

In a keyboarding or computer applications course, students should be introduced to differences in document formats in other countries. When teaching students about spreadsheets, a teacher can download demographic and economic data from various nations and analyze the data for various trends. Foreign trade data may be obtained from the U.S. Census Bureau at www.census.gov/foreign-trade/www/index.html.

In a marketing course, an analysis of variations in consumer behavior in other countries could be included. Students should be aware that collecting marketing research data in some countries might require observation and interviews rather than telephone or mail surveys.

Specialized International Business Courses
A more complete international business approach involves specialized courses and programs that focus primarily on relevant internationalized content (Scott, 1996). These courses may include principles of international business, as well other courses such as economics, marketing, management, and communication with an international emphasis.

COMPREHENSIVE INTERNATIONAL BUSINESS PROGRAMS
Some colleges and universities offer a specialized international business curriculum or major involving various types of international courses and other academic experiences. Such curricula generally include components such as a business core foundation, international electives, foreign language, and experiential learning.

Business Core Foundation
An international business program includes foundation knowledge of business principles in the areas of accounting, finance, human resources, information systems, marketing, and management. In addition, a study of international trade, global marketing, comparative management, global marketing, and cross-cultural communication may be included.

International Electives
Global understanding among students can be enhanced with topics for study, such as Middle Eastern religions, South Africa politics, Latin American music, Chinese art, French literature, Russian history, as well as the study of international culture and geography. Establishing an interdisciplinary collaboration enhances the ability of students to understand better the cultures in which they will be conducting business (Loughrin-Sacco, 2000).

Foreign Language
While many people around the world still consider English the "language of business," extensive evidence exists for the study of a second or third language. Language study is an excellent source of understanding a society's culture and business environment. Second language skills also give applicants an edge in the process both for domestic and international positions (Albers-Miller, Sigerstad, & Straughan 2000). In coming years, English as the native language of Internet users will decline from almost 50% to less than 30% (Languages on the Net, 2001). This prospect implies a need to understand other languages and cultures.

Experiential Learning

Experiential learning includes field research projects, internships and work-study projects, foreign study programs, and service learning.

Field research projects provide students with an opportunity to identify, research, and assess global organization situations in a real-world setting. Internships and work-study programs are viewed very favorably by employment recruiters (Albers-Miller, Sigerstad, & Straughan, 2000). Students gain needed skills and insights by participating in these organizational experiences with international companies, embassies, trade associations, or government export agencies.

Foreign study programs provide opportunities for international travel with a study component. Information about study abroad and exchange programs may be obtained from the American Institute for Foreign Study at www.aifs.org, the Institute for International Education at www.iie.org, as well as at www.studyabroad.com and www.afs.org.

By getting involved in international service learning projects, such as planning and implementing a program to collect clothing, food, and other needed items for organizations, students can serve recent immigrants and others in need. Volunteer time may be used to provide office help, cleaning, repairs, tutoring, or other teaching to support program activities of international service organizations. Fund raising and public relation activities for global programs can also be the basis of an international service-learning experience.

INSTRUCTIONAL STRATEGIES FOR INTERNATIONAL BUSINESS

Learning activities and instructional methods successful in other business education settings are easily adaptable to international courses. These techniques range from lectures and discussions to cultural role playing and team research cases. Various innovative strategies are also available to enhance the effectiveness of student-teacher interactions, including the following activities:

Case Studies and Decision-Making Exercises

International business curriculum specialists advocate the use of global case problems for global instruction (Gibbs, 1994). Company cases and country scenarios help students understand financial, economic, cultural, and political factors that affect global business decisions.

Research Reports

Traditionally, the research paper allowed students to develop knowledge of a topic. Today, online research can enhance this experience. International topics for research reports might include studying the culture of another country, exporting opportunities for small businesses, and comparing stages of economic development, regional economic agreements, and joint ventures.

Company Analysis
Information and financial data for multinational enterprises can be the basis for a research report. Company data may be obtained from Web sites such as www.hoovers.com and www.annualreportservice.com, as well as many others. These Web sites offer needed information for assignments and projects when studying global company activities.

Geography Activities
The use of maps, globes, and atlases are vital for international business instruction. The teacher should encourage students to learn about the location, major cities, waterways, climate, natural resources, and other geographic details for one or more countries. This information gives students a better understanding of trade relations, economic development, and global distribution systems.

Role Playing
Interaction among students can help to understand international business concepts, while developing an appreciation for other cultures. Suggested international role-playing scenarios include the following activities:

- Simulated business negotiations among people from different cultures

- Debates between country representatives supporting and opposing free trade

- Discussions comparing the advantages of exporting and joint ventures for global business activities

- Demonstrations of different greetings, gestures, and other nonverbal communication

Students might create a video of these activities for use in class and for future classes.

Interviews
Students should be encouraged to interview global managers, export assistance specialists, language interpreters, and culture experts to gain practical insight into course topics. Interviews can yield current information about international business activities and foreign markets.

Observations
Observational research is appropriate in various locations. In local settings, ethnic communities and stores can give insight into cross-cultural consumer behavior patterns, international product offerings, and distribution methods. During foreign travel, students can observe shopping habits, interpersonal encounters, recreational activities, and business transactions.

Collections

Analyzing food packages from other countries can create an understanding of culture, economic development, and government regulations. Clothing labels provide information about the locations of global manufacturing facilities. Postage stamps, coins, and paper money from around the world can contribute to an understanding of business activities and culture. Sample bank notes reflecting the culture, geography, history, and business activities of various nations may be viewed at www.collectpapermoney.com and www.banknoteworld.com. Using these and other items, students can create a visual journal or scrapbook with examples of international business key terms and concepts.

Foreign Market Analysis

Country or regional research can be the starting point for a continuing classroom activity. This project requires students to obtain key geographic, economic, cultural, and political information for a nation. The resulting information may be then used to (1) prepare a profile of the foreign business environment and (2) identify potential business opportunities for companies considering this market. The findings from this research could also be used for other assignments during a course.

Useful Web sites with country information include the CIA *Factbook* at www.odci.gov/cia/publications/factbook/index.html, country background notes of the State Department at www.state.gov/r/pa/ei/bgn, and the Library of Congress country studies at http://lcweb2.loc.gov/frd/cs/cshome.html.

Exporting Plan

Creating an export plan is another comprehensive activity with several components. Elements for this project might include (1) identifying business opportunities in foreign markets, (2) developing a product concept adapted for the intended market, (3) planning funding sources, (4) planning human resource needs, (5) creating a distribution and promotional strategy, and (6) developing a time line.

Team Activities

Most employers value prospective employees with team experience. International business courses may include the following team activities:

- Research and prepare a group summary describing the international business activities of a company or discussing the unique characteristics of a foreign market.

- Develop a survey and collect data on globalization, exporting, trade barriers, economic development, e-commerce, and other international trade issues.

- Present a group oral report communicating proposed e-commerce activities that might enhance the global operations of a company.

- Create an electronic newsletter, PowerPoint presentation, video, or Web site with a summary of key cultural facts, current economic data, the political environment, or travel tips for a country.

The team concept can be extended beyond the school setting. Virtual teams involving e-mail, Web sites, and other technology interactions allow students in different geographic locations to collaborate on consulting projects and case problems. These cross-cultural exchanges involve online researching, sharing, discussing, integrating, and reporting information (Chappell & Schermerhorn, 1999a).

E-Mail Exchanges
Online interaction among students in other countries provides a cross-cultural collaboration for gaining cultural and economic knowledge. E-mail exchanges with representatives of company and international agencies can result in current information related to international trade and exporting.

Web Searches
Integration of the Internet into international programs is vital for enhancing information literacy (Matyska, 1998). Searches related to "exporting," "foreign exchange rates," "global stock exchanges," and other topics will help direct students to appropriate information sources. Students can participate in an online information search for answers to questions related to international business concepts, global companies, or countries. A variation of this activity might involve students locating unusual items online; for example, a country flag with an animal on it, the map of a nation with no ocean seaports, or a country in which you cannot buy Coca-Cola.

Locating information about current values of various monetary units is also useful. This information may be found in the business section of newspapers as well as at www.xe.net/ucc and www.x-rates.com. Students should calculate the cost of various items in different currencies and also be able to explain possible reasons for the changing value of a nation's currency.

E-Commerce Projects
Analysis of a Web site based in another country can start the global e-commerce experience. A project that recommends various global e-commerce activities could include one or more of the following components:

1. Identify global business activities that could benefit from e-commerce. These actions might include contacting new customers, offering online product catalogs, locating a local distributor, ordering online, maintaining inventory control, promoting new products and services, or providing customer service.

2. Locate Internet examples of global companies and other organizations that use online activities for various business functions. Analyze the effectiveness of Web

sites for providing information, selling goods, promoting an organization, and other basic business operations. Determine if the use of e-commerce is better for consumers or saves money for the company.

3. Develop a flowchart that communicates e-commerce uses in various departments and processes of a business or other organization.

Electronic Portfolio

An electronic portfolio on a CD-ROM or a Web site can serve as a culminating outcome for various activities. Portfolio components might include research findings, data collection results, links to related Web sites, PowerPoint presentations, proposed package designs and advertising messages, and a resume. An electronic portfolio serves several purposes: (1) as an assessment tool for instructors, (2) as a promotional device for a school and its international business program, (3) as an initial contact for potential employers, and (4) as sample projects for students who will take the course in the future (Chappell & Schermerhorn, 1999b).

GLOBAL BUSINESS RESOURCES

Multiple resources are readily available to provide basic information, as well as current updates on global business topics. These resources include curriculum guides, journals and periodicals, reference books, multimedia and community contacts, and various agencies.

Curriculum Guides

"The Role of International Business in Business Education" in the *National Standards for Business Education* (NBEA, 2001) lists performance expectations for the creation of courses. The National Council on Economic Education (www.ncee.net) offers curriculum guides and teaching ideas for international trade and global economics.

Journals and Periodicals

Articles about teaching international business appear regularly in the *Business Education Forum* published by the National Business Education Association. The *Journal of Teaching in International Business* provides research-based studies related to curriculum planning, faculty development, and instructional strategies. The business and travel sections of daily newspapers offer an inexpensive source of current international business information. Weekly newsmagazines and other periodicals provide economic, political, and cultural news from around the world. Specialized publications addressing specific international business topics and geographic regions include *Export America* (http://exportamerica.doc.gov), *World Trade* magazine (www.worldtrademag.com), *Latin Trade* (www.latintrade.com), *Mexico Business* (www.mexicobusiness.com), *Far Eastern Economic Review* (www.feer.com), and *Euromoney* (www.euromoney.com).

Reference Books

Many reference books are available to provide current international business information. Useful books about global business culture include *Kiss, Bow or Shake Hands* (Morrison, 1994); *Do's and Taboos Around the World* (Axtell, 1993); *International Business Etiquette: Asia & Pacific Rim,* part of a series with volumes also covering Europe and Latin America (Sabath, 1999); *When Cultures Collide* (Lewis, 1999); and *Working Across Cultures: Applications and Exercises* (Gannon, 2001). Travel guides provide information about a country's history, geography, culture, and business activities.

Multimedia and Community Contacts

Information about global business and cross-cultural management videos may be obtained at www.bwvideo.com, www.films.com, and www.insight-media.com. Videos regarding culture and globalization may be obtained at www.bullfrogfilms.com and at www.pbs.org. Speakers from global companies and international agencies can enhance the learning environment. Company representatives are often willing to share their experiences with students.

Government Agencies

Several U.S. government agencies address exporting and international trade issues. These services range from providing loan advice to monitoring trade agreement violations. Agencies most useful for international business teaching include the International Trade Administration (www.ita.doc.gov), the U.S. Trade Center (www.usatrade.gov), the Small Business Administration (www.sba.gov), and the Foreign Agricultural Service of the U.S. Dept of Agriculture (www.fas.usda.gov). In addition, state departments of economic development or state departments of commerce may provide exporting and international trade information.

International Agencies

Various global organizations facilitate trade relations among countries. The World Trade Organization (www.wto.org) encourages countries to eliminate tariffs and other barriers that discourage free trade. The International Monetary Fund (www.imf.org) and World Bank (www.worldbank.org) analyze economic situations, suggest trade policies, and provide loans to encourage economic development and to maintain stable foreign exchange rates. Embassies and consulates are a vital link between the United States and other nations. Foreign embassies (www.embassy.org) commonly have a commercial division or economic development department to promote international trade activities.

FACULTY DEVELOPMENT ACTIVITIES

Foreign travel and international study programs can enhance global business knowledge and cultural awareness. Faculty internships with global companies, government agencies, and trade associations can provide international experience. Each year, several universities with a Center for International Business Education and

Research (CIBER) present Faculty Development in International Business (FDIB) programs. These professional development seminars provide opportunities for faculty members to internationalize their teaching. Information about FDIB programs is available at http://ciber.centers.purdue.edu.

Various organizations offer conferences, seminars, and other professional development activities. The Academy for International Business (www.aibworld.net), the International Society for Business Education (www.siec-isbe.org), and the North American Association of Small Business International Trade Educators (www.nasbite.org) offer opportunities to exchange curriculum ideas and instructional strategies through conferences and publications.

Local and regional trade association programs provide updates on exporting, trade barriers, and foreign business environments. Information may be obtained from the World Trade Centers Association (www.wtca.org) with more than 200 affiliates in over 100 countries. Other international trade organizations may be contacted at www.fita.org.

SUMMARY

The constantly changing political, economic, and technological environment must be considered when selecting international topics and learning experiences for students. The fundamental knowledge of every business student should include international trade concepts, the global business environment, methods for conducting international business, global marketing activities, international finance, and global risks. Planning international business instruction based on appropriate content and student-centered learning activities will help ensure that every student is prepared to be a consumer, worker, and citizen in the global economy.

REFERENCES

Albers-Miller, N. D., Sigerstad, T. D., & Straughan, R.D. (2000). Internationalization of the undergraduate curriculum: Insight from recruiters. *Journal of Teaching in International Business, 11*(4), 55-80.

Amin, S. G. (1996). British students' perceptions of ethical issues in international marketing: An empirical investigation. *Journal of Teaching in International Business, 8*(1), 45-62.

Axtell, R. (1993). *Do's and taboos around the world* (3rd. ed.), New York: John Wiley & Sons, Inc.

Chappell, D. S., & Schermerhorn, J. R., Jr. (1999a). Introducing international business experience through virtual teamwork. *Journal of Teaching in International Business, 10*(3/4), 43-58.

Chappell, D. S., & Schermerhorn, J. R., Jr. (1999b). Using electronic student portfolios in management education: A stakeholder perspective. *Journal of Management Education, 23*(6), 651-662.

Dlabay, L. R. (1998). Integrated curriculum planning for international business education: Analysis of global business trends. *The Delta Pi Epsilon Journal, 40(3)*, 158-165.

Dlabay, L. R. (2001). Global e-commerce: Issues, implications, and instructional strategies. *Journal for Global Business Education, 1*, 38-49

Dlabay, L. R., & Scott, J. C. (2001). *International business* (2nd. ed.). Cincinnati, OH: South-Western Educational Publishing.

Gannon, M. J. (2001). *Working across cultures: Applications and exercises.* Thousand Oaks, CA: Sage Publications, Inc.

Gibbs, M. C., Jr. (1994). Contemporary strategies for internationalization of the business curriculum. *Journal of Teaching in International Business, 5(3)*, 1-9.

Glenn, J. M. L. (2002). Beyond our doorsteps: Preparing students for an international business environment. *Business Education Forum, 56(3)*, 10-12.

Hill, C. W. L. (2003). *International business: Competing in the global marketplace* (4th. ed.). New York: McGraw-Hill/Irwin.

Hise, R. T., Davidow, M., & Troy, L. (2000). Global geographic knowledge of business students: Update and recommendations for improvement. *Journal of Teaching in International Business, 11(4)*, 1-22.

Javalgi, R. G., Vogelsang-Coombs, V., Lawson, D. A., & White, D. S. (1997). Designing an international business curriculum: A market-driven approach. *Journal of Teaching in International Business, 9(2)*, 31-48.

Languages on the net (2001). *Business 2.0,* November, 121.

Lewis, R. D. (1999). *When cultures collide: Managing successfully across cultures.* London: Nicholas Brealey Publishing.

Loughrin-Sacco, S. J. (2000). Building a bridge to liberal arts. In R. F. Scherer, S. T. Beaton, M. F. Ainina, & J. F. Meyer (Eds.), *A field guide to internationalizing business education* (pp. 107-119). Austin, TX: Center for International Business Education and Research.

Matyska, R. J., Jr. (1998). Online international business. In D. LaBonty (Ed.), *Integrating the Internet into the business curriculum* (Yearbook No. 36, pp. 81-91). Reston, VA: National Business Education Association.

Morrison, T., Conaway, W. A., & Borden, G. A. (1994). *Kiss, bow or shake hands: How to do business in sixty countries.* Holbrook, MA: Adams Media Corporation.

National Business Education Association. (2001). International business. In *National standards for business education: What America's students should know and be able to do in business* (2nd ed.), (pp. 94-107). Reston, VA: Author.

National Business Education Association & International Society for Business Education. (1996). *Creative teaching ideas for international business.* Reston, VA: Author.

Policies Commission for Business and Economic Education. (1992). *This we believe about the role of business education in the global marketplace, policy statement 52.* Reston, VA: National Business Education Association: Author.

Sabath, A. M. (1999). *International business etiquette: Asia & the pacific rim.* Franklin Lakes, NJ: Career Press.

Scott, J. C. (1996). Providing instruction for and about international business. In H. R. Perreault (Ed.), *Classroom strategies: The methodology of business education.* (Yearbook, No. 34, pp. 194-202). Reston, VA: National Business Education Association.

Scott, J. C. (1999). Internationalizing business communication instruction. In P. A. Gallo Villee & M. G. Curran (Eds.), *The 21st century: Meeting the challenges to business education.* (Yearbook, No. 37, pp. 27-46). Reston, VA: National Business Education Association.

Zeliff, N. D., Herbers, D. K., Meyers, K. E., & Sly, T. L. (1999). International business education: What should be taught and by whom? *The Delta Pi Epsilon Journal, 41*(4), 194-203.

Marketing

William J. Wilhelm
Indiana State University
Terre Haute, Indiana

Marketing education programs offer students opportunities to develop career-related skills, civic responsibilities, and leadership competencies when class activities are designed for student participation. These activities include hands-on classroom exercises, cocurricular student organizations, school-based enterprises, and community service.

This chapter addresses the goals, methods of instruction, and resources for teaching marketing education. The chapter also discusses curriculum organization of marketing education programs, outlines national standards, identifies performance expectations, describes specific strategies for instruction, and suggests numerous resources.

THE MARKETING EDUCATION CURRICULUM

The marketing curriculum is a continuum that begins with the basic or beginning marketing course at the secondary level, introducing students to the foundations and functions of marketing and related business skills. Advanced marketing explores these foundations, functions, and business-related skills in greater detail; this course prepares the student for entry-level marketing employment upon high school graduation or serves as a foundation to continue more specialized study of marketing at a community college or university.

Marketing programs at the community college level offer basic courses, as well as specialized courses in marketing fields such as sales management, real estate sales, industrial sales, and insurance. University-level marketing programs also introduce students to the basic concepts of marketing but allow marketing majors to explore both domestic and international marketing theory in greater detail.

Marketing education at the secondary level is based on four foundational content areas detailed in the National Marketing Education Curriculum Standards (MarkED, 2002) that must be mastered in order for marketing-specific content to have relevance to student learning: (1) economics; (2) business, management, and entrepreneurship; (3) communication and interpersonal skills; and (4) professional development. The curriculum emphasizes oral and written communication, mathematical applications, problem solving, and critical thinking, as these skills relate to distribution, financing, marketing-information management, pricing, product/service management, promotion, and selling.

Performance standards for the foundations course vary from state to state. Table 1 presents a common distribution of performance expectations for each content standard for a two-year marketing education program (Indiana Department of Education, 2002).

Table 1. Content Standards and Performance Expectations for Two-Year Marketing Programs

Foundation Marketing Course	Advanced Marketing Course
Business, Management, and Entrepreneurship Content Standard: Understands fundamental business, management, and entrepreneurial concepts that affect business decision making.	
Performance Expectation Concepts: Describe, explain, analyze business activities, marketing and its importance, types of business ownership, marketing functions and related activities, the concept of utility, and marketing strategies.	**Performance Expectations:** Demonstrate understanding of risk management. Explain the concepts of management, production, accounting, and marketing and the relationship between business and society. Identify current business trends, the impact of technology, laws, diversity, ethics, and social responsibility in business.
Communication and Interpersonal Skills Content Standard: Understands concepts, strategies, and systems needed to interact effectively with others.	
Performance Expectations: Demonstrate effective communication in writing, in person, and by telephone, voice mail, and e-mail. Write different forms of business correspondence,	**Performance Expectations:** Write business letters, reports, and employee publications. Demonstrate effective communication by giving directions for completing job tasks,

using computers, fax, and the Internet. Develop personality traits important to business, including a positive attitude, participation as a team member, enthusiasm, responsibility, honesty, and integrity.	conducting staff meetings, and demonstrating initiative. Set personal goals, use time-management principles, show empathy for others, handle difficult customers, demonstrate problem-solving skills, and participate as a team member.

Distribution Content Standard: Understands the concepts and processes needed to move, store, locate, or transfer ownership of goods and services.

Performance Expectations: Compare and contrast channels and scope of distribution, receiving, warehousing, and inventory control systems.	**Performance Expectations:** Calculate inventory shrinkage and maintain unit inventory control systems.

Economics Content Standard: Understands the economic principles and concepts fundamental to marketing in an international environment.

Performance Expectations: Explain the concept of economics and economic activities, differentiate between economic goods and services, compare and contrast the types of economic systems, explain the concepts of private enterprise and supply and demand. Calculate profit/ loss and analyze its importance in the marketplace in relation to risk and competition.	**Performance Expectations:** Explain the concepts of productivity, specialization/division of labor, organized labor and business, and international trade.

Marketing Information Management Content Standard: Understands the concepts and systems needed to access, synthesize, and evaluate information for use in making business decisions.

Performance Expectations: Describe the nature and scope of marketing information management and the nature of marketing research.	**Performance Expectations:** Describe sources of primary and secondary data, research approaches, methods of data collection, sampling, and test marketing. Describe the organization of a marketing research report and the presentation of marketing research findings.

Math Content Standard: Solve mathematical problems that present themselves in marketing.	**Financing Content Standard:** Understands the financial concepts used in making business decisions.
Performance Expectations: Demonstrate basic mathematical skills. Solve mathematical problems involving percentages. Calculate tax, discounts, miscellaneous charges for purchases, and make change.	**Performance Expectations:** Explain the nature and scope of financing and the purposes and importance of credit and credit applications. Explain installment loans, mortgage loans, credit statements, profit-and-loss statements, and financial ratios.

Pricing Content Standard: Understands concepts and strategies for determining and adjusting prices to maximize return.

Performance Expectations: Explain the nature and scope of pricing and the factors affecting selling price. Solve math problems related to pricing.	**Performance Expectations:** Explain the psychological effects of pricing. Calculate merchandising-related discounts, final costs, net sales, and break-even point.

Product/Service Management Content Standard: Understands the concepts and processes needed to develop, maintain, and improve a product or service mix in response to market opportunities.

Performance Expectations: Explain the nature and scope of product service planning and the product life cycle.	**Performance Expectations:** Explain and plan product mix, warranties and guarantees, branding, packaging, purchasing, and the buying process.

Professional Development Content Standard: Understands and applies concepts and strategies needed for personal and professional growth in marketing.

Performance Expectations: Assess personal interests and skills, conduct a career/job search, analyze current employment trends, and set personal goals. Prepare a resume, a letter of application/cover letter, and complete job applications. Interview for a job. Develop civic consciousness, exhibit social skills, and develop leadership skills.	**Performance Expectations:** Explain the use of trade journals/periodicals, professional/trade organizations, and trade shows. Develop civic consciousness, exhibit social skills, and develop leadership skills. Update resume and portfolio.

Promotion Content Standard: Understands the concepts needed to communicate information about products, services, images, and/or ideas to influence behavior.	
Performance Expectations: Explain the role and types of promotion and the promotional mix.	**Performance Expectations:** Explain the types of media, calculate media costs, select promotional media, plan publicity and community activities, and write a news release.
Selling Content Standard: Understands the concepts needed to respond to client needs and wants through planned, personalized communications that influence purchase decisions and ensure satisfaction.	
Performance Expectations: Explain the purpose and importance of selling, the selling process, and the sales presentation. Demonstrate all the steps of the sale.	**Performance Expectations:** Demonstrate customer follow-up techniques and explain key factors in building a clientele.
Note: Adapted from the Indiana Department of Education, Curriculum Materials/ Standards for Business and Marketing Education, Office of Career and Technical Education (2002).	

A marketing education program is designed to prepare students for employment in various sales, customer service, and/or first-line supervisory positions in wholesale, retail, and service establishments. A student who completes a marketing education program should possess the technical knowledge and skills associated with sales, marketing, and related activities for broad categories of products and services. In addition to the required technical skills, students should acquire advanced employability, critical thinking, applied academics, and life management, business, economic and leadership skills required for employees in sales and marketing occupations (Mason, Furtado, & Husted, 1989). Occupational clusters include the following areas of marketing:

- Advertising

- Fashion marketing

- Financial services marketing

- Industrial sales

- Marketing of business and personal services

- Property management and sale

- Purchasing

- Restaurant management

- Sales: marketing, management, and research

- Shipping, receiving, and stock clerking

- Travel and transportation marketing

Depending upon local economic bases and community needs, many state-approved marketing programs include analogous courses in marketing specializations, such as sports, recreation, and entertainment marketing; hospitality, travel and tourism marketing; financial service marketing; and entrepreneurship.

ORGANIZATION OF THE MARKETING EDUCATION CURRICULUM

All educators preparing to teach marketing courses at the secondary level should become familiar with their state's marketing education course descriptions, content standards, and performance expectations before developing their lesson plans. Although these foundational elements of the curriculum may be similar in the various states, sequences of learning objectives and instructional activities may differ. School districts may also vary the marketing education course offerings available to students. Whereas one district may offer a marketing foundations course at the sophomore level, continue courses through the junior year, and culminate with an advanced marketing course in the senior year, other districts may offer the marketing foundations course only at the junior level, followed by advanced marketing at the senior level.

The basic two-year high school marketing curriculum aims to provide program completers with a foundation of (1) business knowledge grounded in free enterprise economics, (2) a comprehension of general business management practices, and (3) a thorough understanding of marketing functions applied to all levels of the distribution hierarchy. Figure 1 depicts the curriculum of a typical two-year high school marketing education program.

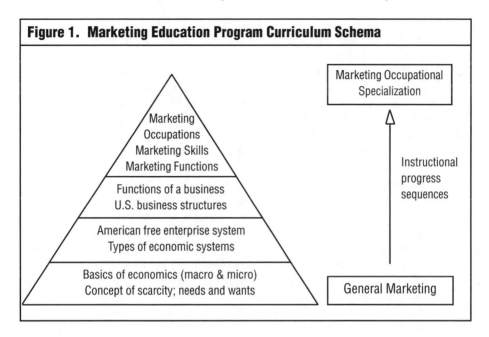

Figure 1. Marketing Education Program Curriculum Schema

Marketing Occupational Specialization

Marketing Occupations
Marketing Skills
Marketing Functions

Functions of a business
U.S. business structures

American free enterprise system
Types of economic systems

Basics of economics (macro & micro)
Concept of scarcity; needs and wants

Instructional progress sequences

General Marketing

The curriculum model presented in Figure 1 demonstrates the importance of teaching marketing concepts as they relate to American businesses. A beginning course in marketing is usually a high school student's first exposure to concepts of economic scarcity, microeconomic and macroeconomic theories, and the American free enterprise system. After introducing basic economic theory and the American free enterprise system, the teacher should present an overview of business functions, followed by marketing functions and the relationship of those functions to the success of a business venture.

INSTRUCTIONAL STRATEGIES FOR MARKETING EDUCATION

Instructional strategies may include traditional classroom instruction, a school-based enterprise, computer/technology applications, real and/or simulated occupational experiences, or projects in the marketing functions, such as those available through the DECA program of activities. (DECA, the marketing education student organization, is discussed in Chapter 19.) Content standards provide a solid basis for determining unit and lesson objectives. Carefully written performance objectives serve as the targeted outcomes for which instructional activities are selected.

Marketing topics are typically interesting and exciting to students. The marketing education teacher is fortunate that most marketing students are there by choice, as marketing is an elective. In planning lessons, however, the teacher should ensure that he or she has developed an effective *anticipatory set* or *set induction*. These terms refer to what a teacher does at the outset of a lesson to get the students' undivided attention, to arouse their interest, and to establish a conceptual framework for the information that follows (Moore, 1999). For example, attracting students' attention by asking them what they know about the early days of Coca-Cola or McDonalds is an effective anticipatory set. Biographical books about successful entrepreneurs are available at most public libraries. A simple catalog search using the keyword "entrepreneur" can generate a bibliography of relevant books. As an example, *Entrepreneurs, the Men and Women Behind Famous Brand Names and How They Made It* (Fucini & Fucini, 1990) presents a good selection of short biographies about entrepreneurial beginnings of many brands with which students can identify.

Effective and humorous advertisements appeal to a broad range of people, and students respond to effective advertisements. Marketing teachers should look to their local business community to find interesting topical subjects that relate to their planned lessons on advertising. Retailers are often willing to give out-of-date or even new point-of-purchase promotional materials to local business teachers to use in their classrooms. Guest speakers from the business community can be asked to bring print advertisements or videos, company products, samples, and other visual stimuli to their guest speaking appearances.

Lecturing

Lecturing is an excellent way of presenting background information when building a unit frame of reference or when introducing a unit, particularly when dealing with abstract concepts about which students have no empirical knowledge (Moore, 1999). For example, lecturing would be useful to introduce the different types of economic systems throughout the world. Most high school students have little or no prior understanding of socialism or communism as they relate to economic decision making.

Supplementary tools to support effective lecturing, such as Microsoft PowerPoint, Internet connections, and other presentation media software, are effective in capturing and maintaining student interest. Particular attention should be given to planning the related content into a meaningful framework and presenting it to students in a relatively short period of time. Following the lecture, a student-centered activity can help reinforce the learning.

Questioning Techniques

To check for understanding, a variety of questioning techniques are used. These techniques may include focused or broad questions, convergent or divergent questions, probing questions, and redirecting (Moore, 1999). *Focused questions* usually ask only for factual recall or specific correct answers, whereas *broad questions* cannot be answered in simple one- or two-word responses. *Convergent questions* allow for only a few right responses, whereas *divergent questions* allow for many correct responses. *Probing questions* aim at correcting, improving, or expanding a student's initial response and compel the students to think more thoroughly about their initial responses. *Redirecting* is useful for increasing the amount of student participation, because it allows a teacher to draw students into a discussion by asking them to respond to a question in light of a previous response from another student.

The *Socratic method* is another very effective questioning technique that requires considerable practice before successful implementation. This method involves teaching by systematically asking questions and applying inductive reasoning that leads students to see a logical conclusion and to discover contradictions. For example, in a discussion about comparative economic theories (e.g., capitalism, socialism, and communism), the teacher may ask questions about how students, acting as a society, would deal with extreme disparities of wealth, control of resources, and ownership of production by only a few individuals. Most students grappling with this situation, when first asked probing questions about economic inequality in a society, will discover the motivational factors and logical justifications that drive economic systems based on socialistic and communistic concepts. Guiding students' thinking through economic decision-making scenarios using Socratic questioning, can help them to not only comprehend the divergent value systems used in other countries, but to also develop a better understanding of the free-market rationale for the U.S. economic system.

Demonstrations

A teacher can use the demonstration method as an effective strategy for modeling presentation techniques that students can employ effectively in classroom and DECA competitive role-play events. A *demonstration* is a technique of teaching by using materials and displays; the teacher or individual conducting the demonstration generally is the only person directly involved with the materials. However, an effective way to arouse more interest is to involve one or more students in replicating or participating in the demonstration.

A marketing teacher can find many learning situations that are appropriate for effective use of the demonstration method. The teacher should model all interpersonal performance outcomes, including selling, prospecting, or handling customer complaints through the use of demonstrations before requiring students to perform their own demonstrations.

Class Discussions

Class discussions are carefully planned interactions and exchanges of ideas among students directed toward a specific goal (Moore, 1999). Whole-class or group discussions are especially useful with issues that have no single correct answer but are derived from various attitudes, values, and behaviors. Other variations of the discussion method include panel discussions and debates.

Acting more as facilitator than participant, the instructor should specify before the discussion begins that ground rules for discussions preclude unacceptable expressions of disapproval or domination by one or a few individuals, and include acceptance of everyone's right to express an opinion. Ethical issues such as promotional pricing techniques, warranties, collusion, and employee pilferage are just a few examples of the types of topics to which most students can relate. After learning about basic management theory and labor history, students can discuss philosophical differences between management and labor. Truth in advertising is another area that typically generates a broad range of opinions.

Problem-Based Learning

One of the most realistic and effective methods of teaching in a marketing education classroom employs the problem-based learning method, also referred to as *discovery learning*. This instructional strategy involves projects that present students with simulated real-world dilemmas that include a number of variables that students must address to resolve a situation. The instructor must invest considerable time in planning, refining, and defining the project to make it as realistic as possible. These projects fit well as end-of-unit capstone learning activities, because they can combine a wide variety of learning outcomes during the process.

In a problem-based learning activity, the teacher presents a well-developed scenario to the students, who may work alone or in groups. For example, after the concepts of U.S. free enterprise, basic marketing principles, consumer behavior, advertising media and media pricing are taught, a problem-based activity may involve students working in teams of four to five members in the role of an advertising agency. Their responsibilities could include analyzing a product of a fictional company, utilizing a budget provided by the instructor, and formulating a detailed advertising strategy to market the product to consumers. In such a problem-based learning project, learning goals may include process-oriented outcomes such as explaining, describing, generalizing, paraphrasing, brainstorming, discussing, rating, ranking, constructing, designing, budgeting, comparing, contrasting, and justifying; all higher order thinking skills of analysis, synthesis, and evaluation (Bloom, Engelhart, Furst, Hill, & Krathwohl, 1956). The DECA competitive events provide many similar projects to engage students in actual problem solving.

Field Trips

To facilitate learning during a field trip, the instructor should give a specific assignment and review it with the students before the field trip experience. For example, during a trip to a new regional mall, the instructor could arrange for a presentation by the head of marketing operations for the facility and ask students to write a summary of the presentation. In visiting stores or behind-the-scenes operations, students could be assigned to record specific data about their experiences and write a report. Students could also be required to interview sales people during such a field experience.

Simulations and Games

Students often find learning through simulations and games to be fun as well as educational. *Simulation* presents an artificial situation or event that represents a real life situation but removes the risk to individuals involved in the activity (Moore, 1999). Two basic types of simulations include human simulations, such as role-play events, and person-to-computer simulations. DECA provides opportunities for both types of simulations at DECA competitive events, which include various role-playing components. The DECA Web site (www.deca.org) has links to proprietary simulations; for example, Virtual Business Retailing and Virtual Business Management allow DECA students throughout the world to engage one another in marketing-related decision making on an interactive basis. The Marketing Education Resource Center (MarkED, 2002) has a wide variety of interactive computer-based lessons and simulations tailored for the marketing education classroom.

Games can make learning more enjoyable for beginning as well as advanced marketing students. The Monopoly® game (Hasbro, 2002) can serve as a familiar platform for beginning marketing students to "experience" the advantages and disadvantages of trading in different economic systems. Marketing educators can use several variations on the basic free enterprise structure of Monopoly® to help students develop an appreciation of the freedoms of U.S. capitalism. A lesson typically follows a simple sequence. On the first day, students play Monopoly® using the traditional rules and record their properties and cash at the end of the class. On the second day, students receive a new set of teacher-developed instructions based on socialistic economic principles. These new, more financially restrictive rules specify the manner in which students must disperse their possessions in a more egalitarian society. New tax rates, Community Chest and Chance instructions, and board movement rules are designed to provide less money for the player, but more for the government. On the third and final day, the teacher gives the students another set of rules for trade practices allowed under a society controlled by communism. These rules are even more constricting of the students' freedom to acquire and trade property and gain monetary success. Since private property is theoretically not permitted in a communistic society, players wind up rolling the dice and simply proceeding around the board without motivation or initiative. After completing this game, students have a much better appreciation for and understanding of the importance of individual incentive and profit in a free enterprise system. New instructors should ask veteran marketing teachers to share their rules variations, as most marketing teachers are willing to share their resources.

Service Learning

Service learning is a character building educational strategy that links classroom learning with service to the community. Perhaps the greatest benefit to students from participation in service-learning activities is that they learn to address real community needs. Several states have service-learning projects funded by the Corporation for National Service (www.cns.gov), which was created under the National Community Service Trust Act in 1993 (Otten, 2000). Service-learning projects for student groups or individual student placements should be designed to enhance the educational goals of the course and to serve the public good. Students involved in service learning make a commitment to engage in a service project or to complete a specified number of hours of service work. Students may be required to integrate their service experience with other course components through reflection and analysis. The teacher should link concepts and connections of the service-learning project to the course content, and the students should write their reflections about the service-learning project guided by these concepts. This reflective process permits students to see the relevance of the course content to the community and enhances their understanding of their civic rights and responsibilities. Finally, the teacher should facilitate group discussions as students share their reflections in class. (Weis, 2000, p. 26).

DECA has long been a student organization that has encouraged service learning and provided opportunities to its members through national, state, and regional projects. Most DECA chapter charters include a service-learning component. National DECA also offers incentives for chapter participation in community-based service-learning projects by providing opportunities for local chapter projects to receive regional and national recognition and honors through the DECA Civic Consciousness Project. The purpose of the Civic Consciousness Project is for DECA chapter members to develop a better understanding of the role that civic activities have in society, to make a contribution to a community service or charity, and to learn and apply the principles of marketing management (DECA, n.d.). The Civic Consciousness Project provides an opportunity for the participants to demonstrate the skills necessary in planning, organizing, implementing and evaluating a civic consciousness project.

E-Commerce

E-commerce is defined by the U. S. Department of Commerce as goods and services sold online whether over open networks such as the Internet or over proprietary networks running systems such as Electronic Data Interchange (EDI) (U. S. Department of Commerce, 2002). E-commerce is an established mode for selling between businesses and is rapidly gaining acceptance as a mode for consumers to buy from businesses. As e-commerce has an important market niche and is continuing to grow, marketing educators should include this topic in the marketing curriculum. (King, 2000, p. 46).

The high school marketing educator must first gauge the technical acumen of his or her students in order to create hands-on educational activities that will result in learning rather than student frustration. Introductory activities can focus on evaluating Web site qualities, including content interest, ease of navigation, effectiveness of advertising, assurances of security, ease of ordering, and general user-friendliness. Such activities can generate class discussions, as students express their opinions about the sites they visited.

After students have learned the basics of navigating the Web, the students can "comparison shop" online for a particular product, while considering factors such as purchase price, taxes, shipping, and other charges (King, 2000). Teams of students can design a mock or actual Web site using PowerPoint, FrontPage, or another similar software application and develop pages for product promotion, inventory management, ordering, credit approval, and shipping. If students generate many ideas for Web sites, they can be given a "budget" and asked to prioritize their ideas within the parameters of their budget (O'Connor, 2002). For another project, students could develop a school-based enterprise to sell school store or fund-raising merchandise online. In all of these examples, students can discuss concepts such as attributes of an effective Web site and concerns such as privacy, legality, safety, theft, and other security issues.

School-Based Enterprises

School stores and other school-based enterprises have traditionally been a part of high school marketing education programs. Educational benefits include applying and extending knowledge acquired in the classroom, solving problems in the context of real social transactions, and working in teams. These activities provide many students their first work experience; for others, they provide an opportunity to build management, supervision, and leadership skills. Well-developed and well-managed school-based enterprises offer opportunities for students to learn skills and competencies in business management including retail operations, inventory control, personnel operations, customer service, advertising and promotion, market research, bookkeeping and accounting, and interpersonal skills. Any school-based enterprise, whether housed on campus, off campus, or online, should be an actual learning laboratory and, therefore, tied directly to the marketing education curriculum. Student learning outcomes should be defined in relation to the marketing performance standards stipulated in the curriculum adopted by the school district, which generally are state and national standards. Based on these defined performance outcomes, the teacher can select appropriate learning activities and specify the areas of student participation in the enterprise. Whenever transactions involving money take place, the teacher should emphasize appropriate procedures, authority, and assigned responsibilities.

Educators interested in investigating the possibility of establishing a school-based enterprise can download the highly informative *Guide For Starting and Managing School-Based Enterprises* from the DECA Web site: (http://www.deca.org/). This document presents a thorough plan of action for researching the market potential for a school-based enterprise and how-to guidance for operating one. Well-planned school-based enterprises not only provide a successful learning laboratory, but they can also be a profitable funding tool to support DECA chapter activities and a program development tool, projecting a positive image to potential marketing students.

Cooperative Work Experience

Customarily included as a component of a senior-level advanced marketing class, *cooperative work experience* gives students already grounded in the basic marketing concepts an opportunity to apply these concepts as a part-time paid employee in an established business. Cooperative education provides planned learning experiences structured by the advanced marketing instructor/work experience coordinator and the employer to ensure that the student receives exposure to a breadth of business operations over the course of the program, usually a full academic year. Chapter 18 discusses cooperative work experience programs.

Other Organizations

Toastmasters International is a nonprofit organization dedicated to helping people speak more effectively. At Toastmasters, members learn by speaking to groups and working with others in a supportive environment. Toastmasters International has long supported marketing education programs. Local Toastmasters clubs offer programs for their members to conduct a series of planned public speaking meetings in the marketing classroom. At these meetings, students learn and practice the art of public speaking, an essential skill for success in marketing. Toastmasters' programs for schools enable students to have fun, while overcoming fear and mastering public speaking. Educators can usually find a local phone listing for a Toastmasters International club in their area or contact the national organization at http://www.toastmasters.org/index.htm.

Junior Achievement is a not-for-profit organization sponsored by corporate and individual contributors that "seeks to educate and inspire young people to value free enterprise, business, and economics to improve the quality of their lives" (Junior Achievement, n.d.). Junior Achievement volunteers bring to the high school classroom a range of different programs that teach concepts about business and economics of the sports, arts, and entertainment industries, business in our society, international trade, business concepts through math exercises, personal finance goals, interpersonal effectiveness, and problem solving. The volunteers are usually employees of local companies who bring real-life business experience and guidance into the classroom. Marketing educators should contact their local Junior Achievement office and ask to meet with a volunteer to discuss the range of educational programs available from the local organization. The local Junior Achievement organization may be found in the telephone directory or by accessing the national Web site at http://www.ja.org.

Professional Associations

One of the best ways that a teacher can model leadership to students is by actively participating in professional marketing associations. Marketing associations offer a plethora of opportunities for the educator to learn and share new technologies and teaching strategies. Membership benefits extend beyond the cognitive benefits and include the rewards of serving as an officer in a leadership role and the personal reward of affiliating with like-minded professionals. The marketing educator should not only be an active member in DECA, but should also participate in his or her state's professional marketing and business education associations. In some states these associations are separate; in others they are the same. In addition, the following national associations offer unique opportunities to marketing educators.

The *American Marketing Association* (AMA) is a network of more than 40,000 marketing practitioners in industry and education. The association's academic division offers resources specifically for marketing educators; members can choose from a variety of special interest groups. The association's Academic Council consists of marketing academicians who are members of the AMA. The primary purpose of this group is to develop and improve its members' capabilities for instruction in marketing subjects (http://www.ama.org).

The *National Marketing Education Association* (MEA) is an organization of educators and business people committed to the career development of youth and adults in the areas of marketing, management, and entrepreneurship (http://www.nationalmea.org).

The *National Business Education Association* (NBEA) is the nation's largest professional organization devoted exclusively to serving individuals and groups engaged in instruction, administration, research, and dissemination of information for and about business (http://www.nbea.org/). This organization is discussed in Chapter 20.

These organizations represent only a few of the many professional organizations available to marketing educators. New teachers should network with veteran marketing instructors to obtain their perspective on the benefits of various professional organizations that are active in their geographic area.

SUMMARY

The basic two-year high school marketing curriculum aims to provide program completers with a foundation of business knowledge grounded in free enterprise economics, a comprehension of general business-management practices, and a thorough understanding of marketing functions applied to all levels of the distribution hierarchy. Students completing a marketing program have several options available to them. They are prepared for entry-level employment in many areas of the marketing function, they can build upon their foundation skills by pursuing more specialized training in industry-specific marketing areas in community colleges, or they can thoroughly explore marketing theory in a four-year university in preparation for entry-level marketing management positions.

A range of instructional strategies are used in the marketing education classroom, including traditional methods such as lecture, directed questioning, demonstration, and class discussion, as well as student-centered activities, such as problem-based learning, hands-on activities—role-play and computer simulations, project construction, and participation in the DECA student organization. Outside the classroom, cooperative work experience programs, service-learning projects in the community, and school-based enterprises such as school stores are also sound instructional methods.

The marketing educator has a wide range of resources to support his or her efforts in the educational process. By remaining active in discipline-related professional associations, marketing educators can stay abreast of these rapidly changing resources.

REFERENCES

Bloom, B. S., Engelhart, M. D., Furst, E. J., Hill, W. H., & Krathwohl, D. R. (1956). *Taxonomy of educational objectives, volume 1: Cognitive domain.* White Plains, NY: Longman Press.

DECA, An Association of Marketing Students. (n.d.). Retrieved February 10, 2002, from http://www.deca.org

Fucini, J. J., & Fucini, S. (1990). *Entrepreneurs, the men and women behind famous brand names and how they made it.* Boston: G.K. Hall.

Hasbro. (2002). *Monopoly.* Retrieved February 2, 2002, from http://www.hasbro.com/

Indiana Department of Education. (2002). *Business and marketing education, office of career and technical education, curriculum materials/standards, marketing education.* Retrieved January 15, 2002, from http://doe.state.in.us/octe/bme/curriculum/ contentstandardsme.html

Junior Achievement. (n.d.). *Who we are: Our mission.* Retrieved February 10, 2002, from http://www.ja.org/about/about_who.shtml

King, P. A. (2000). The impact of e-commerce on marketing education. *Business Education Forum, 54*(3), 46-49.

Leventhal, J. I. (1999). Marketing education and the development of leadership skills. *Business Education Forum, 54*(2), 44-45.

MarkED. (2002). *Marketing Education Resource Center.* Retrieved February 2, 2002, from http://www.mark-ed.com/

Mason, R. E., Furtado, L. T., & Husted, S. W. (1989). *Cooperative occupational education and work experience in the curriculum.* Danville, IL: The Interstate Printers & Publishers, Inc.

Moore, K. D. (1999). *Middle and secondary school instructional methods* (2nd ed.). Boston: McGraw-Hill Companies, Inc.

O'Connor, M. C. (2002). The role of technology in learning marketing and management concepts. In A. Remp (Ed.), Technology, methodology, and business education (Yearbook No. 40, pp. 148-163). Reston, VA: National Business Education Association.

Otten, E. H. (2000). *Character education.* Bloomington, IN: ERIC Clearinghouse for Social Studies/Social Science. (ERIC Document Reproduction Service No. ED444932).

Weis, W. L. (2000). Enriching business education through community service. *Business Education Forum, 55*(1), 25-26.

U. S. Department of Commerce. (2002). *E-stats.* Retrieved June 2, 2002, from http://www.census.gov/eos/www/papers/estatstext.pdf

Cooperative Education and Work-Experience Programs

Patti K. Beltram

Mesquite High School

Gilbert, Arizona

Allen D. Truell

Ball State University

Muncie, Indiana

Quality business and marketing education programs will include a career and technical education student organization, such as Business Professionals of America, DECA, or Future Business Leaders of America; a cooperative education/work-experience component; and related class instruction. This chapter provides an overview of the cooperative education and work-experience components of business and marketing education programs. Specifically, the chapter presents the history and benefits of cooperative education and work-experience programs, introduces various approaches to cooperative education and other work-experience programs, outlines the roles of teacher-coordinators, discusses legal issues related to cooperative education and work-experience programs, explains the role of advisory committees, and describes the related class.

HISTORY OF COOPERATIVE EDUCATION AND WORK-EXPERIENCE PROGRAMS

The first cooperative education and work-experience program in the United States was established at the University of Cincinnati in 1906. In that year Herman Schneider, a professor of engineering, proposed a new method of instruction, whereby his college students studied both in classes and in paid work settings. Schneider believed that many concepts and skills could not be mastered without real work experience. The first year 27 students participated in the cooperative education program. The next year more than 400 students applied to the cooperative education program. Schneider's program was so successful that other institutions followed by developing their own versions of what became know as the "The Cincinnati Plan." Nearly 30 years after

Schneider started his cooperative education program, it was cited as the single most important development in engineering education (Solvilla, 1998).

By the 50th anniversary of Schneider's founding of cooperative education at the University of Cincinnati, more than 60 colleges and universities had established similar programs. The growth of cooperative education continued, as organizations such as the Thomas Alva Edison Foundation and The Ford Foundation's Fund for the Advancement of Education promoted and researched its value. Additional support for cooperative education was achieved with the founding of the Cooperative Education & Internship Association (CEIA) in 1963 (http://www.ceainc.org). Growth of cooperative education continued through the 1980s, when an estimated one-third of all U.S. colleges and universities reported having cooperative education programs (Solvilla, 1998).

The earlier success with cooperative education programs at colleges and universities gave rise to cooperative education and other work-experience programs in secondary schools. Today secondary schools offer a variety of cooperative education and work-experience programs. For many of the same reasons that Herman Schneider established cooperative education at the University of Cincinnati in 1906, secondary programs combine related class instruction with that of practical work experience.

The *National Standards for Business Education* (National Business Education Association, 2001) notes the importance of career development. The standards addressed by the career development component include career research, career strategy, lifelong learning, school-to-career transition, self-awareness, and workplace expectations. All of these concepts are addressed through cooperative education and work-experience programs at the secondary level. Because cooperative education and other work-experience programs serve as a connection between the related class instruction and practical work experience, they are an ideal setting for teaching the career development standards.

DESCRIPTION OF WORK-EXPERIENCE PROGRAMS
Work experiences can be integrated into the learning process in a variety of ways. These approaches include apprenticeships, cooperative education, job-shadowing experiences, internships, and service learning.

Apprenticeships
The U.S. Department of Labor's Employment and Training Administration (ETA) coordinates apprenticeships. *Apprenticeships* combine both work experience with related class instruction to foster development of the attitudes, knowledge, and craft needed for a skilled trade. More than 800 occupations have been approved as apprentice-suitable (U. S. Department of Labor, n.d.). Depending upon the occupation, apprenticeships take from one to four years to complete. At the completion of apprenticeship programs, participants are awarded either a certificate or an associate degree.

Employers and labor unions, individual employers, and/or employer associations sponsor apprenticeship programs jointly, depending upon the occupational area. The Bureau of Apprenticeship Training (BAT) or a State Apprenticeship Council (SAC) registers program standards for each occupation. Only a small percentage of secondary students are involved in apprenticeship programs.

Cooperative Education Programs

Cooperative education programs are typically school-year long, part-time paid work experiences at training sites related to occupational areas of interest to students. Teacher-coordinators place students at training sites that best develop the attitudes, knowledge, and skills needed in students' chosen occupations, while providing a related class instruction component. The cooperative education process is formalized and guided by signed training agreements and training plans prepared for each student. Training agreements and training plans require that students be provided learning experiences at the training site and frequent teacher-coordinator visits to solicit and provide feedback about their performance. Students earn academic credit based on the completion of required work hours and on their work performance (Ascher, 1994; *Career/Technical Education*, 2000; *Cooperative Education Policies*, 2000; Mason & Husted, 1997). Because policies for granting credit vary from state to state, teacher-coordinators should contact appropriate state department of education personnel for specific requirements. Cooperative education programs may be referred to as cooperative office education (COE), cooperative vocational education (CVE), or vocational office training (VOT), among others (Calhoun & Robinson, 1991). Some business teachers in schools that are too small to support separate business or marketing education cooperative education programs coordinate *diversified cooperative education (DCE)* or *interdisciplinary cooperative education (ICE)* programs. These programs offer a wide variety of educational experiences in business and nonbusiness occupations such as automotive mechanics, food preparation, and childcare.

Job-Shadowing Experiences

Job-shadowing experiences are often completed as career exploration activities. Students typically shadow an employee in a company for a few days to learn about a specific occupational area. Because job-shadowing experiences are short-term, students may explore a number of occupational areas. Students normally job shadow during their middle and junior high school years. This introduction to occupational options in middle and junior high school allows students to make more informed decisions when selecting tentative occupational courses to study in high school (*Work-Based Learning*, n.d.).

Internships

Students participate in *internships* in their occupational area of emphasis. Students may or may not earn pay but do earn academic credit for their internship participation. Unlike cooperative education programs, internships usually have no concurrent related class. However, students generally complete one or more courses related to their internship prior to their internship experience. Internships normally take place near the end of formal coursework and provide students with opportunities to practice what they have learned. Internships are most often found at the postsecondary level and are sometimes called *practicums* (Mason & Husted, 1997).

Service-Learning Options

Service learning students participate in community service positions for extended periods of time. Students are usually placed in organizations that focus on fulfilling a community need. Careful planning and management of service learning experiences are essential, so that students learn from the experience. Students learn by developing the attitudes, knowledge, and skills needed for work, while participating in service to the community. Documentation of learning is frequently achieved through journal reflections and portfolio preparation (*Work-Based Learning*, n.d.).

BENEFITS OF WORK-EXPERIENCE PROGRAMS

Cooperative education and other work-experience programs provide many benefits to stakeholders, including businesses, communities, schools, and students. By understanding the advantages of cooperative education and work-experience programs, teacher-coordinators can better position their respective programs to serve all stakeholders.

Business Benefits

Business personnel assist cooperative education programs by serving on advisory committees, providing student training sites, speaking to student groups, and working with student organizations. The many benefits to business include providing input into developing the local workforce, developing potential employees, portraying a positive image in the community, and developing positive workplace behaviors, such as increased attendance and productivity among prospective workers (*Career/Technical Education*, 2000; *Work-Based Education*, 2002).

Community Benefits

Cooperative education and other work-experience programs provide numerous benefits to the local community. Advantages to the community include greater linkages between school and work, better citizenship development and civic responsibility, encouragement of students to remain in school, and promotion of closer community and school relationships (*Career/Technical Education*, 2000; *Vocational Cooperative Education*, 1993).

School Benefits

Schools benefit from the positive relationships that are built from program successes, as students begin to see the relevance of what they are learning in their work settings. In addition, by placing students at community-based training sites, resources such as expertise, equipment, and facilities that are not available at the school site now become available for use in student learning (*Career/Technical Education*, 2000;

Vocational Cooperative Education, 1993; *Work-Based Education*, 2002). Employers often assist schools in other ways, by serving on advisory committees; providing guest speakers; donating funds, equipment, and scholarships; working with student organizations, and partnering with schools on special projects.

Student Benefits

The benefits of cooperative education and work-experience programs to students include the fostering of positive safety and work attitudes, the providing of the opportunity to apply what was learned in the related class at work, the promoting of portfolio development, the providing of opportunities to receive training in a selected occupation in the community, and the smoothing of the transition from school to career. (*Career/Technical Education*, 2000; *Vocational Cooperative Education*, 1993; *Work-Based Education*, 2002).

TEACHER-COORDINATOR ROLES

Teacher-coordinators serve in many roles when completing their daily tasks. Among the roles described in this section are those of coordinator, documenter, program promoter, instructor, and training site developer.

Coordinator

As coordinators, teachers are actively involved in the cooperative method of instruction. Coordination responsibilities include aligning related class curriculum with the work experiences of students, assessing students' work performance, placing students at training sites, and selecting and developing training sites (Redesigning Cooperative Vocational Education, 1996).

Documenter

An essential responsibility of teacher-coordinators is to maintain appropriate program and student documentation. Documentation is needed to meet various federal, state, and local accountability, follow-up, and reporting requirements. Among the documents teacher-coordinators need to maintain are training agreements and training plans.

Training agreements establish the formal relationships among students, parents, training sponsors, and teacher-coordinators (Stone, 1995). Training agreements outline the duties of all parties—parents, students, training site personnel, and teacher-coordinators. Written training agreements serve to reinforce the responsibilities to which all parties have agreed. In addition, to protect a student's civil rights, the training agreement should include a nondiscrimination statement (Rader & Kurth, 1999). A sample training agreement is shown in Table 1.

Completion of the training plan is probably the most important step in job placement (Stone, 1995). Teacher-coordinators develop training plans cooperatively with parents, students, and employers. Training plans connect related class instruction with

Table 1. Cooperative Education Training Agreement

Student Name: _____

Home Address: _____

Home Phone: _____

Training Site: _____

Address: _____

Training Supervisor: _____

Phone Number: _____

Student's Career Interest: _____

(Include an appropriate civil rights statement here.)

Student Agrees

1. To be regular in attendance, both in school and at work, and, unless permission is granted, not to report for work on a day when absent from school.
2. To perform the training station and classroom responsibilities to the best of his/her abilities.
3. To furnish the teacher-coordinator with necessary information about his/her training station and to complete all required reports promptly.
4. To abide by the rules and regulations of the training station.
5. To consult with the teacher-coordinator about any difficulties arising at the training station or related to the training program.
6. To provide his/her own means of transportation to the training station.
7. Not to terminate employment with the training agency without approval of the teacher-coordinator.
8. To relinquish the job if he/she withdraws from school or from the cooperative education program.

Training Sponsor Agrees

1. To provide a variety of work experiences for the student-learner that will give the student the opportunity to progress in competency achievement.
2. To endeavor to schedule the student-learner for at least an average of 15 hours per week.
3. To abide by all federal and state regulations regarding employment.
4. To assist in the evaluation of the student-learner.
5. To consult with the teacher-coordinator about any difficulties arising at the training station or related to the training station that involve the student-learner.

6. To reinforce safety instructions and practices related to the job.
7. To cancel this training agreement at any time, provided due notice is given to all parties concerned.
8. Not to discriminate in employment practices on the basis of sex, race, color, handicap, or national origin.
9. FOR HAZARDOUS OCCUPATIONS ONLY:
   a. The work of the student-learner in occupations declared hazardous shall be incidental to his/her training, shall be intermittent and for short periods of time, and shall be under the direct and close supervision of a qualified and experienced person.
   b. Safety instruction shall be given by the school and correlated by the employer with work site training.

Parent/Guardian Agrees

1. To encourage the student-learner to carry out effectively his/her duties and responsibilities both in the classroom and at work.
2. To be responsible for the actions of the student-learner while at work.

Teacher-Coordinator Agrees

1. To provide related classroom instruction, including safety instruction for hazardous occupations.
2. To periodically observe the student-learner at work and to visit with the training supervisor in order to aid in the student-learner's development.
3. To consult with the training supervisor in the evaluation of the student-learner.

Student: _____

Date: _____

Parent: _____

Date: _____

Training Site: _____

Date: _____

Teacher-Coordinator: _____

Date: _____

work activities in the desired occupational areas of students (Caton & Buck, 1990). These plans provide summaries of the competencies students are to develop in their selected occupational areas. Training plans should be reviewed frequently to retain the focus of the students and training sites and should include specific safety instruction objectives with instructional responsibility clearly defined. A safety checklist is recommended for all co-op students. Topics on the safety checklist may include appropriate work behaviors, correct lifting techniques, electrical safety procedures, fire and severe weather procedures, safety symbols and markings, and what to do during a robbery (Rockefeller & Zikmund, 1990). A sample training plan is shown in Table 2.

In addition to documenting and maintaining training agreements and training plans, teacher-coordinators manage other documentation including pay stubs, safety test results, student work evaluations, student program applications, training site visit records, wage and hour forms, and work permits. Because states vary on documenta-tion policies, teacher-coordinators should obtain their state handbook or policy for cooperative education and work-experience programs for specific requirements. These various state requirements generally specify how long these documents need to be retained (typically from three to five years).

Program Promoter

Promoting cooperative education and work-experience programs is an essential task of teacher-coordinators. A well-designed promotional program targets businesses, parents, school personnel, and students (*Vocational Cooperative Education*, 1993). Each entity is important to program success and must be included in any well-organized, teacher-coordinator promotional effort.

Without the support of businesses, cooperative education and work-experience programs could not exist. Businesses provide staff service on advisory committees, support for career and technical education student organizations, and training sites. Promotional activities targeted to this group are very important, as the teacher must outline the value of the program and secure support for it. Teacher-coordinators frequently place displays in local businesses highlighting student achievements, present to civic and professional groups, provide certificates of appreciation to contributors to the program, and work with local media to foster public relations by writing feature stories about students in the program and their training sites. In addition, at least one training site/student appreciation event is held each year. The appreciation event is typically a banquet or luncheon where students and employers receive recognition for their accomplishments (*Vocational Cooperative Education*, 1993).

Parents play an important role in making cooperative education and work-experi-ence programs successful, and promotional activities directed at keeping them in-formed are essential. One way to promote to this group is through direct mail, with letters outlining the benefits of cooperative education and work-experience programs sent to parents of students taking one or more courses in an occupational area served

Table 2. Sample Training Plan

Student: _____

Date of Hire: _____

Training Site: _____

Supervisor: _____

Degree of Responsibility (place next to progress rating)
* Demonstrates in a timely fashion
** Demonstrates with a positive attitude

Degree of Progress:
1. Demonstrates without assistance.
2. Demonstrates with minimal assistance.
3. Demonstrates with assistance.
4. Needs additional training to demonstrate.
5. Not applicable at this time.

Competencies to be Developed	Grading Period			
Specific Occupational Competencies to be Developed at the Training Site	1	2	3	4
Specific Safety Competencies to be Developed at the Training Site				

Comments/Feedback: _____

Student Signature: _____

Date: _____

Teacher/Coordinator Signature: _____

Date: _____

Training Site Signature: _____

Date: _____

by the program. Promotional videos can be prepared so that parents can view the benefits of cooperative education and work-experience programs. Placing articles in school newsletters and local newspapers explaining the benefits of the program and supplying supporting statistics about program completers and their successes may inform parents of middle and junior high students about the program. Holding an open house for parents of prospective students is another option available to teacher-coordinators (*Vocational Cooperative Education*, 1993).

Positive relationships with school personnel at all levels, including administrators, counselors, faculty, and staff are important to the success of cooperative education and other work-experience programs. Administrators and counselors are frequently invited to attend training site/student appreciation events. Brochures explaining program goals and benefits can be distributed to all administrators, counselors, faculty, and staff. These promotional efforts are essential because school personnel are typically unfamiliar with cooperative education and other work-experience programs. Annual reports for administrators and counselors highlighting program accomplish-ments are another useful promotional device (*Vocational Cooperative Education*, 1993).

Various promotional activities can be effectively designed for students. Students can deliver presentations to classes or assemblies. English classes are often used as a setting for presentations, since all students take English classes. Student interest surveys are another effective promotional strategy. Students who identify a tentative career interest in occupational areas served by the program can be contacted directly. Promotional flyers or brochures can be created and distributed for the occupational areas served by cooperative education and work-experience programs. These flyers may contain information such as program descriptions and employment outlook information for the areas served. Posters can be placed in various locations in the school and at feeder schools. These promotional materials serve to raise awareness of the program and provide contact information for interested students. Other promo-tional activities include inviting middle and junior high students to visit the program, providing interest stories about student successes at work, holding an open house during appropriate times of the year, and promoting the program via the public address system (*Vocational Cooperative Education*, 1993).

Instructor

Teacher-coordinators direct student learning in the related class. They foster learning environments in which students develop the attitudes, knowledge, and skills needed at work. Thus, teacher-coordinators perform a variety of instructional tasks, such as aligning related class instruction with work skills; assisting students in develop-ing their occupational competencies; providing guidance as it relates to career, school, and work issues; and advising the career and technical education student organization (*Redesigning Cooperative Vocational Education*, 1996).

Training Site Developer

The development of training sites includes finding appropriate job placements in the community for students and working closely with employers to achieve program goals. Students participate in cooperative education and work-experience programs to develop occupational-specific competencies in a supervised environment. For cooperative education and work-experience programs to function effectively, the teacher-coordinator must familiarize all employers with program goals and strategies for achieving these goals.

Teacher-coordinators provide the linkage between the training station site and the school. They coordinate work site training with classroom instruction, work with training sites to ensure supervision of students, evaluate training site experiences, and prepare reports required by the state and the school district (*Vocational Cooperative Education*, 1993).

Training sponsors have a variety of responsibilities, including orienting the student to the job, providing supervision and training for the student, providing the student with a variety of learning experiences that foster maximum learning, evaluating and providing feedback to the student, counseling the student on job-related matters such as good attitude and work ethic, and communicating with the teacher-coordinator regularly about job-related concerns (*Vocational Cooperative Education*, 1993).

LEGAL ISSUES RELATED TO WORK EXPERIENCE PROGRAMS

Teacher-coordinators are responsible for assuring that their programs comply with related federal, state, and local laws and regulations. The major federal laws and regulations include the Americans with Disabilities Act, the Civil Rights Act, the Fair Labor Standards Act, the Immigration Reform and Control Act, the Occupational Safety and Health Act, and the Occupational Safety and Health Act (Rader & Kurth, 1999).

Americans with Disabilities Act (ADA)

The ADA provides workers with protection from discriminatory hiring practices against individuals with disabilities. More specifically, the ADA provides civil rights protection to individuals with disabilities by guaranteeing equal opportunity in public accommodations, employment, transportation, government services, and telecommunications (*The Americans with Disabilities Act*, 2001). Information about the ADA is available on the U.S. Department of Justice Web site at http://www.usdoj.gov/crt/ada/qandaeng.htm.

Civil Rights Act

The Civil Rights Act protects minorities and women from discriminatory workplace hiring practices. A statement indicating that the training site does not discriminate on the basis of race, religion, ethnicity, national origin, age, disability, marital status, or veteran status should be included on all program forms for cooperative education programs. Information on the provisions of the Civil Rights Act is found on the Equal Employment Opportunity Commission Web site at http://www.eeoc.gov.

Fair Labor Standards Act (FLSA)

The FLSA was enacted in 1938 and is enforced by the Wage and Hour Division of the U.S. Department of Labor (DOL). The FLSA protects the health and safety of youth workers by establishing working hour standards and prohibiting employment in hazardous occupations. Under the FLSA, 14- and 15-year-olds may work outside school hours in various nonmanufacturing, nonmining, nonhazardous jobs under certain conditions. Permissible work hours for 14- and 15-year-olds are (a) 3 hours on a school day, (b) 18 hours in a school week, 8 hours on a nonschool day, (c) 40 hours in a nonschool week, and (d) between 7 a.m. and 7 p.m. From June 1 through Labor Day, 14- and 15-year-olds may work from 7 a.m. to 9 p.m. The number of hours or times or times of day for workers 16 and older is not limited by the FLSA.

In addition to being well-informed about working hour regulations, teacher-coordinators must be aware of hazardous occupations in which their students cannot be employed. For example, occupations that are generally prohibited for 16- and 17-year-olds include driving a motor vehicle and operating power-driven hosting equip-ment (U.S. Department of Labor, 2002). Teacher-coordinators must be knowledgeable of what their students can and cannot do at training sites. Exceptions to some FLSA standards have been made for youth employed in agricultural occupations (Handy, 1994). Information on FLSA is available at the FLSA Web site at http://www.lectlaw.com/files/emp39.htm. Current information on federal child labor laws is available at the U.S. Department of Labor Web site at http://www.dol.gov/dol/topic/youthlabor/index.htm.

Immigration Reform and Control Act (IRCA)

The IRCA of 1986 requires that only U.S. citizens or aliens lawfully authorized to work be employed in the United States. The documentation requirements necessary to work in the United States are the same for both adult and youth employees. A social security number and two forms of approved identification are needed to complete the I-9 form, making a person eligible to work in the United States. The Immigration and Naturalization Service is responsible for enforcing the IRCA (*The Immigration Reform,* n.d.). Additional information may be found on the IRCA Web site at http://www.usda.gov/oce/oce/labor-affairs/ircasumm.htm.

Occupational Safety and Health Act (OSHA)

OSHA regulates workplace safety. Teacher-coordinators need to be knowledgeable about OSHA regulations when placing students at training sites. Safety hazards such as chemical use, crime, fire, and operation of dangerous equipment all fall under OSHA's auspices. Cooperative office education students may be exposed to common chemicals such as ink and toner cartridges, glue, or correction fluid, both at school and at training sites. Teachers and students should be aware of *Material Safety Data Sheets* (MSDS), which list chemical ingredients, warning statements, precautionary measures, and emergency fist-aid procedures. MSDS forms should be located in conspicuous places in the classroom and workplace for easy access in case of emergency. OSHA also requires safety training for all workers exposed to hazards. As a result, safety is an essential component of instruction at both the related class and training site (Rader & Kurth, 1999). Information on OSHA is available at the OSHA Web site at http://www.osha.gov.

State Laws and Regulations

In addition to being knowledgeable about the various federal laws and regulations governing student workers, teacher-coordinators must also be well informed about student work issues in their respective states. A list of state-level contacts and Web sites containing state youth employment information is available on the U.S. Department of Labor Web site at http://www.dol.gov/esa/contacts/state_of.htm.

ADVISORY COMMITTEES

Advisory committees are essential to the success of cooperative education and work-experience programs. Advisory committees provide occupational standard updates, support for career and technical student organizations, training site recommendations, and updates on workplace practices and expectations. Members of advisory committees generally include businesses, current students, parents, program alumni, school professionals, and training site representatives. Advisory committees vary in size depending on the tasks that need to be completed, but membership is normally 7 to 12 people. Formal meetings are usually held two or three times a year. Teacher-coordinators often meet informally with advisory committee members on an individual basis throughout the school year (*Career/Technical Education*, 2000; Mason & Husted, 1997).

RELATED CLASS

Related classes are those in which instruction is tied to the attitudes, knowledge, and skills developed while working at a training site. Instruction in the related class is usually both general and specific. General instruction seeks to develop the attitudes, the knowledge, and the necessary skills for all students, regardless of occupational area. Specific topics might include career development, credit, fringe benefits, dressing and grooming for success, insurance, money management, safety, saving and investing, study habits, taxes, and working relationships. To make the related class most effective, teacher-coordinators must be well supplied with resources to make learning realistic. Teacher-coordinators have the advantage of working closely with training sponsors and other community-based organizations that are rich sources of instructional information, materials, and assistance. These community business/professional organizations include Toastmasters, Junior Achievement, Chambers of Commerce, and other professional groups (*Career/Technical Education*, 2000; Mason & Husted, 1997).

SUMMARY

Valuable work experience can be provided to secondary and postsecondary business and marketing students through apprenticeships, cooperative education, job shadowing, internships, and service learning. Cooperative education and other work-experience programs provide numerous benefits to students, businesses, schools, and communities.

Teacher-coordinators serve many roles, including documenter, program promoter, instructor, and training site developer. Essential documents include training agreements and training plans. Employers and schools must comply with various federal and state laws affecting work-experience programs. Advisory committees provide assistance for cooperative education and other work-experience programs. The related class provides instruction in essential academic concepts and skills that parallel the work experience component.

REFERENCES

Ascher, C. (1994). Cooperative education as a strategy for school-to-work transition. *CenterFocus Number 3*. Retrieved November 19, 2002, from http://ncrve.berkeley.edu/CenterFocus/cf3.html

Calhoun, C. C., & Robinson, B. W. (1991). *Managing the learning process in business education*. Bessemer, AL: Colonial Press.

Career/technical education: Teacher/coordinator manual. (2000). (Bulletin 2000, No. 18). Montogomery, AL: Department of Education, Career and Technical Education.

Caton, J., & Buck, C. (1990). Interning, co-oping, and programming alternatives: Successful partnerships and funding. In S. L. O'Neil (Ed.), *Strategic planning for the 1990's*, (Yearbook No. 28, pp. 142-150). Reston, VA: National Business Education Association.

Commonwealth of Virginia. Department of Education. (1993). *Vocational cooperative education: Guide for teacher-coordinators*. Richmond, VA: Author.

Cooperative education policies & procedures manual. (2000). Public Schools of North Carolina, State Board of Education, Department of Public Instruction, Workforce Development Education.

Equal Employment Opportunity Commission/U.S. Department of Justice Civil Rights Division. (2001). *The Americans with Disabilities Act: Questions and answers*. Washington DC: U.S. Government Printing Office.

MarkED. (2002). *Work-based education: Tips guide*. Columbus, OH: Author.

Mason, R. E., & Husted, S. W. (1997). *Cooperative occupational education: Including internships, apprenticeships, and tech-prep*. Danville, IL: Interstate Publishers, Inc.

National Business Education Association. (2001). *National standards for business education: What America's students should know and be able to do in business* (2nd ed.). Reston: VA: Author.

Rader, M. H., & Kurth, L. A. (1999). Federal workplace laws: Are business work-experience programs in compliance? *Business Education Forum, 53*(4), 26-29.

Redesigning cooperative vocational education. (1996). (Project No. 94-133-110-8). University of Missouri, Columbia: Instructional Materials Laboratory.

Rockefeller, D. J., & Zikmund, D. G. (1990). Protecting students on the job. *American Vocational Education Journal, 65*(2), 30-31.

Sovilla, E. S. (1998). Co-op's 90-year odyssey. *ASEE Prism, 7*, 18-23.

Stone, J. R., III. (1995). Cooperative vocational education in the urban school: Toward a systems approach. *Education and Urban Society, 27*(3), 328-352.

Tennessee Department of Education. (n.d.). *Work-based learning: Policies, procedures, and resources.* Nashville, TN: Author.

U.S. Department of Justice. (n.d.). *The Immigration Reform and Control Act (IRCA) prohibits employment discrimination: What you should know.* Washington, DC: U.S. Government Printing Office.

U.S. Department of Labor, Employment Standards Administration, Wage and Hour Division. (1994). *Handy reference guide to the Fair Labor Standards Act.* Retrieved November 19, 2002, from http://www.dol.gov/esa/regs/compliance/whd/hrg.htm

U.S. Department of Labor. Employment and Training Administration. (n.d.). Retrieved June 4, 2002, from http://www.doleta.gov/individ/apprent.asp

U.S. Department of Labor. Youth & Labor. (n.d.) Retrieved November 14, 2002, from http://www.dol.gov/dol/topic/youthlabor/index.htm

Sponsoring Student Organizations

Janet M. Gandy

Arizona Department of Education

Phoenix, Arizona

Donna Green

Mingus Union High School

Cottonwood, Arizona

Business and marketing teachers looking for innovative ways to inspire students and bring curriculum to life have found sponsoring student organizations to be an effective and rewarding approach to teaching and learning. Secondary and postsecondary business and marketing instructors who have integrated a nationally recognized student organization into their programs have successfully enhanced classroom learning and bridged the gap for students between school and career.

This chapter presents an explanation of the purpose and benefits of cocurricular student organizations when they are integrated with business and marketing instructional programs. It provides a brief description of the career and technical student organizations—Business Professionals of America, DECA, and Future Business Leaders of America/Phi Beta Lambda and discusses the teacher's many responsibilities as an organization adviser. The information presented offers veteran student organization advisers a fresh perspective and new advisers some practical approaches to sponsoring student organizations.

CAREER AND TECHNICAL STUDENT ORGANIZATIONS
The new term "career and technical education" (CTE) has replaced the term "vocational education" at the national level, as discussed in Chapter 2. Organizations serving students in these programs, formerly known as *vocational student organizations* (VSOs), have been renamed *career and technical student organizations* (CTSOs) (Association of Career and Technical Education [ACTE], 1999a, p. 8).

The common purpose of career and technical student organizations is to bring business/industry and education together in a working relationship and as an integral part of the school curriculum. The United States Department of Education recognizes the Business Professionals of America, DECA, and Future Business Leaders of America/ Phi Beta Lambda as the national career and technical student organizations serving business and marketing education programs. The Department recommends support of all educational leaders for career and technical student organizations and strongly endorses the objectives of the career and technical student organizations in the following policy statement: "The United States Department of Education recognizes the educational programs and philosophies embraced by the career and technical student organizations as being an integral part of vocational and technical education instructional programs" (ACTE, 1999b, pp. 38-39).

Integration of Learning

Career and technical student organizations are not clubs, but rather are an integral part of instruction that makes learning relevant to the student while incorporating academic standards. Student involvement in career and technical student organizations reinforces what is learned in the classroom and helps students see a correlation among instruction, competitive events, and workplace skills (Williams, 2001). *Integrated learning* is "an approach to designing learning objectives to connect areas of study to enrich classroom learning, promote programs, and reinforce curriculum focus" (Penn & Williams, 1996, p. 20).

Student organizations provide experiences that inspire young people to realize their potential, to investigate business careers, and to assume responsibilities of adult life. These organizations give students the opportunity to develop their confidence, self-esteem, leadership abilities, and spirit of cooperation by participating in competitive activities (National Advisory Council on Vocational Education, 1982, as cited in Newton, 1992). The national Policies Commission for Business and Economic Education (1997) affirmed its support of career and technical student organizations with the following statement: "Vocational student organizations serve a cocurricular purpose with projects correlated to classroom instruction while providing opportunities for leadership and personal development, social responsibility, and business skills" (pp.61-63).

Although often categorized as extracurricular activities, student organizations serve a cocurricular purpose, with projects and activities correlated closely to classroom instruction. *Cocurricular activities* are defined as "planned activities, which are part of the school curriculum and occur during the school day and, therefore, fall under a state's constitutional authority for public education" (Ladd & Ruby, 1997, pp. 41-44).

Local and state chapters of student organizations affiliate with the national organization. State chapters recognize local chapters, which operate under charters granted by the national organization.

Business Professionals of America

Business Professionals of America (BPA) was founded in 1971 as the Office Education Association, and in 1988 changed its name to Business Professionals of America. The mission of this organization is to contribute to the preparation of a world-class workforce, through the advancement of leadership, citizenship, academic, and technological skills (Business Professionals of America [BPA], 2002).

In fiscal year 2001-2002, BPA had 2,500 local chapters with more than 52,000 dues-paid members (BPA, 2002). Membership divisions include secondary, postsecondary, associate (for middle-school students and members with special needs), alumni, and professional division membership (for individuals who support the organization but have no previous affiliation).

Chapters develop projects and activities focusing on employability, leadership, civic service, and technical skill development. Chapter members compete in events at the regional, state, and national levels. The Workplace Skills Assessment Program reinforces the workplace skills taught in the classroom, while developing the employability skills necessary for the transition from school to work. Additional information is available at the BPA Web site at www.bpa.org.

Future Business Leaders of America/Phi Beta Lambda

The formative years of Future Business Leaders of America/Phi Beta Lambda (FBLA/PBL) took place during World War II. The organization began in 1940, and the first chapter was organized in 1942. Its mission is to bring business and education together in a positive working relationship through innovative leadership and career development programs (Future Business Leaders of America/Phi Beta Lambda [FBLA/PBL], 2002).

During the 2001-2002 fiscal year, FBLA/PBL had over 13,000 local chapters with 240,000 members in 48 states, the District of Columbia, U.S. Virgin Islands, Puerto Rico, the Department of Defense—Europe, and Canada (FBLA/PBL, 2002). Membership divisions include middle school, secondary, postsecondary, and the professional division, which includes alumni members and individuals who have not affiliated but support the organization.

Areas of emphasis include chapter projects and activities, integrated curriculum that includes leadership development, service learning activities (volunteerism), and reinforcement of job skills. In addition, leadership development activities are enhanced through the National Fall Leadership Conferences and the National Leadership Conference. The competitive events program reinforces curriculum aligned with the *National Standards for Business Education*. Additional information is available at the FBLA Web site at www.fbla-pbl.org.

DECA and Delta Epsilon Chi

DECA (formerly named Distributive Education Clubs of America) is an association of marketing students founded in 1946. The mission of the organization is to enhance the cocurricular education of students who have an interest in marketing, management, and entrepreneurship. DECA supports and contributes to classroom learning through its cocurricular materials and chapter activities (DECA, 2002).

During the 2001-2002 membership year, DECA had 170,000 student members, faculty advisers, professional, and alumni members, 3,700 affiliated secondary and postsecondary local chapters in 50 states, and the District of Columbia, Guam, and Puerto Rico. Membership divisions include DECA for secondary members and Delta Epsilon Chi for postsecondary and alumni members. Professional Division members are individuals who support the goals of DECA and do not qualify under any other membership category.

Areas of emphasis for DECA chapters include career and professional development, civic service, and leadership skills. Additional information is available at the DECA Web site at www.deca.org.

BENEFITS OF STUDENT ORGANIZATIONS

Everyone benefits when student organizations succeed. These organizations provide numerous opportunities for students by promoting programs, teaching workplace skills, recognizing achievement, developing leadership, encouraging professionalism and social skills, and participating in community service. Business and marketing departments enhance their reputations through student success; schools generate positive publicity through student organization efforts and achievements; and the community-at-large takes pride in the accomplishments of youth who will enter the community prepared to contribute as responsible citizens. Businesses that need better trained and better prepared employees are willing to work with schools to offer learning opportunities.

Promoting Business Education Programs

Student organizations promote enrollment in business and marketing programs. CTSOs are especially important at a time when fewer elective courses, such as business and marketing, are available to students at the secondary level. Student members of the organizations are the best advocates for business and marketing education programs because of their related activities on and off campus. These student projects increase the visibility of the program and promote its benefits.

Reinforcing Workplace Skills

The programs and activities of student organizations reinforce the goals of business and marketing education—preparing students for the workplace by developing the skills that employers seek. Employers want employees who can identify and solve problems, set and achieve goals, communicate effectively, apply new information, negotiate with others, and work in teams. These skills are reinforced by student organization activities. Participation in CTSOs motivates students to achieve in class, develop leadership skills, set and accomplish goals, and become competitive both inside and outside the classroom. CTSO activities also provide students opportunities to stay abreast of changes in business and technology. Student organizations create an atmosphere that emphasizes excellence, inspiring students to develop the workplace skills necessary for secondary, postsecondary, and career success.

Recognizing Student Achievement

Career and technical student organizations serve as a catalyst for recognizing student achievement at the individual, team, and chapter levels. As students meet and compete with other business and marketing students from their state, region, and the nation, they take pride in realizing that their studies have been relevant and meaningful.

Students develop proper attitudes toward competition through CTSO events. Learning how to compete successfully gives students an advantage in other competitive arenas, such as applying for jobs or college admission upon graduation from high school. The competitive events are designed to mirror the curriculum. These events, which reinforce the skills learned in the classroom, afford students opportunities to experience both low-risk failure and success. These experiences prepare students for the competitive environment they will encounter throughout their lives. Competitive events offered by each of the CTSOs are found on their respective Web sites.

Developing Leadership

Leadership development is a hallmark of career and technical student organizations. Students are elected by their peers to fill officer roles within the local, state, and national chapters of the student organization. Officers learn the roles and responsibilities of their office. Additionally, they are taught to plan and conduct meetings utilizing parliamentary procedures and other techniques for effective meeting management.

Effective chapters ensure that all members share in the responsibilities of meeting chapter goals and objectives by including each of its members in committee and project work. Every student should be encouraged to learn, to gain self-confidence, and to develop as a future leader. Chapter officers and members learn together through experience, conflict management, communication skills, teamwork, and resource management, as they plan and accomplish their chapter's goals.

Preparation of young people for positions of leadership is the chief aim of career and technical student organizations. Gary Hannah, former President of the Business Professionals of America, observed, "Some say leaders are born, not made. There are some people who are leaders but never surface because they do not have the opportunity—we provide the opportunity" (NBEA, 1997).

Today, leadership is an attribute valued by employers. The qualities of a leader include the ability to inspire others; to do one's best in producing quality results; and to exhibit honesty, sense of humor, passion, risk taking, respect for diversity, energy, organizing skills, and vision (NBEA, 1997). To prepare business leaders, educators must provide leadership opportunities to enable students to demonstrate leadership skills. Student organizations provide motivation in the classroom and encourage leadership among students and teachers. Teachers serve as role models of professionalism and provide positive influences on student attitudes.

Dr. Edward D. Miller, former President and CEO of Future Business Leaders of America/Phi Beta Lambda, comments, "Advisers recognize student leaders by their ability to get involved, their effective questioning, and their ability to follow through, delegate, and set goals. Teachers draw students out by encouraging them to take assignments and progressively accept more responsibility. Leadership is hard work for individuals to reap personal and professional rewards" (NBEA, 1997).

Encouraging Professionalism and Social Skills
Career and technical student organizations offer students opportunities to recruit members, to become involved in running a campaign, and to run for an elected office that represents the members at the local, state, or national level. Participation in elections, as candidates or voting delegates, offers students insight into the electoral process. In addition, students are provided with the opportunity to develop social awareness, communication abilities, and organizational skills while learning time management and pride in the their accomplishments.

Participating in Community Service
Students discover how classroom learning can be applied through community service projects and activities. Examples of these types of projects might include having students assist in the managing and staffing of a cooperative food store, or writing a business plan and preparing a marketing strategy for a nonprofit agency. Service opportunities like these allow students to become involved in real-world situations that cannot be replicated in a classroom. Students participate in community service programs, linking them to the course curriculum and opening opportunities for business and education partnerships. The common thread is reciprocity—performing service in exchange for shared expertise and hands-on learning.

CURRICULUM INTEGRATION
Integration of student organizations such as BPA, FBLA/PBL, and DECA with the business and marketing instructional programs can improve the effectiveness of instruction (Beltram, Green, Harvey, & Harris, 1999). Integrating student organizations into business and marketing programs through projects and activities can enrich classroom learning. Reinforcing connections between classroom learning, involvement

in student organizations, and achievement in the workplace increases students' chances for success in all three.

Teachers who take the initiative to integrate the goals of student organizations with curriculum standards enhance the teaching objectives of the business and marketing programs. The teacher/adviser who takes the initiative to integrate the CTSO projects and activities with the standards can reinforce the importance of business and marketing education by demonstrating how students learn critical academic standards. The *National Standards for Business Education* for marketing provides guidance in linking standards with various business subjects to make learning relevant for students. The standards represent the interrelationship of business functions and demonstrate a higher level of learning in the context applied knowledge and skill (National Business Education Association, 2001).

Making the Classroom Relevant

Opportunities to involve students in diversified projects can reach beyond the educational boundaries of the ordinary classroom by providing assignments that are authentic rather than simulated. Teaching such basic concepts as appropriate time management and pride in a finished product is more easily accomplished when the students know that their work is actually being utilized. Teachers are encouraged to offer their students' services in the performance of tasks such as designing, inputting, and maintaining databases; designing Web pages; preparing and mailing form letters; developing spreadsheets; completing tax returns; and preparing resumes.

Organization advisers develop unique lessons and activities to engage students in solving problems with creative solutions not always found in textbooks. Through various projects and activities, student organizations reinforce what is learned in the business and marketing classrooms and provide students with the opportunity to apply in the community what they have learned in the classroom. Academic concepts are more relevant to students when they are applied through leadership development, career exploration, community service, and fundraising activities.

Extracurricular Approach

If the local school district does not support the student organization as a cocurricular activity, advisers must use their ingenuity to bring this educational component to students as an extracurricular activity. An extracurricular CTSO generally requires the adviser to meet and work with students before school, after school, during the lunch hour, or within an activity period.

In order for meetings to hold the interest of the students, a regular meeting day, time, and place should be established. Although the adviser should be in attendance at all chapter meetings, the students should run them in order to practice parliamentary procedure, adherence to an agenda, and the rules of meeting protocol. Local officers should meet separately prior to general membership meetings to establish the agenda and prepare for a meaningful meeting. In addition to conducting regular business at each meeting, the students should arrange a short educational program such as a guest speaker, a video clip, or information on educational Web sites.

Program of Work

Organizations are most effective when highly motivated members plan and implement a realistic chapter program of work. State and local chapters adopt projects and programs within the framework of the national organization with application to their local communities. The adviser must teach business and marketing students how to plan effectively, as they develop an annual program of work and a calendar of activities.

The goal of each chapter should be to develop a balanced program that facilitates the development of students' civic responsibility, social skills, leadership, and business knowledge. The program of work includes professional activities that reinforce leadership skills—preparing and conducting meetings and programs, managing chapter funds, and budgeting and fundraising; civic and service activities that develop an understanding of civic responsibilities; social activities that promote social skills and etiquette; promotional activities that involve students in public relation efforts both inside and outside the school; and competitive activities that sharpen students' business skills.

Traditional school systems typically develop their program of work around a September to June calendar; however, with the myriad of school calendars and schedules throughout the nation, each school must make its particular adjustments. Table 1 illustrates a typical program of work, taking into consideration that each of the three CTSOs operates within its own rules and regulations with organization-specific time frames and deadlines.

Table 1. Typical Programs of Work	
September	Meet with officers prior to first general meeting. Reserve rooms and meeting dates on school calendar. Hold first general meeting. Recruit new members. Initiate members. Collect local, state, and national dues. Establish the program of work for year. Develop a budget. Establish committees. Delegate responsibilities. Hold parent/guardian information meeting.

October	Submit membership dues and other necessary paperwork to state and national offices. Continue member recruitment. Hold a fundraising activity. Participate in a schoolwide activity. Review bylaws and make needed changes.
November	Conduct service activity associated with national and/or state goals.
December	Hold a social activity for members. Evaluate progress to date; adjust program of work, if necessary.
January	Take members on a field trip. Hold additional fundraising activity.
February	Begin work on state and national competitive events. Conduct local community service project.
March	Select competitors and officer candidates. Work on campaign materials. Submit all necessary paperwork for state and national conferences and events.
April	Attend State Leadership Conference. Host employer/employee banquet.
May	Elect officers for next school year. Hold officer installation and awards banquet. Conduct officer training. Complete all state and national reports. Close out all accounting records.
June	Attend National Leadership Conference. Make presentation to school board. Evaluate year-end effectiveness of program of work.
July/August	Maintain student contact and enthusiasm with social gatherings and service work; use time to recruit new members.

RESPONSIBILITIES OF THE ADVISER

Mary Lynn Fracaroli (1988) of the New Jersey State Department of Education recommends that advisers adopt a personal philosophy about student organizations and set goals for the organization based on that philosophy. Whatever particular mission the adviser envisions for the organization he or she assists, certain responsibilities are common to all: general, legal, travel, and communication responsibilities fall under every adviser's purview.

General Responsibilities

Serving as an adviser of a student organization includes, but is not limited to, the following responsibilities:

- Becoming knowledgeable about the policies and procedures related to the specific organization including its history, mission, goals, policies, bylaws, ceremonies, programs, and activities, and then passing on this knowledge to the students

- Organizing a process for the selection of local officers and then properly training them

- Holding regular organization meetings and ensuring that each runs efficiently and for a purpose

- Assisting students in the development, coordination, and implementation of a well-defined yearly plan of action

- Being consistent in the enforcement of the student organization's rules and guidelines, as well as the policies of local schools

- Informing the school administration, governing board, parents, and community of chapter activities and student success

- Preparing students for participation in local, state, and national activities and competitive events

- Supervising the financial operation and fundraising activities of the organization

- Providing instruction for students in leadership and personal development

- Maintaining continuity, stability, and membership as students graduate and leadership changes

Legal Responsibilities

Each of the student organizations provides suggested and/or required traveling forms, medical releases, insurance information, parental/guardian release statements, and other documents required by the school district. All legal documentation must be properly signed, duplicated, and distributed to the necessary individuals and officials annually. The adviser should place these documents in a binder and take them to all off-campus functions. Additionally, schools may require specialized district permission forms and other documentation.

Advisers should also secure parental/guardian releases for students' pictures and all information that may be included in school and organization publications, such as newspapers, brochures, Web sites, and videos.

Out-of-School Travel Responsibilities

The involvement of students in service projects, fundraising, and competitions frequently involves off-campus travel. The adviser should accompany students to all of these activities. Parents/guardians should be informed well in advance of these trips about specific dates, travel times, location, and phone contacts.

School districts require prior notification and parental permission for student travel, and the adviser must follow all required district procedures. Trip preparation may include filling out a requisition for a bus and driver, requesting a substitute teacher, or making a presentation to the school board. In some schools, the trip may necessitate driving a school van to transport students, which may require the teacher to secure a special category of driver's license. Additionally, districts may have specific guidelines for the ratio of teachers to students and specific requirements for male and female travelers.

Overnight trips offer a new level of responsibility. The adviser must arrange accommodations and address a set of guidelines and rules concerning room assignments, curfews, and bed checks. The adviser should arrange hotel details in advance, including issues such as placement of students in nonsmoking rooms, the number of individuals per room, the presence of connecting doors between rooms, telephone usage, locked beverage bars, and blocking of access to rental movies. Provisions should also be made as to method of payment, as many school districts operate with purchase orders rather than credit cards, and some lodging establishments may be unwilling to accept this form of payment.

The adviser should review with students common courtesies and protocols, such as checking in luggage at the airport, proper table manners, tipping procedures, and what not to remove from a motel room. Some students may be experiencing their first stay at a hotel, eating out at their first sit-down restaurant, taking their first airplane flight, or riding in an elevator for the first time. The adviser should discuss appropriate behavior in advance of each out-of-town trip and address all expectations with the students.

Parent/Guardian Communication

Parent/guardian communication is vital in maintaining a strong student organization. Students are often called upon to perform community service projects or participate in fundraising activities away from school. These opportunities may require students to work beyond school hours, often late into the evening, and possibly in settings unfamiliar to the parents. The teacher should communicate with parents/guardians and ensure that they are aware of and approve of their child's whereabouts at all times. Advisers also must know who has legal permission to pick up a student from an activity.

An effective method of communication is to invite parents/guardians to a beginning-of-the-year social event and explain the goals and purposes of the organization and the planned activities. At this meeting, the parents can complete all necessary legal documentation and the adviser can address parents' concerns.

SUPERVISION OF FUNDRAISING ACTIVITIES

Fundraising for purposes such as financing membership dues, creating travel funds, and conducting service projects is necessary for most CTSOs. Through fundraising, students learn leadership, organization, promotion, and marketing. In addition, these experiences teach them how to work as a team. The students should select the project, set realistic goals, and identify skills and interests associated with the chosen project. As the fundraising project progresses, students learn to employ marketing strategies, to evaluate their work by presenting a final analysis of income and expenses, and to examine the strengths and weaknesses of the project.

School Policies and Procedures

Many schools have strict guidelines for fundraising that may exclude certain activities. Established policies may regulate the number and type of activities, or the duration, location, and time these events are held. The student organizations must secure permission for all activities according to school guidelines. Additionally, the intake of funds must be closely monitored, processed, and accounted for. School policy generally specifies records that must be completed and distributed appropriately for receipt and disbursement of funds.

Community Regulations

Off-campus activities typically involve compliance with additional policies and procedures. The adviser should be aware of community regulations and legalities that may be involved. Some fundraising activities may require food handler permits or event licenses. Other regulations such as curfew ordinances may be an issue when student activities occur in the evening. To ensure compliance, the adviser should maintain a close working relationship with local government entities including police chiefs, fire marshals, and health inspectors.

Social and Political Standards

Before taking students out into the community, the teacher should be aware of norms and acceptances of the local community regarding social and political standards, religious beliefs, and local customs. Student activities should be well researched for all possible implications, negative as well as positive, before investing time and energy into a project that may be considered too controversial.

SERVICE LEARNING ACTIVITIES

Through service activities, students learn the importance of honesty and integrity, exercise their leadership skills, and develop the ability to work as members of a team. Service-learning activities also help students to develop a respect for people of various ages, ethnic backgrounds, education, and income. In-school activities can range from volunteering to help campus instructors with paperwork, to picking up trash, to tutoring incoming freshmen.

In community service projects such as researching the history of a local community and developing a Web site from the information collected, or assisting with local voter registration efforts, the adviser acts as an ambassador of education in the community. Students develop self-worth and a sense of belonging when they reach out into their local communities. Service projects teach students valuable skills such as time management, organization, attention to deadlines, and effective communication. Working with civic organizations or providing service to needy individuals or groups fosters support for the involved student organization and helps to present the youth of the local community in a positive light.

Specific projects both on the state and national levels are designated by each of the individual organizations. Each local chapter should build activities to support each of these projects into their annual program of work. Participation in these state and national projects helps to educate local chapter members about the larger purpose of their organization.

PREPARATION FOR COMPETITION

The competitions offered through student organizations are a capstone for many of the students and a reason that many students become members. The adviser is responsible for preparing students to perform to the best of their ability.

Students should be prepared and coached for competitions. The teacher should instruct students in testing basics, such as darkening the spots on an answer sheet properly, listing the complete school name instead of using acronyms or abbreviations, printing neatly and legibly, not folding or damaging a score sheet, and printing a full first and last name instead of nicknames.

The adviser should apprise students of all the guidelines and requirements for each event. Completing entry forms correctly, proofreading documents for grammatical or spelling errors, submitting the correct number of copies, addressing documents properly, and labeling event folders accurately are essential. A student or team may be disqualified for minor infractions such as completing a job application form in pencil instead of pen, exceeding a required performance time limit, submitting a report with an improper cover, or appearing in improper attire.

Advisers should provide students with all the necessary guidelines for each of the competitive areas well in advance of the competition. The students should arrange study sessions before competitions, rehearse speeches and presentations, scrutinize their own attire, and double check supplies and materials.

The students should be encouraged to compete in a variety of events, as competition encourages students to reach their potential. To be a winner, a student does not have to win a trophy. The most important benefit is the experience gained, the learning acquired, and the knowledge that the student gave his or her best effort.

PROMOTION OF THE ORGANIZATION

Creating, building, and maintaining a strong chapter are a constant challenge to the adviser. The adviser and the students are all responsible for promoting the organization. These efforts include student recruitment, administrative support, and advertising media.

Student Recruitment

The adviser, with the assistance of current students, must reach out to bring new students into the group. Recruitment can be accomplished in a number of ways, including promotions at student career fairs and school open houses, classroom presentations, personal letters of invitation, incentive challenges with current members, audiovisual presentations, brochures, guest speakers, or field trips. Recruitment should begin early in the school year when students are enthusiastic and not yet committed to other activities.

Administrative Support

A student organization's continued success is only as strong as the support provided to the adviser and students by the school administration. The adviser must constantly work to inform new administrators about the importance of the student organization by publicizing students' involvement and success through newsletters, faculty meeting presentations, student presentations, e-mails, invitations to social events, and in-service workshops.

Advertising Media

Advisers and students should continually advertise their success stories to all stakeholders. Student members' achievements should be used to publicize events on a regular basis. News releases and pictures should be sent to local newspapers, as well as to publications in community venues such as school newspapers, church bulletins, and newsletters of local civic organizations. The adviser should encourage students to create and regularly update a chapter Web site. If the school has its own television broadcast capability, it should be utilized. Students can prepare speeches, aided by the use of presentation software, and contact local civic groups and neighboring schools to make presentations. Officers can join the local Chamber of Commerce and attend monthly meetings. A student organization will flourish if the adviser, officers, and members persistently work to promote its activities.

SUMMARY

A strong student career and technical organization enriches the business and marketing education curriculum. Membership in student organizations such as Business Professionals of America, DECA, and Future Business Leaders of America enhances learning through practical applications. Benefits of student organizations include promoting business and marketing education programs, reinforcing workplace skills, recognizing student achievement, developing leadership, encouraging profession- alism and social skills, and participating in community service activities. The goals of the student organization should be integrated with the business and marketing curriculum. Organization meetings and other activities may occur during school (cocurricular approach) or after school (the extracurricular approach).

The adviser's responsibilities are many. In addition to general responsibilities for supervising chapter activities, the adviser has many legal responsibilities when students participate in out-of-school activities, including traveling to competitions and super- vising fundraising activities. Advisers are also responsible for communicating with parents, complying with community regulations, organizing and supervising service- learning activities, and preparing students to be successful in competitive events. With the assistance of students, advisers must promote their organization and recruit new members by reaching out to the community.

REFERENCES

Association for Career and Technical Education. (1999a). *CTSO guide to accessing federal Perkins funds: For the support of career and technical student organizations.* Washington, D.C.: Author.

Association for Career and Technical Education. (1999b). Policy of the United States Department of Education for career and technical student organizations. *CTSO career and technical student organizations, a reference guide* (2nd ed.). Washington, D.C.: Author.

Beltram, P. K., Green, D., Harvey, M. M., & Harris, C. R. (1999). Business student organizations: Bridging the gap. *Business Education Forum, 54*(2), 49-51.

Business Professionals of America. (2002). Retrieved February 18, 2002, from http:// www.bpa.org/history.html

DECA, An Association of Marketing Students. (2002). Retrieved February 18, 2002, from http://www.deca.org/ introduction/info.html

Fracaroli, M. L. (1988). Integrating student organizations into the business education curriculum. *Business Education Forum, 42*(4), 23-25.

Future Business Leaders of America/Phi Beta Lambda. (2002). Retrieved February 18, 2002, from http://www.fbla-pbl.org/about_main.asp?featureid=687

Ladd, P. D., & Ralph, R., Jr. (1997). Statewide responsibility and its effect on due process. *Business Education Forum, 52*(2), 41-44.

McFarland, L. J., Senn, L. E., and Childress, J.R. (1993). *21st century leadership: Dialogues with 100 top leaders.* New York: The Leadership Press.

National Business Education Association. (1997). Leadership: A skill for everyone. *Keying In*, 7(4). Reston: Author.

National Business Education Association. (2001). *National standards for business education: What America's students should know and be able to do in business.* Reston, VA: Author.

Newton, L. (1992). *Youth organizations and their role in enhancing elements of the hidden curriculum.* (Yearbook No. 30, pp. 176-195). Reston, VA: The National Business Education Association.

Penn, A., & Williams, D. (1996). *Integrating academic and vocational education: A model for secondary schools.* Alexandria, VA.: Association of Supervision and Curriculum Development.

Policies Commission for Business and Economic Education. (1997). Policy Statement No. 30. *This we believe about the role of student organizations in business education,* pp. 61-63. Reston, VA: National Business Education Association.

Williams, K. L. (2001). Student organizations and business education: A winning combination. *Business Education Forum, 56*(2), 56-57.

Lifelong Professional Development

James Calvert Scott
Utah State University
Logan, Utah

Change occurs at a rapid rate, leading quickly to obsolescence. This twenty-first century truism certainly applies to business educators, who are professionally prepared for a world that all too soon may vanish before their eyes. To keep abreast of all of the changes in contemporary life, business educators must continue to learn and grow. This chapter discusses a variety of means by which business educators can choose to engage in the lifelong professional development that is critical to keeping up with changing times.

PROFESSIONAL DEVELOPMENT THROUGH LIFELONG LEARNING

For the purposes of this chapter, *lifelong learning* is defined as ongoing learning. While lifelong learning begins at birth, lifelong learning in the professional sense extends from formal profession-related education through the working life of a teacher, a time period that might last forty or more years. Lifelong learning is based on a holistic view of the evolution of a teacher from novice to master practitioner, rather than on the development of a teacher through a series of separate and distinct stages ("Reconceptualizing Professional," 1995). Imel (1990) envisioned this professional development as a continuing series of carefully planned and managed activities that contribute to professional growth throughout the teacher's working years. Such activities should be part of an integrated, cumulative process that is focused on achieving optimum performance, instead of a series of disjointed, unrelated activities (Livneh & Livneh, 1999). These activities should provide opportunities for professional growth and enrichment (Chin, 1996). Since a teacher may engage in some professional development activities independently and apart from immediate colleagues, a personal professional development model that includes initiating, planning, managing, and evaluating may be one viable approach to lifelong professional development (Imel, 1990).

The need for lifelong professional development is an important reccurring theme in education literature (Edwards & Usher, 2001; Naylor, 1997; Nicholls, 2000). It also appears in business education literature (e.g., Neal, 1997; Scott, 1987). The need for lifelong professional development was reiterated for business educators by the Policies Commission for Business and Economic Education in its Policy Statement No. 68 entitled, "This We Believe about the Emerging Roles of the Business Educator" (Policies Commission for Business and Economic Education, 2001); and by the National Association for Business Teacher Education in its *Business Teacher Education Curriculum Guide & Program Standards* (National Association for Business Teacher Education, 1997). Cochrane (2001) stated the case for lifelong professional development succinctly: "Professional development is a vital way to ensure that we [business educators] stay on the cutting edge of our field and that we have the knowledge and skills to prepare students for success in tomorrow's workplace" (p. 6).

According to Livneh and Livneh (1999), the need for ongoing education and development has been intensified by such factors as (a) the surge in information and technology, (b) legislative educational mandates, (c) the public's demand for competent teachers, (d) regulatory board and professional association standards, (e) emphasis on reflective professional practice, (f) pride in professional work, and (g) the need for a skilled workforce.

Lifelong professional development for teachers includes some combination of the following major components: (1) undergraduate teacher education, (2) graduate teacher education, (3) reading of professional literature, (4) peer relationships, (5) inservice training, (6) work-experience placements, (7) professional certification or licensure, (8) travel, (9) sabbatical leave, and (10) membership in professional organizations. Business educators will likely choose different mixes of these components to meet their lifelong professional development needs, reflecting differences in work assignments, interests, and the like.

Undergraduate Teacher Education
Undergraduate teacher education provides a prospective business educator with basic preparation for a teaching career and is the foundation upon which lifelong professional development is built. Besides the general university or liberal arts requirements, undergraduate teacher education typically includes both business and education requirements, the specifics of which vary somewhat from one educational institution to another and from state to state. The purposes of the business requirements are to expose a prospective teacher to the knowledge, skills, and attitudes necessary to perform effectively in the major functional areas of business and to develop basic mastery of the business subject matter that he or she might be asked to

teach, as reflected in the *National Standards for Business Education* (National Business Education Association, 2001). The purposes of the education requirements are to develop in prospective business educators the teaching-related knowledge, skills, and attitudes necessary to effectively deliver business subject matter in educational settings. The education requirements include both academic work and student teaching experiences in public school settings. Successful completion of undergraduate teacher education typically leads to a bachelor's degree and initial teacher certification or licensure.

Graduate Teacher Education

Graduate teacher education provides additional opportunities for academic and professional advancement. Depending on the type of graduate program pursued, it may focus on increased understanding of business subject matter, business teaching methodology, general education methodology, or some combination of the three, through traditional and/or electronic delivery of instruction. Regardless of the focus, the program will build upon the basic undergraduate background and strengthen it by broadening and refining the capabilities of the business educator and by developing one or more areas of expertise. Graduate teacher education often has some type of research-related component, especially at the doctoral level. Major reasons for earning an advanced degree include professional advancement, better job opportunities, and an increase in salary.

Professional Literature

Professional literature functions as the foundation of the profession by offering a wealth of information and guidance. A business teacher who regularly reads both business and business education literature can acquire a great deal of information without returning to a collegiate-level institution. For example, to learn more about some aspect of business education, a teacher can conduct a search of relevant data-bases, such as ERIC or ABI-Inform. Professional literature is a particularly important source of professional development for those who teach in a small department, without the benefit of frequent interaction with colleagues who teach the same subjects.

A business teacher should be not only a thoughtful consumer of literature in the field, but also a contributor to business education literature. Every business educator, regardless of the level at which he or she works, has valuable insights about and strategies for effectively delivering business subject matter that would be beneficial to others. Whether the results of scholarly research or practical teaching tips, that information can—and should—be shared with others through the appropriate business education publication (see Arosteguy, 1999; Blaszczynski & Green, 1999; Scott, 1998, for manuscript-preparation tips). A business teacher should submit a manuscript to a publication outlet that has an audience for whom the message is relevant. For example, the results of a scholarly research investigation might best be disseminated through *The Delta Pi Epsilon Journal* or the *NABTE Review,* while practical teaching tips might be best disseminated to others through *Business Education Forum,* National

Business Education Association's quarterly, or *Instructional Strategies: An Applied Research Series*, a Delta Pi Epsilon publication.

Peer Relationships

A *peer relationship* exists when business educators help one another to grow and succeed. A prospective teacher typically forms early peer relationships with preferred fellow students and instructors and with the cooperating and university supervising teachers during student teaching. Later, a teacher typically forms peer relationships with colleagues, especially those with whom he or she regularly works or associates in other academic settings. Sometimes peer relationships grow from the professional level to the personal level, which further enriches a mutually beneficial and personally satisfying relationship that can last for the remainder of a lifetime.

As a teacher matures professionally, he or she begins to serve as a mentor to others. A novice business educator can benefit considerably from the nurturing provided by a more experienced business educator. The quality of this mentoring is often a factor that influences whether a novice continues to be a business educator (Neal, 1997). Two key issues for new teachers who apprentice to a master are first, whether or not the mentor provides personal support during those difficult days when little seems to be going right in the classroom, or whether or not the novice receives practical guidance about classes that the novice is teaching for the first time. Well-intentioned support and advice can bolster the morale of the novice and contribute to classroom success. Having a mentor who genuinely cares about the welfare of a novice business educator prevents the novice from having to learn everything through the school of hard knocks, which can be debilitating for both the teacher and the students. An inexperienced teacher can reciprocate the support with a mentor, since the novice is likely better versed than the mentor in some matters—perhaps the latest technologies, the newest teaching methodologies, some business subject matter, or possibly the culture of the students.

To show gratitude for the generous assistance received from other business educators, a teacher can repay in kind by reaching out and helping others who can benefit from assistance, but who may not feel always feel comfortable asking for it. A good peer relationship is like a two-way street with traffic flowing in both directions on a regular basis.

Inservice Training

Inservice training is training provided for teachers typically on a schoolwide or districtwide basis by local school district personnel, and occasionally on a regional or statewide basis by college/university faculty or by state department of education personnel. It allows a teacher to update knowledge, skills, and attitudes in a setting that is usually close to work and home, at little or no cost other than the investment of time and effort. Often inservice training is provided a few hours at a time after school, during a teacher release day, or immediately before or after the regular school year. In some cases participation in inservice training may count toward a salary increase and/ or toward maintaining or upgrading teaching certification or licensure.

To be effective, inservice training should (a) focus on competency-based approaches that consider the knowledge, skills, attitudes, and experiences of teachers as assets; (b) allow adequate teacher time for analytical and reflective learning; (c) emphasize learning together rather than in isolation; and (d) support what practicing teachers believe is important and needed ("Reconceptualizing Professional," 1995).

Work-Experience Placements

Work-experience placements are opportunities to apply previously learned knowledge, or to acquire new knowledge, skills, and attitudes, while functioning as an employee of an organization. Work-experience placements provide real-world settings in which to hone the qualifications that are necessary for employment. By having multiple work-experience placements, a business educator better understands how the business subject matter that is being taught applies in today's business world.

An enterprising business teacher can find relevant work-experience placements domestically or internationally. Work-experience placements ideally are full-time, since such placements are more realistic and typical of employment in the business world, but even part-time placements can provide valuable insights about the way in which the business world actually functions. Although a business educator is more likely to undertake a work-experience placement when school is not in session, other configurations are possible. A part-time placement can be completed after school hours, on weekends, or during days off from school. Occasionally, a business educator may qualify for release time or a sabbatical leave devoted to learning about contemporary business practices, by engaging in business activities related to his or her teaching assignment. By devoting time to learning about contemporary business practices, the teachers can refresh their classroom repertoires and renew their teaching energies. That block of time might be one summer, one semester, two semesters, or one year. While work-experience placements can be paid or unpaid, the paid type provides a monetary reward beyond the intrinsic knowledge, skills, and attitudes and can further motivate a teacher to choose them as viable means of professional development.

Professional Certification or Licensure

Professional certification or licensure is the endorsement of a teacher as having met the professional standards set by an awarding body, such as a state or its designee, a vendor, or a profession-related organization. Professional certification or licensure is a stamp of approval that indicates that a business educator is a qualified practitioner.

Required professional certification or licensure to teach in the public schools is typically granted by the teacher certification division of a state or by its designee, such as an approved teacher-training institution or department. Although requirements vary from state to state, they typically include successful completion of coursework in a specified content area, and education topics and student teaching in the public schools. In the past, teacher certification or licensure may have been granted for life, but now, in a number of systems, a business educator must provide continuing evidence of having updated knowledge, skills, and attitudes through additional education, training, and work experience to remain certified or licensed. States often grant teacher certification or licensure in stages—from provisional to basic to standard certification or licensure—that approximate the transition from novice to experienced teacher.

Many states are experimenting with alternative certification or licensure programs because of a shortage of teachers, and because many people who want to teach have not graduated from traditional teacher-training programs. Since alternative certification or licensure is controversial, the National Association for Business Teacher Education (NABTE) has drafted a model for alternative certification or licensure to guide states as they develop their respective standards for qualifying someone with a nontraditional background to practice as a business teacher (National Association for Business Teacher Education, 2001).

Some technology vendors used by business educators have their own optional vendor-sponsored certification programs for those who pass a series of examinations. The purpose of such proprietary certification is to regulate qualifications, so that those who claim to possess certain proficiencies are, in fact, well-qualified and competent. Vendors such as Microsoft, Novell, and Cisco have their own certification programs for businesspeople and their teachers (D. J. Green, personal communication, December 6, 2001). A state-certified business educator who is extensively involved with technology might also choose to pursue vendor-sponsored certification to increase his or her understanding, proficiency, and visibility within the business world.

Some professional organizations have their own optional profession-related certification programs for those who pass a series of examinations. The purpose of such professional certification is, again, to regulate qualifications and ensure that the holder of a particular professional designation is well-qualified and competent. Such professional organizations as the American Institute of Certified Public Accountants (AICPA) and the International Association of Administrative Professionals (IAAP) set the qualifications and examinations, allowing members who meet their standards to use the professional designations of Certified Public Accountant (CPA) or Certified Professional Secretary (CPS) and/or Certified Administrative Professional (CAP, respectively, after their names (C. Blaszczynski, personal communication, December 6, 2001).

Travel
Business educators can also grow professionally through domestic and international travel. While business educators can learn much about business by reading, listening, and watching training films, he or she can learn even more by experiencing that business activity in person. Teachers can broaden and deepen their understanding

about the business world by carefully observing how business is conducted and by asking businesspeople thoughtful questions. Since not all types of businesses operate in all localities, business teachers should look beyond their own doorsteps to develop a more comprehensive understanding and appreciation of how business is practiced domestically and internationally. The information gathered from travel not only increases the knowledge base of business educators, it also enhances their ability to deliver high-quality business education through exposure to multiple ways of doing business and/or educating, and through selection of the more effective content and delivery.

Sabbatical Leaves

A *sabbatical leave* is an opportunity for a teacher to be released from a regular teaching assignment, typically every seventh year, to engage in developmental activities that benefit both the teacher and his or her employer. During a sabbatical leave a business educator might return to college for more advanced study, work in a business or at another educational institution, conduct a full-time research project, or engage in any other activities that are agreeable to both the business educator and the employer.

The terms of a sabbatical leave vary from one educational institution to another. Typically, a teacher will be released for one semester, two semesters, or one year to pursue approved activities. He or she might receive partial or full pay, depending on the policies of the educational institution. In most cases, a condition for being granted a sabbatical leave is a requirement that the teacher return to the educational institution at the sabbatical's end for a period of time, often for one academic year.

Since business is increasingly conducted on a global basis, a business educator who qualifies for a sabbatical leave should seriously consider spending at least one the leaves abroad. Scott (1997) identifies a wide variety of international opportunities and their related sources of information, including educational fellowships and teaching opportunities. While a sabbatical leave abroad is not for everyone, it can be highly successful and rewarding if it is carefully planned and thoughtfully implemented. Scott (1992) provides practical tips for planning a sabbatical leave, getting a sabbatical leave approved, and implementing a sabbatical leave in another country. Living and working abroad can be a profound personal and professional growth experience—an unparalled opportunity for a business educator and accompanying family members to experience a new culture firsthand.

Professional Organization Memberships

A *professional organization membership* is an affiliation with others who share similar work-related interests and goals. This linking together of like-minded people allows them to achieve goals collectively that would not be feasible for them to achieve individually. The three primary functions of a professional organization are to (1) offer professional development opportunities for its members, (2) link members with others who have shared interests, and (3) serve as advocates for the profession and its members. Professional organization membership typically includes most or all of the following advantages: (a) leadership that looks after the best interests of the profession and its members, (b) publications that meet the needs of the members, (c) networking opportunities that facilitate interaction with others with similar interests, (d) standards that influence the profession and its members, (e) research-based information and publications to guide members, (f) conferences that meet the needs of the members, (g) legislative advocacy to safeguard the interests of the profession and its members, and (h) workshops that address the concerns of the profession and its members. About seven out of ten U.S. workers are members of at least one professional organization, and about one out of four U.S. workers are members of four or more professional organizations (Anderson, Mitchell, & Erthal, 2001).

The highlight of membership in professional organizations is attendance at conferences, be they local, state, regional, national, or international, because conferences serve as a focal point for lifelong professional development. A typical business education professional conference includes a variety of sessions designed to meet the divergent needs and interests of members. That meeting will often include sessions with speakers from the business world, sessions to meet the practical needs of business educators at various instructional levels, sessions to present new research findings and implications, meals and social functions to promote networking among attendees, exhibits of textbooks and technology to help teachers gain access to the resources they need, and tours of business and industry to promote better understanding of the business world.

Attending professional organization conferences is a wonderful way to meet old friends and to make new friends who are interested in promoting business education. This networking can lead to the acquisition of much useful information. Teachers should attend conferences of professional organizations to learn about business trends, teaching methodologies and materials, curriculum updates, business education research, new textbooks and technologies, professional publications, professional organizations, and legislative developments, to name but a few.

PROFESSIONAL DEVELOPMENT THROUGH SPECIFIC ORGANIZATIONS

A business educator can make effective use of the benefits of membership in a wide variety of business education-related professional organizations to foster lifelong professional development. This section of the chapter briefly highlights six professional organizations that can contribute extensively to lifelong professional development.

National Business Education Association

The *National Business Education Association (NBEA)* is the largest U.S. organization devoted to those interested in education for and about business. Its members are engaged in all aspects of business education, including instruction, administration, research, and dissemination of information about business education. Although NBEA is primarily a national organization, it does have five regional divisions and international linkage to the International Society for Business Education (ISBE) through ISBE's U. S. chapter (National Business Education Association, 2001).

The benefits of NBEA membership include both regular and special publications, such as the quarterly journal *Business Education Forum*; the *NBEA Yearbook*, which addresses a different educational theme each year; and the quarterly newsletter, *Keying In*. NBEA offers regional association membership, annual national and regional conferences, free and low-cost professional liability insurance, a group insurance plan, a professional awards program, International Society for Business Education linkage, legislative advocacy, and a credit card program. For additional information communicate directly with NBEA by mail at 1914 Association Drive, Reston, VA 20191-1596; by telephone at (703) 860-8300; by facsimile at (703) 620-4433; by e-mail at nbea@nbea.org; or on its Web site at www.nbea.org (National Business Education Association, 2001).

National Association for Business Teacher Education

The *National Association for Business Teacher Education (NABTE)* is the institutional arm of NBEA, providing nationwide leadership and service to business teacher educational institutions and business teacher educators. Its members are colleges and universities that have state-approved business teacher education programs and individuals interested in business teacher education. The NABTE functions throughout the year, and its research conference and annual meeting are held concurrently with the annual conference of NBEA (National Business Education Association, 2001).

Membership benefits from NABTE include its regular and special publications, including *NABTE Review;* an annual research conference and annual business meeting; curriculum guides and program standards; a model for alternative licensure/certification; and an award of merit program for outstanding undergraduate business teacher education graduates. For additional information communicate directly with NABTE by mail at 1914 Association Drive, Reston, VA 20191-1596; by telephone at (703) 860-8300; by facsimile at (703) 620-4433; by e-mail at nbea@nbea.org; or on its Web site at www.nbea.org (National Business Education Association, 2001).

International Society for Business Education

The United States Chapter of the *International Society for Business Education (ISBE)* is the international arm and linkage for NBEA to the international aspects of business education. Its members are NBEA members who are particularly interested in promoting and strengthening business education around the world. Although the United States Chapter of ISBE functions throughout the year, its main events occur during the annual convention of NBEA and during the annual international convention of ISBE (National Business Education Association, 2001b), which is known abroad by its French name and acronym, Societe Internationale pour l'Enseigenement Commercial (SIEC) (International Society for Business Education, 2001).

Membership benefits from SIEC-ISBE include its regular and special publications, such as *International Review for Business Education, Journal for Global Business Education*, and *International Society for Business Education Network*. SEIC-ISBE offers an annual international conference, an annual U. S. chapter meeting, networking possibilities with business educators and trainers domestically and internationally, and various opportunities for the international exchange of business education information. For additional information communicate directly with SIEC-ISBE by mail at P.O. Box 20457, Carson City, NV 89721; by telephone at (775) 882-1445; by facsimile at (775) 882-1449; by e-mail at secretary@siec-isbe.org; or on its Web site at www.siec-isbe.org (International Society for Business Education, 2001).

Delta Pi Epsilon

Delta Pi Epsilon (DPE) is a professional honor society devoted to the scientific study of business education through scholarship, leadership, and service. Its members include business educators, administrators, researchers, and businesspeople, all of whom have education at the graduate level and share a common interest in business education research. DPE functions at both the chapter and national levels (Delta Pi Epsilon, n.d.).

The membership benefits at DPE include its regular and special publications, including *The Delta Pi Epsilon Journal* and *Instructional Strategies: An Applied Research Series*. DPE also sponsors chapter meetings, an annual research and teaching conference, conference research awards, chapter activity awards, national graduate and independent research awards, and research grants funded by the Delta Pi Epsilon Research Foundation, Inc. For additional information communicate directly with DPE by mail at P.O. Box 4340 Web site at www.dpe.org (Delta Pi Epsilon, n.d.).

Pi Omega Pi

Pi Omega Pi is the business-teacher education honor society. Its members are undergraduate and graduate business education majors in the top 35 percent of their classes and people who meet the alumni, faculty, associate, and honorary membership requirements. Although Pi Omega Pi is a national organization, its largest concentration of chapters is in the Midwest (Pi Omega Pi, 2001). Contact the organization in Little Rock, AR 77714; by telephone at (501) 219-1866; by facsimile at (501) 219-1876; by e-mail at dpe@ipa.net; or on its Web site at www.dpe.org (DPE, n.d.)

Membership benefits of belonging to Pi Omega Pi include its regular and special publications, such as the newsletter *Here and There*, chapter meetings, biennial national convention held in conjunction with the NBEA convention, and chapter award competition (Pi Omega Pi, 2001). For additional information communicate directly with Pi Omega Pi by mail in care of Dr. Nancy Zeliff at Computer Science/Information Systems Department, Northwest Missouri State University, Maryville, MO 64468; by telephone at (660) 562-1292; by facsimile at (660) 562-1963; by e-mail at nzeliff@ mail.nwmissouri.edu; or on its Web site at www.nwmissouri.edu/~oisbe/piomegapi (N. Zeliff, personal communication, December 11, 2001).

Association for Career and Technical Education

The *Association for Career and Technical Education (ACTE)*, the largest U.S. association that focuses on education, prepares people for careers within a competitive workforce. ACTE members include students, educators, administrators, counselors, and local and state employees and represent 13 diverse divisions, including business education and marketing education, and five geographic regions (Association for Career and Technical Education, 2001).

Membership benefits of belonging to ACTE include its regular and special publications, such as *Techniques* and *Career Tech Update*, an annual convention and related trade show, a national policy seminar, regional workshops, an awards program, professional resources, a legislative action center, professional liability insurance, and a life insurance plan. For additional information communicate directly with ACTE by mail at 1410 King Street, Alexandria, VA 22314; by telephone at (800) 826-9972; by facsimile at (703) 683-7424; by e-mail at acte@acteonline.org; or on its Web site at www.acteonline.org (Association for Career and Technical Education, 2001).

SUMMARY

To keep up with the changing times, business educators must actively engage in lifelong professional development through a variety of means. Among the options from which business educators can choose when crafting their personal professional development plans are the following: (a) undergraduate teacher education, (b) graduate teacher education, (c) professional literature, (d) peer relationships, (e) inservice training, (f) work-experience placements, (g) professional certification or licensure, (h) travel, (i) sabbatical leaves, and (j) professional organization memberships. If business educators carefully plan and thoughtfully manage selected professional development activities, they can achieve optimal professional performance through growth and enrichment year after year.

REFERENCES

Anderson, M., Mitchell, R., & Erthal, M. (2001, November). *Professional associations: Their value as perceived by members.* Paper presented at the 2001 Delta Pi Epsilon National Conference, Nashville, TN.

Arosteguy, S. L. (1999). Strategies for illustrating a research article. *The Delta Pi Epsilon Journal, 41*(4), 212-218.

Association for Career and Technical Education. (2001). ACTEonline. Retrieved December 11, 2001, from http://www.acteonline.org

Blaszczynski, C., & Green, D. J. (1999). Strategies for writing quantitative and qualitative research articles. *The Delta Pi Epsilon Journal, 41*(4), 204-211.

Chin, B. A. (1996, January). How to employ professional development for lifelong learning. *Curriculum Review, 35,* 5.

Cochrane, D. J. (2001). Meeting the professional development needs of today's business educator. *Business Education Forum, 56*(2), 6.

Delta Pi Epsilon. (n.d.). Delta Pi Epsilon. Retrieved October 24, 2001, from http://www.dpe.org

Edwards, R., & Usher, R. (2001). Lifelong learning: A postmodern condition of education? *Adult Education Quarterly, 51*(4), 273-287.

Imel, S. (1990). *Managing your professional development: A guide for part-time teachers of adults: ERIC digest* (Report No. EDO-CE-90-98). Washington, DC: Office of Educational Research and Improvement. (ERIC Document Reproduction Service No. ED321155)

International Society for Business Education. (2001). Societe Internationale pour l'Enseigenment Commercial—International Society for Business Education. Retrieved December 10, 2001, from http://www.siec-isbe.org

Livneh, C., & Livneh, H. (1999). Continuing professional education among educators: Predictors of participation in learning activities. *Adult Education Quarterly, 49*(2), 91-106.

National Association for Business Teacher Education. (1997). *Business teacher education curriculum guide & program standards.* Reston, VA: National Business Education Association.

National Association for Business Teacher Education. (2001). *Draft—model for alternative licensure/certification for business teachers developed by National Association for Business Teacher Education (NABTE):* Author. (Available from Dr. Dennis LaBonty, President, National Association for Business Teacher Education, Department of Business Information Systems, College of Business, Utah State University, 3515 Old Main Hill, Logan, UT 84322-3515)

National Business Education Association. (2001a). *National standards for business education:* Author.

National Business Education Association. (2001b). NBEAonline. Retrieved October 24, 2001, from http://www.nbea.org

Naylor, M. (1997). *Vocational teacher education reform: ERIC digest no. 180* (Report No. EDO-CE-97-180). Washington, DC: Office of Educational Research and Improvement. (ERIC Document Reproduction Service No. ED407572)

Neal, D. A. (1997). Retain, retrain and reward business educators. In C. P. Brantley & B. J. Davis (Eds.), *The changing dimensions of business education* (Yearbook No. 35, pp. 130-135). Reston, VA: National Business Education Association.

Nicholls, G. (2000). Professional development, teaching, and lifelong learning: The implications for higher education. *International Journal of Lifelong Education, 19*(4), 370-377.

Pi Omega Pi. (2001). Pi Omega Pi. Retrieved October 24, 2001, from http://www.nwmissouri.edu/~oisbe/piomegapi

Policies Commission for Business and Economic Education. (2001). This we believe about the emerging roles of the business educator. *Business Education Forum, 56*(1), 14-15.

Reconceptualizing professional teacher development: ERIC digest. (1995). (Report No. EDO-SP-94-2). Washington, DC: Office of Educational Research and Improvement. (ERIC Document Reproduction Service No. ED383695)

Scott, J. C. (1987). Enhancing the image of business teachers. In M. P. Gregory & W. Daniel (Eds.), *Business education for a changing world, National Business Education Association* (Yearbook No. 25, pp. 153-162). Reston, VA: Author.

Scott, J. C. (1992). Planning and implementing a sabbatical leave abroad. *Journal of Education for Business, 67*(4), 238-242.

Scott, J. C. (1997). International opportunities for business educators. *Business Education Forum, 51*(4), 25-27.

Scott, J. C. (1998). Using the author-date documentation system: Some useful guidance for writers. *The Delta Pi Epsilon Journal, 40*(1), 3-9.